ASSEMBLED
FOR USE

THE HENRY ROE CLOUD SERIES ON
AMERICAN INDIANS AND MODERNITY

Series Editors:

Ned Blackhawk, Yale University;

Joshua L. Reid, University of Washington;

Kate W. Shanley, University of Montana; and

Kim TallBear, University of Alberta

SERIES MISSION STATEMENT

Named in honor of the pioneering Winnebago educational reformer and first
known American Indian graduate of Yale College, Henry Roe Cloud (Class
of 1910), this series showcases emergent and leading scholarship in the field
of American Indian Studies. The series draws upon multiple disciplinary
perspectives and organizes them around the place of Native Americans
within the development of American and European modernity, emphasizing
the shared, relational ties between indigenous and Euro-American societies.
It seeks to broaden current historic, literary, and cultural approaches to
American Studies by foregrounding the fraught but generative sites of inquiry
provided by the study of indigenous communities.

ASSEMBLED FOR USE

INDIGENOUS COMPILATION
AND THE ARCHIVES OF
EARLY NATIVE AMERICAN LITERATURES

Kelly Wisecup

Yale
UNIVERSITY PRESS
New Haven & London

Published with assistance from the foundation established in memory of Henry Weldon Barnes of the Class of 1882, Yale College.

Yale University Press books may be purchased in quantity for educational, business, or promotional use. For information, please e-mail sales.press@yale.edu (U.S. office) or sales@yaleup.co.uk (U.K. office).

Set in MT Baskerville & MT Bulmer type by Newgen North America, Austin, Texas.
Printed in the United States of America.

Library of Congress Control Number: 2021904101
ISBN 978-0-300-24328-4 (hardcover : alk. paper)

A catalogue record for this book is available from the British Library.

This paper meets the requirements of ANSI /NISO z39.48-1992 (Permanence of Paper).

10 9 8 7 6 5 4 3 2 1

CONTENTS

ACKNOWLEDGMENTS

This book had its origins in Texas, and I'm grateful for conversations, feedback, and friendship from Gabriel Cervantes, Nora Gilbert, Matt Heard, Ryan Skinnell, and Jae-Jae Spoon. Many thanks to Dahlia Porter for many dog-walk conversations about lists. The book came to completion in Chicago, and I'm grateful to my colleagues in the Department of English for welcoming me to Northwestern University. Thank you to Nick Davis and Jay Grossman for asking just the right questions about this book, to Wendy Wall for generous and penetrating feedback, to Jeffrey Masten for advice at several critical moments, to Harris Feinsod, Nitasha Sharma, Carl Smith, and Tristram Wolff for reading chapters, and to Shaundra Myers for writing sessions that kept me in the book at what seemed an impossibly busy time. Thank you to Department of English chairs extraordinaire Susan Manning and Laurie Shannon for your support of this book, in ways big and small. Thanks also go to English Department colleagues Katy Breen, Brian Bouldrey, Averill Curdy, John Alba Cutler, Betsy Erkkilä, Kasey Evans, Lauren Jackson, Rebecca Johnson, Jim Hodge, Michelle Huang, Jules Law, Justin Mann, Juan Martinez, Susie Phillips,

Helen Thomson, Viv Soni, Julia Stern, Will West, and Ivy Wilson. I have been fortunate to learn from my graduate and undergraduate students' brilliant work: thank you especially to Lois Biggs, Bonnie Etherington, Bradley Dubos, Harrison Graves, Erin Leary, and Nina Moon, and to the students in the ENG 471 graduate courses in spring 2016 and winter 2020. Much gratitude to Lois Biggs for research assistance on the Johnstons as well as good cheer and conversations on an epic midwestern research trip. Thank you to Ilana Larkin and Cameron Schell for excellent research assistance on Simon Pokagon. Across campus, I'm grateful for conversations with Lydia Barnett, Corey Byrnes, Gerry Cadava, Laura León Llerena, Doug Kiel, Emily Maguire, Beatriz Reyes, Nicole Spigner, Kim Marion Suiseeya, and Mary Weismantel. It is my good fortune to work alongside and learn from the Native women at the Center for Native American and Indigenous Research: Patty Loew, Jennifer Michals, and Pamala Silas.

In Chicago, the scholars in the Chicagoland NAIS Working Group have created a remarkable space for sharing research, and I'm grateful to Leila Blackbird, Melissa Adams Campbell, Janet Dees, Sarah Jessica Johnson, Matthew Kruer, Fred Hoxie, Sam Maza, Rose Miron, Hayley Negrin, Teresa Montoya, Cassy Smith, and Isaiah Wilner. Thanks especially to Hayley, Sarah, and Rose for reading several chapter drafts. Conversations with Haku Blaisdell, Andrea Carlson, Heid E. Erdrich, Meranda Roberts, Heather Miller, Isabella Twocrow, and Debra Yepa-Pappan about archives, contemporary art, and museums have helped me think through the stakes of literary archives: thank you.

While writing the book, I was fortunate to work on several grants related to Native American archives and Native American and Indigenous Studies. Thanks go to Heather Miller and Dave Spencer at the American Indian Center of Chicago, as well as Monica Boutwell and Naomi Harvey-Turner, and at Northwestern, John Bresland, Matt Taylor, and Josh Honn, all part of the NEH Common Heritage Grant project "The American Indian Center of Chicago and Urban Native American Histories." Thanks to Dorene Wiese and Melanie Cloud at the American Association of Illinois, and to Allison Connor, Josh Honn, and John Dorr, all part of the Collections as Data "NAES College Digital Library Project." Thanks to everyone in the Humanities Without Walls "Indigenous Art and Activism in Changing Climates: The Mississippi River Valley, Colonialism, and Environmental Change" project (Sara Černe, Vicente Diaz, Bonnie Etherington, Andrew Freiman, Doug Kiel, Samantha Majhor, Robert Morrissey, Chris Pexa, Jacki Thompson Rand, Agléška Cohen-Recountre, Phillip Round, and Caroline Wigginton). Each of you shaped my thinking about archives, about NAIS research, about the responsibilities of collaboration.

Several seminars on book history, NAIS, and colonialism were crucial immersions in these fields, and I'm grateful to the instructors and students in each seminar: thank you to Mary Fuller and participants at the 2011 NEH summer seminar on "English Encounters with the Americas, 1550–1610"; to Phillip Round, for putting together a formative syllabus and list of guest speakers for the 2013 "Indigenous Cultures of Print in Early America" History of the Book seminar at the American Antiquarian Society; thanks as well to the participants in that seminar and to Paul Erickson for cultivating the seminar and its afterlives. And thank you to Michael Kelly, Kiara Vigil, and participants for the 2018 Rare Book School class on "A History of Native American Books & Indigenous Sovereignty."

The book benefited immensely from conversations with librarians and archivists at tribal libraries, tribal historians, and Native American community members. Thank you to Courtney Cottrell and Megan Fulopp for feedback on chapter 1, and to Courtney, Megan, David Freeburg, Jason Mancini, Kathleen Brown-Perez, and Melissa Tantaquidgeon Zobel for conversations about Samson Occom. Thank you to Daniel Heath Justice and Mary Kathryn Nagle for exchanges about John Ridge, and to Patrick Del Percio for discussions about the Cherokee syllabary. I'm grateful to James Francis, Sr. and Charles Norman Shay for conversations about Joseph Nicolar and Penobscot history, and to Rhonda Besaw, Lisa Brooks, Margaret Bruchac, Daniel Nolett, and Richard O'Bomsawin for conversations about Joseph, Stephen, and Octavie Laurent. Thank you to John N. Low, Kyle Malott, and Michael Zimmerman, Jr., for discussions about Simon Pokagon and Pokagon Potawatomi history, and to John for his generosity in both Ohio and Chicago. Thank you to Chris Pappan for discussing his installation at the Field Museum and to Debra Yepa-Pappan for generously making a way for me and my students to see the exhibit. I am grateful to these interlocutors for sharing their time and knowledge; any mistakes or errors are mine.

ACKNOWLEDGMENTS

This book would not have been possible without the librarians who generously paged books, pointed me to sources I would not otherwise have read, and discussed questions of provenance. Thank you to Trisha Roylston at the New London County Historical Society and to Peter Carini and the staff at the Rauner Special Collections Library. Thank you to the staff at the American Philosophical Society, especially Brian Carpenter and the late Timothy Powell, for conversations about Indigenous vocabulary lists and archives, and to Tim, especially, for laying out the stakes of NAIS research in an influential conversation in 2014. Thanks to the amazing staff at the American Antiquarian Society, including Ashley Cataldo (thank you for the cart of vocabularies!), and to Meredith Sommers at the Bayliss Public Library. Thanks to Michael Kelly at Amherst Special Collections for bringing out a copy of Laurent's book at a key moment. Thank you to directors, staff, and librarians at the Newberry Library's D'Arcy McNickle Center over the years—Rose Miron, Patricia Marroquin Norby, Scott Manning Stevens, Sarah Jimenez, Patrick Del Percio, Madeleine Krass, Analú Maria López, Seonaid Valiant—as well as to Catherine Gass, Will Hansen, Juan Molina Hernandez, Brad Hunt, and the Newberry's unsurpassed Special Collections staff. Thanks to the librarians at the Burton Historical Collection at the Detroit Public Library, the Chicago History Museum, Huntington Library, the Library of Congress, Martha's Vineyard Museum, Minnesota Historical Society, the National Archives, National Museum of Health and Medicine, the New-York Historical Society, and the Massachusetts Historical Society. Closer to home, to the interlibrary loan staff at Northwestern Libraries, thank you for your tireless assistance; it would not have been possible to write this book without you. Many thanks to Northwestern subject librarians Scott Garton, Josh Honn, and Gina Peterson, and to Special Collections librarians Jason Nargis and Scott Krafft, as well as to Martin Antonetti.

Funding for travel to these archives was indispensable, and I thank the University of North Texas for a Research Initiation Grant in 2010 to support research on Samson Occom's "Herbs & Roots" that was the seed for this book, and to UNT for a 2014 Scholarly and Creative Activity Grant. Further research was supported by an NEH Summer Stipend, an Andrew W. Mellon / Lloyd Lewis Fellowship from the Newberry Library, and short-term fellowships at the American Antiquarian Society and the

American Philosophical Society. Thank you to Northwestern's Kaplan Institute for the Humanities for a publication subvention grant.

I'm grateful to faculty and students at the following institutions for invitations to discuss the book: University of West Florida, Bard College, the Newberry Library, University of Maryland–College Park, University of Mississippi, Purdue University, University of Tennessee, San Jose State University, Ohio State University, University of Chicago, Trinity College, Tulane University, University of Minnesota, University of Kansas, and University of Illinois, Urbana-Champaign.

In the community of NAIS and early American studies scholars, I'm especially indebted to Kristina Bross and Hilary E. Wyss for laying pathways in early American studies and for your ongoing mentorship. Thank you to Ivy Schweitzer for your hospitality and conversation about Occom and archives at the beginning of this project, and many thanks to Lisa Brooks for generous conversations about Joseph Laurent. I owe immense thanks to Hester Blum and Caroline Wigginton for reading the entire manuscript and for thoughtful feedback and questions. I'm also grateful to Angela Calcaterra, Katy Chiles, Christian Crouch, Christine DeLucia, Drew Lopenzina, Alyssa Mt. Pleasant, Dan Radus, and Caroline Wigginton for conversations about Indigenous literatures, early America, and NAIS, many of which took place at Ralph's, in swamps and forests, and sometimes at conferences. Thank you to Ralph Bauer, Matthew Crawford, Stacey Dearing, Molly Farrell, Teresa Strouth Gaul, Alanna Hickey, Frank Kelderman, Heather Kopelson, Laura Mielke, Christen Mucher, Margaret Noodin, Jean O'Brien, Robert Dale Parker, Jason Payton, Josh Piker, Cassander Smith, Laura Stevens, Marie Balsey Taylor, and Coll Thrush for smart and productive questions and generous conversations.

I'm very grateful to the two anonymous reviewers for Yale University Press for their comments and to series editors Ned Blackhawk and Josh Reid for accepting this book into the Henry Roe Cloud Series on American Indians and Modernity. Thanks go to Sarah Miller for overseeing the early stages of the manuscript review process, to Adina Berk for editorial guidance in the final stages, and to Ash Lago for assistance all along the way. Selections of this work have previously appeared as "Medicine, Communication, and Authority in Samson Occom's Herbal," *Early American Studies* 10, no. 3 (Fall 2012): 540–65, and as ' "Meteors, Ships, Etc.':

Native American Histories of Colonialism and Early American Archives," *American Literary History* 30, no. 1 (2018): 29–54. I thank these journals for permission to republish.

Thanks, finally, to Wayne Marko for steadfast patience and partnership through it all.

A NOTE ON TERMS

———————

Whenever possible, I refer to Indigenous peoples with specific tribal national affiliations. I use "Indigenous" and "Native American" interchangeably, and I use the term "Indian" when it appears within legal terms (such as "federal Indian policy"). I refer to people of European descent in the Americas as colonists or settlers. While some scholars align "colonist" and "colonial" exclusively with the period before the United States' existence, when parts of North America were British colonies, my use of "colonist" indicates that the colonization of Indigenous lands did not end with the formation of the United States.

TIMELINE

———◆———

INDIGENOUS COMPILATIONS	COLONIAL ARCHIVES
1754, Samson Occom (Mohegan) gathers the recipes in "Herbs & Roots" while serving as a teacher at Montauk.	
1775, Emigration to Brothertown begins, is interrupted by the American Revolution, and resumes in 1784.	
1780, The "Cherokee archive" of Attakullakulla and Oconostota is stolen by a Virginia colonist.	
1785, Brothertown is formally established.	1785, In *Notes on the State of Virginia*, Thomas Jefferson calls for settlers to found libraries to hold lists of Indigenous-language words.
1788, Occom may have sold his copy of *Up-Biblum God* to Thomas Shaw around this time.	1791, Massachusetts Historical Society founded.

INDIGENOUS COMPILATIONS	COLONIAL ARCHIVES
	1804, New-York Historical Society founded.
	1809, Publication of volume 10 of the Massachusetts Historical Society's *Collections*, featuring many stories recorded from Native people in the Northeast, including Samson Occom's "Account of the Montauk Indians."
	1812, American Antiquarian Society founded.
1816, George Johnston (Anishinaabe) begins keeping a commonplace book.	1815, The American Philosophical Society's Historical and Literary Committee makes Indigenous languages its primary area of focus.
1819, John Ridge (Cherokee) makes a commonplace book while at Cornwall Mission School in Connecticut.	
1825, John Ridge goes to Washington to help renegotiate the Treaty of Indian Springs.	1825, Albert Gallatin and James Barbour receive federal support for a collecting project focused on Indigenous languages.
1826, John Ridge writes two letters in response to Albert Gallatin's query list, passed on to him by Thomas McKenney.	
1826, Charlotte Johnston (Anishinaabe) exchanges versions of the "Ojibwe Maid" song with Thomas McKenney and other U.S. men, using her album to gather these versions.	
1826–27, Jane Johnston Schoolcraft (Anishinaabe) and possibly other Johnston siblings co-edit the *Muzzeniegun / Literary Voyager*, along with Henry Rowe Schoolcraft.	1827, Thomas McKenney publishes *Sketches of a Tour to the Lakes, of the Character and Customs of the Chippeway Indians, and of Incidents Connected with the Treaty of Fond du Lac.*
1828, The *Cherokee Phoenix* newspaper begins publishing, printing John Ridge's "Strictures" in two 1828 issues.	1828, The first edition of Washington Irving's *History of the Life and Voyages of Christopher Columbus* published.

INDIGENOUS COMPILATIONS	COLONIAL ARCHIVES

1829, William Apess (Pequot) publishes *Son of the Forest*, including the appendix of extracts (with a second edition in 1830).

1830, Pierre Paul Wzokhilain (Abenaki) publishes *Wobanaki kimzowi awighigan* with Boston publisher Crocker and Brewster.

1833, Charlotte Johnston and William McMurray accompany Shingwaukonse's community as they move to lands claimed by British Canada.

1833, Jesuit priest Sébastian Rasles's Abenaki dictionary published in the *Memoirs of the American Academy of Arts and Sciences.*

1835, Working with Mashpee Wampanoag leaders, William Apess publishes *Indian Nullification of the Unconstitutional Laws of Massachusetts Relative to the Marshpee Tribe; Or, the Pretended Riot Explained.*

1836, Albert Gallatin publishes some of the results of his linguistic and historical research in the American Antiquarian Society's transactions, *Archaeologia Americana*, vol. 2.

1826–50s, Charlotte Johnston continues compiling her albums, adding poetry and hymns in Anishinaabemowin and English to the Ojibwa Book. It is likely that Jane Johnston Schoolcraft penned the undated acrostic poem "Album" during these years.

1836–44, Publication of McKenney's and Hall's *History of the Indian Tribes of North America, with Biographical Sketches and Aanecdotes of the Principal Chiefs. Embellished with One Hundred and Twenty Portraits, from the Indian Gallery in the Department of War, at Washington.*

1839, Henry Rowe Schoolcraft publishes the Johnstons' translations of Anishinaabe stories, alongside his commentary, in *Algic Researches.*

1848, William Whipple Warren (Anishinaabe) receives Henry Rowe Schoolcraft's list of 347 queries from the trader Henry M. Rice, for whom Warren worked as a clerk.

1849, Minnesota Historical Society founded.

1849, Warren's initial, unrevised research on Anishinaabe histories is published in the *Minnesota Pioneer* newspaper.

1852–53, William Whipple Warren completes his history of the Ojibwes and seeks a publisher for his manuscript.

1851–56, Henry Rowe Schoolcraft publishes *Historical and Statistical Information Respecting the History, Condition, and Prospects of the Indian Tribes of the United States,* drawing on information returned in query lists like the one sent to Warren.

INDIGENOUS COMPILATIONS	COLONIAL ARCHIVES
	1851, John William De Forest publishes *History of the Indians of Connecticut, from the Earliest Known Period to 1850, Published with the Sanction of the Connecticut Historical Society*.
	1870, New London County Historical Society founded.
	1879, Bureau of American Ethnology founded.
1884, Joseph Laurent (Abenaki) publishes *New Familiar Abenakis and English Dialogues* and sends one copy to James Pilling at the Bureau of American Ethnology.	1885, William Whipple Warren's *History of the Ojibway People* published posthumously in Minnesota Historical Society *Transactions*, sandwiched between a preface and additional histories written by Minnesota settlers.
1884–1917, Joseph Laurent travels to the Abenaki camp at Pequaket, in Intervale, New Hampshire.	1887, Newberry Library founded.
	1887, Franz Boas and Otis T. Mason debate methods for representing the human past in an issue of *Science*.
1893, E. Pauline Johnson (Mohawk) publishes "A Red Girl's Reasoning."	1891, James Pilling publishes *Bibliography of the Algonquian Languages*.
1893, Simon Pokagon (Pokagon Band of Potawatomi Indians) circulates *The Red Man's Rebuke / Greeting* at the World's Columbian Exposition in Chicago, where he also travels in October 1893.	1893, Chicago hosts the World's Columbian Exposition, bringing Indigenous people from across the globe to the city.
	1894, The Field Museum is founded, repurposing some of the displays created for the Columbian Exposition.
1916–22, Carlos Montezuma (Yavapai Apache) publishes his newsletter *Wassaja*, in which he calls for abolishing the Bureau of Indian Affairs. Around this time, he assembles a scrapbook of Albert Payton Terhune's "50 Famous American Indians" newspaper articles.	1899, William DeLoss Love publishes *Samson Occom and the Christian Indians of New England*.
1921, Gertrude Bonnin (Yankton Dakota) publishes *American Indian Stories*.	

INTRODUCTION

———————◆———————

Sifting, Procuring, Collecting: Indigenous Compilations

In 1848, the Anishinaabe man William Whipple Warren received a list of 347 queries about Indigenous histories, languages, and life. Created by the ethnographer Henry Rowe Schoolcraft and passed along to Warren by a trader for whom he worked as a clerk, the list was designed to extract and return information to Schoolcraft in discrete, organized categories that he could analyze to produce a government-sponsored census and ethnographic report. Yet rather than play the informant or assistant, Warren turned the query list to different ends, by embarking on his own process of gathering and recirculating Anishinaabe histories. He described this work as "sifting and procuring corroborative testimony from various sources, the traditions which have been orally transmitted from father to son, for generations past."[1] For events that remained within the remembrance of living people, Warren chose from the "mass of information which [he] has been collecting during several years past, such portions as may truly be considered as historical and worthy of presenting to the world."[2] His studies required a "most intimate acquaintance" with Anishinaabe people, and he accordingly foregrounded the conversations on which his work relied by presenting stories told "verbatim" from their sources.[3] Warren's sifting and gathering extended to nonalphabetic records as well: he cited a copper plate on which one family kept pictographic genealogies, quill-worked and painted buffalo robes, and the "lodge stories" that he heard from his grandparents as a child.[4] Finally, Warren contrasted his acts of sifting and procuring and the resulting "mass of information" he gathered with the "superficial" claims made about Indigenous peoples in books by U.S. settlers, which relied, he said, on "mere temporary observations."[5]

Warren's turn from the ethnographic query list to collecting Anishinaabe histories and from colonial print networks to intimate acquaintances and lodge stories are turns toward Anishinaabe media, conceptions of history and nationhood, and relationships. In making this turn, Warren participated in an extensive eighteenth- and nineteenth-century practice of textual production in which Indigenous people made texts by sifting, procuring, and amassing materials to make new meanings out of the collected parts. Like the Cheyenne, Kiowa, Lakota, and other Indigenous men who used lined pages from account books as surfaces for ledger art, Indigenous writers arranged words, images, and excerpts in ready-made and documentary forms. These forms are made to receive and store information, from documentary forms like the list or catalogue to ready-mades like albums, scrapbooks, or accounting ledgers. Indigenous people listed plant knowledge in medicinal recipes, collected previously published poems in albums, gathered tribal histories on scraps of paper, and made vocabulary lists of words in their languages. They described this work as accumulating and arranging distinct pieces from Indigenous and, sometimes, colonial sources to make new texts.

In addition to Warren's language of "collecting" and "sifting," there is John Ridge's (Cherokee) 1828 account of "open[ing]" colonial texts to reinterpret and correct the state of Georgia's claims to Cherokee lands. In the 1820s and 1830s, the Anishinaabe woman Ogenebugoquay/Charlotte Johnston understood the work of assembling poetry albums as "twining" both published and unpublished materials together, and Pequot William Apess described the materials from colonial newspapers and Indigenous petitions that he excerpted, gathered, and juxtaposed in his 1835 book *Indian Nullification* as "extracts."[6] This book is about how, in the eighteenth and nineteenth centuries, Native people made, used, and circulated intentional assemblages—texts made by opening, collecting, and twining materials—which I call "Indigenous compilations" and about the relation of those compilations to both Indigenous and colonial archives.

In *Assembled for Use: Indigenous Compilation and the Archives of Early Native American Literatures* I read Indigenous compilations on a spectrum that extends from collections of previously published excerpts in scrapbooks and albums to arrangements of words and images in lists, account books, recipes, and preprinted blanks (figures I.1 to I.4). Focusing on compilations made by Mohegan, Cherokee, Anishinaabe, Abenaki, and Potawatomi people between the 1750s and 1890s, I study Indigenous compilations as experiments in translation, combination, and recirculation. While, as Schoolcraft's list of 347 queries demonstrates, documentary and ready-made forms have a history as ethnographic, bureaucratic documents, I trace a story of Indigenous people using those forms' capacity to generate meaning through proximity and juxtaposition in order to make alternate arrangements and new readings of the assembled parts.[7] These compilations served particular uses within Indigenous communities, from recipes for medicinal treatments to scrapbooks that made opportunities for textual or material exchanges.

Indigenous compilations proliferated in a period of colonial archive making, a time when many of the local, state, and national archives now in existence in the U.S. were founded and when colonists were imagining those archives as places for stabilizing and authorizing their interpretations of Indigenous literatures and histories. Like Warren in his commentary on colonial books, Indigenous compilers characterized colonial archives as sites of power and deception and as places where settlers established geopolitical and historical boundaries within which they tried to contain Native nations. Indigenous people also saw colonial archives as sites of intervention, and they sometimes sent their compilations into those archives. They made these decisions for varying reasons—from financial need and friendship to political advocacy for their nations. Indigenous compilations consequently reckon with the history of the word "compilation," which has referred both to textual accumulation and to plunder.[8] I attend to the adjacency of plunder and accumulation in these etymologies to register how Native people made compilations in the midst of colonists' efforts to

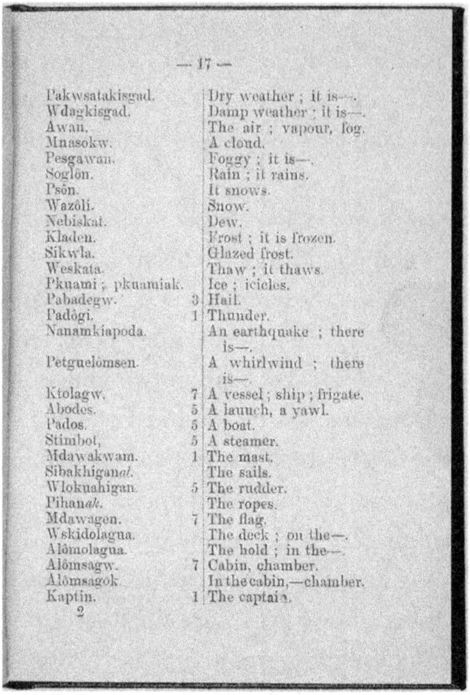

— 17 —

Pakwsatakisgad.		Dry weather ; it is—.
Wdagkisgad.		Damp weather ; it is—.
Awan.		The air ; vapour, fog.
Mnasokw.		A cloud.
Pesgawan.		Foggy ; it is—.
Soglôn.		Rain ; it rains.
Psôn.		It snows.
Wazôli.		Snow.
Nebiskat.		Dew.
Kladen.		Frost ; it is frozen.
Sikwla.		Glazed frost.
Weskata.		Thaw ; it thaws.
Pkuami ; pkuamiak.		Ice ; icicles.
Pabadegw.	3	Hail.
Padôgi.	1	Thunder.
Nanamkiapoda.		An earthquake ; there is—.
Petguelômsen.		A whirlwind ; there is—.
Ktolagw.	7	A vessel ; ship ; frigate.
Abodes.	5	A launch, a yawl.
Pados.	5	A boat.
Stimbot,	5	A steamer.
Mdawakwam.	1	The mast.
Sibakhigan*al*.		The sails.
Wlokuahigan.	5	The rudder.
Pihan*ak*.		The ropes.
Mdawagen.	7	The flag.
Wskidolagua.		The deck ; on the—.
Alômolagua.		The hold ; in the—.
Alômsagw.	7	Cabin, chamber.
Alômsagok.		In the cabin,—chamber.
Kaptin.	1	The captain.

2

FIGURE I.1. Joseph Laurent's word lists, in *New Familiar Abenakis and English Dialogues* (1884). Kim-Wait / Eisenberg Native American Literature Collection, Archives and Special Collections, Amherst College Library.

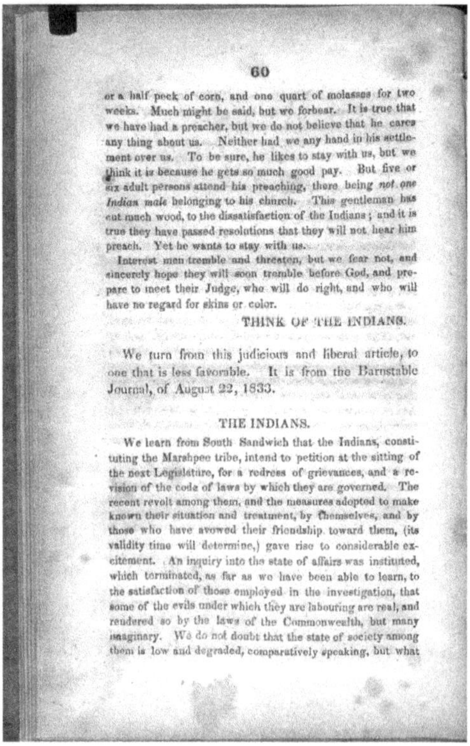

60

or a half peck of corn, and one quart of molasses for two weeks. Much might be said, but we forbear. It is true that we have had a preacher, but we do not believe that he cares any thing about us. Neither had we any hand in his settlement over us. To be sure, he likes to stay with us, but we think it is because he gets so much good pay. But five or six adult persons attend his preaching, there being *not one Indian male* belonging to his church. This gentleman has cut much wood, to the dissatisfaction of the Indians ; and it is true they have passed resolutions that they will not hear him preach. Yet he wants to stay with us.

Interest men tremble and threaten, but we fear not, and sincerely hope they will soon tremble before God, and prepare to meet their Judge, who will do right, and who will have no regard for skins or color.

THINK OF THE INDIANS.

We turn from this judicious and liberal article, to one that is less favorable. It is from the Barnstable Journal, of August 22, 1833.

THE INDIANS.

We learn from South Sandwich that the Indians, constituting the Marshpee tribe, intend to petition at the sitting of the next Legislature, for a redress of grievances, and a revision of the code of laws by which they are governed. The recent revolt among them, and the measures adopted to make known their situation and treatment, by themselves, and by those who have avowed their friendship toward them, (its validity time will determine,) gave rise to considerable excitement. An inquiry into the state of affairs was instituted, which terminated, as far as we have been able to learn, to the satisfaction of those employed in the investigation, that some of the evils under which they are labouring are real, and rendered so by the laws of the Commonwealth, but many imaginary. We do not doubt that the state of society among them is low and degraded, comparatively speaking, but what

FIGURE I.2. "Extracts" in William Apess's *Indian Nullification of the Unconstitutional Laws of Massachusetts Relative to the Marshpee Tribe: or, The Pretended Riot Explained* (1835). Kim-Wait / Eisenberg Native American Literature Collection, Archives and Special Collections, Amherst College Library.

FIGURE I.3. Title page for Charlotte Johnston's Journal, with illustration signed by Chrs. S. F. [Charles S. Frailey]. Courtesy of the Judge Joseph H. Steere Room, Bayliss Public Library, Sault Ste. Marie, Michigan.

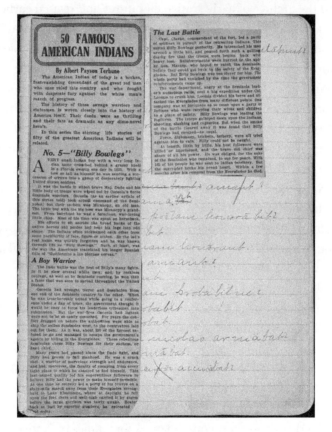

FIGURE I.4. Carlos Montezuma's scrapbook, with clippings from "50 Famous American Indians" by Albert Payson Terhune (1889–1935). Ayer Modern MS Montezuma, Box 4, Folder 219, Newberry Library, Chicago.

relocate Indigenous words, literatures, and histories into archives, often doing so, as Warren observed, without their knowledge. At moments when colonists were attempting to transform Native people into "things" that could be studied on paper, Indigenous compilations generated opportunities for Native people to *do* and *assert* things within their own communities, things like treating ill bodies, sharing hospitality with other Indigenous people, defending their communities from land theft, and maintaining relations to other Indigenous people.[9]

In its attention to assembled texts and archival interventions, this book joins scholarship in Native American and Indigenous Studies (NAIS) and early American studies that, over the last several decades, has dramatically expanded the archive of early Native literatures and revised earlier narratives of scarcity and inauthenticity. Scholars have shown how early Native writers' petitions, letters, sermons, poems, journals, and autobiographies were informed by Indigenous textual practices in multiple languages and media. Writing in English was a practice with which Indigenous people worked on behalf of their communities and nations, whether by defending land rights with petitions and letters or by using copyright and their own printing presses to determine representations of their communities and histories.[10] Building on this scholarship, *Assembled for Use* contributes to early Native literary histories both by reading texts usually considered to be utilitarian and documentary as significant to Native literary histories and by illuminating how Indigenous compilations served uses specific to Indigenous communities while also fostering critiques of colonial archives. I offer as well a history of Indigenous archival creation and intervention that stands both as a foundation for recent efforts to decolonize museums and archives and as a point from which to reflect on scholarly methodologies for approaching colonial archives. In the sections that follow, I first survey how compilations were assembled and used within Indigenous communities. I then follow Indigenous compilations as their makers circulated them into colonial archives and to Indian officials, settler anthropologists, and colonists. In the final section, I turn to Indigenous compilations' archival afterlives and their consequences for studies of Native American literature and early American archives, asking how Indigenous archival interventions might bear on contemporary scholarly practices of reading in those same archives.

Making, Reading, and Using Compilations

If Indigenous compilations stand as a textual relative to ledger art, they have nonetheless obtained a reputation not as artistic or literary works but as utilitarian texts entangled with colonial practices of ordering and de-contextualizing. This reputation emerges in part from an extensive history in which colonists made lists, catalogues, taxonomies, and blank forms—many of the same forms Indigenous people used to make compilations—in order to facilitate exploration and dispossession. In North America, this history ranges from English explorer James Rosier's lists of Abenaki words and their English translations, which he completed with linguistic knowledge obtained from five Abenaki men the English took captive in 1605, to the minister Experience Mayhew's 1727 "catalogue" of deathbed testimonies gathered from Wampanoag people on Noepe (currently Martha's Vineyard). In the nineteenth century, settlers recorded their division of collectively held Native lands into individual allotments in lists like the so-called Dawes Rolls, and Indian boarding school administrators filled in blank forms with Native children's personal information and disciplinary records.[11] Indian agent-ethnographers like Henry Rowe Schoolcraft even made blank forms into a metaphor. He wrote that Native history "is such a blank," imagining a historical "blank" that could be documented and visualized in the ubiquitous paper blanks created by printed forms (figure I.5).[12] In Schoolcraft's formulation, the blank references printed lines awaiting inscription, which stand here as a metaphor for the supposed absence of Indigenous histories, a blank Schoolcraft's six-volume history purported to fill in. Unsurprisingly, colonists' use of forms like the blank, list, and catalogue have figured in studies of settlers' scientific and theological debates over Indigenous peoples' origins and languages. Recent scholarship positions colonists' lists and catalogues as historical texts that provide access into the past or as ethnographic texts that participate in U.S. and European intellectual histories.[13] Colonists' documentary forms offer, as literary scholar Laura J. Murray argues of word lists, "windows" into "dynamics of cross-cultural talk and translation" and "dramas of encounters with strangeness."[14]

While keeping colonial science, bureaucracy, and their material effects on Indigenous peoples' lives in view, I turn from histories of collecting and

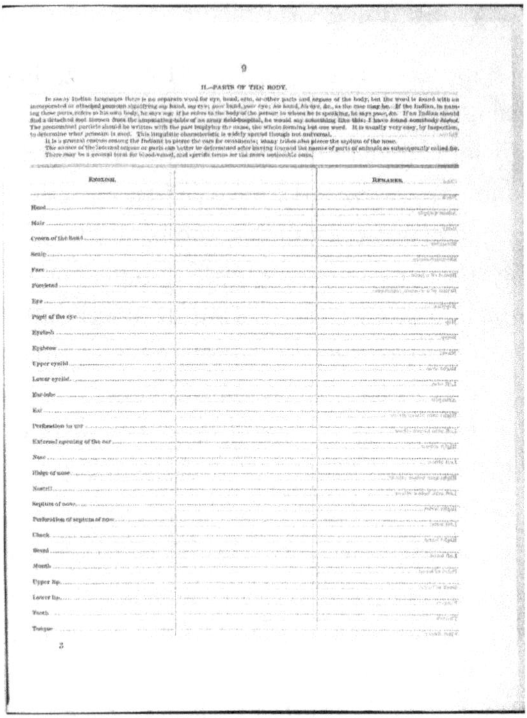

9

II.—PARTS OF THE BODY.

In many Indian languages there is no separate word for eye, hand, arm, or other parts and organs of the body, but the word is found with an incorporated or attached pronoun signifying my hand, my eye; your hand, your eye; his hand, his eye, &c., as the case may be. If the Indian, in naming these parts, refers to his own body, he says my; if he refers to the body of the person to whom he is speaking, he says your, &c. If an Indian should find a detached foot thrown from the amputating-table of an army field-hospital, he would say something like this: I have found somebody his-foot. The pronominal particle should be written with the part implying the name, the whole forming but one word. It is usually very easy, by inspection, to determine what pronoun is used. This linguistic characteristic is widely spread though not universal.

It is a general custom among the Indians to pierce the ears for ornaments; many tribes also pierce the septum of the nose.

The names of the internal organs or parts can better be determined after having learned the names of parts of animals as subsequently called for. There may be a general term for blood-vessel, and specific terms for the more noticeable ones.

ENGLISH.		REMARKS.
Head		
Hair		
Crown of the head		
Scalp		
Face		
Forehead		
Eye		
Pupil of the eye		
Eyelash		
Eyebrow		
Upper eyelid		
Lower eyelid		
Ear-lobe		
Ear		
Perforation in ear		
External opening of the ear		
Nose		
Ridge of nose		
Nostril		
Septum of nose		
Perforation of septum of nose		
Cheek		
Beard		
Mouth		
Upper lip		
Lower lip		
Teeth		
Tongue		

3

FIGURE I.5. Printed blanks for collecting vocabulary words. John Wesley Powell, *Introduction to the Study of Indian Languages with Words, Phrases, and Sentences to Be Collected* (1877). Ayer 402 .P8 1877, Newberry Library, Chicago.

of colonial bureaucracy, in which Indigenous peoples appear as objects of study. Instead, by making Indigenous compilations the focus of my research, I foreground Indigenous people's acts to collect, excerpt, open, and twine texts together. This turn does not seek to peer through Indigenous compilations to the past so much as it positions those compilations as texts Indigenous people themselves read and that bear the traces of their making and reading. Instead of reading through compilations, I read their pages, trace the origins for the assembled materials, and follow compilations as they travel into different hands and spaces. My approach draws on NAIS methodologies to investigate Indigenous compilations within tribally specific understandings of textual making and use, and I bring NAIS together with textual studies' attention to reading as a social activity and as one of several things people might do with textual material, particularly compilations.[15] Such textual studies scholars as Ann M. Blair, Ellen Gruber Garvey, and Jeffrey Knight argue that some compilations, like scrapbooks, commonplace books, and aggregated books (individual books purchased and then bound together by their owner), reflect the readerly acts with which individuals tamed information or charted their own routes through books, newspapers, and manuscripts.[16] At the other end of the spectrum, compilation's documentary forms—lists, blanks, catalogues—are said to lack readers but to have uses; they operate as utilitarian technologies of decontextualization, stasis, and inertia, forms in which, as media studies scholar Lisa Gitelman puts it, "things [are] stopped forever."[17] These documentary forms store and present information to support acts like making agreements, paying debts, or entering into contracts. As a result, scholars argue, blanks and other documentary forms "transformed daily life without necessarily having any connection to reading."[18] The forms of reading and writing that blanks did elicit, Gitelman writes, have little to do with the "readerly subjectivity" or "identification" associated with printed forms like the novel and newspapers. Instead, blanks rationalize, dehumanize, and stabilize information, separating that information from affect and agency.[19]

In *Assembled for Use* I ask what we might learn by reading texts long assumed both to lack readers and to elicit use rather than reading. I approach Indigenous compilations as assembled texts for which making, reading, and using are interrelated rather than opposing actions. Native people made compilations out of documentary forms that were designed to standardize information—as well as more readerly forms like scrapbooks and commonplace books—and in the process they turned those information-storing and -stabilizing functions to other ends. Indigenous compilers assembled medicinal, political, poetic, linguistic, and historical materials within lists, recipes, albums, and scrapbooks, in this way gathering environmental and linguistic knowledge, sharing poetry and songs in English and Indigenous languages, and circulating stories. It was in *reading* and *using* those compilations that Native people activated them as medicinal guides, political commentary, poetic experiments, and tribal histories. In this sense, making compilations was also an act of "making do," of using materials in ways that departed from their imagined, intended uses.[20]

In 1884, for example, Abenaki leader Joseph Laurent compiled a book of vocabulary lists featuring parallel columns of Abenaki- and English-language words. Vocabulary lists do not feature subjects, sentences, or plots; instead, they store information for future use, stabilize meaning, and often detach words from their contexts of use. But in *New Familiar Abenakis and English Dialogues,* Laurent arranged Abenaki-language words in lists that represent Abenaki people hunting, writing and painting, playing music, and traveling North America and the Atlantic Ocean. Imagined dialogues in Abenaki and English evoke conversations among bilingual speakers, envisioning not just the survival of the Abenaki language but also English speakers learning Abenaki. Laurent's word lists demonstrate the intimate relations between reading and using compilations, as the lists elicit uses that range from reading and speaking the words aloud to passing the book back and forth (see figure I.1).

Indigenous compilations plumb the multiple ends to which textual forms and materials might be put, the different reading practices Native people might employ, and the objects that might be created by assembling elements that direct attention to, around, and off the page. Take the manuscript poetry albums compiled by the Anishinaabe translator Charlotte Johnston in the mid-nineteenth century, which juxtapose poems, songs, hymns, and illustrations. The people who interacted with the albums included those who read and contributed poems as well as those who were singers, churchgoers, patients, friends, and language learners, figures who often receive only passing notice in histories of Native literature. As Johnston's albums show, many Native people had a "functional understanding" of how writing and publication worked, that is, an understanding of textual circulation and its social power across many languages and forms, whether in alphabetic orthographies or forms such as pictographs, syllabaries, and wampum belts, or strings made of quahog shells.[21] Johnston's poetry albums generated readings of the assembled poems while also inviting other interactions with the albums, from contributions to their pages, to acts like hymn singing, tears of affection, and expressions of friendship. As the albums suggest, Indigenous compilations are not oriented just by their documentary or ready-made forms or even by alphabetic literacy but by using and circulating those forms. Indigenous compilations illuminate the many people involved in making, reading, and using alphabetic texts but who less often appear in literary histories oriented around familiar literary genres, such as the sermon, autobiography, poem, journal, and novel, and their corresponding conceptions of authorship. The texts I assemble in the following chapters bear the contributions and actions of well-known authors, scarcely known writers, and the Indigenous people all but absent from literary historical narratives as authors, editors, or publishers but who interacted with compilations as makers, contributors, and readers.

Indigenous compilations require expansive understandings of use that exceed the utilitarian, informational functions scholars attribute to documentary forms: use as inscription (arranging letters and words on a page), assemblage (forms and materials from colonial texts remixed alongside Indigenous knowledges, genres, and words), and practice (circulating, handling, sharing).[22] These uses are not misunderstandings of writing, such as those colonists frequently attributed to Native people, and they exceed the obedient, devotional reading practices that colonial ministers sought to teach their Native pupils.[23] Instead, Indigenous compilations demonstrate the argument of Creek literary scholar Craig Womack that Native literatures are as much about action as about representation. As he writes, "Native artistry is not pure aesthetics, or art for art's sake: as often as not Indian writers are trying to *invoke* as much as *evoke*."[24] In the case of assembled texts, using an Indigenous compilation invoked relations among Native people: these relations include social exchanges, feelings, and common causes shared among people in different places and nations. Indigenous compilations also reorient Womack's account of aesthetics as "art for art's sake," for they do important work on the page.

In Indigenous compilations, linguistic and aesthetic meanings are not separate but rather amplify the meanings they accrue through use within a set of "material, social and institutional relations" specific to Indigenous families, tribal nations, and intertribal communities.[25] Indigenous compilations were made in response to and for use by those communities, and compilations consequently generated specific meanings that both built on and existed in excess of the materials assembled on the page. A focus on Indigenous compilations reconceives of Native American literatures in ways that attend to Native peoples' uses for texts, uses that certainly include, even while they also go beyond, reading and writing. This history transforms narratives of non-reading and of Indigenous objects of collection and study into one of creative making, recontextualizing, and using within

Native communities. And the uses for compilations, as the next section shows, extend to interactions with colonists and colonial archives.

Circulating Compilations

The Indigenous compilations I examine throughout *Assembled for Use* reside in colonial archives today because their makers made a decision to send them to an archive or to a settler who was collecting materials related to Indigenous peoples' lives. Records of how Indigenous writing came to reside in colonial archives do not always exist—as is true for many texts—and certainly many Indigenous literatures exist in colonial archives because of plunder, coercion, and extraction. In the case of Indigenous compilations, following their archival pathways shows that intentional circulation into colonial archives is one of their defining features. As I noted above, Native people had different reasons for making these decisions to circulate compilations into colonial archives: some people sought to affirm tribal national sovereignty, express friendship, or maintain a correspondence, while others made decisions influenced by coercion, financial need, and threats of land dispossession. Indigenous peoples' acts to circulate compilations produced critical reflections on and corrections of settlers' assumptions and archives, and these acts make pathways for approaching the colonial archive through Native peoples' uses for and readings of those institutions. The decision to circulate Indigenous compilations acknowledged how colonial archives produce and delimit knowledge about Indigenous peoples even as those compilations made alternate interpretations of those archives possible. In what follows, I place histories and theories of colonial archives alongside the circulations of Indigenous compilations, in order to consider their implications for fields that, like early American studies, rely on colonial archives as sites of knowledge production and critical analysis.

As book historian Lindsay diCuirci remarks in her study of early American historical reprintings, the mere presence of a book or manuscript in an archive does not necessarily correlate to an intentional act of preservation.[26] Instead, the archive itself endows objects with significance as records of the past, as texts that illuminate an origin.[27] In the case of Indigenous peoples, colonists explicitly imagined archives as sites of preservation for

edge production but held no guarantees that colonists would change their reading practices or claims.

Circulating Indigenous compilations repositioned colonial archives within what Osage literary scholar Robert Warrior calls Indigenous "intellectual trade routes": both the physical trails and pathways Indigenous people follow in their travels and the routes that their ideas and books take.[34] Consider, for example, the routes of Laurent's *New Familiar Abenakis and English Dialogues*. Laurent brought copies of the book along as he traveled from his home at Odanak, in Quebec, to a camp in Wabanaki homelands within New Hampshire, where he sold baskets and other materials (possibly including copies of the *Dialogues*) to non-Native tourists. As it circulated, the *Dialogues* helped maintain linguistic and kinship ties among Abenaki people living in the U.S. and Canada while also fostering Laurent's conversations with university anthropologists and tourists who visited the camp to satisfy their interest in "Indians" and who often left those conversations having revised their inquiries. As we can see from the circulation of Laurent's *Dialogues*, Indigenous compilations amassed (and still accrue) layered meanings as Native people sent them into motion among their own communities and into settlers' hands as well.[35]

Tracing compilations' travels along such intellectual trade routes is essential to telling more complete stories, both of Indigenous compilations and of colonial archives.[36] Seen from the networks that Indigenous compilations made as they circulated, archives are both "scenes of apprehension" and places within Indigenous homelands. From this view, compilations' archival interruptions create routes that look much like the "third space of sovereignty" that Bruyneel describes as refusing the boundaries with which colonists sought to "map out [Native] people's relationship to time and space in North America."[37] This third space exists as a supplemental one, "inassimilable to the institutions and discourse of the modern liberal democratic settler-state and nation."[38] Similarly, while Indigenous compilations circulate through and are often physically held in colonial archives, they make a third space of literary experimentation and critique that remains unassimilated by colonial archival and disciplinary institutions.

As I trace how Indigenous peoples' interventions into colonial archives necessitated critical reflections on archives at the moments of compilations' circulation, I also ask what forms of practice and interpretation Indigenous compilations might require of scholars in order to reflect on the temporal, geopolitical, and literary historical boundaries colonial archives still produce today. Lisa Brooks has observed that scholars can reproduce the categories with which colonists demarcated Indigenous homelands and relationships as foreign as we "create spaces of foreignness and familiarity through our interactions with texts . . . as readers and teachers, we can unwittingly be participants in this construction of foreignness."[39] Conceptions of the familiar and the foreign are produced and reproduced, initially by colonists who established practices for reading Indigenous literatures and lands within colonial intellectual frameworks, geographies, and temporalities. These forms of knowledge may be reproduced as scholars make choices about the language we use to introduce texts, delimit literary histories, and describe places.

As a non-Native, settler scholar trained in graduate school as an early Americanist, I work within a field and from a position that has participated—and sometimes still participates—in constructing and perpetuating the forms of archival elimination and misrepresentation that eighteenth- and nineteenth-century Indigenous compilers critiqued. This participation ranges from the active forgetting of Indigenous presence produced by settler educational systems, cityscapes, and systems of representation to early American studies' privileging of literary histories oriented around colonial texts and intellectual histories. NAIS scholarship—to which graduate training also introduced me—makes visible and challenges these disciplinary and everyday forms of forgetting Indigenous presence and of constructing Indigenous nations and literary histories as foreign. Especially important is NAIS's emphasis on the continuation of Native literatures and settler colonialism across multiple literary historical periods, the importance of place- and tribally-specific research, and the need for research that is in dialogue with and beneficial to Indigenous communities.

My reading of Indigenous compilations' pathways to colonial archives asks how those circulations might challenge how early American studies scholars perceive and define the field's familiar objects of study and our conceptions of where and what archives are. How do the forms of order and arrangement with which colonists sought to document and archive

Native words and writing continue to shape assumptions about the past or about which texts figure in literary histories? What are the responsibilities, for contemporary, non-Native scholars, of working within the archives assembled to justify settler boundaries placed onto Native nations? How might scholars, and especially early American studies scholars, make our research responsive to texts and histories that, if often marked as foreign by disciplinary structures, might nonetheless ground alternate relations to the past and ways of producing knowledge from and about the archives of early Native American literatures? I take up these questions not only to reflect on early American studies but also to write a literary history of Indigenous compilations that makes those compilations and Indigenous peoples' uses for them the orienting point for reading in the colonial archive. To do so, I both relied on NAIS scholarship and sought out conversations with Indigenous community members, including tribal historians, tribal historic preservation officers, and language experts, as well as descendants of some of the Native writers I discuss throughout this book. These consultations not only expanded, challenged, or changed the questions I considered; they also provided insight into the contexts in which Indigenous compilations were made, read, and used, and into the ways those compilations are still used and circulated today, as they continue to generate collaboration, exchanges of affection and care, and political critique.

My reflections on colonial archives, their histories, and my own research and relation to those histories are indebted to the work of tribal historians, archivists, and museum curators who are themselves reshaping archives and museums, whether with museum exhibits that emphasize both the violence of colonialism and Native peoples' persistence or with projects to send digital copies of archival holdings to the Indigenous communities where they originated.[40] It is telling that several archives and libraries have recently hosted seminars on NAIS, providing a space for training graduate students and faculty for whom NAIS was or is not a programmatic part of their curriculum (as was my case). These seminars attest to how those institutions are actively reframing the histories and policies informing their collections.[41] As Margaret M. Bruchac (Abenaki) and Kiara Vigil (Dakota/Apache heritage) have shown in their studies of Indigenous people who worked to contest and determine the terms with which indigeneity has been represented, these efforts originated in the political and kinship networks that Indigenous people formed in the twentieth century, in organizations like the Society of American Indians and within the discipline of anthropology.[42] Indigenous people wielded these networks to act as "intellectuals" rather than as objects of study.[43] *Assembled for Use* builds on Bruchac's and Vigil's scholarship on the twentieth century by examining an earlier period, to ask how Native people interacted with colonial archives at their moments of formation and expansion and to consider how those interactions might inform contemporary understandings of the knowledge those archives continue to produce. Well before recent digital projects to open colonial archives and museum renovations that center Indigenous stories, Native people circulated compilations to generate alternate ways of reading and using colonial archives.

Chapter Map

The chapters of this book traverse 150 years, from the 1750s to the 1890s, as Indigenous people made compilations while colonists were simultaneously forming literary, antiquarian, and ethnographic archives. Interludes between the chapters map compilation's capaciousness as a textual practice across early Native literatures and provide hinges between the chapters. Throughout, Indigenous compilations form the center of gravity, with each chapter spiraling outward to trace their processes of creation, examine the meanings that arise through the arrangement and juxtaposition of materials and as Indigenous people read and used them, and move with the compilations as they traveled through different hands. While each chapter focuses on one or several people as compilers, I follow the uses for each compilation to a broader community of readers and users, some of whom left traces on the page and others whose actions I recover by reading deeply across historical records. I also follow these pathways as they manifest in contemporary Native American literatures, digital projects, and archival interventions in which Indigenous writers, scholars, and community members continue to use, engage with, and make new texts out of eighteenth- and nineteenth-century Indigenous compilations. Each chapter is also located in part in a colonial archive or institutional space, its formation or expansion in the eighteenth or nineteenth century, and Indigenous compilations' afterlives within that space.

I trace Indigenous compilations across five chapters, examining lists (recipes, numerical accounts, and vocabulary lists), albums (scrapbooks and poetry albums), and excerpted texts (both small- and large-scale extracts of existing texts). The first three chapters take up manuscript compilations in which Native writers arranged words or extracts of previously published texts into the recipe, the letter, and the album, respectively. These chapters trace an arc in which Indigenous compilations increasingly bear visible traces of collaborative making and use. While each of the Indigenous compilations I examine was collaboratively assembled, they move toward forms that increasingly enact and demonstrate collaborative use in their materiality, from recipes assembled for personal use, to support acts of medical care and community-building, to albums that, with entries in different hands and different contributors' signatures, materially bear the signs of collaborative creation.

As shown in chapter 1, Samson Occom's medicinal recipes, made in 1754 to record medicinal knowledge he learned from the Montaukett man Ocus, require reading not just his lists of medicinal preparations but plants, leaves, roots, and bodies. As Occom used the recipes to treat Native and non-Native people, his actions helped bind northeastern Native peoples together into intertribal communities, such as the Brothertown Indian Nation. I begin the story of Indigenous compilation with Occom's recipes because they exemplify how compilations carried and communicated Indigenous environmental knowledge while also generating uses that created and sustained Indigenous communities. The recipes are also a starting place because their current archival locations are symptomatic of settler antiquarians' desires to archive and reprint Occom's manuscripts and Native American writing more generally, desires that fueled the founding of regional historical societies in the 1790s and that were reconfigured as categories of arrangement in national archives in the 1870s and 1880s.

In chapter 2 I turn to compilations that recontextualize colonial lists, blanks, and ethnographic categories to make them, rather than Indigenous nations, objects of analysis. It examines two 1826 letters by the Cherokee lawyer John Ridge addressed to Albert Gallatin. Gallatin anticipated that the information from Ridge would advance a government-funded initiative to use Indigenous languages and histories to locate Indigenous nations in place and in relation to the U.S. Instead, Ridge extracted colonists'

documentary forms and claims and read them against a capacious Cherokee archive that included official papers and personal archives. In chapter 3 I examine poetry albums kept by the Anishinaabe translator Charlotte Johnston in the late 1820s and early 1830s, into which acquaintances
and family members throughout the Great Lakes region transcribed original poems, drew images, and copied previously published texts. Acts of
assembling and using the albums generated feelings of friendship and generosity shared among Johnston and other Anishinaabe people, and these
feelings frustrated colonists' desire to imagine Johnston as a specimen of
Indigenous vanishing.

Chapters 4 and 5 take up printed compilations—lists and account books
—that invoke manuscript inscriptions or spoken conversation to recirculate
Indigenous histories of colonization. While the book chapters move from
manuscript to printed compilations, they resist any manuscript-to-print
narrative, for Ridge and Johnston copied and arranged printed materials
in manuscript compilations, and chapters 4 and 5 show how printed compilations generated manuscript notes and responses. Printed compilations
did greatly expand the communities who read and used them, for the multiple copies afforded by print allowed Native people to send Indigenous
compilations into colonial archives and simultaneously to circulate copies among their own communities. These chapters follow printed Indigenous compilations as they traveled into colonial archives that were also
proliferating—with settlers displaying and consuming Indigenous writing,
people, and belongings at world's fairs and in tourist markets—and being centralized in government agencies, universities, and museums. By the
late nineteenth century, Indigenous compilations traced multiple routes
and had parallel, though very different, uses in both colonial archives and
Indigenous communities.

In chapter 4 I examine Abenaki leader Joseph Laurent's book of Abenaki
grammar and word lists, *New Familiar Abenakis and English Dialogues* (1884).
Laurent embedded Abenaki histories of colonization in the word lists, so
that using the book circulated the histories in dialogues between language
learners and speakers. Laurent placed the book into tourist and ethnographic networks at a moment when tourism both objectified Indigenous
people and provided avenues for maintaining long-standing Indigenous relationships across settler nation-state borders. The circulations of *Dialogues*

disrupted geographic, racial, and linguistic maps of Abenaki and other Indigenous peoples. At the end of the nineteenth century, as seen in chapter 5, Potawatomi writer Simon Pokagon thematized Indigenous compilation by taking account books—lists of debts and payments—as a genre for his *Red Man's Rebuke* (also titled *Red Man's Greeting*, 1893). Pokagon used compilation to create a critical perspective on global and local histories of colonialism, by reading both the archives of colonialism and the exhibits at the 1893 World's Columbian Exposition held in Chicago, where he circulated the *Rebuke/Greeting.* Pokagon's use of compilation as both a genre and a material practice presaged its transformation into a narrative perspective in early twentieth-century fiction and nonfiction, particularly narratives critical of colonial bureaucracy by such writers as Carlos Montezuma/Wassaja (Yavapai Apache) and Gertrude Bonnin (Zitkála-Šá, Yankton Dakota). In an epilogue, I examine compilation's afterlives in contemporary Indigenous interventions into archives and museums.

Assembled for Use is an archival and literary history that reads compilations within Indigenous networks of relation, from the familial to the tribal national to the transnational. Indigenous compilations are essential to understanding the formation of colonial archives and the knowledge they produce, for compilations reframe the questions colonists posed about Indigenous pasts and futures and scholarly assumptions about compilation forms. One result of following compilations and their uses, I hope, is a more capacious and more complete sense of what we mean by Native American literature, of the Native people who made, read, and used compilations, and of how we might read archives of Native American literature today.

The ethnographic categories that colonial collectors devised as they amassed and organized archives hardened across the nineteenth century into modes of anthropological reading, subsequently deployed in searches for authentic indigeneity, cultural hierarchies, and progress (or, more often, their absence) in Indigenous literatures. This process left Indigenous compilations with their reputation as documentary texts or as specimens of reprinting that register colonial appropriation, assimilation, and control, seemingly at odds with the acts of sovereignty expressed in the more familiar literary genres of early Native literary histories, including the autobiography, sermon, petition, novel, and letter. But even as colonists were honing these ethnographic reading practices, Indigenous peoples' acts to make and circulate their compilations critiqued the categories with which colonists delimited Indigenous literatures and, by extension, Indigenous nations and homelands. Attending to juxtaposition, citation, and recirculation as tools for making Indigenous literatures, I show that what might look like a mere copy, colonial appropriation, or a utilitarian form are Indigenous compilations that generate shared acts of textual use among Indigenous people and a range of relations to colonial archives, including both rejecting and repurposing them. Combined, rearranged, and assembled for use, disparate textual materials took on new meanings and became new texts within Indigenous compilations.

CHAPTER ONE

RECIPE

Plant Vocabularies, Indigenous Bodies, and Antiquarian Reprinting

In 1749, the young Mohegan man Samson Occom was learning how to teach his Montaukett pupils on Long Island how to distinguish and arrange the letters of the English alphabet. Some students probably already spoke English as a result of interactions with colonial missionaries who began preaching on Long Island in the 1740s, but Occom found that some students could distinguish the sounds of English-language letters by ear but struggled to identify written letters by sight. Their efforts may have reminded Occom of his own experience learning letters as a boy, when a minister came to his home at Mohegan, in what is now the state of Connecticut, and "Us'd to Catch me Some times and make me Say over my Letters, and I believe I learnt some of them."[1] By 1749, Occom had not only learned his letters but studied for four years with the Congregational minister Eleazar Wheelock in order to gain greater facility in the English language and alphabetic literacy, which, Occom and Mohegan leaders recognized, could be tools for protecting Mohegan lands from Connecticut colonists eager to expand their land base. Occom took a leave from those studies to recover from severe eyestrain and to answer a call from Montaukett people to teach in their community.

Instead of catching and making his students repeat the letters of the alphabet, Occom sketched letters on "Small bits of paper, and Glued them on Small Chips of Cedar." Placing the letters "in order on a Bench, [he] then point to one Letter and bid a Child to take notice of it, and then I order the Child to fetch me the letter from ye Bench." If the child selected the right letter, "it is well, if not it must go again and again till it brings ye right Lr." When they could identify and "bring any Letters," Occom "Just Jumble[d]" them together and asked his students to arrange them in "Alphabetical order," an activity in which they took "Pleasure."[2]

In one reading of this scene, the Montaukett students entered into an arbitrary system of alphabetization that arranged both letters and bodies. For English colonists, writing and reading in English was a sign of the behaviors, knowledge, and bodily comportments they viewed as "civilized."[3] For example, Wheelock expected the Native people who attended his school, even those who, like Occom, were teachers in Native communities themselves, to report on their travels, expenses, and feelings, believing that he could mine their letters for information about their spiritual and cultural status. Wheelock circulated Native peoples' letters along with his own interpretations of them throughout missionary networks, providing his view of the intellectual capacity of Native men, women, and children and casting those writings as evidence of his success transforming Native people into obedient Christians. Alternately, he chastised his Native correspondents if he felt their writing betrayed actions or thoughts he deemed inappropriate or sinful. Wheelock's collection of the journals and letters made by Native students formed part of a manuscript collection that now resides at Dartmouth College, the school for which Occom raised support and funds among Native and white communities in the northeast and in Great Britain. As Wheelock's actions show, alphabetic order was deeply enmeshed with religious and cultural systems that justified colonists' efforts to elicit, analyze, and archive letters and other writings in order to discipline and control Indigenous people.

But another reading of this scene emerges when we turn our attention from the alphabetic and spiritual order valued by ministers like Wheelock to the students' process of selecting, arranging, and jumbling letters. The students learned how to alphabetize letters, to be sure, but they also experienced the pleasure of jumbling letters on the bench, of watching their friends select a letter, and of understanding the letters' many possible combinations. Arranging the letters into alphabetic order was not the final act but one that encouraged subsequent moves to arrange and rearrange, order and jumble. In this lesson, reading is one among several outcomes for encounters with letters, which also include jumbling letters, feeling the cedar chips, and sharing in the game's pleasure. Occom taught his students how the alphabet could order letters and bodies, but he also demonstrated how jumbling might be just as pleasurable and useful as ordering. At a moment when colonists were using writing as a disciplinary tool in Native communities and reading Native writing as an object that could illuminate spiritual and cultural states, Occom's game invoked uses like jumbling and rearranging that eluded those actions that colonists privileged, required, and documented.

While Occom was teaching his students about alphabetic order and the ways it might be jumbled, Occom was himself learning how letters and words might be arranged to reflect and make relations among humans, plants, and bodies. And this process, like the game of jumbling letters, entailed making combinations of letters, plants, and bodies that produced not discipline but care for Montaukett peoples' bodies. A few years after he answered the request to teach school at Montauk, Occom obtained instruction from a Montaukett man named Ocus, from whom Occom learned how to identify plants, the diseases they were "good for," and how to treat some common illnesses, including headaches and "sore eyes," lice, fevers, fluxes, bruises, sores, snake bites, and broken bones.[4] Occom recorded what he learned from Ocus in fifty-two recipes, which he listed across two unbound quires or booklets, held together with two stitches at the centerfold. Occom titled one booklet "Herbs & Roots," and he numbered most of the recipes, starting in the titled booklet and continuing in the second, untitled one. He transcribed plant names using English and Mohegan words, and he included information for identifying plants and instructions for preparing and administering medicinal concoctions and broths. As early modern studies scholars Sara Pennell and Wendy Wall have shown, recipes, far from being utilitarian documents, are dynamic texts that illuminate rich writing cultures and offer instructions for making and doing. Occom's recipes similarly function as such guides to doing, even as they also cultivate practices of making compilations that extend from assembling the entries in the booklets to mixing plants and roots and applying care to both bodies and souls.[5]

Occom's booklets act as compilations in two ways: the recipes gather together medicinal and plant knowledge, and the booklets physically aggregate a host of information, including accounts, a draft letter, and journal entries, alongside the recipes. The titled booklet (which I call booklet one) includes ten recipes; a cover page on which Occom listed a few expenditures and penned the words "Herbs & Roots"; a letter fragment, written upside down relative to the recipe on the facing page; and a journal entry (figure 1.1). The untitled booklet (booklet two) includes recipes numbered 6–51; a longer draft of the letter fragment; and nineteen blank pages (figure 1.2). Its cover is inscribed with signatures, including Occom's and those of other people, notes on debts owed, and tally marks. Like the alphabetic arrangements and jumbled configurations Occom and his students made out of letters, the recipes and material compilation in "Herbs & Roots" gathered together the materials with which Occom entered into relationships with Native nations and with places across the northeast.

"Herbs & Roots" troubles the categories around which the archives and anthologies of early Native literature have been constructed, such as English-language literacy and the genres of the autobiography and sermon.[6] Occom wrote the recipes primarily in English and included at least seven Algonquian-language names for plants, but the recipes are not oriented by the elements of English-language syntax. Instead, the recipes invoke acts of reading words as well as leaves, roots, stems, and bodies. Some entries identify the malady a recipe addresses, and some explain how to administer a concoction to a patient or how to apply a poultice. However, most entries contain far less information: sentences, subjects, plots, and sometimes even objects are not present. Some entries offer only the name of the illness against which the plant is effective, seeming to omit the herb's or root's name. For example, the recipe "Prickly Leav'd and Thorn Rts most of the thorn boild in a bout 3 Quarts of water till Consumed to a Quart—good for Heart burn" seems to offer a description but not a name for the roots.[7]

The recipes' flouting of the sentence as a unit of communication and their attention to plants as well as words as objects of reading frustrate literary studies methodologies of close reading oriented toward the sentence

FIGURE 1.1. Title page of Samson Occom's "Herbs & Roots, 1754–56," with accounts (booklet one). New London County Historical Society, New London, Connecticut.

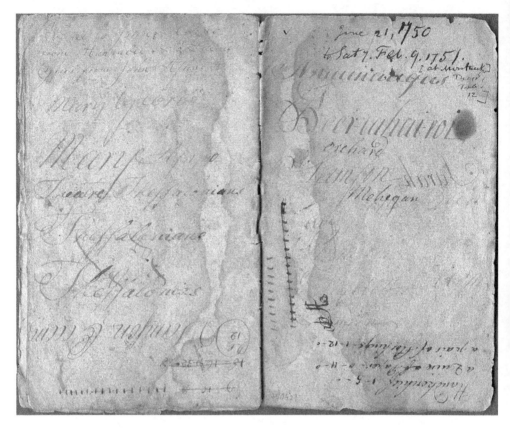

FIGURE 1.2. Title page of "Samson Occom, herbal remedies and letter fragment" (booklet two). Courtesy of Dartmouth College Library.

and figurative language. As literary scholar Siobhan Senier has observed of "Herbs & Roots" in an article on Mohegan understandings of illness and healing, "The herbal, in short, contains nothing to explain or contextualize the remedies for people not already familiar with this kind of plant use."[8] Perhaps as a result, early American studies scholars usually take note of "Herbs & Roots" as a biographical and historical document, reading the recipes as evidence for the contexts through which we might understand Occom's other, more ostensibly literary writings, like his sermons, journals, and autobiographies.

Occom's compilations are also partly obscured by the booklets' two archival locations and by their contemporary publication. The booklets are held separately, in two archives, one at the New London County Historical Society (New London, Connecticut), along with a few other Occom manuscripts, and the other at Dartmouth College Special Collections (Hanover, New Hampshire), among the many manuscripts by and about Occom. The recipes were published in full in 2006, in the complete edition of Occom's writings edited by literary scholar Joanna Brooks.[9] In that volume, Brooks prints the recipes as one text, indicating their separate archival locations in a note at the end of the entry; she also rearranges the order of the recipes in booklet one and omits the paratextual materials.[10] The 2006 publication of "Herbs & Roots" renders it as a cohesive and sequential text, effacing the fragments, drafts, and notes that share space with the recipes and thus its status as a material compilation.

In this chapter I read Occom's recipes and the booklets as compilations that assemble words, textual fragments, plants, and bodies into meaningful relation. "Herbs & Roots" epitomizes the forms of reading that Indigenous compilations generate and require: those that can attend both to the relationships Occom made among words on the page and to the ways the recipes point beyond their pages to relationships among plants, bodies, and maladies. The recipes require an understanding of local plants and their properties in order to use them, and in this chapter I point to some of the ways Occom may have read and used the recipes, by drawing on Occom's own accounts of his medical practices and on published work by Mohegan and Brothertown Indian Nation scholars. I focus on acts of reading and using the recipes, rather than on specific knowledge or medicinal practices, both to model alternatives to reading the recipes as historical documents and to recognize my own lack of knowledge, as a non-Native scholar, regarding Mohegan medicine.[11] I read the booklets alongside Occom's journals to understand how the recipes assisted Occom in responding to requests for both spiritual and physical care and strengthening communities at Montaukett and at the intertribal Brothertown community (now the Brothertown Indian Nation) he helped to found in the 1770s and 1780s.

In addition to traveling with Occom to Indigenous nations, the recipes also traveled into the colonial archives where they now reside. The different locations of the two booklets attest to the ways that Occom sent his compilations to colonists for reasons that included demands for reports from people like Wheelock, financial need, and friendship. The locations of the two booklets recall as well colonists' desire to possess Occom's writing after his death in 1792, and I conclude the chapter by examining the processes by which some of Occom's manuscript writings were archived and published posthumously. In the 1790s, settlers were constructing new categories for understanding Indigenous writing. Crucial to this work was their move to interpret Occom's writing not as texts created to support Indigenous communities and his own family, or to help him provide comfort to people's bodies, minds, and spirits, but as historical documents useful for telling narratives that cast settlers as central actors. I argue that these early acts of creating and organizing archives established a foundation for colonial archives formed later in the nineteenth century, when colonists categorized Indigenous writers like Occom within frameworks for authorship and history oriented around settlers. While these categories have proved durable and influential across centuries, Mohegan and Brothertown tribal citizens maintain their own spaces for reading and understanding Occom's writing and their nations' respective historical and literary archives more generally.

Routes and Relations

Occom's studies of medicinal plants with Ocus deemphasize his schooling with Wheelock as a defining moment in his life, a focus initiated by colonial historians in nineteenth-century biographies of Occom and one many scholars have since reiterated. "Herbs & Roots" turns our attention from Occom's studies of theology and languages (including Latin and Hebrew) with Wheelock to center his studies of plants, while also shifting our focus from Wheelock's school in Lebanon, Connecticut, to center on Mohegan and Montauk. In this, I follow the lead of Mohegan and Brothertown Indian Nation tribal historians and citizens as well as Abenaki scholar Lisa Brooks and literary scholar Hilary E. Wyss. They all position Occom's studies with Wheelock within already existing relations among Mohegan people and between Mohegan and Montaukett people and as critical to Occom's advocacy for Mohegan land rights.[12] In the 1720s and 1730s, when Occom was a child, Connecticut Colony expanded its settlements onto Mohegan lands despite Mohegan petitions to the British crown and legal documents affirming that no lands could be ceded without approval from the Mohegans' trustees.[13] Occom's decision to study with Wheelock emerged at least in part from his and other Mohegans' observation of the ways English colonists used literacy as a tool of dispossession. As Lisa

Brooks notes, while Wheelock's school fostered his "colonial experiment," the school also "provided a space of interaction for Native students who could potentially utilize their education for community empowerment."[14] In Occom's case, that education was a "tool he could use to reclaim land and reconstruct the 'whole' of Mohegan."[15]

Moreover, rather than make a permanent move to Lebanon and Wheelock's school, Occom's journals indicate that he moved between Lebanon, Mohegan, and other northeastern Native communities. Occom noted that his studies with Wheelock began when he went to Lebanon, where he stayed only "about a Week" before he "was obliged to Come away from there again to Mohegan, and stayed a bout a Fortnight at mohgn and then I returned up to Mr Whees again."[16] His journals from the 1740s and 1750s often begin with the phrase "I set out" or "I went away from," tracing routes to and from Mohegan, his journeys to Wheelock's, and his travels to visit Native communities at Nahantick (Niantic), Montauk, Narragansett, and Shinnecock.[17] Occom followed well-established routes among these communities.[18] And it is Mohegan, not Lebanon, that remained the center of these travels: Mohegan was his first stop on leaving Wheelock's, and he often saw his mother and visited friends there before setting out for other communities, again returning to Mohegan before going to Lebanon. Lebanon became one node in a web of Native places, but rather than standing at the center of that map, Lebanon was integrated into an existing network.

Occom's routes indicated Mohegan's centrality, and they show that Occom maintained frequent contact with Native relatives, friends, and travelers.[19] He regularly indicated in his journals that he traveled with other people, using a plural pronoun to explain that "we set out" or "we arrived" and other times indicating specifically that he traveled alone. He did not always specify whom this "we" included, but the fellow travelers he did name are people with whom Occom later collaborated in organizing to protect Mohegan lands and to form Brothertown, including men from Mohegan like Samuel Ashpo and Joseph Johnson, or Montauk men with whom he traveled to visit, fish, be "entertained," and sometimes to have "Meetings together."[20] In November 1748, for example, Occom departed Natick accompanied by two leading men of that community, Jacob Chalkcom and Isaac Ephraim, who traveled with him "3 or 4 miles—and so we parted."[21] In another instance, in June 1750, he met John Ashpo, the son of the Mohegan minister Samuel Ashpo, whom Occom knew well, and traveled with him from Easthampton to South Hampton on Long Island, staying "there amongst our Country Men till Monday June ye 22 . . . and then we Return'd from thence to wards Montauk."[22] Such extensive journeys made Occom a well-known presence in northeastern communities, including Montauk.[23]

Before moving to Montauk in 1749, Occom had joined Montauk men on fishing expeditions, and he had stayed at Montauk on several earlier occasions. As he writes in September 1745, "Many of us Sot out from Mohegan for Long Island and we got so far as New London that Night, & in the Morning we Sot Sail from there, and we got to the place of our Desire in the Evening, and Some of us Lodg'd at [Queen's] Wigwaum that Night, and there we were very kindly Entertained by all of 'em, We had Several Meetings together, and there was Some Stir among 'em—And in the 18th of Sepr we all Return'd home again to Mohegan, and to Several Places where we belong'd."[24] These journeys allowed Occom to participate in seasonal ceremonies that involved knowledge of and relations to plants: in 1750, he hurried back to Montauk from a visit to Mohegan, setting out from the shore to "the Indian Towns, and went among the People to get some Sweet Corn."[25] Joanna Brooks observes that Occom was likely participating in the Green Corn Ceremony, a celebration of the harvest that acknowledged the importance of corn as a "primary crop and a sustainer of life."[26] Like the Mohegans, the Montauketts had faced decades of pressure to give up their lands, and they had confronted colonial policies that restricted their access to resources like firewood as well as colonists who killed their dogs and levied high fines if their livestock escaped.[27] Ministers also discouraged ceremonies like the Green Corn Festival.[28] Its celebration in 1750 thus not only affirmed Montaukett peoples' reliance on corn and gratefulness for the harvest but also insisted on the continuing importance of those ceremonies even in the face of colonial obstructions to planting, harvesting, and celebrating corn. Occom's participation in the ceremony indicates that his relationship with the Montaukett community included the shared recognition of their "relationship to all living and growing things," a relationship that extended to learning medicinal knowledge.[29]

The Vocabularies of Plants

His journeys throughout northeastern Native communities in the 1740s meant that Occom was already known at Montauk by the time he responded to Montaukett people's request to serve them as a teacher in 1749. Wheelock and the Boston Board of Commissioners approved a plan in which Occom either taught school or performed manual labor while he recovered from eyestrain, anticipating that he would then continue his studies at a colonial institution, such as Yale College. But Occom took a different route: he established a school at Montauk and was soon serving Montaukett people in multiple capacities.

Occom's interest in medicinal knowledge may have emerged in part from his own ill health and his desire to obtain "means for [his own] Recovery."[30] The presence of three recipes for treating eyestrain in "Herbs & Roots" may indicate Occom's interest in seeking relief for his own ailments. But it is also likely that Occom asked Ocus to train him in medicinal knowledge in response to requests from Montaukett people, who had recently experienced widespread illnesses.[31] Occom wrote in his autobiographical narrative that his responsibilities to the community grew over time, so that he eventually "read the Scriptures to them and Usd to expound upon some perticular Passages in my own Toung; Visited the Sick and attended their Burials."[32] After six months serving in these capacities, the Montauketts urged him to stay longer, and he continued "till I was Married" to the Montauk woman Mary Fowler. He soon "had additional Service: I kept School as I did before and Caried on the Religious Meetings as often as ever, and attended the Sick and their Funerals, and did what Writings they wanted, and often Sat as a Judge to reconcile and Deside their Matters between them, and had visitors of Indians from all Quarters; and, as our Custom is, we freely Entertain all Visitors."[33]

As Occom's increasing responsibilities to visit the sick and attend the dead at Montauk suggest, the recipes Ocus imparted to Occom were lessons both in using plants to prepare medicinal concoctions and in making relationships with Montaukett people and to Montaukett lands. Occom's recipes not only gather medicinal knowledge, they also encode relationships with plants and other people. Those relations are woven throughout the recipes, compiled in Occom's choice of plant names and modes of identifying illnesses. Several patterns of identification are present in the recipes: Occom described some roots and herbs on the basis of a key characteristic, while he represented others in terms of their ability to heal a particular illness or disorder. In many entries, Occom identified roots and herbs by naming one of their primary or distinguishing features, and he followed this identification with a statement of the malady against which the plant was efficacious. Four examples display this structure explicitly:

wehsuck or Bitter Root good to kill Lise 12 . . .
A Long Notched Leaf good Boil 17 / Master over Witch Rt 18 . . .
Long Fever herb take it the Leaves & throw them into hot water and Put
    them upon the wrsts hollow of the feet and upon the forehead 20 . . .
Prickly Leav'd and Thorn Rts most of the thorn boild in about 3 Quarts
    of water till Consumed to a Quart—good for Heart burn 36[34]

In these recipes, the plant names—wehsuck or Bitter Root, Long Notched Leaf, Long Fever herb, Prickly Leav'd and Thorn Rts—highlight a defining element of the plant's appearance, taste, or texture. As they identify these qualities, the names also establish the plants' healing virtues.

Mohegan people began to place some of their medical knowledge into print publications in the twentieth century, in their own writing and in collaborations with U.S. anthropologists to whom Mohegan people relayed some of the knowledge held in their community for generations. Gladys Tantaquidgeon, the Mohegan medicine woman, educator, anthropologist, and co-founder, in 1931, of the Tantaquidgeon Indian Museum, produced several such publications. Tantaquidgeon was a descendant of Occom's sister Lucy, and as Abenaki scholar Margaret M. Bruchac explains in her study of Indigenous collaborations with settler anthropologists, Tantaquidgeon was "trained in Indigenous knowledge by Mohegan sociocultural authorities, including Nehantic elder Mercy Ann Nonesuch Mathews, medicine woman Emma Baker, and one of the last fluent Mohegan speakers, her great-aunt, Fidelia Fielding."[35] In 1919, Tantaquidgeon began studying anthropology at the University of Pennsylvania, and she worked with Penn anthropologist Frank G. Speck from 1919 to 1933. As Bruchac shows, Speck had been visiting families at Mohegan since 1900, and he wrote several articles on Mohegan medicinal knowledge based on his conversations with Mohegan elders.

Reading Occom's recipes alongside these later publications can illuminate some of the plant vocabularies on which Occom drew to compile
the recipes, while also indicating the continuities between eighteenth- and
twentieth-century medicinal practices. As Tantaquidgeon and Speck explain, one mode of classification in Mohegan medical systems identifies
plants according to their appearance or qualities, which correspond to and
reflect their medicinal properties. This practice is based on the observation that plants visibly signal their virtues and, by extension, their relationship to diseases. Speck discussed these associations in his 1917 account of
"Northeastern Algonquian" medicine, information he drew from conversations with Mohegan people. Speck wrote that "relationships exist between the disease to be treated and either the appearance, the imaginary
quality, smell, taste, or even the name of the herb used in the treatment."[36]
Descriptive names such as those Occom used likely represent these relationships between plants and the diseases against which they were effective. As he gathered plant names and instructions for use within the recipes, Occom made the recipes reflect as well the relations between plants
and illnesses.

Plant names could also signal their appearance and related medicinal
virtues and, consequently, the maladies they addressed.[37] In her writings
on Mohegan medicine, Tantaquidgeon noted that ' "Canker lettuce,' shin
leaf (*Pyrola elliptica*), is steeped and the liquid used as a gargle for sores or
cankers in the mouth," and ' "Peppergrass' (*Bursa bursa-pastoris*) seed pods
are made into a tea for the general benefit of the stomach. Its pungency
is thought to kill internal worms."[38] In these descriptions, as in Occom's
recipes, plants' names act not only as labels for identification but also keys
or clues—"sympathetic associations," as Speck called them—into plants'
powers and uses.[39] In "Herbs & Roots," "Prickly Leav'd and Thorn Rts"
may have possessed traits similar to the inward stings brought on by heart-
burn; they consequently provided an ideal antidote with which to counteract that malady. The name "Long Fever herb" links the herb to an illness; the herb's name indicates that it possessed attributes that suited it to
healing fevers. In some instances, a quality or feature of the plant signaled
its medicinal qualities: for example, "Bitter Root" could counteract lice,
perhaps because its bitterness drove the lice away. The recipes' descriptive
names were not merely identificatory; they also allowed Occom to make

visible on the page the correspondences among plants, their medical qualities, and the illness they counteracted.

Occom's practice of identifying herbs according to their properties may
also have reflected his own location on Montauk. Montauk has several
different "biotic areas," each of which differ "floristically," with coastal
areas, pine woods, and hilly areas supporting different plants.[40] Descriptive names such as Bitter Root or Prickly Leav'd and Thorn Rts were
probably place-specific, perhaps unique to Montauk and certainly referencing plants growing at particular places. Moreover, Occom employed
several Algonquian words—for example, "wehsuck" for "bitter root" and
"Cowachink" for an herb "good for Cole [cold?]"—and these words point
to his knowledge of places and plants as they were known to Montaukett
people and for which, as Courtney Cottrell, PhD, tribal historic preservation officer at Brothertown Indian Nation, suggests, there may not have
been English-language words.[41] Occom would have learned about the appropriate times of year to gather plants and how to dry them in order to
render those plants suitable for medicinal treatments.[42] Identifying plants
in terms of their properties involved recognizing, by their appearance or
other qualities, when plants were ready for gathering or when they were
ready to be ground or hung to dry. The recipes thus also require reading
plants in season- and place-specific contexts, coordinating their medicinal
virtues with their location and with the season.

In a second pattern of identification, Occom provided no information
about the appearance or qualities of the herb or root, instead identifying
plants by naming the malady that they treated. In these instances, the lists
of herbs, roots, and maladies indexed a body of knowledge associated with
each illness and each plant. These listings not only represent relationships
among plants and diseases but also require someone who could interpret
such descriptions to complete the compilation. For example, Occom included entries on:

A Rt. For fits. Pound the Rt and Soke in water about half an hour 4 Rts
   will doe. 19 . . .
an herb good for worms 24 . . .
An herbe good for Rattle Snakes bite 34 . . .
Herb good to heal brocken bones about the fingers and feet 47[43]

FIGURE 1.3. Page of recipes from "Herbs & Roots."
Courtesy of Dartmouth College Library.

In each recipe, the name of the malady stands in for the name of the herb or root; no further instruction for identifying the "Rt." or herb is provided (figure 1.3). The plants listed here seem to be so intimately related to particular maladies that Occom can record that relationship by naming the disorder.

These recipes reference relations between plants and diseases by naming the plant's medicinal properties, which may have been represented by taste or texture or by a sign on the surface of the plant or its root, in markings that pointed to some feature of the malady. Yet rather than identifying these markings in the recipe, Occom named the disease to which the plants' appearance and virtues corresponded. In these cases, he could work back from the malady listed in "Herbs & Roots" to remember and identify the plant. These recipes consequently call into play a practitioner who, like Occom and Ocus, understood the connections between illness and the properties of plants and could apply this knowledge in particular times and places to locate the appropriate herbs and roots.

While the recipes might appear to contain sparse descriptions, they are compilations of the pieces necessary to identify plants, recognize their medicinal properties, observe their readiness for gathering, and see their relations to illnesses. The recipes gather together the components Occom needed to read environmental and botanical signs, especially the relations that endowed plants with healing qualities and made them effective against particular diseases. Occom gathers these relations on the booklets' pages, and the recipes ultimately must be read within the relationships already existing among plants, bodies, and diseases. The compilation on the page relies on another assemblage off the page.

The recipes' patterns of identification parallel the vocabularies on which Mohegans draw to weave and ornament baskets. Gladys Tantaquidgeon and her niece, Jayne G. Fawcett, write that designs on Mohegan woodsplint baskets constitute a "symbolic vocabulary" composed of design elements, or "syntax,"[44] that are arranged in "one or more arbitrary, meaningful codes—languages, to use another term—within Mohegan painted designs."[45] The domes, triangles, dots, bars, leaves, curls, medallions, and stockades that compose this language represent Mohegan people and their relations to their lands at particular moments. But Tantaquidgeon and Fawcett also explain that these "designs . . . are more than simple representations of nature. There is a spiritual force that flows through all things, and if these symbols are true representations of that force, this spirit should be expressed in the designs."[46] Accordingly, Tantaquidgeon and Fawcett interpret "curved lines and rosette figures" that suggest the "flora of the woodland home of the Mohegan-Pequot" as designs that also signify those plants' healing properties: "Plant figures, symbolizing the food that sustained life and the medicine that healed sickness, would see a natural outgrowth of a world in which these elements played so vital a role."[47] Basket makers use this symbolic vocabulary in contexts of shared labor, as they work together to select and soak logs, separate the wood rings, and prepare the splints. Making baskets is a social activity, often, as Cree scholar Stephanie Fitzgerald writes in an article on a Mohegan basket now held at the Connecticut Historical Society, accompanied by "stories and songs, which in turn become part of the basket, joining together two traditions, oral and textual."[48] The basket's symbolic vocabulary is composed of designs and technical knowledge, and it requires a knowledgeable user to interpret and enact the relationships between plants, bodies, baskets, and stories.

Occom's compilation operates according to a similar symbolic vocabulary. When the recipes reference a plant, they also name a network of botanical, environmental, and bodily associations: the plant, its medicinal properties, and the malady for which it provided relief. And the recipes, like the designs on baskets, require a knowledgeable interpreter to read and activate the vocabulary of plants. The forms of reading the recipes require are oriented more by symptoms, seasons, and plants than words, sentences, and paragraphs. Just as basket makers rely on environmental, artistic, and literary historical knowledge to make and ornament a basket, so treating illnesses required Occom to identify plants, know the right times of year and how to harvest them, how to dry and prepare them, and how to apply them to the diseases they were "good for." The recipes act as guides to reading and using plants, for they hold within their lines a vocabulary for the relations among people, illnesses, and plants.

Learning about plants' medicinal properties and using the recipes incorporated Occom into the social relations through which plant knowledge and requests for healing circulated at Montauk and throughout other Indigenous communities. In the following section, I examine the recipes in motion, as they traveled with Occom throughout the northeast. Tracing the recipes' uses and circuits shows how visualizing relations between bodies and plants on the page also generated actions that provided relief for bodies and gathered people together. The travels of the compilations illuminate how Occom used the recipes throughout his life, and their journeys into their current locations in colonial archives underscore the extent of the Indigenous networks through which Occom traveled.

Gathering Plants and Communities

Reading the recipes alongside Occom's journals can indicate how he put the recipes to use. His reports of providing medical care during his travels indicate that the relations between plants and illnesses compiled in the recipes in turn created relations in social space. Occom recorded treating disease at two key moments: one cluster of medical care centers on his treatment of Montaukett people, and a second cluster appears in the 1780s, during his travels from Mohegan to Oneida territory to establish the intertribal community of Brothertown, where Occom and other Brothertown members hoped Indigenous lands would be protected from colonial control and dispossession.[49] At Montauk, learning herbs and roots allowed him to fulfill requests to serve as a healer as well as a teacher, writer, judge, and reader; thirty years later, medical care affirmed existing relationships among Native nations, including at Niantic, Narragansett, Pequot, and in Haudenosaunee territories, and built new relationships, as people from several communities reimagined their relationships to one another to form Brothertown. The recipes derived from relations centered around plants and bodies even as they prompted additional forms of relation. These uses mean that the recipes are less ethnographic items or utilitarian records than compilations that assembled and generated pieces of a network extending from Occom's page to plants, places, and individual bodies.[50]

Connections between medicinal treatments and other forms of care appear in the narrative Occom transcribed for the Montaukett woman Temperance Hannabal, who had been skeptical of colonial missionaries but who in the spring of 1754 called Occom to her bedside. In the narrative she relayed to Occom, Hannabal noted that she "was Sick for Some Time, and in my Sickness, I Begun to Query, What would become of my Soul, if I Shoud [*sic*] Die in this State and Condition, and these thoughts threw me into Fright."[51] Hannabal's illness raised concerns about her body even as it created a state in which she questioned her "condition," her physical and spiritual future.

Hannabal's account of how her illness aligned with her concern about her future state hints at the ways that Occom offered advice and comfort for various concerns, bringing relief to frightened minds concerned about the future and perhaps using the recipes to create a concoction that would attend to physical maladies. He may also have transcribed Hannabal's conversion narrative as part of doing "what Writings they wanted."[52] Perhaps Hannabal wished to give an account of her conversion to other Montaukett people, or perhaps she hoped to share with Occom her feelings of fear, illness, and concern. Or perhaps Occom sought out Hannabal for her story, asking to transcribe her words in order to create a written account of the people to whom he provided care, similar to the accounts of expenses he jotted throughout his booklets. Given that Hannabal's narrative is dated 1754, the same date for "Herbs & Roots," Hannabal's narrative suggests that Occom may have begun to learn and employ plant knowledge alongside the work of providing many other kinds of aid to people at Montauk.

After Occom left Montauk, he continued to provide medical care to people—Native and non-Native alike—whom he met on his travels. Throughout his journals for the 1780s, Occom recorded his travels from Mohegan to other northeastern Native nations as well as to Oneida and other Haudenosaunee nations. Visits to ill people, primarily women, punctuate these journeys. Requests to attend to the sick often delay, halt, or direct his travels, as he stopped to provide medical care for someone, retraced his route to answer a request for treatment, or stayed a little longer than planned in one place because someone was near death, perhaps anticipating the need to speak at a funeral. In January 1786, he visited an ill woman, agreeing to stay on with the family that night after they requested that he do so. They "Sot up very late," and in the morning Occom answered another call from a man who "desird me to go back a little way to See a woman put to bed last Night in Child Birth." He prayed with these "Dutch Folks" before returning to his host's home at Groton.[53] At other times, ill people provided motivation to visit a place, as when he went "to Nahantick in Lyme, to see the Sick, got to Rope Ferry just after Sun Sit, and heard, my Aunt widow Hannah Justice was Dead and Buried."[54] Occom's aunt had married into the Poquiantup family at Niantic, and this kinship relation, as well as Occom's frequent visits to the town in the

1740s, made him a well-known friend and relative. It may have been this kinship relation that motivated him to go to Nahantick specifically to "see the Sick," where he would have treated people he knew well.

The recipes likely traveled with Occom on these journeys, and Occom must have consulted the recipes as he responded to requests for treatment. The medical care he provided frequently involved treatments recorded in the recipes, from setting broken bones, bleeding people, and providing relief to women who had just given or were about to give birth. Sometimes he encountered difficulties, as when he tried to bleed Sally Skeesuck, a Narragansett woman who broke her arm when her horse threw her, but, he wrote, "I Cou[l]d not make out."[55] At other times, he bled people without comment on the process, as when he "Stopt at Jo Ashpo's and bled his Daughr Mercy She was very Sick."[56] Occom probably traveled with some of the herbs and roots he had learned to identify and use, plants he may have gathered near his home at Mohegan, carefully dried, and then packed among his belongings. He may also have supplemented these herbs with plants he collected on his travels to Oneida territory, such as the ginseng David Fowler and other Native men harvested as they traveled with Occom in August 1786.[57] Throughout these travels, the recipes took on a role not just as a guide to plants and illnesses but also to actions that knit together existing and new communities.

Occom's medical care continued to complement spiritual care throughout these travels. In July 1785, he "Stopt at one Mr John Shoolers to See a Sick Woman, found her very much Distrest both Body and Mind, I gave her Some Councill and prest to believe on the Lord Jesus Christ, and prayd with her and then went on my way."[58] A few months later, he stopped along his way to "Shursbury" (Shrewsbury, Vermont) in January 1786, "to see Mrs Burnham She was lately taken with a fit, and she is very Sick—I prayed with her, and then went on to the meeting H[ouse?]."[59] The "Councill" and prayer Occom provided for these women's minds may have been accompanied by medicinal care for their bodies, allowing him to treat multiple sets of symptoms. Praying and attending to illness took place in the same spaces, for Occom sometimes held a religious meeting at an acquaintance's house because of a sickness, as he did in August 1786: "Had a meeting at Abraham Simons on account of his Wife's Sickness; he was not at Home, he has been gone five weeks tomorrow."[60]

Seeing a sick person participated in and supported relations of reciprocity among Occom and the families and individuals with whom he collaborated to establish and sustain the Native community at Brothertown, on lands they were granted by the Oneida.[61] The people Occom recorded providing medical care for in his journals were frequently members of families who provided lodging and food for him on his travels, when he was raising support for Brothertown and when he was serving that community and the one nearby at New Stockbridge.[62] Acts of hospitality intersected with medical and spiritual care in these moments. For example, when the Mahican Stockbridge woman Catherine Quinney experienced a physical and spiritual illness in July 1787, Occom responded as he did in cases when people had broken bones and other bodily injuries, by going to see her and assessing her symptoms:

> Catherine Quenney was taken very Strangely at once her Breath was most gone all of a Sudden, and Capt Hindreck [Aupaumut, the Stockbridge Mahican leader] and his Wife, got up and went to See her, and I lay Still, and told them, if She Continued so, let me know, and the Capt Came back directly, and desired me to go over, and I got up and Drest me and went over, and when I got into the House, I went right to her Bed Side, and Sot down, she lay very Still, only Breathe with Struggle, and Sigh'd once in a While; and I asked her Whether She was Sick; She Said no, What then is the matter with you, and She Said, with Tears, I want to Love god more, and Serve him better; and I Said to her, if She really Desired and Askd for it She Shud have her desire granted, for it was a good Desire, & gave her Some further advice and Councel.[63]

At the call of his host, Stockbridge Mahican diplomat Hendrick Aupaumut, Occom got up from his bed, dressed, and went to see Quinney in the middle of the night. Assessing her physical state—that she breathed with difficulty—he began a series of queries to determine "what is the matter" with her. Giving her "Some further advice and Council," Occom attended to both her spiritual and physical needs.

Occom articulated the relations among physical, social, and spiritual bodies in a description of Brothertown from November 7, 1785, when he imagined the town as a healthy body composed of individual members acting in relation to each other and when he consented to make the town his "Home and Center." He wrote:

We proceeded to form into a Body Politick—We Named our Town by the Name of Brotherton, in Indian Eeyawquittoowauconnuck—J. Fowler was chosen Clarke for this Town Roger Waupieh, David Fowler, Elijah Wympy, John Tuhy, and Abraham Simon were Chosen a Committee or Trustees for the Town, or a Year and for the future the Committee is to be Chosen Annually,—and Andrew Acorrowcomb and Thomas Putchauker Were Chosen to be Fence Vewers to Continue a Year. Concluded to have a Centre near David Fowlers House the main Street is to run North and South & East and West, to Cross at the Centre Concluded to live in Peace, and in Friendship and to go on in all their Public Concerns in Harmony both in their Religious and Temporal Concerns, and every one to bear his part of Public Charges in the Town,—They desired me to be a Teacher amongst them, I consented to Spend some of my remaining with them, and make this Town my Home and Center.[64]

Occom's vision of Brothertown as a "Body Politick" characterized by "peace and friendship" and the promise to live in "harmony both in their Religious and Temporal Concerns" took the healthy body a metaphor for Brothertown.[65] Binding people together required cooperation, harmony, peace, and friendship among the parts. The "Body Politick" rested on what Brothertown Indian Nation scholar and lawyer Kathleen A. Brown-Pérez calls a "common vision of unity as a means to survival," a vision that imagined shared goals, labor, and understandings, and on bodies working separately but in tandem to achieve those goals.[66] Occom's actions to provide care for bodies experiencing physical and spiritual maladies created relations among people that in turn contributed to the new forms of community that Occom and other Native people envisioned.[67] The acts of medical care enabled by "Herbs & Roots" also generated conversations about bodies, souls, and community formation, and those conversations in turn built the alliances on which Brothertown depended to bring people together in a new community.[68]

Occom's physiological metaphor for Brothertown takes on additional significance when we consider that most of the people Occom recorded healing in the 1780s were women and that he transcribed multiple conversion narratives from women.[69] As his journals make clear, Occom healed men as well as women, and he described visiting entire communities suffering from illness. But in his journal entries, it is primarily women he recorded as requesting and receiving his medicinal care. Given Native women's historical and ongoing roles as keepers of medical knowledge, we might see these moments less as one-directional treatments than as conversations in which Occom and women from several tribal nations discussed the state of bodies and spirits. Native women's bodies and their accounts of physical and spiritual illness were central to personal and intertribal relations, and women's calls for healing—of spiritual and physical conditions—provided an impetus for the actions that helped form new relationships. And when considered within Mohegan medicinal practices, in which, as Bruchac explains, "healing was best effected by embedding one even more deeply within one's culture, and applying appropriate Indigenous pharmacological, physical, and spiritual interventions to encourage some restoration of balance or accommodation to both the individual, and the community," these conversations contribute to forming intertribal political bodies and to making relations among members of a community.[70] While scholars have sometimes viewed Brothertown as a male-dominated enterprise—and certainly its visible leaders were men—Occom's accounts of healing suggest that women and their calls for and use of medicinal knowledge were central to the relations that formed new Indigenous communities. Occom's recipes and his uses for those recipes throughout his life uphold practices in which, as Siobhan Senier puts it, "traditional Mohegan values and communities accept, care for, and benefit from those who are sick and disabled."[71]

Indigenous Compilations and Colonial Archives

If consulting the recipes as a guide constituted one form of use and an engine of their mobility, Occom also sent the recipes into motion as material compilations. In that capacity, the compilations obtain different kinds of uses than the treating, transcribing, and comforting the recipes supported. As material compilations, the booklets functioned as gifts, objects for purchase, and documents that represented Occom's actions. As I explained above, the two recipe booklets now reside in separate archives, with booklet two held at Dartmouth College, among papers by and about Occom, many of which were gathered by Eleazar Wheelock, and booklet one held at the New London County Historical Society, along with one of Occom's journals from 1786, and a letter from Occom to Nathaniel Shaw, a New London merchant and shopkeeper whom Occom knew well. Occom and his wife, Mary Fowler, purchased household goods from Shaw and his son, Nathaniel Shaw, Jr. Shaw built the house in which the historical society now resides. While provenance records for both booklets are incomplete (if they exist at all), examining their locations alongside Occom's relationships with the Shaw family and Wheelock can indicate how circulating compilations—in addition to reading them—could generate support for Native communities, even as settlers sought to give those texts new meanings within colonial archives.

The New London location of booklet one is significant for its proximity to both Montaukett and Mohegan. New London is located down the Thames River from Mohegan, on ancestral Mohegan lands, which Connecticut colonists bought and, in some cases, seized from Mohegan people. Occom often passed through New London on his travels to and from Mohegan and Montauk, and his journals indicate that he sometimes lodged at Nathaniel Shaw's house. Shaw regularly received money and other donations for Occom in his absence, holding them until Occom returned from his travels. On several occasions, Occom requested that Nathaniel Shaw, Jr., assist his family with material support when Wheelock was failing to fulfil promises to provide for Occom's wife and children. When Occom was in Great Britain from 1765 to 1768 preaching and raising funds for schools for Native communities, Occom asked that Shaw, Jr., loan money to Occom's wife, Mary Fowler Occom, at a moment when Wheelock was remiss in providing assistance.[72] Writing from London in 1767, Occom stated that he was "much obligd to [Shaw] for your Care and assistance to my Family, in my absence" and assured Shaw, Jr., that he would repay the loan. Occom concluded the letter with a postscript in which he requested that Shaw "supply my wife with Money if she wants 10 . . . [pounds] let her have it."[73]

It is unclear exactly how one recipe booklet came to the New London County Historical Society, but Occom's frequent references to the Shaws throughout his letters and journals suggest that the manuscript may have been held with the papers of Nathaniel Shaw, Jr., and moved with them to the Historical Society's current location.[74] Occom may have decided to give the booklet to Shaw, Jr., perhaps for safekeeping, to pay a debt, or as a gift. Or, perhaps the recipes came into the Shaw family along with other texts Occom sold to another Shaw son, Thomas. Occom sold to Thomas

Shaw his copy of the 1685 second edition of *Mamusse Wunneetupanatamwe Up-Biblum God,* the Wôpanâak Bible translated by Wampanoag men working with minister John Eliot and printed by the Nipmuc man Wawaus, or James Printer. The Bureau of American Ethnology clerk James Pilling's *Bibliography of the Algonquian Languages* describes this copy in 1891, noting that Thomas Shaw had deposited it at Yale College in 1790. An inscription in the Bible indicates that Occom was its previous owner: "On one of the blank leaves at the end is written: 'Samson Occom ooskcoweeg Sepr ye 27 AD 1748:' also 'Thos Shaw's'; and in the upper corner, '17 6 53.' Below these names is the inscription: 'Purchased of the Revd Samson Occom by Thomas Shaw Esquire of New London & by him presented to Yale College Library AD 1790."[75]

If Occom sold the bible to Thomas Shaw in 1788, as Christine DeLucia suggests, he would have done so at a time when he was advocating and raising funds for Brothertown.[76] Shaw's possession of the Bible suggests that the family's relationship with Occom extended to the exchange of books and manuscripts, raising the possibility that "Herbs & Roots" may have been part of a similar transaction. The booklet's current residence at New London may reflect the decisions Occom made throughout his life about where to send his books and manuscripts and how to provide for his family and extended Native community, decisions that were shaped by and that reflect his travels and the connections important to his family's and community's well-being.[77] In this sense, circulating the booklets paralleled using the recipes: compilations on the page and at the level of the booklet made and strengthened relations among people.

The second booklet resides at Dartmouth College, along with letters Occom sent to Wheelock and Wheelock's records from the school that served Native students, Moor's Indian Charity School. The second booklet's location may attest to Occom's relationship with Wheelock before he broke ties with Wheelock in 1771, as well as to Wheelock's own desires to collect and interpret Occom's writing. Provenance records for Occom's manuscripts held at Dartmouth do not appear to exist, but Occom sent many letters to Wheelock as part of their correspondence. Wheelock demanded financial accounts and spiritual ones, texts that he could analyze for their status as writing specimens and records of Native students' "Progress [and] Success."[78]

Wheelock's insistence that his students create written reports for him aligned with eighteenth-century pedagogical practices even as it also emerged from his belief that he must make his Native students account-able to colonial overseers (even if he never succeeded in this project, as Hilary E. Wyss has shown).[79] In a comment that colonists would echo throughout the nineteenth century and that I take up in more detail in chapter 3, Wheelock claimed that Native people had "no care for Futu-rity" and "they are as unpolished & uncultivated within as without."[80] His view of his Native students as possessing misplaced or uncontrolled desires and their failure to "care" for the future motivated Wheelock's decision to apply his own strategies of "constant care," which he understood as oversight and discipline.[81] To take just one example, Wheelock wrote to Occom in 1764 with a series of instructions about how to account for his actions and expenses:

> Don't fail to write to me of your Progress, Success, and any Occurrence that may be entertaining, by every Opportunity, as you know Friends at Home will be glad to hear. Send me an Account of what Labour you have or shall hire upon my Credit at Mohegan; and what you desire me to do for your Family while you are gone.[82]

Wheelock defined "progress" in financial and spiritual terms: he insisted that Occom report on events that may prove "entertaining" to the school's "Friends" and supporters.[83] It may have been to satisfy this demand that Occom kept lists of expenses on the blank pages of the "Herbs & Roots" booklets, where he charted expenses for plowing and carting and carefully listed everything from a "fawn skin and Cote" given by a man named Thomas on September 15, 1761, to the "3 Dollars for Marrying a Cupple" he received on Monday September 5.[84] Later in the nineteenth century, as chapter 2 shows, colonial ethnographers continued Wheelock's practice of reading Indigenous writing as a portal to the writer's abilities and "civiliza-tion," arguing that Indigenous literatures could offer a guide to hierarchi-cal stages of human development.

"Herbs & Roots" shares space at Dartmouth College with many other writings by Occom, including letters, journals, and sermons. Private col-lectors evidently sold some of Occom's writings to the college throughout the nineteenth century, in this way affirming its status as a repository for

Occom's writing.[85] Occom's letters to the minister Nathaniel Whitaker, with whom Occom traveled to Great Britain in 1765, were reportedly donated to Dartmouth College by one of Whitaker's descendants, and the *Springfield Republican* reported in 1898 that the letters had "been in the possession of one family since the founding of the college."[86] In most cases, records of such donations and their sources are sparse: an 1825 account of a contribution to the Connecticut Historical Society simply noted that a "gentleman" had obtained "sundry tracts, sermons and other papers of the Rev. Sampson Occum," without specifying who the man was or how he obtained the documents.[87] Yet these reports show that Wheelock's gathering of his students' writing lasted beyond their deaths and even his own, as later collectors and librarians added Occom's manuscripts to Wheelock's papers. Even so, it is ironic that so much of Occom's oeuvre resides at Dartmouth, for one of Occom's reasons for breaking with Wheelock was that the minister had moved the school from Connecticut to New Hampshire, away from the Native communities Occom was committed to serving. Instead, Wheelock refocused the school's mission on training colonial students rather than the Native youth he had initially claimed an interest in teaching.

Booklet two's Dartmouth location reflects the ways that Wheelock and other colonists sought to possess Native writing and determine its meanings by claiming authority over where those texts resided and who could access them. Yet considered alongside booklet one's location in New London, the disciplinary web Wheelock sought to weave at Dartmouth is countered by Indigenous networks that extend to and incorporate colonists in ways that support Native families and communities. The Shaw family's provisioning of the Occoms is one facet of those networks; Thomas Shaw's purchase of the Bible, possibly to support the emigration to Brothertown, may have been another outcome. In the case of the booklet held in New London, Occom's decision to give or leave the recipes there kept them on ancestral Mohegan land, close to the plants listed in the recipes, and close to descendants of the people to whom Occom provided medical and spiritual care.

The recipe booklets' circuits to different archives were followed in the 1790s by intensive historical archiving and reprinting practices on the part of colonists. They sought to establish their own readings for Occom's— and other Native peoples'—writings, as texts that could illuminate North

America's past, in this way transforming them from compilations that generated relations with plants and people to ethnographic and historical portals to the past. Colonists' reading and cataloging of Occom's work influenced both literary histories and ethnographic research in the late eighteenth century and through the end of the nineteenth. These posthumous acts of archiving and reading Occom's work created ethnographic and archival categories that proved persuasive far beyond Occom's lifetime.

Making Archives of Native American Literature

By the late eighteenth century, settler antiquarians were representing Occom as a person central to the northeast's history, and they embarked on projects to publish some of his writing shortly after his death in 1792. Turning from Wheelock's interest in reading his students' letters and journals to monitor their actions, colonial antiquarians sought Occom's writings as materials for their efforts to construct a settler history for the continent and nation. The early archiving of Occom's work intersected with a monumental project of reprinting, whereby settlers sought to secure a past for the United States. As book historian Lindsay DiCuirci points out in her study of nineteenth-century historical reprinting, this was a time when "colonial sources we now consider authoritative were simply unavailable," and antiquarians sought to accumulate and reprint historical documents.[88] As I argue in this section, Native peoples' writings and stories figured in this project of what DiCuirci calls "antiquarian reprinting" in several ways, first as evidence of a colonial past and later as ethnographic documents.[89]

One of the first posthumous publications of Occom's manuscripts occurred in 1809, when the Massachusetts Historical Society (MHS) published his "Account of the Montauk Indians," in the tenth volume of its *Collections*.[90] When he wrote the "Account," in the late 1750s or early 1760s, Occom may have been describing his work at Montaukett to satisfy missionary commissioners' demand to know the results of his labor on Long Island.[91] In 1757, Wheelock wrote a letter asking Occom to "Represent to Them [ministers] The State of The indians at Muntauck and Desire Said Ministers to Manyfest to us wheather They approve of our Proseeding according to The foregoing Vote of Comifs:rs &c."[92] The "Account" is likely Occom's answer to the question of "The State of The indians at Muntauck." Paralleling the subjects on which Wheelock asks Occom to comment, his "Account" describes Montaukett practices for marriage, funerals, and the naming of children while also describing the current state of Christian belief.

Yet the "Account" is not entirely determined by the ministers' request, for the topics under discussion in the "Account" correspond to the duties Occom performed at Montaukett people's request, reflecting his role as a teacher who also attended the sick, assisted at funerals, provided teachings about "gods" and humans' "future state," joined other parents as they celebrated the births of their children, and perhaps baptized those children. When considered within the context of its creation at Montauk, the "Account" reflects the actions and roles that shaped Occom's relations with Montaukett people. From that vantage point, the "Account" described Montaukett as a community that maintained long-standing practices for celebrating life and marking death, even as some of those practices changed over time. The "Account" makes clear that the presence of Christianity did not eradicate preexisting Montaukett ways of life.

But as the "Account" circulated within colonial archives, colonists read it as an ethnographic document. The *MHS Collections* presents the "Account" as a report about what the society called "ancient Indians," despite the fact that Occom was describing living peoples and that the "Account" reflected his own participation in the community, rather than an attempt to document disappearing practices or peoples.[93] The "Account" may have achieved this label as an ethnographic text in part through the process by which it was incorporated into the MHS's archives. The minister John Devotion sent the "Account" to his cousin Ezra Stiles (also a minister and later the president of Yale College).[94] It is not clear how or when Devotion came into possession of Occom's manuscript, but an accompanying letter indicates that he hoped to contribute to Stiles's project to gather information about the northeast's Native peoples and colonial towns. Stiles requested original manuscripts relating to the region's history from his network of contacts throughout the northeast, and he took copious notes on Native peoples in the course of his own travels. He gathered information about "Indian customs," place names, histories, and populations, information he himself sometimes "took on the spot among the Wigwams."[95]

It is equally unclear how the MHS came to be in possession of Occom's "Account" in order to print it (the manuscript is not extant, to my knowledge).[96] It is probable that the manuscript traveled to the historical society along with Stiles's manuscripts, which compose much of the *Collections'* volume 10. That volume is filled with "memoirs," "numbers," and accounts of Native nations that were "Collected from the Itineraries and Other Manuscripts of President Stiles" after his death, as part of the society's acquisition of private libraries to increase its own holdings.[97]

For the MHS, publishing the "Account" in 1809 contributed to a larger project to create an archive of the region's history. Founded in 1791, a few years after Thomas Jefferson's call in his *Notes on the State of Virginia* (1785) to deposit lists of Indigenous-language words in public libraries in order to study them for evidence of Native peoples' origins, the MHS sought to obtain Native peoples' writings, place names, and histories as evidence of the ancient past. If Jefferson hoped to gather Indigenous-language words and Native peoples' belongings in order to articulate the relations between the United States and Native nations, the MHS focused on the local unit of the town, and its collectors viewed Native people as central to that study. In a 1791 letter, the society urged colonists to submit information in response to several queries, including their town's "Indian name; when the settlement began; whether it was interrupted, and by what means."[98] The second query requests information about colonists' experiences in wars, calling for "particular accounts of devastations, deaths, captivations, and redemptions."[99] Query eight calls for "Monuments and relicks of the ancient Indians: number and present state of any remaining Indians among you."[100] While this latter query is the only one to request materials explicitly belonging or related to "ancient Indians," Native peoples are an assumed object of study throughout other queries. They provide place names and constitute unnamed protagonists in stories of interrupted settlement, captivities, and redemptions—actions that from Native points of view might look more like defending homelands and insisting that English colonists abide by their own agreements.

The Massachusetts Historical Society initiated a process of reframing the complex, rich documents created by and related to Native peoples—from land deeds to Native stories of the northeast's geologic formations and Occom's "Account"—as disparate remnants that signal loss, decline, and disappearance. Colonial historians then located the northeast's history and literature in manuscripts written by colonial ministers like John Eliot, Roger Williams, Jonathan Edwards, and Experience Mayhew. In this way, the Massachusetts Historical Society and its *Collections* established a select set of colonists as central figures and sources for the northeast's literary history while making their writings newly accessible. Meanwhile, the *Collections'* dedication to gathering place names, stories, and demographic data from Native peoples in order to tell *colonial* histories participates in what Jean M. O'Brien has called "firsting," the claim that European colonists were the "first people to erect the proper institutions of a social order worthy of notice" in order to "assert . . . [Native peoples'] extinction."[101] In the *Collections,* Native peoples exist in the past, giving shape to the northeast but only as they interact with and are documented by settlers.

Occom's writings hold a special place within these claims of firsting: for Stiles and the *Collections'* editors (among them the ministers and MHS founders Jeremy Belknap and John Eliot), Occom was significant because his life and writings provided information about colonial missionary projects, constituting an important case in a narrative of colonial firsts. Categorizing Occom as part of colonial histories avoided addressing the question of settlers' encroachment on Mohegan, Brothertown, and other Native nations' lands as well as the contexts of dispossession that galvanized Occom's decisions to pursue studies that would assist with advocacy for Mohegan lands and later to move his family to Brothertown. The nineteenth-century framings of his writings as a chapter in missionary narratives attempt to paper over the long-standing relations of reciprocity, care, and knowledge of place that Occom's compilations fostered.

Settlers' antiquarian archiving has a long afterlife in both colonial histories and ethnographic archives. By the mid-nineteenth century, colonial historians were replicating the *Collections'* narratives about Native people and colonial missionaries as self-evident facts in their studies of Occom's life and work. Those historians produced posthumous publications of Occom's writings by relying on the *Collections* to generate their interpretive frameworks. The writer (primarily of novels and travel narratives) John William De Forest cited the *Collections* almost exclusively in the opening chapters of his *History of the Indians of Connecticut, from the Earliest Known Period to 1850, Published with the Sanction of the Connecticut Historical Society* (1851), a book about the early history of what became the colony and state of Connecticut and one of the earliest biographical studies of Occom. Like the *Collections,* De Forest began his story with colonists' "first discovery," and he relied on the *Collections* for historical evidence of those events.[102] Similarly, in his biography of Occom, the minister and historian William DeLoss Love framed Occom's writings within a story that follows "these Indians in detail from barbarism along the trail of civilization for a century and three quarters, an opportunity which is afforded by no other North American Indians."[103] Love began his story of the "trail of civilization" in 1620, with what he described as colonists' attempt to convert the Wampanoag men Tisquantum and Hobbomock. As Love claimed, "The civilization of the American Indians, to whom our land from sea to sea once belonged, is an endeavor nearly three centuries old. At no time since the forefathers came to New England have they or their descendants been wholly unmindful of this obligation."[104] Love presented Wheelock's life as part of this story of colonial "obligation," one that emphasizes colonial rather than Native actions. Like the *Collections*' focus on Native histories and place names to illuminate New England's past, Love positioned Occom's work and writings within a story about the "civilization" of "New England," a story beginning with and directed by colonists.

Ethnographic researchers later recirculated these narratives, transforming them from arguments about New England's origins into categories for organizing information about the past. In the 1880s and 1890s, researchers turned again to the *Collections* for source material. The Bureau of American Ethnology's focus on theories of cultural change converted colonists' histories from exceptional texts or emblems of New England's religious commitments into ethnological resources affording insight into Indigenous languages and histories. To take just one example, Bureau of American Ethnology clerk and bibliographer James Pilling consulted the Massachusetts Historical Society's publications to describe copies of Indigenous-language texts for his 1891 *Bibliography of the Algonquian Languages.* Occom's entry in the *Bibliography* reads simply: "Occom (Samson). See Edwards (J)," a direction that leads one to Jonathan Edwards's entry, which includes a description for Occom's best-selling *Sermon, preached at the execution of Moses Paul, an Indian* (1772), a copy of which Edwards donated to the Connecticut Society of Arts and Sciences.[105] Occom's work remains categorized in terms of and within entries for colonial ministers, and in terms of colonial ministers' possession of his publications, despite the *Sermon's* best-selling status and Occom's own active role in directing its wide circulation.[106] Pilling's bibliography made colonial missionaries and writers into framing categories and contexts for reading Native literatures as nineteenth-century ethnology recapitulated eighteenth-century antiquarian reprinting. If the reason for Eliot's, Mayhew's, and Edwards's prominence shifted by the 1890s, their ongoing centrality to publications and bibliographies of Native literatures is indebted to the eighteenth- and early nineteenth-century publications defining the New England town as a space with an Indigenous past and a settler future.

Colonial archiving and reprinting practices transformed what were, at their moment of creation, settlers' arguments for particular ways of seeing the past or reading documents into pieces of evidence and informational categories that rested on but obscured those historical arguments. These categories reframed Occom's writings within genres ranging from the missionary history to the ethnographic report, and these categories in turn downplay and efface the multiple roles and relations that shaped Occom's writings and that his writings helped to generate. Colonists carried these acts of reading ethnographically forward into the nineteenth century, as they analyzed Indigenous literatures for insight into various objects: the past, Indigenous peoples' intellects, and cultural hierarchies, as I show in subsequent chapters. These readings also, like the MHS's interest in claiming Indigenous homelands in the northeast as settler towns, established colonial boundaries through which colonists sought to confine Indigenous peoples in place and time. The archiving histories I have sketched here establish several dynamics that would continue to characterize colonial archives in the nineteenth century: colonists solicited and gathered Indigenous writing to read it as a portal into the past or for insight into ethnographic questions. And, they honed reading practices oriented by temporal and geographic boundaries with which they sought to frame Native peoples and writings.

Settlers' archival categories influenced generations of scholarship on Occom and other Native American writers, and they are one of the archival structures that historians and archivists in tribal archives, university special collections, and national archives are seeking to revise, with more accurate search terms or subject headings and with archives that relocate Native writings and documents within tribal national contexts.[107] Before those contemporary decolonizing efforts, nineteenth-century Indigenous people made and circulated compilations in moments when colonists were attempting to determine and impose those boundaries, even as Indigenous compilations also emerge from environmental and Indigenous interpersonal networks, as Occom's "Herbs & Roots" did. The mobility that characterized Occom's recipes continued to be a feature of Indigenous compilations throughout the nineteenth century, and as Indigenous people circulated compilations, they disrupted and reconfigured colonial categories formed in archives like the MHS and the Bureau of American Ethnology.

Conclusion

Stories of settler classification and interpretation are far from the final chapter in the creation and use of compilations by Mohegan and Brothertown peoples. Citizens of both tribal nations return to and read Occom's writings and those of Joseph Johnson, Thomas Commuck, and other Brothertown members. Despite settler antiquarians' work to relocate Occom's writings to historical societies and archives, many documents and copies of documents related to Brothertown's history were—and still are—held and cared for by Brothertown citizens. Love remarked in his history that his research relied in part on Brothertown community members, "in whose homes many items have been gathered."[108] Since Occom passed away at New Stockbridge in 1792, it is no surprise that some of his writings remained nearby at Brothertown. The Brothertown homes in which these writings were kept constitute an archive made by and for Brothertown citizens, to remember Occom and their own history, separate from the settler archives and publications that pursued ethnographic ends in reading Occom's writings.

Brothertown Indian Nation citizens continue to recirculate Occom's writings in such blogs as *Occom's Footsteps* and *The Life of the Brothertown Indians,* written and maintained by Brothertown Indian Nation citizen Megan Fulopp. Each blog invites readers to engage actively with the writings and histories of Occom and other Brothertown citizens. From December 2015 to November 2017, *Occom's Footsteps* republished transcriptions of Occom's journal entries about his travels in Great Britain exactly 250 years after Occom wrote them, allowing readers to retrace Occom's travels.[109] *The Life of the Brothertown Indians* hosts a "digital library" with articles about and records from Brothertown, as well as a chronology, digitized documents, transcriptions of Occom's and other Brothertown citizens' writings, and historical research. The blog, as the "About this Site" page explains, is a "learning tool" as well as a "place for our community (members and friends of the Brothertown) to meet and get to know one another"; it is a social space as well as a space for encountering writing by Brothertown founders and citizens.[110] In 2020, the Brothertown Indian Nation's declaration of July 14 as Samson Occom Day recognized his "sizeable role in the organization and the propagation of the Brothertown tribe." As Fulopp reported on *The Life of the Brothertown Indians* blog, Brothertown citizens took multiple approaches to honoring and remembering Occom's life:

> To commemorate this special day, tribal citizens will be offering up prayers in gratitude to God for the gift of Samson Occom's life; speaking with their family members "about [his] story and what he stood for"; reading portions of his journals, letters, and sermons; watching YouTube videos about him; and, in imitation of one of the ways in which Occom supported his family financially, one person is planning to carve a wooden spoon."[111]

Similar to Brothertown citizens' creation of their own archives and virtual spaces for discussing their histories, contemporary Mohegan writers model a turn away from colonial archives and books, looking instead to the relations with plants like those Occom learned and reflected in "Herbs & Roots." In her 2004 futuristic novel *Oracles,* the Mohegan writer Melissa Tantaquidgeon Zobel, Gladys Tantaquidgeon's great-niece, imagines a world in which corporate greed is transforming social and natural worlds alike. Most children have never seen a tree, instead experiencing the world through digital interfaces that provide a full sensory experience of everything from nature shows to news. Schools make yearly outings to a reservation—modeled on the Mohegan reservation in Connecticut—to see the only trees left in the area. Those trees remain, Zobel writes, because Native people had "failed at being good corporate Americans"—failed, in other words, to commercialize their lives and lands.[112] But opportunists are seeking to extract and commodify Native knowledge: a group Zobel calls the New Lighters have established a "spiritual space station" where they aim to make Native knowledge available to high-paying customers for a "blockbuster admissions fee."[113] For the New Lighters, Indigenous knowledge can "save" the world from ecological disaster and individual despair when it is detached from Mohegan people and lands and transformed for consumption.

Within this world, the young Indigenous woman Ashneon decides to end her studies in anthropology at a nearby university and instead learn from the stories in objects—from baskets to tools to rattles and plants—for which her great-uncle and grandmother care at their home and the tribal museum. Recognizing the animacy of these belongings and the static, incomplete nature of information in archives and books, Ashneon can "hear" objects in ways her anthropology professor refuses to. As a result, she comes to an understanding of the objects' deep histories and the relations they generate among people and between people and nonhuman beings. As she says to her professor, "Each artifact's story holds multiple layers. Books are so primitive." Instead, she can consider a "reality that I almost missed by thinking knowledge came from books. Now I read objects and they speak volumes."[114]

Ashneon's turn from reading books to reading objects—like the turn "Herbs & Roots" makes from sentences to plants, and like the Ojibwe historian William Whipple Warren's turn from colonial query lists to assembled histories with which this book begins—raises questions of what and how we read, of where knowledge is located, and of the relationships in which it is enmeshed. Zobel makes these questions central to a world shaped by environmental catastrophe, the corporatization of information transmission and experience, and the conquest of space. In an ironic wordplay, Zobel also links these questions to the forms of colonialism experienced by Mohegan people across multiple centuries: the "New Lights" is also a name for the eighteenth-century ministers and missionaries who emphasized feeling as a sign of conversion during the Great Awakening and who established missions trying to convert Native people, including Mohegans.

Ashneon's claim that "books are so primitive" might also describe how colonial institutions like the Massachusetts Historical Society and its *Col-*

lections make Native writings play roles as static representatives of Indigenous pasts. Instead, Ashneon attends to the relations embodied in the tribal museum's objects, much as generations of Mohegan medical practitioners learn to read plants in relation to the seasons, illnesses, and bodies. Importantly, Ashneon's turn away from anthropology and books to the tribal museum and her grandmother's botanical lessons is not an anti-technological move, for her grandmother watches the "cy" (a television-like machine that transmits sensations along with images) in addition to caring for plants. Ashneon rejects colonial claims to authoritative knowledge and order to emphasize other outcomes for reading and other possibilities for knowing.

Interlude

William Apess's Bright Gleams

In the early nineteenth century, colonial greed threatened the health of Native bodies and body politics like those Occom and others in the Brothertown Indian Nation worked to sustain. When the Pequot writer and intellectual William Apess visited the Mashpee Wampanoag community on Cape Cod in summer 1833, he described finding strange, sickly faces occupying the Mashpee meetinghouse, which had been a site of Indigenous activism and governance since the early eighteenth century. Apess "turned to meet my Indian brethren and give them the hand of friendship" but was "disappointed" by the people he met: "All the Indians I had ever seen were of a reddish color, sometimes approaching a yellow; but now, look to what quarter I would, most of those who were coming were pale faces, and, in my disappointment, it seemed to me that the hue of death sat upon their countenances. It seemed very strange to me that my brethren should have changed their natural color, and become in every respect like white men." The people he found sitting in the Mashpee meetinghouse were not the Wampanoag people he expected but white settlers who had "crowd[ed]" the Mashpee out of their meetinghouse and took the books intended for "little red children," who were "virtually bidden to stand aside."[1] Apess described whiteness as a hue of sickness: the hue of colonial dispossession and greed, which he found written on the faces of the white men, women, and children who occupied the Mashpees' meetinghouse and who were illegally harvesting timber from Mashpee lands.

Apess identified the cure for this sickness as the return to Wampanoag people of their governance and of their lands and meetinghouse. To make this case to Massachusetts officials, he illuminated colonists' duplicity and mistreatment of Mashpee Wampanoag people. He argued that the sickness at Mashpee originated with "oppressive" laws and the "systematic course taken to degrade the tribe from generation to generation."[2] To unveil this "systematic course" of degradation, in 1835 Apess published *Indian Nullification of the Unconstitutional Laws of Massachusetts Relative to the Marshpee Tribe: or, The Pretended Riot Explained.* The book is composed of what Apess called "extracts," selections from newspapers, petitions, firsthand accounts, and legal proceedings that "mark out the state of public feeling," often vitriolically opposed to Mashpee and to Apess and often insistent that degradation was a natural state for Mashpee people.[3] Apess assembled these extracts in *Indian Nullification,* adding his own comments and interspersing the extracts with "multivoiced" narratives of events at Mashpee, collectively authored by Mashpee leaders.[4] He arranged the extracts so that they expose the distance between colonists' words of concern for Mashpee people and their actions; colonists' "injustice" and deceit were illuminated as people read the extracted texts alongside one another and petitions from Mashpee.[5] As Apess explained, "If the reader will take the trouble to examine the laws regarding the Marshpees, he will see those causes of the inevitable and melancholy effect, and, I am sure, will come to the conclusion that any people living under them must necessarily be degraded."[6] The extracts illuminated both the Mashpee community's experiences under unjust laws and colonists' blindness to the ways those laws produced degradation (see figure I.2).

Deceitful claims about Native lands and communities were, as Apess was arguing in the 1830s, given weight and power in colonial archives and publications. In his autobiography, Apess addressed at length the processes by which colonial writers circulated false and harmful claims about Native people, which they transformed into foundations for legal policies seeking to limit Native homelands and rights. He concluded both editions of *Son of the Forest* (1829 and 1831), with a lengthy appendix, a compilation of what he again called "extracts."[7] The appendix fills nearly half of the published book: in it, Apess assembled extracts from colonial histories that reflect Native people's hospitality in the early seventeenth century and colonists' repayment of that generosity with theft and accusations of violence. Like *Indian Nullification,* the appendix is an Indigenous compilation that exposes the fallacies of colonial histories of Indigenous degradation by extracting and rereading them against themselves.

Apess remarked on the appendix's extract-oriented nature, noting: "He is conscious that they [the extracts] are thrown together without that order that an accomplished scholar would observe—and he takes this means of saying, that he is indebted in a great measure to the works of the venerated BOUDINOT, late president of the American Bible Society, BRAINARD, COLDEN, and several other gentlemen, as well as to the newspaper press and missionary journals, for many of the interesting facts &c. which will be found in this department of his work."[8] By stating that the appendix lacks the "order" an "accomplished scholar would observe," Apess contrasted his compilation with colonial histories. Those writings occupied a space of order and authority by virtue of being located in archives, cited by other colonists, and recirculated in the publications of historical societies and at commemorative events or in courtrooms. But Apess disrupted these citational expectations to tell an alternate history, one that does not observe "order" but that he created by cutting up, reassembling, and critiquing colonial histories. His compilation created a different view of colonial archives and of history: as he noted, colonists' "annals" are "rude," characterized by their "obloquy" of Native character, but some "bright gleams will occasionally break through" those dark spots, gleams that Apess's compilation illuminated.[9]

Indian Nullification and the appendix to *Son of the Forest* exemplify Apess's use of extracting as a form of archival critique. The assembled extracts illuminate the false premises on which colonial claims to Native lands rest: deceitful claims about Native peoples' lack of humanity that accrued power as they circulated through newspapers, popular town histories, and the laws designed to produce degradation among Indigenous people. Apess's compilations exposed the duplicity and damaging effects of colonial documents, while rejecting the archival structures—from genres like colonial histories to physical places like libraries and the cultural weight given to colonial publications—that endowed colonists' claims with authority. And as Apess extracted and recombined colonial archives, he recontextualized those extracts within Indigenous knowledge and experience, including his own observations of and participation in Mashpee people's collective acts to protect their meetinghouse and timber.

Extracting and recontextualizing colonial documents manifested as a practice of Indigenous compilation during the early nineteenth century, when Indigenous writers observed that settlers were amassing and reprinting colonial histories of the continent and seeking to pose their own claims about Native nations, languages, and histories. These settler publications sought not just to claim a past for the United States but also to use that history to justify taking Indigenous land and resources, like the timber from Mashpee, and to assimilate Native nations into U.S. political structures. Indigenous writers used their compilations of extracts to expose how colonial histories functioned as engines of dispossession. These archival interventions occurred alongside Indigenous communities' own collaboratively authored petitions and histories. In these compilations, Native people juxtaposed extracts from colonial publications with Indigenous communities' own archives and writings. A few years before Apess extracted newspaper articles and colonial histories to expose colonial duplicity, John Ridge, one of the Cherokee men who at times appeared alongside Apess in public speeches insisting on Indigenous rights, was extracting colonial documents and documentary forms to question their legitimacy and to assert multivocal Cherokee articulations of history and nationhood.

CHAPTER TWO

EXTRACT

Cherokee Nationhood and Indigenous Archives of Diplomacy

———◆———

Tucked among Albert Gallatin's voluminous papers at the New-York Historical Society (NYHS) and catalogued under the heading "Indian Languages" lies a fifteen-page letter that is not, in fact, about "Indian Languages." The Cherokee lawyer and spokesman John Ridge sent the letter to Gallatin in the spring of 1826. At the time, Ridge was in Washington, D.C., having traveled there in 1825 to assist Creek leaders in their successful renegotiation of a fraudulent treaty that had ceded thousands of acres of Creek lands to the U.S.[1] Hearing that Ridge was in Washington, Gallatin (a former secretary of the Treasury and by the 1820s an aspiring collector of Indigenous-language words) corresponded through Superintendent of Indian Affairs Thomas McKenney, sending Ridge seven sets of queries about Cherokee people and their relationship to what Gallatin called "civilization," and requesting translations of vocabulary words and the Lord's Prayer into several Indigenous languages.[2] Ridge took several weeks to write back, but he eventually sent Gallatin a letter in answer to the queries along with a set of word lists.

The letter now misleadingly cataloged at the NYHS has a twin, a draft letter in which Ridge considered how to engage Gallatin's queries and tested out arguments. In the draft, he tried out phrasings, crossed out words, left ink smudges and blots, and inserted new sentence structures and paragraphs with superscript x's. The draft letter now resides in the John Howard Payne Papers at the Newberry Library in Chicago. A playwright and aspiring magazine editor, Payne received permission in 1835 from Cherokee Principal Chief John Ross to record Cherokee accounts of their history, their philosophies, and the invention of the Cherokee syllabary by Sequoyah. Payne worked closely with the missionary Daniel S. Butrick to gather an archive of manuscript notes that Cherokee people directly shaped and oversaw.[3] At some point, Ridge's draft letter—along with writings he completed at mission schools in the Cherokee Nation and in Connecticut—came to rest in Payne's papers, and these manuscripts remain in Chicago today, distant from the letter sent to Gallatin.

After anthropologist William C. Sturtevant transcribed and published the NYHS letter in the *Journal of Cherokee Studies* in 1981, that letter became the text with which Ridge is most often associated. In 1995, historians Theda Perdue and Michael D. Green included the Newberry letter in their volume *The Cherokee Removal: A Brief History with Documents.* Perdue and Green read Ridge's draft as "virtually identical" to the NYHS letter, although they suggest that the draft "contains more spontaneous—and perhaps more accurate—descriptions than the final version."[4] Following these publications, scholars have read the letters through Ridge's decision in 1835 to sign the Treaty of New Echota, which ceded Cherokee lands to the United States and allocated funds to remove Cherokee people to Indian Territory. That decision was informed by decades of violence from Georgia settlers against Cherokee people and the state's refusal to uphold the Supreme Court decisions of 1831 and 1832 affirming Cherokee sovereignty and formalizing a nation-to-nation relation with the federal government. Twenty Cherokee men, including Ridge, his father Major Ridge, and his cousin Elias Boudinot, signed the treaty, whereas Principal Chief John Ross and a majority of Cherokee people opposed it. Cherokee men assassinated the Ridges and Boudinot in Indian Territory in 1839, in keeping with Cherokee law making it a capital offense to cede lands without the approval of the Cherokees' representative government.[5]

The events of the 1830s tend to orient scholarship on nineteenth-century Cherokee literatures, which ranges from framing the Cherokee Nation as split between "traditional" and "progressive" parties to presenting the changes the Nation made in the late eighteenth and early nineteenth centuries as ones that absorbed it into U.S. forms of nationhood.[6] From this perspective, the letters to Gallatin appear to offer an example of how Ridge "lauded Cherokee progress toward 'civilization'" and "readily embraced white ways."[7] Similarly, when Ridge's letter is read as foreshadowing the Treaty of New Echota, it participates in a narrative in which Ridge and other Cherokee men adopted settlers' own practice of evaluating the Cherokee Nation through categories like "civilization" and "improvement." But as Cherokee scholars Kirby Brown, Daniel Heath Justice, Joshua B. Nelson, and Julie L. Reed have recently shown, linear narratives moving from the Cherokee Nation's early nineteenth-century political and social reorganizations to the Treaty of New Echota in 1835 and forced removal risk effacing how Cherokee people continued to live, govern, and care for each other across and beyond those changes.[8] While Ridge, Boudinot, Ross, and some other Cherokee people adopted some U.S. cultural and economic practices, including the English language, Christian religious beliefs, and owning enslaved African-descended people, these changes did not—the desires of U.S. officials aside—entail political or cultural assimilation. In fact, Ridge strongly opposed removal and land cessions throughout the 1820s and much of the 1830s, and he wrote and spoke publicly in defense of Cherokee sovereignty. When his letters to Gallatin are read alongside Cherokee histories and actions leading up to 1826, rather than events that had not yet occurred, different readings of the letters emerge. In that context, the letters participate in a decades-long and ongoing Cherokee insistence that U.S. and European nation-states recognize and respect Cherokee sovereignty.

In this chapter I reunite Ridge's draft and sent letters, reading them as compilations in which he excerpted, copied, and recontextualized Gallatin's query list and its categories alongside extracts from U.S. periodicals and Cherokee Nation records. In addition, his letters extract and combine several documentary forms, including censuses, blanks, and lists. Like William Apess's appendix of extracts "thrown together" in *Son of the Forest*, Ridge's manuscript compilations engage practices of reprinting, such as those utilized by newspapers and literary journals that filled their pages by reprinting materials (for example, the *Cherokee Phoenix* reprinted articles from U.S. newspapers alongside original articles in the Cherokee sylla-bary).[9] He also joined such Black and Black/Indigenous writers as Pauline Hopkins and Robert Benjamin Lewis, who extracted—often at enormous scales—and recombined U.S. and European histories and ethnologies to place Africa at the center of global histories and kinship narratives.[10] Ridge juxtaposed extracted texts from popular periodicals with Galla-tin's query list, in the process revising Cherokee peoples' relation to those documentary forms and refusing the categories into which settlers sought to place Cherokee people. Recognizing that Ridge's letters are composed of extracts changes how we read them, by showing that they are neither straightforward reflections of Ridge's own opinions or his viewpoints on "civilization" nor concessions to the query list's categories but Indigenous compilations that recontextualize and create new uses for the extracts.

While Ridge's letters might seem to respond most immediately to Galla-tin's query list, his acts of extracting followed Cherokee diplomatic prac-tices going back at least to the eighteenth century, when leaders assembled, arranged, and circulated materials as part of strategies of interacting with British and U.S. officials. Starting as early as 1750 and until around 1778, the Cherokee leaders Oconostota and Attakullakulla sent and received let-ters, wampum, and peace medals to and from British Indian agents and government officials, and they stored these materials in what scholars call the "Cherokee archive."[11] Virginia colonist Arthur Campbell stole that archive in 1780 or 1781, in one of several attacks on Cherokee communi-ties during the American Revolution, and he sent some of the materials to Thomas Jefferson, then governor of Virginia.[12] Now held in the National Archives in Washington, D.C., Oconostota's and Attakullakulla's archives consist of around eighty pages (the wampum and medals have since been separated from the letters). The materials document and maintain Chero-kee relationships with colonial representatives: the letters record promises colonists made to Cherokee leaders, admonitions from both sides to ab-stain from violence, admissions that colonists infringed on Cherokee lands, attempts to establish boundaries between the British and the Cherokee Nation, and requests from both Cherokee and British leaders for alliances.

The Irish trader James Adair described part of Attakullakulla's archive before its theft. At that time, the archive contained letters from the colonial governor of South Carolina, and Adair reported that Attakullakulla found the governor to be untrustworthy, adding that he himself had "repented of trusting to the governor's promises."[13] He explained that the Cherokee leader received from the governor

> a considerable number of letters, which he said were not agreeable to the old beloved speech. He kept them regularly piled in a bundle, according to the time he received them, and often shewed them to the traders, in order to expose their fine promising contents. The first, he used to say, contained a little truth, and he excused the failure of the greater part of it, as he imagined much business might have perplexed him, so as to occasion him to forget complying with his strong promise. "But count, said he, the lying black marks of this one:" and he descanted minutely on every circumstance of it. His patience being exhausted, he added, "they were an heap of black broad papers, and ought to be burnt in the old years fire."[14]

Adair's comment suggests that one of Attakullakulla's purposes for keeping the letters was to make a record of the governor's words that could expose his duplicitous actions and writing. Attakullakulla could consult the letters to reveal the "lying black marks" contradicting the governor's actions, certainly a common scenario in the mid-eighteenth century, when colonists broke agreements with Cherokee leaders by encroaching on their lands. The proposal to burn the letters in the "old years fire" as a response to their "lying marks" may have aimed to purify Attakullakulla's relationships with colonial leaders, to set the relationship on a path in which honest, straightforward communications, or the "old beloved speech," would characterize interactions. Attakullakulla's reference to the "old years fire" may invoke the ceremonial fire that purifies and prepares the people for the new year. The Cherokee Nation's six major ceremonies begin with a lighting of a sacred fire, which symbolically begins the year anew. Fire renews social relations and roles and the peoples' reliance on the land for sustenance.[15] By suggesting that he would burn the letters, Attakullakulla may have hoped to purify the governor's words of deceit and his "lying black marks," to set the relationship on more honest footing. And Attakullakulla's reference to the fire shows how Cherokee practices of purifying words and actions informed his archive keeping.

This diplomatic archive was not limited to paper, for Cherokee leaders used wampum to maintain political relationships, as a letter to Oconostota from British Indian agent Alexander Cameron indicates: "I shall hide nothing from you, & do everything in my power for you & your Nation, in Token of which I send you this white string of wampum."[16] For his part, Oconostota sent a peace medal and string of wampum to endow a message to the British Indian agent John Stuart with the force of his presence. In return, Stuart thanked Oconostota for "your Medal and Commission with a String of white wampum," which the Cherokee leader had sent with a messenger who relayed Oconostota's message in his absence. Stuart stated that while he would have been glad to have "shaken hands and smoked with" Oconostota, he "looked upon your medal to be the same as if you were present in Person."[17] In these exchanges, wampum and medals act not as accessories to written letters but as messages that verify the letters' trustworthy status. Wampum fulfilled a role it had long performed in Cherokee communities, which Cherokee scholar Ellen Cushman describes as functioning "as texts, an archiving system of sorts, which chronicled events, negotiations with other tribes and colonists, and Cherokee philosophies."[18] The Cherokee leaders kept an archive of colonists' letters, wampum, and peace medals to maintain and affirm diplomatic relations and to insist that officials honor their promises. Campbell's theft of Oconostota's and Attakullakulla's papers and wampum during the American Revolution acknowledged those archives' power—the ability of medals, wampum, and paper to expose colonial duplicity and enact Cherokee leaders' authority.

Following this history of Cherokee archiving into the nineteenth century, this chapter tells a story of Indigenous compilations that draw on, reconfigure, and circulate through both Cherokee and colonial archives. Ridge's decision to write to Gallatin shows how some Indigenous compilations intervened in the assumptions embedded in colonists' inquiries, even while the ends of those interventions remained uncertain and subject to misinterpretation. Reading Ridge's two letters and following their travels move us from Indigenous compilations made for personal use (like Samson Occom's recipes) to public compilations made for circulation and composed of texts already circulating. As Ridge assembled materials from printed and manuscript sources authored by colonists and from Cherokee Nation archives, he continued Cherokee practices of making archives out of colonists' own words to hold them to their promises. Yet colonial archives are only one of the contexts relevant for reading the letters, for as Ridge engaged in compilation making as a form of diplomacy, he also represented how Cherokee people across the Nation used and made archives. Many such archives—for example, records transcribed in the syllabary, the histories kept by Cherokee knowledge keepers, and the stories inscribed in places like earthworks and caves—remained largely out of colonists' sight.[19] Reading Ridge's letter in relation to these archiving projects shows how his compilations represented and drew on some of those internal records even while keeping them from Gallatin's view.

Colonial Queries and Cherokee Compilations

By 1826, when he wrote to Gallatin, Ridge had observed many manifestations of what Gallatin's query list called "civilization" and its consequences for him and other Cherokee people. Born in 1803, Ridge grew up with the effects of the civilization policy instituted by the new U.S. nation. Initiated in the 1790s by George Washington's administration and continued by subsequent presidents, the civilization policy sent missionaries, traders, and Indian agents to the Cherokee Nation and other southeastern Indigenous nations with the goal of transforming gendered divisions of labor, generating debt and dependency on the U.S., and encouraging land cessions. The promise of citizenship—understood as incorporation into the U.S.—was attached to the changes the U.S. demanded of the Cherokee Nation.[20] Ridge attended schools established in the Nation by missionaries, who were charged with overseeing Cherokee peoples' adoption of western agricultural, domestic, and religious practices.[21] Ridge and his sister Nancy both went to mission schools within the Cherokee Nation, and they were bilingual in Cherokee and English languages. Ridge also attended schools in Knoxville, Tennessee, and Cornwall, Connecticut. Like his father, Ridge adopted forms of agriculture and commerce that white men used to accrue wealth, including owning enslaved Black people.[22] And Ridge married a white woman, Sarah Bird Northrup, whom he met while a student in Connecticut, a marriage to which the town of Cornwall responded with vitriolic racist threats.[23]

Ridge also encountered settlers' expectations as he worked to generate support for the Cherokee Nation, such as when he spoke in northeastern cities alongside his cousin Elias Boudinot and, on occasion, William Apess.

In these instances, settlers judged his appearance and speech against categories of "civilization" and an imagined Indianness. An observer summarized an 1832 speech Ridge gave in Boston in an issue of *The Liberator*, promising to satisfy "those who feel curious to know how a civilized and well bred Indian talks."[24] As the observer represented it, Ridge's "language was strongly figurative, though not strictly grammatical, but the more impressive, perhaps, on that very account, from its conformity to the Indian mode of expression: his voice distinct, and his action and elocution such as would grace an orator of the schools."[25]

As he confronted these categories of civilization and of Indianness, Ridge made compilations, transforming assignments or situations meant to order his thoughts and actions into assembled texts that critiqued those forms of order. In 1819, as a student at Cornwall Mission School in Connecticut, he kept a commonplace book into which he arranged moral axioms and religious poems, many of which he may have copied from *The American Reader* (1812), the instructional text written by his schoolmaster Herman Daggett.[26] The commonplace book does not seem to contain any original poems by Ridge; instead, it reflects the qualities of formality, regularity, and cleanliness through which the school sought to evaluate its Indigenous students.[27] Ridge inscribed his own name five times throughout the book, each script just a bit different in its placement of flourishes, a variation that suggests that he may have been experimenting with how to represent himself on the page and within—as well as outside—the school's constraints.

Ridge continued to make compilations throughout the 1820s, increasingly using them to make his own arrangements and interpretations out of colonial texts.[28] In 1828, he published several articles in the *Cherokee Phoenix*, critiquing a state of Georgia document laying claim to Cherokee lands. In "Strictures on 'The Report of the Joint Committee on the State of the Republic,'" he explained that he "open[ed]" publications by British and U.S. writers to refute their fallacious claims. Ridge observed that a Georgia committee had consulted Swiss legal theorist Emmerich de Vattel's 1758 *Law of Nations* to support its claims to Cherokee lands, commenting, "It affords one pleasure that the Committee counseled this work, which is open to me also for the same use."[29] Ridge opened colonists' writings by extracting quotations from the original state of Georgia "Report" and arranging the excerpts alongside pieces from colonial histories and legal texts like

Vattel's. In the process, he created a new text out of the disassembled parts, one that countered the original. "Strictures" is a brilliant piece of legal analysis, in which Ridge used European and settler texts to argue against the doctrine of discovery.

When Ridge decided to write to Gallatin in 1826, then, he did so in a context in which settlers were reading his body and words through their own expectations for Indigenous people as well as from the position of a young Cherokee man who was experimenting with how to speak and write against those expectations. At the War Department, where he went in 1825–26 to assist with the renegotiation of the Treaty of Indian Springs, he would have seen Thomas McKenney's Indian Gallery, which included Charles Bird King's portraits of Native leaders as well as "Indian dresses, ornaments, petrefactions, minerals" that McKenney and other officials had collected.[30] Ridge must also have known that when McKenney commissioned King to paint Ridge's own portrait in 1825, he was likely recruiting the young man as an object to add to the Indian Gallery. Non-Native visitors to the gallery viewed the portraits as objects that would allow them to read Native American people within racial systems of classification. An 1830 guidebook description of the gallery argued that Native people needed to be "*seen* to be known," presenting the gallery as a place to interact with "scenes which are past."[31] The guidebook noted that the portraits were "arrayed, in tasteful order" and offered the "likenesses of one hundred and thirty Indian chiefs, in their native costume."[32] King's attention in his portraits to the "relative proportions of the head—and the central hemispheres . . . in which are supposed to lie those governing powers which lift man so far above the lower orders of beings" supposedly allowed readers to make "another link in the long chain of the *history of man.*"[33] Despite the fact that King painted many Native diplomats who were in Washington as part of tribal delegations, the Indian Gallery purported to offer a record of an allegedly vanished people within a racial and temporal classificatory system focused on the question of what "an Indian" is or was.

Gallatin's queries for Ridge relied on similar assumptions. Expanding the Massachusetts Historical Society collectors' focus on the town to the scale of the continent, Gallatin had just launched a project to collect hundreds of Indigenous-language word lists. He eventually published his conclusions in 1836, in the second volume of the American Antiquarian Society's publication *Archaeologia Americana: Transactions and Collections of the American Antiquarian Society*. But in 1826, when he wrote to Ridge, Gallatin had only recently received federal support for this project. Against the advice of his friend Peter du Ponceau, the philologist and secretary of the Historical and Literary Committee at the American Philosophical Society, who warned that presidents and secretaries of state would not "condescend to be a Collector of Grammars and Vocabularies," Gallatin persuaded President John Quincy Adams to sponsor the massive linguistic collecting project.[34] Working with Secretary of War James Barbour, Gallatin developed a list of about six hundred "primitive words which can hardly have been borrowed from other languages," and he distributed them to Indian agents, traders, and travelers, with instructions to fill in the blanks and return the lists.[35] Barbour and Gallatin explained that it was crucial "to know the name, and the meaning of the name, (when it has any,) given by each tribe to the rivers known to them. And there are some rivers which, could we know by what nation, or in the language of which nation they are called by the name they now bear, or which they did bear when first known to us, would assist us in finding out the ancient boundaries of certain tribes." Gathering these words would, the men believed, allow them to place Native peoples within geographic boundaries, for Gallatin and Barbour argued that linguistic study constituted the "best mode of finding out, with certainty, to whom debatable country did belong, and to what class lost languages did pertain."[36] The word list functioned as an imagined taxonomy, one that would ideally produce unique linguistic units that colonists could compare and arrange on the basis of their similarities and differences, thus illuminating what they believed were the "characteristic features" of Indigenous languages.[37] It was on the basis of these features that Gallatin and Barbour proposed to arrange Native peoples in place, a desire that reappeared in the 1870s and 1880s when officials at the Bureau of American Ethnology proposed to use language to place Native nations on reservations. (I discuss this proposal in chapter 4.)

Gallatin utilized a similar taxonomic form in his correspondence with Ridge, turning to the query list to solicit information about the "characteristic features" of Cherokee life and to ensure that he could file this information into preexisting categories.[38] Query lists systematized collection, ensuring—at least in theory—that data about very different places and peoples would return in a form that allowed it to be systematically aggregated. The goal of such queries, as historian of science Elizabeth Yale has pointed out, was to produce a "complete picture of nature": each query would result in "natural facts" that could be compared with other results.[39] Gallatin arranged his queries into seven categories: population, agriculture, manufactures, commerce, government and laws, religion, and knowledge, and he included three to five questions under each heading. These categories reproduced hierarchical social orders in which U.S. religious, agricultural, and educational practices were positioned as the most advanced.

By framing Ridge's response through the queries, Gallatin's list also attempted to naturalize these hierarchies and make them into interpretive frameworks for reading Cherokee lives. By separating topics into discrete, numbered categories, the queries suggest that the topics are ontologically different, that is, that religion and knowledge, agriculture, and government and laws are separate matters. In this way, the categories attempt to circumvent any suggestion that Cherokee people might be able to maintain their own practices alongside their adoption of some U.S. ones. Yet Gallatin's categories also sought to preclude change as a regular part of Cherokee life. If change occurred, within this vision it would transform Cherokee people into assimilated members of the United States who were, as a result, unable to form a sovereign political entity as the Cherokee Nation.[40] Gallatin's queries are requests for information that also attempt to locate the Cherokee Nation within the United States and to constrain Cherokee peoples' future as citizens of the Cherokee Nation.

These queries and the readings they enable had (and still have) political consequences. The query list implicitly posed the question of whether the Cherokee Nation was an "autonomous state . . . over which the U.S. could not claim authority" and what the responsibility of the United States was with regard to Cherokee people.[41] Two Supreme Court cases in the 1830s moved to define those responsibilities and rights: the Supreme Court ruled in 1831 in *Cherokee Nation v. Georgia* that the Cherokee Nation and other Native nations were "domestic dependent nations" over whom the United States would act as a "guardian."[42] The court's decision in *Worcester v. Georgia* (1832) recognized the Cherokee Nation's sovereignty over their lands, ruling that states like Georgia did not possess jurisdiction within the

Cherokee Nation. These decisions established the tenets of federal Indian law, while supposing that the United States was the only sovereign nation within the borders of the lands it claimed.[43] The decisions mandated that political relations between the U.S. and Native nations occur through the framework of the ostensible political superiority of the U.S., one that, as political theorist Kevin Bruyneel has observed, attempts "to narrowly bound indigenous political status in space and time."[44] In the 1820s and 1830s, however, colonists still sometimes admitted the possibility of other relations. Gallatin himself contemplated one such possibility in his 1836 "Synopsis," writing: "We may indeed say, that, if a scrupulous regard had always been paid to the rights of the Indians, this nation [the U.S.] would not have sprung into existence."[45] Recognizing—even if momentarily—that the political and temporal frameworks of the settler nation were not a given, Gallatin acknowledged the existence of other sovereignties. A decade earlier, in 1826, Gallatin's queries about civilization sought to envision and solidify relations between the U.S. and the Cherokee Nation at a moment when the U.S. could not assume it had authority on Cherokee lands.

By the time he corresponded with Gallatin, Ridge had seen how U.S. audiences read Native bodies, speech, and writing within limiting categories. He knew that many U.S. colonists perceived Cherokee people not as members of an Indigenous nation but as people whose lands were conquered by Europeans and whose future as Cherokees was limited. Ridge must also have known that replying to Gallatin's queries was not a task simply of delineating the changes Cherokee people had confronted in the late eighteenth and early nineteenth centuries but an action with repercussions for how the United States perceived Cherokee territories and governance. He may have hoped that sending a compilation to Gallatin would allow his response to circulate beyond the United States, to an audience that would prove a useful international ally to the Cherokees. Writing to Thomas McKenney in early March 1826, Gallatin complained that Ridge had not replied to his initial request for information, and he requested McKenney to "press him in that subject."[46] He also suggested that McKenney present Gallatin's demands as an opportunity for international publication, writing: "If published by Humboldt, this essay written by a native Indian may have a public opinion both here and abroad. I have already verbally conversed with you; and I may add that it gives an opportunity to Mr Ridge to obtain a general reputation."[47] Two weeks after Ridge dated his sent letter, Gallatin wrote to Alexander von Humboldt, whose travels throughout the Americas had inspired his own interests in Indigenous languages and histories. Gallatin praised Ridge's letter, even as he offered his own reading of it, writing that the letter was, "written by his hand, without my changing or adding a single word. There is probably a bit of exaggeration; but you will find the real and exalted sentiments of the Indians and their desire to subsist as a civilized and independent nation."[48] Ridge may have hoped that his letter's travels through international circuits would—much like Attakullakulla's desire to burn the governor's letters in the old year's fire and like the wampum and medals Oconostota sent to colonial officials—set relations between the U.S. and Cherokee Nation on an honest path.

"By Choice and Necessity": Extracting the Queries

In his letters to Gallatin, Ridge extracted the material forms and claims through which colonists sought to locate Cherokee people within U.S. political and cultural categories, including the query list in which Gallatin placed his request, forms like printed blanks that received and ordered information, and representational forms like those in McKenney's Indian Gallery. Ridge extracted these forms from their original contexts to insist on alternate ways of reading colonists' own words and, by extension, to insist on a space for Cherokee history and sovereignty. Opening Gallatin's query list, like opening Vattel's *Law of Nations* and other European texts and using them for his purposes in "Strictures," was not a straightforward or easily resolved undertaking, as differences between the draft and sent letters indicate. The draft letter is clearly a working draft, in which Ridge crossed out phrases, substituted others, and marked the insertion of paragraphs with asterisks, while the sent letter is largely clean of ink blots and strikeouts, written in a neat hand. Some revisions are minor, involving changes at the level of syntax and the placement of sentences or phrases. But the changes also extend to significant revisions to the content in the draft. Ridge seems to have debated how to describe Cherokee life when he knew colonists were likely to seek evidence for their preexisting assumptions and when the stakes of representing topics like spiritual beliefs and

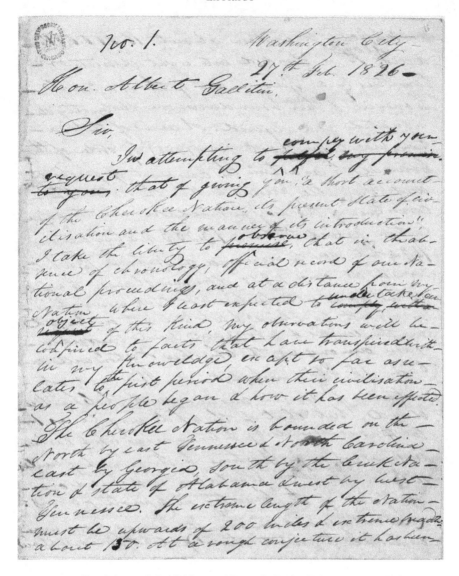

FIGURE 2.1. Draft letter, John Ridge to Albert Gallatin, February 27, 1826, vol. 8, folder 4, John Howard Payne Papers, Ayer MS 689, Newberry Library, Chicago.

agricultural practices included dispossession. The differences between the letters reflect Ridge's process of determining how to answer the queries, a process in which we can see him moving from describing the contexts in which Cherokee people interacted with the civilization policy to using textual extracts to oppose and redirect Gallatin's queries (figures 2.1 and 2.2).

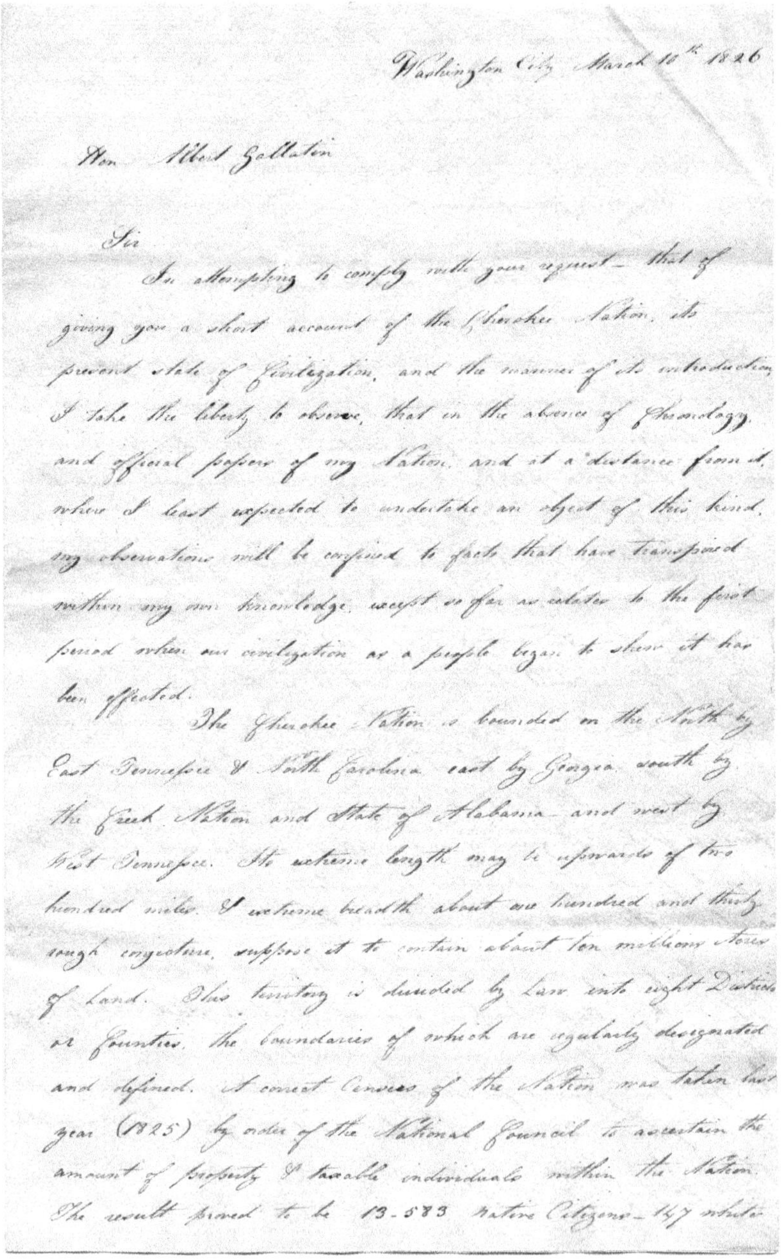

Washington City March 10th 1826

Hon Albert Gallatin

Sir

In attempting to comply with your request— that of giving you a short account of the Cherokee Nation, its present state of Civilization, and the manner of its introduction I take the liberty to observe, that in the absence of Chronology and official papers of my Nation, and at a distance from it, where I least expected to undertake an object of this kind, my observations will be confined to facts that have transpired within my own knowledge, except so far as relates to the first period when our civilization as a people began to shew it has been effected.

The Cherokee Nation is bounded on the North by East Tennessee & North Carolina east by Georgia south by the Creek Nation and State of Alabama and west by West Tennessee. Its extreme length may be upwards of two hundred miles & extreme breadth about one hundred and thirty rough conjecture, suppose it to contain about ten millions Acres of Land. This territory is divided by Law into eight Districts or Counties, the boundaries of which are regularly designated and defined. A correct Census of the Nation was taken last year (1825) by order of the National Council to ascertain the amount of property & taxable individuals within the Nation. The result proved to be 13-583 Native Citizens— 147 white

FIGURE 2.2. Sent letter, John Ridge to Albert Gallatin, letter dated March 10, 1826. Albert Gallatin Papers, Indian Languages, Manuscripts Collection, New-York Historical Society. Photography © New-York Historical Society.

Both letters answer Gallatin's question about how "civilization" was "introduced" to the Cherokee Nation by emphasizing the contexts in which Cherokee people made decisions regarding the civilization policy. Ridge wrote in both letters that "the hardest portion of manual labor is performed by the men & the women occasionally lend a hand [to the men] in the field, more by choice, and necessity than any thing else."[49] This comment referenced the process whereby many (but not all) Cherokee men added farming to existing sustenance practices after pressure from Indian agents who sought to change matrilineal clan structures. His statement that women performed such labor "by choice, and necessity" identified how that policy attacked women's power as cultivators and keepers of land. Ridge also identified the nature of Cherokee peoples' decisions to change some of these practices: these were decisions made by necessity, in the face of colonial settlement and encroachment, disregard for Cherokee boundaries, and attacks on Cherokee towns following the departure of their British allies after the American Revolution. As historian Tiya Miles explains, "Failure to visibly adopt the changes of the U.S. civilization program could have meant a decrease in material aid and loss of promised protection from white intruders, both of which Cherokees sorely needed."[50] The decisions made by "choice and necessity" are similar to what the Ojibwe literary scholar Scott Richard Lyons calls an "x-mark": "a contaminated and coerced sign of consent made under conditions that are not of one's making. It signifies power and a lack of power, agency and a lack of agency. It is a decision one makes when something has already been decided for you, but it is still a decision."[51] The "choice" for Cherokee men to work in the fields was one constrained and made by "necessity," in the wake of ongoing threats to Cherokee land.

In both versions of the letter Ridge continued to emphasize constrained choices when discussing changes to the Cherokees' system of government, explaining that the Cherokees had made decisions to protect the Nation from colonial land theft. He wrote in the draft letter, "Their chiefs were numerous and their responsibility was as trifling. Lands then could be obtained of them at a price most convenient to the U. States as their commissioners with the assistance of their agent could always procure a majority for a session & when this was done, all yielded [for a share of the Booty] to secure their shares for the trifling equivalent. At length the eyes of our

Nation were opened to see their folly."[52] Ridge may have been referring to several late eighteenth-century land sales, when Kentucky settlers persuaded a few Cherokee leaders to sell nearly thirty thousand square miles of land in exchange for trade goods, a move that violated both English and Cherokee laws.[53] Over the early decades of the nineteenth century, the Cherokee Nation took action to oversee how land cessions were made, to place the authority to make and pass laws with two governing bodies, and to locate control of the treasury in the Nation rather than with the Indian agent. As Julie L. Reed explains of these measures, the Nation "took coercive steps to limit the ability of individuals to harm the entire community."[54] Ridge's letters reminded Gallatin that the Cherokees created these governing bodies to protect their lands from dishonest, land-hungry settlers and government agents. He emphasized the contexts in which Cherokee people adopted practices settlers might want to deem "civilized," contexts that included settlers' threats to Cherokee lands and actions taken to protect Cherokee sovereignty. The letters thus insist that any inquiry into the Cherokees' "present state of civilisation" must account for Cherokee experiences of settler violence and pressures to cede land and Cherokee Nation actions to secure its citizens' protection.[55]

While his emphasis on context and constraint is shared across both letters, Ridge made a series of revisions in the sent letter that refuse Gallatin's queries and their logic. Many queries sought to quantify Cherokee life, requesting information about the "proportion"—a term Gallatin repeats throughout the queries—of manufactured goods made in the Nation or of Cherokee people who rely on agriculture or live on separate farms.[56] The draft letter contains paragraphs in which Ridge responded to this request for quantitative data by enumerating aspects of Cherokee life, from tableware to domesticated animals like sheep and horses. By contrast, in the sent letter, Ridge refused the logic of quantification. For example, he removed the draft sentences in which he listed tableware, writing instead in the sent letter: "I am sorry that I have not with me the estimate of the respective number of live property & their value, as well as the number of ploughs, brooms, wagons, Saw and grist mills &tc in the Nation."[57] Turning from the draft letter's more earnest tabulation, in the sent letter Ridge deferred, emphasizing that he lacked access to the information needed to answer Gallatin's query and in the process refusing the queries' request for statistics. He framed his knowledge as limited early in each letter, writing, "I take the liberty to observe, that in the absence of Chronology, and official papers of my Nation, and at a distance from it, where I least expected to undertake an object of this kind, my observation will be confined to facts that have transpired within my own knowledge, except so far as related to the first period when our civilization as a people began to show it has been effected."[58]

He expanded on this strategy of refusing to supply information as Gallatin requested it throughout the sent letter by answering queries with extracts from printed sources then circulating in the U.S. In the sent letter, Ridge discussed a query about the effect of religion on what Gallatin termed "love of revenge, drunkenness" by quoting a short article published in the Philadelphia publication *Weekly Magazine*, "Anecdotes of Teedyuscung," which claimed to present knowledge from a Delaware leader.[59] The article presents Teedyuscung as a purveyor of simple yet wise observations about colonists. Ridge quoted Teedyuscung's comments about drunkenness from the article: "Intemperance, like Love, is found in the Halls of the great and in the wig wam of the Indian—with this difference—'Indians consider it no harm to drink, but the whites do, and drink notwithstanding'__."[60] In the draft letter, Ridge had answered the query in terms that echoed Gallatin's assumptions, writing, "In regard to Intemperance, we are still as a nation grossly degraded. We are however on the improve."[61] By contrast, the sent letter refused Gallatin's query, instead answering with an extract from another source. In this way, Ridge addressed the logic of the question without answering it. He amplified the extract's meaning in the sent letter by criticizing Gallatin's query directly, writing: "In regard to the love of revenge the Indians have been represented in the grossest colours. I never could have the audacity to ascribe inconsistency to any portion of God's creation. The various Nations of the Earth were created for noble purposes, endowed with sensibility to feel their own wrongs and sympathize for another's woe."[62] Ridge refused to state whether Christianity—one of the central facets of the civilization program—had made Cherokee people "love . . . revenge" less and instead exposed the query itself as founded on inaccurate assumptions, part of a racist system of representation that, as Ridge explained, categorized Cherokee people as "savages of the human race" on the same level as the "beasts of the Forests."[63] By answering

Gallatin's queries with extracts, Ridge's sent letter cast "civilization" itself as an invented framework and documented how such categories produced racist representations.

Ridge's extracts turned the categories of the query list back on the United States, to render it an object of observation and to destabilize the category of the nation as Gallatin deployed it. He made this turn in the sent letter when noting, in the discussion of temperance, that he "cannot call the Cherokees a civilized people and perhaps in this respect it would baffle our expectations if we were to look for it, in any Nation on the face of the Earth."[64] This comment undercut the very premise of Gallatin's query list, that the Cherokee Nation would eventually disappear, whether by incorporation into the United States or other means. Instead, Ridge suggested, the category of "nation" included multiple, distinct political entities. By including both the United States and the Cherokee Nation within the category of the "nation," Ridge indicated that both were subject to historical change, changes that he emphatically described as affecting each nation alike, writing, "all Nations have experienced change."[65] Ridge placed Cherokee temporalities into relation with the category of the "nation" while insisting on a Cherokee reading of that category that refused the theories of nationalism then circulating in the U.S., in which change led to vanishing for Native people.[66]

The content-level differences between the two letters reflect a process of revision and experimentation regarding how to interact with Gallatin's queries and claims about Cherokee people. Ridge's revisions may reflect conversations in which he debated the content of the letters with his friend David Vann and members of the Creek delegation who were also in Washington. The two letters may also represent a spectrum of Ridge's own thinking about the best way to address requests like Gallatin's. Their differences show that decisions about how to refute U.S. claims to Cherokee lands and expectations regarding "civilization" were not unanimous or linear but involved questions that Cherokee people weighed and disagreed over and about which they changed their minds. The letters' differences also indicate the constraints that documentary forms like the query list put on Indigenous compilations. Gallatin's query list attempted to define the content and the form of Ridge's writing for settler audiences, and Ridge's revisions reflect a careful calculation, experimentation, and possibly some uncertainty about how to write in the midst of those limitations. The differences between the letters show Ridge making decisions about how to represent the Cherokee Nation, even as reading the letters alongside the query list shows that these are not choices made free of constraints but actions made, as Ridge himself put it, by choice and necessity.

As Ridge experimented with using extracts to refuse and redirect the query list in the sent letter, he also expanded his extracts from quotations to archival forms. He invoked the forms with which colonists ordered information about Cherokee people, particularly the blank forms used to solicit and store information, which he cited by strategically inserting dashes throughout the sent letter.[67] In the draft letter, the dashes are limited and serve primarily as punctuation, connecting words split across a line and sometimes connecting sentences. In the sent letter, by contrast, dashes proliferate, serving several functions: they set off excerpted information, reference acts of the Cherokee National Council, and indicate Ridge's reliance on Cherokee Nation sources. These more capacious uses for dashes in the sent letter parallel the multiple rhetorical functions dashes and blanks performed in nineteenth-century U.S. manuscript and print cultures. Blanks and dashes could indicate absence while calling for inscription; they could emphasize presence or alienation; they could order and stabilize information or conceal it. Perhaps the best known examples are Emily Dickinson's dashes, which scholars have read as lending emphasis to a pause, indicating a question, or reflecting the writer's alienation from the text.[68] Dashes hid or omitted information, as well, as in works where a dash withheld a last name (Mr. R——), in ways that reflect the "abstraction and depersonalization" of print, or effaced an act deemed too scandalous or traumatic to name.[69] In Ridge's exchange with Gallatin, the dashes also evoke the blank. As Henry Rowe Schoolcraft's commentary on the blank (discussed in the introduction) shows, blanks had a particular resonance in the eighteenth and nineteenth centuries, as the white space on paper awaiting inscription represented Indigenous peoples' supposedly absent histories and invited settler histories in their place. Gallatin himself frequently used blanks throughout his manuscript records of Indigenous-language words: blanks on printed word lists delineated the words Gallatin wished his sources to gather, and in his manuscript notes on those lists, blanks signaled a missing word, a space requiring more collection.

Read alongside his textual extracts and nineteenth-century uses for blanks, Ridge's dashes are marks of compilation in at least two ways: first, they indicate when he gathered materials from Cherokee Nation sources, and they gesture to archives that remained separate from and unassimilated to the queries. On the sent letter's first and second pages, he set off data from a Cherokee Nation census by placing it between dashes that, like blanks, store and separate information: "13,583 Native Citizens__147 white men married with Indians & 73 white women do [ditto].; & African slaves 1,277__to which if we add 400 Cherokees who took their Reservations in North Carolina & not included in the Census and who have since merged again among us—the Cherokee Nation will contain 15.480 inhabitants." The dashes separate Cherokee, white, and enslaved people within the Nation, creating blanks that place quantitative information in discrete units and create categories of citizens and noncitizens. These lines come closest to imitating the blank's information storage function, while indicating how creating discrete categories of information contributed to the early nineteenth-century hardening of racial categories and differences between Cherokee and African-descended people within the Nation. While Ridge moved on from the blank's stabilizing and ordering functions in the rest of the letter, his use of those functions here emphasized the Cherokee Nation's authority to define who its citizens were (which it had recently asserted in laws passed in 1819 and 1825), definitions that for Ridge rested on what Tiya Miles calls a "triangular relationship among white women, Cherokee men, and black slaves."[70]

The dashes also mark the presence of Cherokee archives that exist beyond Ridge's own compilation and, by extension, beyond the scope of Gallatin's queries. Like the census records, some of these archives are governmental and bureaucratic: Ridge represented the work of the Cherokee National Committee and the National Council by using dashes to emphasize those bodies' legal actions. He wrote that all such actions began with a performative act of collective decision making, and he emphasized this act by placing it within dashes: "__'Be it resolved by the National Committee and Council of the Cherokee Nation'__."[71] The dashes represent the authority of the National Committee and Council as manifested in both the action of resolving—marked by the dashes—and in the written document recording the resolution. Ridge's dashes require readers to look beyond

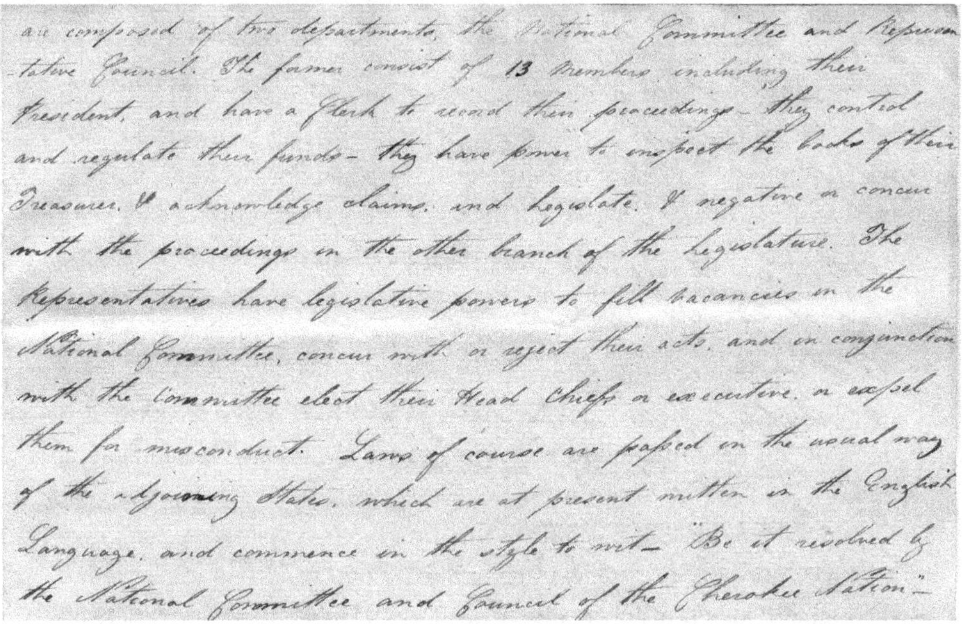

FIGURE 2.3. Dashes in Ridge's sent letter (dashes appear in lines 3 and 4, and in the last two lines of the image). John Ridge to Albert Gallatin, letter dated March 10, 1826. Albert Gallatin Papers, Indian Languages, Manuscripts Collection, New-York Historical Society. Photography © New-York Historical Society.

the page to archives created by the Nation's leaders and to their embodied acts of resolution (figure 2.3).

These embodied archives extended to materials and actions performed not just by Cherokee leaders but by many people throughout the Nation. Ridge referenced plans to establish a printing press and newspaper published in Cherokee and English languages (the *Cherokee Phoenix,* which published its first volume in February 1828) and the existence of a library, "attached" to the Moral and Literary Society of the Cherokee Nation.[72] He used dashes to set off an account of Sequoyah's invention of the Cherokee syllabary, explaining in another passage unique to the sent letter that "Mr. Guess [Sequoyah] is an Indian unacquainted with the English language__but an untutored Philosopher, who has succeeded in a few months as it were to educate a Nation. . . . Among those unacquainted with the English it [the syllabary] is very much esteemed__Portions of the bible are

translated & read and Hymns are sung in that character. With the Cherokees of the Arkansas they correspond regularly by letter in Guess' character."[73] Ridge emphasized the syllabary's difference from English and positioned it as a uniquely Cherokee system, by stating that Sequoyah created
the writing system without recourse to alphabetic models.[74] Ridge likewise
used dashes to mark out several Cherokee translation projects, including
a translation of parts of the Bible and hymns into the Cherokee syllabary.

By inserting dashes throughout the sent letter, Ridge acknowledged the
blank's status as a tool of information management, a function evidenced
most clearly in the census data, where the dashes delineate citizenship and
racial categories. He combined those uses with the dash's function as a
mark of emphasis and elision in his references to national and individual
archives. In this way, he extracted not just the language of Gallatin's query
list but also colonial archival forms that ordered Native histories and lives
on paper. In the process of extracting and recontextualizing the dash and
the blank, Ridge transformed their meaning. His blanks point readers off
the page, acknowledging the presence of Cherokee archives that complement and even supersede his report to Gallatin. His references to official
documents and libraries, hymnbooks and personal letters, newspapers, and
writing systems gesture to the practices with which Cherokee people created documents and archives for their own uses. Some of those archives,
like the syllabary texts and letters—remained illegible to most settlers even
as they served ends specific to individual Cherokee people. Glimpses of
some of those archives appear in collections that settler ethnographers created later in the nineteenth century: in the late 1880s, Bureau of American
Ethnology anthropologist James Mooney found himself overwhelmed by
family archives kept by Eastern Band Cherokee people. Mooney commented on the extensive manuscripts in the syllabary that were protected
by Cherokee families, often the children of the people who created the
documents, and he noted that "it was with a feeling akin, to despair that we
viewed the piles of manuscript which had to be waded through and classi-
fied."[75] While Mooney approached the manuscripts with a desire to order
and classify them, his comments indicate that Cherokee families created
and kept archives for their own purposes and in their own homes.

Ridge's letters call for being read alongside contexts and spaces that
are glossed but not fully described on the page. Like Occom's recipes, the

letters' meanings are fully present only when an interlocutor could place them in relation to the papers, histories, and exchanges of the Cherokee Nation. These are archives created by and for Cherokee people to govern, learn, sing, and interact with each other. In Ridge's compilation, the dashes also elide the exact details of those archives for readers who would try to contain them within the query list's categories. By pointing readers off the page, Ridge's dashes demonstrate how these embodied archives remain unassimilated by query lists and their categories. Ridge's blanks reference—even as they keep from full view—some of the practices that maintain peoplehood, or what Daniel Heath Justice defines as a "relational system that keeps the people in balance with one another, with other peoples and realities, and with the world."[76] Several of these internal archives were being constructed within the Cherokee Nation at the same time Ridge wrote to Gallatin, as Cherokee leaders made decisions to circulate histories of the Nation in multiple media. Their archives, like Ridge's letters, avoid claiming completeness, instead highlighting the extract both as a sign of the effects of settler colonialism on Cherokee history keeping and a mark of colonial archives' failure to contain Cherokee experiences.

"Their proper connection": Making Cherokee Archives

In 1826, as Ridge was composing his letters, Cherokee Nation assistant chief Charles R. Hicks wrote several letters to John Ross, who would later be selected as principal chief in 1828. Hicks stated that he hoped to educate Ross about Cherokee history, and he compared his attempt to "give an outline of the traditions of this nation which have been handed down from our forefathers from time immemorial" to the task of picking through the rubbish from a fire and attempting to arrange the "cinders" so that they gave "light" into Cherokees history.[77] Hicks explained to Ross,

> Even when the rubbishes are examined, and [one] happens to find a spark among them, it is only in detached parts, [much] as to render it difficult to form their proper connection, to enable one to have clear insight in[to] the progress of their emigration; and may justly be remarked that we have only the body like a tree left, with the branches lopt off, that might have related to many particulars in regard to their original institutions, when they arrived in this country.[78] (brackets in original)

For Hicks, transmitting histories entailed searching for a spark among "rubbishes" and "detached parts," and then sorting and piecing those parts together into the "proper connection" to find "clear insight" into the past. Once compiled, the rubbishes, detached parts, and sparks constitute an account of Cherokee origins and, in Hicks's metaphor, reignite a fire. Hicks also emphasized the difficulty of finding connections among "detached parts" and of telling a history without the "particulars" that formed its "branches." His metaphors of cinders, rubbishes, trees missing branches, and detached parts cast the process of remembering and passing down histories as one of seeking for missing pieces and of making structures that remained incomplete. Hicks explained that these histories had been "handed down from our forefathers from time immemorial" but that "their institutions began to decline when their intercourse commenced with the whites."[79] Read in relation to Ridge's compilations of extracts, Hicks's letter shows that extracts are sometimes fragments or cinders that remain difficult to reassemble, and that acknowledging incompleteness, as Ridge did, can avoid claims to authoritative knowledge but can also be a repercussion of colonial theft and settlement. The archive Hicks and Ross built by compiling rubbishes and detached parts resisted the corrosive effects of "intercourse . . . with the whites," even as Hicks also marked the difficulties of passing down histories in a context shaped by colonialism.

Hicks's description of Cherokee history as a fire aligns this history telling with the Cherokees' responsibility to keep sacred fires burning and with the eighteenth-century archives of Attakullakulla and Oconostota. As Daniel Heath Justice has argued, keeping council fires lit is both a central metaphor and an action: "The survival of the People—of the nation itself—is thus directly linked to their thoughtful attention to their responsibilities as keepers of the sacred fire."[80] The *Cherokee Phoenix* is named after the mythical bird that rises from the ashes, suggesting that fire creates new avenues for creativity, diplomacy, and communication. As Justice notes, "The Phoenix, a spirit-bird of living and continually renewing flame, has been such an enduring symbol of Cherokee nationhood since the early nineteenth century. The spirit of the fire is also the spirit of the nation."[81] Hicks and other Cherokee leaders like Attakullakulla foregrounded these responsibilities when they used fire as a figure for correcting deceitful speech and remembering Cherokee history, thus aligning their compilations with the work of supporting the Nation's spirit and survival.

After he became principal chief, Ross directed another archival project, in which he gave permission for colonists to hear and transcribe some Cherokee histories. In 1835, as noted at this chapter's opening, Ross granted John Howard Payne permission to conduct research in the Nation. Payne collaborated with the missionary Daniel S. Butrick, who had lived in the Cherokee Nation since 1818 and who had received permission earlier that year from Ross to record some Cherokee histories and philosophical beliefs. Butrick sent his manuscripts to Payne after Cherokee leaders had reviewed, corrected, and approved them. Unlike Gallatin's and Barbour's project to gather Indigenous-language words in their libraries and then use their conclusions to map Indigenous homelands, Butrick and Payne undertook a project directed and controlled by Cherokee people. Butrick at times described his interviews with Cherokee people as preserving information that would otherwise be lost, and certainly Butrick and Payne created an archive that holds many documents of importance to Cherokee histories. Yet Ross described their research not as the work of preservation but as a project that supported the Nation, in this way imagining an archive that, like Attakullakulla's and Oconostota's papers, might foster honest relations with U.S. settlers. In 1835, amidst increasing, violent harassment from Georgia settlers, including arrests, occupations of Cherokee peoples' houses, withholding annuities that led to starvation, and violence against Cherokee women, the stakes of such relations were incredibly high. Ross addressed "All the aged, and wise Antiquarians of the Cherokee Nation" in a letter regarding Butrick's request for information, noting that:

> This is to inform you that our believed Friend RႿ (Revd Mr. Butrick) [Mink] has conversed with me on the subject of making a research into the Original Customs & Manners of our Nation and to let you know that I approve of his intention on this subject, also to tell you that his object will not in the slightest degree affect the private or political rights and interests of the Cherokee people, but on the other hand his work will be interesting and useful. And perhaps, may be of advantage to us__As our beloved Friend has no intention to publish the information which he may collect on this subject, previously to

exhibiting it before 𝐑𝐘𝐏 (Mr Lowry) and myself for inspection, it is my wish
and request that you will render him all the facility in your power, for the
accomplishment of his undertaking, by communicating to him freely all the
information that you may possess of the Original Customs and Manners of
our departed Sires__and by recommending him to others who may be well
informed on this subject__It is desireable that the most correct and full information now extant in the Nation may be collected.[82]

Ross framed exchanges with Butrick (and, by extension, Payne) as acts
that would work to the "advantage" to Cherokee people, and he assured
Cherokee "antiquarians" that he and George Lowry would oversee the
colonists' work.[83] This was a project for Cherokee people first, one that
would not circulate among non-Cherokee audiences before Ross and others reviewed it and whose ends would benefit the Nation.

Butrick and Payne soon learned that their notes were only one version
of a Cherokee embodied and material archive that existed separately from
their papers, much as the embodied actions to which Ridge's dashes point
exist off the page. In one instance, Payne wrote that he transcribed the "life
of George Gist" [George Guess, or Sequoyah] as it was "read & translated
to me in the cabin of the Principal Chief of the Cherokee Nation one
evening during the Session of the Council, Oct. 1835." He described a
process in which the entire Council listened carefully to confirm the story
or debate the translation:

> The room was full of Indians, who listened with great attention. Many who
> knew facts detailed in the narrative confirmed them as the interpreter pro-
> ceeded. The translation was conveyed in turn by several who understood
> English; sometimes the exact interpretation would be discussed, and some-
> times one would explain a sentence for which another could not find words.
> It was written by Major Lowry, second Principal Chief, who was present,
> assisting in the translation. . . . I have a copy in the original Cherokee, written
> out by John Huss a native preacher.

At one point, the Cherokee men discovered that "part of the manuscript
was missing." After searching for it, Payne reported that finally the men
came to a decision about what to do:

> "No matter," said Major Lowry__It was only what the Bark told me & the
> Bark is hereabout__We will go fetch him, exclaimed a dozen voices, and
> presently the Bark appeared:

It is remarkable that when the fragment was afterwards found, it was almost verbatim what the Bark repeated and no correction was thought necessary on comparison.[84]

What Payne viewed as "remarkable"—that a spoken version of a history
matched a written document "almost verbatim"—was for Lowry, the Bark,
and other Cherokees part of the process of history keeping. The document
that Payne eventually consulted was only one part of an extensive archive,
kept by people like the Bark, in the syllabary, and sometimes in English.[85]
The convergence between the Bark's story and Lowry's manuscript indicates the interplay and exchange among different media in Cherokee archives while also giving a glimpse into the processes with which Cherokee
people reviewed written documents made by colonists in order to ensure
that they were satisfactory. These actions generated the pieces necessary
to remember and tell the syllabary's story, which does not exist solely in
one location but is produced by collective work. The manuscript fragment
about the Cherokee syllabary resonates as well with the pieces, fragments,
and extracts with which Hicks, Ross, and Ridge related Cherokee histories, and the story Payne recorded about the manuscript fragment and the
Bark's version provides yet another meaning for such pieces. In this case,
fragments exist in relation to oral and embodied memories; they can also
be strategic withholdings from colonial archives.

By the time Payne and Butrick were conducting their research, Ridge
had seen how colonists could misread his work or put it to ends at odds with
those he pursued. Gallatin's letter to Humboldt makes clear that he read
Ridge's letter not as a compilation of extracts that required a reconsideration of Gallatin's own queries but as evidence of Cherokee desires for civilization. Some of Gallatin's conclusions about the Cherokee Nation were
published in 1826, in French, absent any reference to Ridge and his letter.[86]
Ridge and other Cherokee leaders had also seen how the Nation's diplomatic archives were under attack: just as Attakullakulla's and Oconostota's
archives were stolen during war, some of Ross's and Payne's papers were
stolen by the Georgia Guard when they were arrested in November 1835,
as part of Georgia's defiance of Cherokee sovereignty.[87] Cherokee leaders'
interventions into colonial queries—along the spectrum of intentions and
methods represented by Gallatin and Payne—worked to make colonial
archives serve ends useful to Cherokee people. Yet as Ridge's exchange

with Gallatin shows, this did not guarantee that colonists would embrace different understandings of the Cherokee Nation's sovereignty. Amidst archival theft, colonists' willful misreadings and refusals to enforce laws, and Cherokee leaders' own different positions on how to respond to the threat of removal, making compilations and archives provided one means with which Cherokee leaders interrupted and critiqued the political, cultural, and temporal constraints settlers sought to place on the Nation.[88]

Conclusion

Questions of how to protect the Cherokee Nation and assert its sovereignty continue to orient Cherokee literatures today, as seen in the play *Sovereignty* (2018 premiere, 2020 publication) by Mary Kathryn Nagle, a Cherokee Nation citizen, playwright, lawyer, and descendant of John Ridge. *Sovereignty* moves between the past of the 1820s and 1830s and the present of 2018. The play follows John Ridge, Elias Boudinot, Major Ridge, and John Ross as they fight for Cherokee sovereignty before President Andrew Jackson and the Supreme Court and as the Ridges and Boudinot come to the decision to sign the Treaty of New Echota in 1835. Nagle continues this story in 2018, with Sarah Ridge Polson, a descendant of John Ridge and like him a lawyer. Sarah returns to Tahlequah, Cherokee Nation, to take a job with the attorney general's office, headed by Jim Ross, a descendant of John Ross. She does not tell her new boss of her relation to John Ridge due to the conviction among some Cherokee people that he betrayed the Nation by signing the Treaty of New Echota. For Sarah, John Ridge's decision was one that acted "to save Cherokee Nation" from harassment, violence, murder, and dispossession.[89] And she attributes her own dedication to serving the Nation to her ancestor's actions.

John Ridge and Sarah Ridge Polson each use documents from the U.S.—its periodicals, its constitution, its court's decisions, its paper claims to superiority—to articulate Cherokee sovereignty and in Sarah's case, to defend her sovereignty over her own body. Nagle imagines an 1832 exchange between John Ridge and attorney William Wirt, who represented the Cherokee Nation in *Worcester v. Georgia*. Ridge has written a brief for Wirt that "starts with an analysis of article two, section two, clause two of your Constitution."[90] Surprised, Wirt responds, "I didn't expect you to have prepared arguments based on *our* Constitution," to which Ridge replies, "It's a very straightforward document."[91] Reflecting the ways that Ridge used extracts from colonial documents to defend Cherokee people and the Nation, his legal commentary in the play analyzes the U.S. Constitution to build a case for Cherokee sovereignty. Similarly, Sarah represents Cherokee Nation before the Supreme Court in a case against her ex-fiancé for assaulting her on Cherokee lands. As part of her argument, she provides a history of Cherokee sovereignty and of U.S. violence against Cherokee citizens, particularly Cherokee women. Much as Ridge insisted in his letters to Gallatin that settlers recognize the contexts and decisions made by "choice and necessity" that shaped the Nation's early nineteenth-century history, so Sarah insists that the court understand her case in light of a long history both of Cherokee sovereignty and of U.S. violence against Cherokee women that attempted to strike at the heart of that sovereignty.[92] As she tells Ross when she makes the decision to take a case to the Supreme Court: "I have to fight this. If he can erase my sovereignty over my body, he can erase the sovereignty of my nation."[93]

The play weaves together past and present as it moves between the nineteenth and twenty-first centuries, positioning John Ridge's and Sarah Ridge Polson's actions as echoes and extensions of each other. Sarah's case challenges U.S. court rulings that refuse to recognize tribal jurisdiction over non-Native assailants who commit certain violent crimes on tribal lands. Sarah fears that the Supreme Court will not recognize *Worcester v. Georgia*'s 1832 affirmation of Cherokee sovereignty and will consider only subsequent limitations to tribal jurisdiction (in cases like *Oliphant v. Suquamish Indian Tribe* in 1978). She explains the stakes of her decision, saying: "We could lose our jurisdiction. The court could say tribal jurisdiction over non-Indians is unconstitutional."[94] Similarly, in the scenes set in the 1830s, John Ridge fears that the U.S. will refuse to enforce Cherokee jurisdiction, even after the Cherokee Nation's victory in *Worcester v. Georgia*. In a scene set in 1832, Ridge asks John Ross, as they discuss the ongoing incursions on Cherokee sovereignty even after their legal victory: "What good is a right that will never be enforced? . . . What use will our land be once we've all been killed?"[95] Ridge argues for moving west to protect the Cherokee Nation: "I do not say this lightly. I see no other way for our nation to survive. If we agree to move west, we'll lose our lands, but we'll preserve the nation. Intact."[96] Finally, in scene 10, 1835 and 2018 occupy the same space: Sarah Ridge Polson watches on stage as John Ridge and his wife Sarah Bird Northrup discuss his decision to sign the Treaty of New Echota. Sarah Bird Northrup asks a question that reverberates across the centuries: "Now I ask, who is more savage? A nation who makes laws and abides by them, or a country who makes laws and refuses to enforce them?"[97]

The play's temporal movement between past and present and the temporal collision in scene 10 depict the ongoing consequences of the refusal by the U.S. in the nineteenth century to respect Cherokee sovereignty and the consequences of refusals, like Gallatin's, to revise assumptions about Cherokee people, such as those embedded in the query list. The play demonstrates how those consequences specifically target Cherokee women, for Nagle shows how the violence against Native women committed by non-Native men on Cherokee lands in the present may be traced back to the 1820s and 1830s. As Sarah explains in her argument before the U.S. Supreme Court, "It took one hundred and forty years to fully come into effect, but Andrew Jackson's campaign to eliminate tribal jurisdiction has reaped devastating, life-and-death consequences for Native women."[98] Nagle draws a line between Jackson's refusal to uphold *Worcester* and the conviction of Sarah's ex-fiancé that Cherokee laws do not apply to him. Moreover, the temporal boundaries within which Gallatin's query list attempted to contain Ridge's answers echo in the ex-fiancé's assumption that Cherokee sovereignty is confined to the past and superseded by that of the United States. Yet *Sovereignty* also suggests that John Ridge's work to extract and open the confining categories set by the U.S. for Cherokee people is carried on today by lawyers like Sarah Ridge Polson (and Nagle herself). The play locates this work of opposing U.S. policies and laws as oriented not around the U.S., its temporalities, and legal statutes, but around Cherokee peoplehood and its continuance.

Interlude

E. Pauline Johnson's Wild Flowers

In 1893, the Mohawk writer E. Pauline Johnson dramatized colonists' desire for "Indian relics" as an acquisitive practice with particular consequences for Indigenous women. In Johnson's short story "A Red Girl's Reasoning," a young Métis woman, Christine Robinson, marries a white Canadian man, Charlie McDonald. Charlie traveled to Hudson's Bay as a census agent for the Department of Agriculture, a position that Johnson describes as a logical extension of the "Indian relic-hunting craze" that gripped him as a youth. If as a young boy he "studied Indian archaeology and folk-lore," searching for "relics" and reading ethnological accounts of Indigenous peoples, as a young man Charlie "consummated his predilections for Indianology, by loving, winning and marrying the quiet little daughter of the English trader at Hudson's Bay, who himself had married a native woman twenty years ago."[1] What began as a hobby, or a "craze" for relics, continued with Charlie's work of counting Indigenous people and evolved into a desire to possess Indigenous women.[2] The marriage consummates both his desire for Christine and his enumeration of her community.

In the discussion between Christine's father and Charlie that opens the story, Mr. Robinson, who is an English settler, warns Charlie that Indigenous women must be treated carefully, and that only when Charlie has ' "owned for eighteen years a daughter as dutiful, as loving, as fearless, and, alas! as obstinate as that little piece you are stealing away from me to-day' " will he understand Indigenous women.[3] This transaction between white men mirrors interactions among colonists who vied for "pieces" that they might own, exchange, steal, buy, and trade, transforming people and belongings into objects to be possessed and arranged in displays. Johnson aligns multiple forms of possession in the act of relic hunting, suggesting that the moves to knowledge made by "Indianology" are replicated in the census's quantitative authority and a husband's claims: possession as the power to know, to order, to represent, to speak for, to marry.

After their marriage, the couple returns to the "provincial capital," where Charlie displays Christine (or Christie, as she is called) like one more relic. She never leaves home except with her husband, who displays her "in the drawing-rooms of the wives of pompous Government officials." Christie is called the ' "sweetest wildflower' " and ' "a dolling little appil blossom' " and was "the centre of interest among all the women in the room," a living collectible that Charlie exhibits as a relic of his work at Hudson's Bay.[4] These epithets, and the fact that the story was also published under the alternate title "A Sweet Wild Flower," demonstrate the interchangeability of flowers, ethnographic specimens, and Native women for Charlie and other urban settler elites. For them, Native women are beautiful flowers plucked from the wilderness to be displayed as specimen of their "wild" roots. In these acts of display, Charlie claims to define what an "Indian" is, just as his census claimed to delineate who is and is not "Indian." His desire for relics and Indigenous women alike is a desire to make claims about their histories and lives that position him as a master cataloger and enumerator.

Yet when it emerges at one of these social events that Christie's parents were not married by a priest, Charlie is embarrassed by what he sees as his wife's illegitimate birth and accuses her of disgracing him. Her alleged wildness contributes to her desirability as a specimen while threatening his status through its proximity to practices Charlie sees as dishonorable. His anger exposes his interest in Christie as someone who can be possessed and exhibited but who does not require him to account for Indigenous "rites," histories, or relations. Charlie's interest in "Indianology" extends to Indigenous people as objects of display insofar as they do not require him to alter his understanding of relationships like marriage. In return, Christie leaves him, asking why she should "recognize the rites of your nation when you do not acknowledge the rites of mine."[5] Christie's repudiation of Charlie and her refusal to return to the marriage—even when, stricken by her departure, he again declares his love—is also a repudiation of the categories in which he attempted to know and possess her.

Johnson's alignment of "Indianology," census taking, and marriage to Indigenous women in the story powerfully illuminates the gendered dimensions of colonial archives and acts of collecting and their repercussions for Indigenous women. "A Red Girl's Reasoning" illustrates how settlers' gaze of desire is also a gaze of possession honed in relic hunting and then applied to Indigenous women's bodies. This gaze, as the story elaborates, casts Indigenous women's bodies as specimen, like so many "wildflowers" and "blossoms" available for consumption, as represented by Charlie's statement, "You are mine—*mine*."[6] Indigenous women have long confronted such desire from white men who sought to possess them and through them, Indigenous lands: from the English colonial narratives justifying the capture, baptism, and marriage of the Powhatan girl Matoaka/Pocahontas in the seventeenth century, to the white men whose relationships with Cherokee women prompted the Cherokee Nation to pass laws in the early nineteenth century to protect Cherokee women and their homelands, or the men who in the early twentieth century married Osage women and murdered their relatives to gain access to oil reserves under Osage lands. Christie's defiance of Charlie—her insistence that "we *are not married now*" because he refused to recognize Indigenous forms of relation—is also a refusal of these claims of possession, in marriage and in relic hunting.[7] Christie's rejection of marriage is also a rejection of Charlie's attempts to know and control her.

Building on Johnson's keen analysis of the gendered violence of colonial knowledge production, in chapter 3 I examine Indigenous compilations made and circulated in instances when settler ethnographers and Indian agents sought to collect Indigenous women as specimen. In the 1820s and 1830s, Indigenous women's albums—arrangements of poems, songs, and illustrations in ready-made books, those already bound and featuring blank or lined pages awaiting inscription—were shared texts that those women used to shape their interactions with settler men and women, tourists and ethnographers alike, and to affirm relations with other people. E. Pauline Johnson kept one such album, into which she copied her poems, pasted clippings of published poems, and shared the pages with others for commentary. Her albums participate in a literary history of making compilations in albums that stretches across the nineteenth century and in which Indigenous people of many ages and occupations participated. Native young people assembled albums at Indian boarding schools, where they experimented with ways of recording the friendships they made and their experiences at the school, placing physical objects meant to order their lives and behaviors next to messages representing their friendships with Native people from their own and other tribal nations. For example, the Stockbridge-Munsee boy James E. Johnson pasted dozens of report cards from Carlisle Indian School on page after page of a thick album, where the cards share space with notes exchanged with friends, newspaper clippings from his time on the Carlisle football team, and on one album page, a slender sheet of birchbark.[8] Albums were also critical sites of composition, commentary, and literary generation: Indigenous authors, such as the Creek writer and editor Alexander Posey, kept journals and scrapbooks where he arranged poems and stories, both printed and in manuscript, drafted materials, and where he (and sometimes acquaintances) inscribed notes.[9] The Seneca man and first Native commissioner of the Bureau of Indian Affairs Ely S. Parker and the Yavapai Apache writer Carlos Montezuma (who called for abolishing the Bureau) each kept albums—Montezuma's albums stitched together by hand, Parker's in scrapbooks patented by Mark Twain—in which they each pasted newspaper clippings about Native American people, assembling and tracking mass media representation.[10] Like John Ridge's and William Apess's compilations of extracts, these albums gathered texts already circulating in manuscript or print into new relationships. Some albums, such as Parker's and Montezuma's, juxtaposed colonial texts in order to revise their meaning or expose their deceit, but albums also held original works as well as texts copied from periodicals. Albums are experiments in translation between languages and between poetic and narrative traditions. And albums were Indigenous compilations assembled, circulated, and used to sustain the rites and relations of their makers' own nations.

CHAPTER THREE

ALBUM

Reading and Recirculating Poetry in Anishinaabe Networks

———————◆———————

One of the poems transcribed in Anishinaabe woman Ogenebugoquay/
Charlotte Johnston's album begins self-referentially with the lines, "Yes,
I would add one humble leaf / To the bright chaplet thou art twining."[1]
The poem imagines Johnston's album as a garland and the poem as a
"leaf" that she will weave together with other poems, hymns, and illustrations into a "wreath."[2] For Johnston, "twining" likely glossed a range of
actions. She probably followed the poem's logic by thinking about acts of
excerpting and transcribing poems in the blank, lined pages of her album.
In this case, the Buffalo, New York, woman Sarah Wilkeson contributed
the poem about twining in 1830, while Johnston was visiting the city and
Niagara Falls. She may also have envisioned the bright garland of roses a
contributor drew on one album's title page, into which he wove tiny letters
spelling "REMEMBER Chrs. S. F" (see figure I.3). She may have called to
mind the sheets of paper she stitched into quires for a visiting Presbyterian
minister one May evening in 1832, and she may have pictured the birchbark makaks (baskets or boxes) that her mother Ozhaawshkodewikwe
stitched and adorned.[3]

"Twining" evokes acts of arranging words, images, and objects together, placing materials into relation without collapsing their differences. Twining also indexes the collaborative actions an album invites, from selecting a blank page, choosing a poem to copy in ornamental handwriting, inscribing a name or initials and marking the transcription's date, looking at the poem as an object on the page, and perhaps reading its content. Twining encompasses practices of flipping through the album in order to read the poems nonsequentially or to select a blank page on which to add a new entry. Johnston's act of twining poems stitched those entries into new arrangements within her album, much as the act of stitching leaves makes a garland or, if those leaves are sheets of paper, a book, and, if they are sheets of birchbark, a makak.

Charlotte Johnston twined two albums: the first, begun around 1826, contains about eighty previously published poems and a few illustrations. I refer to this book as Johnston's Book, after the three inscriptions of her name on the cover and title pages, where her name appears as "Miss C. Johnston" (cover), "O-ge-ne-bug-'o'-qua" (title page), and "Miss Charlotte O. Johnston" (title page).[4] A second book, which she titled "Charlotte Johnston's Ojibwa Book, 1828," includes contributions made primarily between 1827 and 1833 and a cluster transcribed in the 1850s. Both blank books are bound and have cloth covers. Across both albums, many poems and songs are in English, one entry is in French, and sixteen are in Anishinaabemowin. Some poems are by well-known English authors, for example, the English poet Lord Byron and the English hymnist Charles Wesley, and most, but not all, had already seen publication in literary magazines and newspapers. Several poems anticipate their twining with such titles as: "Written in a Lady's Album," "Remember Me," "Written in a Common-Place Book," and "For a blank leaf in a New Bible."

From their embellished covers and hand-illustrated title pages to their excerpting of popular poetry, Johnston's compilations share much with the manuscript miscellanies, gift books, and albums that U.S. and British women filled with axioms and poems from friends and acquaintances. In those circles, albums were fashionable literary objects that displayed one's taste while functioning as portable monitors with easily accessible moral axioms; they were also engines of republication, recirculation, and sociability.[5] In British Romantic and American literary histories, these albums served to stage conversations and "materialize . . . new community," by eliciting and representing friendships.[6]

Unlike albums made by white women in British and U.S. circles, how-ever, Johnston twined her albums at Bow-e-ting, a place in Anishinaabe territories between the continent's eastern and western waterways (now known as Sault Ste. Marie, Michigan).[7] Bow-e-ting was the territory of the Anishinaabe community known as the Sauteurs. It was also a place of sea-sonal gatherings, for many Anishinaabe people traveled there in the spring and summer to make maple sugar and catch whitefish. And it was a pas-sage for Native people moving between Lake Huron and Lake Superior, as well as for British, French, and U.S. people—from traders to Indian agents to missionaries—who sought relationships with the Anishinaabe and Dakota nations to the west. Johnston's mother, Ozhaawshkodewikwe, moved from her home at Chequamegon (called La Pointe by the French, now Ashland, Wisconsin) to Bow-e-ting in 1793, following her marriage to the Irish trader John Johnston. She was accompanied by her relatives Waishkey and Keewyzi, whose families also lived at Bow-e-ting and along-side whom Johnston and her siblings grew up.[8] In the mid-1820s, when Johnston began to keep her albums, the Sauteurs' forty to fifty lodges far outnumbered the British and French occupants, mostly traders who had married Indigenous women.[9] John Johnston's and Ozhaawshkodewikwe's successful trading network depended on their kin relations with these Anishinaabe communities and those to the west.[10] Despite U.S. officials' claims to control the region, as the Ojibwe historian Michael Witgen and Garden River First Nation scholar Karl S. Hele have shown, Bow-e-ting and the lands to the north and west to which it was connected by water-ways remained Anishinaabe places, oriented by Anishinaabe social forma-tions and political alliances until well into the nineteenth century.[11]

Johnston twined her albums at a time when U.S. and British Canadian officials were entering the Anishinaabe world at Bow-e-ting in increasing numbers, hoping to realize their respective nation's claims to the region. Much like the census agent and amateur collector Charlie McDonald in E. Pauline Johnson story "A Red Girl's Reasoning," these men sought to make Johnston (and other Anishinaabe women) into specimen they could display and study, threatening to entangle Johnston in representations of Indigenous women as exotic and sexually available and in the political claims of settler nation states to possess Anishinaabe territories. As these officials made Anishinaabe people, languages, and literatures objects of study, they created influential archives of ethnographic and literary materials. A central figure in this history is Henry Rowe Schoolcraft, who arrived at Bow-e-ting in 1822 as the newly appointed U.S. Indian agent for Michigan Territory. Henry embarked on an extensive study of Anishinaabemowin and of Anishinaabe traditional stories, histories, and material culture, hoping thereby to establish himself as an authority on Indigenous peoples and Indian policy. He proposed that reading Anishinaabe literatures would open a window through which settlers could view something he called the Indian mind and by extension Indigenous peoples' past and possible futures. He used his relationship with the Johnston family in these pursuits: he married Charlotte Johnston's older sister Jane in 1823, and he gathered Anishinaabe words, songs, and stories from the Johnstons over the next few decades.

Henry's manuscript archives have made possible recent recoveries of early Indigenous literatures, most centrally Jane Johnston Schoolcraft's poems. With a few exceptions, these poems remained unpublished until the twenty-first century, living within Henry's manuscript collections at the Library of Congress. A 2007 collection edited by literary scholar Robert Dale Parker put Johnston Schoolcraft on the literary map as the "first known American Indian literary writer, the first known Indian woman writer, by some measures the first known Indian poet, the first known poet to write poems in a Native American language, and the first known American Indian to write out traditional Indian stories."[12] Yet if Henry has long claimed a place in the histories of anthropology and American literature, and if Johnston Schoolcraft's many "firsts" establish her centrality to Native American literary histories, Charlotte Johnston remains a quieter presence, largely overlooked by literary historians.[13] This is in part because her compilations resemble twining more than authoring: she collaborated on, translated, transcribed, and recirculated already existing texts rather than writing original poetry. Her published translations remain unacknowledged, such as her work with her husband, the minister William McMurray, to translate religious texts like *Ojibway Muzzeniegun; The Catechism of the Church of England; Written in the Ojibwa (or Chippewa) Language* (1834)—a work attributed only to McMurray in bibliographies and library catalogs.[14] In addition, her textual productions tended to be ephemeral: many existed only in spoken forms, like the sermons she translated for white ministers and the hymns she composed and sang.[15] But her liminal literary historical place is also, as this chapter shows, a result of the fact that Johnston made compilations that generated feelings she shared with other Anishinaabe people and, sometimes, with British and U.S. people as well. Those feelings register in colonial accounts as wasted time, or as confusing interactions colonists could not access or refused to understand. In this chapter, I read against those colonial accounts to examine how Indigenous compilations obtained expansive meaning in their uses by Johnston and other Indigenous people, meanings that can exceed the content of materials entwined on the page and colonists' readings of those materials.

Johnston's albums are Indigenous compilations that twined together songs and shared feeling among members of communities connected by kinship relations, language, shared interests, and affection. Because the pages bear the traces of multiple contributors, they indicate how albums invoked multiple, collaborative uses, and they demonstrate the communal making and using that Indigenous compilations supported, especially from the 1820s to the 1890s. Whereas, as seen in chapter 2, John Ridge gestured at the interactions and shared texts that expressed relations among Cherokee people in his letters to Albert Gallatin, Johnston's albums directly elicited such acts and materially represent communal acts of making and using texts. Those collaborations ranged from Johnston's friendship with Anishinaabe missionaries who contributed hymns to the Ojibwa Book to her interactions with U.S. soldiers and officials, who transcribed poems in the albums even as they sought to possess Johnston and her attention. And Johnston made her albums not in a center for U.S. diplomacy like Washington, D.C., as Ridge did, but at home. Finally, in contrast to the albums kept by U.S. and British women, Johnston's albums wrestle with how to make compilations in the midst of colonial specimen making.

Johnston's albums, along with the Indigenous compilations I consider in chapters 4 and 5, also reframe and reorient studies of nineteenth-century reprinting. Indigenous people have been largely absent from such studies, in striking contrast to the rich scholarship on U.S. authors and newspapers and on juxtaposition and citation within African American novels, scrapbooks, and newspapers. Perhaps this is because much Indigenous reprinting still remains circumscribed within colonial discourses of the ethnographic specimen or tourist souvenir. Indigenous compilations both reckon with and repulse these frameworks, providing a counterpoint to settlers' use of reprinting as what Phillip H. Round has called an "appropriative strategy" that undermined Indigenous intellectual and cultural sovereignty.[16] Johnston made and circulated her albums not through the anonymous circuits reprinting often afforded but in embodied, highly personal contexts in which settlers viewed both the albums and Johnston herself as souvenirs or, alternately, sought to determine the poems' meanings by reprinting them within their own books and magazines. But the albums are not reducible to those framings, for Johnston twined texts and feelings that redirected U.S. bureaucratic, literary, and ethnographic structures at a moment when U.S. officials sought to contain Anishinaabe women—and through them Anishinaabe nations and lands—within and outside U.S. temporal and political boundaries.

Books and Needlework at Bow-e-ting

As Robert Dale Parker has observed, Johnston's books provide a glimpse of the English-language texts that circulated through Bow-e-ting in the early nineteenth century.[17] And the albums do allow us to open a window into the books and newspapers that Johnston was reading and excerpting and more broadly into the Johnston siblings' immersion in European, U.S., and Anishinaabe literary traditions. Colonial commentators like Henry Rowe Schoolcraft romanticized the siblings' reading, finding in them surprising evidence of "civilization" among the "remote" wilds of the Great Lakes.[18] But while the albums might tell us something about what Johnston read, she made the albums not just by reading but also by stitching, translating, and listening. This section positions Johnston's albums within a family history of album making, in order to illuminate the actions with which Johnston made compilations and by extension the range of uses for books and manuscripts at Bow-e-ting. If albums, as literary scholar Andrew Piper has argued, privilege readers over authors by making it "the reader who provided the intellectual threads that connected the book's diverse parts," the Johnstons' compilations wove relations among books and stories circulating at Bow-e-ting.[19] In particular, Johnston's albums embrace recirculation as a mode of compilation by placing reading into relation with a series of actions related to twining.

Charlotte, Jane, and their older brother George Johnston each made several albums over five decades, in which they experimented with translating words and stories in English and Anishinaabemowin and with bringing poems, plants, and languages into relation on the pages of their books. Using both ready-made books like Johnston's albums and those they bound by hand, the siblings made compilations of the poetry, languages, songs, illustrations, and printed media that they encountered in the early nineteenth century. Some materials came from their father's library, which was evidently quite large, inspiring one guest to estimate with surprise and admiration (and possibly some inflation) that it contained "a thousand well-bound and well-selected volumes, French and English, evidently much in use, in winter especially; and not gathered together in these days of cheap literature."[20] George Johnston probably copied excerpts from books in this "much in use" library into the "Memorandum Books" he began compiling as early as 1816, filling them with excerpts from the Bible, Horace, and Virgil. He also used his Memorandum Books to keep accounts related to his work as a trader and Indian subagent at La Pointe, to collect journal entries, and to transcribe Anishinaabe stories. One book bears the faint traces of plants once pressed between pages of journal entries; elsewhere in that same book, George devoted entire pages to pressing plants, identifying their Anishinaabemowin names and adding recipes for plants' medicinal use.[21]

Likewise, Jane compiled several manuscript poetry collections, in addition to writing her own verse. She filled one manuscript album (stitched together by hand, like George's) with sixty-eight pages of hymns by an unidentified author and transcribed her father's poetry in a blank book she titled "Poetic Remains, John Johnston Esqr."[22] Between 1826 and 1827, Johnston Schoolcraft collaborated with her husband in editing the manuscript magazine *Muzzeniegun / Literary Voyager,* which circulated among family and friends at Bow-e-ting and in Detroit and Mackinac, Michigan, and to some of Henry's contacts to the east. Johnston Schoolcraft also contributed her own poetry to the magazine, often written under the pseudonym Leelineau; she may have read *Muzzeniegun* articles aloud and listened to others read them in a "reading society" organized around the magazine.[23]

Unlike Jane, Johnston transcribed relatively few of the entries in her albums, and unlike George, she rarely added her own writing alongside others' contributions. Johnston's Book contains entries transcribed by other hands; Johnston transcribed some of the entries in the Ojibwa Book but signed only one with her initials, "C.O.J."

Accounts of reading in the Johnston household uncover the constitutive role of twining—from stitching pages and birchbark to arranging poems—in Johnston's engagements with print. Schoolcraft described one such moment in his biography of John Johnston, writing that John "gather[e]d his family around the table, and while his daughters were employed at their needlework, he either read himself, or listened to one of his sons, adding his comments upon any passages that required it, or upon any improprieties or deficiencies in emphasis, punctuation, or personal manners."[24] In this scene, reading is a pedagogical exercise that teaches personal comportment. While Schoolcraft gendered the act of reading— placing the brothers as readers and direct receivers of John's instruction and the sisters as occupied not with books but with needles, Johnston and her sisters expand reading to include listening. The sisters' listening is active: they received instruction in elocution and presentation by listening to their father's instructions, even as they also performed their own acts of designing texts, with needles rather than pens. Occupied with sewing *and* with sentences, the sisters drew reading into relation with other ways of making and using texts.

A second account of reading shows in more detail the texts that Johnston and her siblings stitched while they or others were reading. The Presbyterian minister Jeremiah Porter noted in his journal of his several months' stay with the Schoolcrafts in 1832 that he stopped at Ozhaawshkodewikwe's home one night on his way to his lodging. On that May evening, while he "completed the incidents of the day," or wrote his daily journal entry, "C. stitched my paper, & I selected & wrote my text which was about the amount [of his work on the sermon]. As Maria J & Miss Haliday, are staying at Mr. S.s & are singers, they sing a hymn at our evening devotions & then retired to bless our heavenly Father for his continued mercies."[25] Here, needlework extended to book making, and it existed alongside singing and praying by Johnston's younger sister Maria and their friend Mary Haliday, actions that might suggest the presence of a hymnbook. In all of these actions, the women's bodies—hands, fingers, voices—were active in listening to, possibly reading, transmitting, and stitching texts.

These scenes of reading and stitching indicate that it was not just John Johnston's library that informed the Johnston siblings' album making but also Anishinaabe women's practices of stitching. When Porter accompanied Johnston to visit Ozhaawshkodewikwe at her sugaring camp on Sugar Island (in what is now called St. Mary's River) in April 1832, he noted that "the Indian women are all around sewing mococks, made from birchbark, to contain the sugar."[26] Sewing was a practical and a social act on Sugar Island, where it may have renewed relationships among Anishinaabe women who were catching up after their families returned to summer planting and hunting lands. Anishinaabe women shared the makaks they sewed with family members and guests. Jane Johnston Schoolcraft enclosed a makak filled with maple sugar from Ozhaawshkodewikwe with a witty note to Henry before they were married, sending her mother's gift alongside her own Shakespearean puns.[27] Superintendent of Indian Affairs Thomas McKenney described a makak Ozhaawshkodewikwe gave him in 1826, writing that "the smaller ones are ornamented with porcupines quills, died [*sic*] red, yellow, and green. These ornamented mococks hold from two to a dozen table spoons of sugar, and are made for presents, or for sale, to the curious."[28] And Johnston wrote to her brother George in 1833 that their mother had prepared makaks for him in anticipation of his return to Bow-e-ting.[29] Johnston's own needlework likely extended from books to makaks, beadwork, and clothing: she probably sewed her own and her sisters' clothing, including pieces that visitors described variously as "such as we see in our cities"[30] and as outdated by a decade,[31] as well as fashions like Ozhaawshkodewikwe's "blue petticoat, of cloth, a short gown of calico, with leggins worked with beads, and moccasins."[32]

These scenes indicate the centrality of stitching and sewing to Johnston's compilations, placing the albums into relation with other objects made through twining—from quires to clothing to makaks and quillwork. Acts of twining emphasize Anishinaabe women's creative work alongside libraries and reading, placing makaks alongside books as objects of sociality and instruction. That work, as the scene on Sugar Island shows, is deeply collaborative, stitching people together though the exchange of material objects, care, knowledge, and food. Far from a passive girl bent over her needlework while her brothers read from her father's library, Johnston used twining as active, creative work that generated many uses for texts, including reading, listening, sewing, singing, and book making.

Anishinaabe Women and Ethnographic Specimen

While Johnston experimented with twining textual materials, she found that the settler men and women who contributed poems to the albums could transform sharing into extraction. Beginning in the mid-1820s, increasing numbers of missionaries, traders, and tourists stopped at Bow-e-ting for supplies and news on their travels to Anishinaabe territories to the west. For these visitors, the Johnston family home was a central site of social exchange and diplomacy. Non-Native travelers to Bow-e-ting often remarked on the Johnstons' hospitality, noting that John Johnston and Ozhaawshkodewikwe invited them to share meals and often to spend the night at their home, and this generosity extended to Native travelers as well.[33] Yet many colonists also viewed these acts of hospitality as openings for obtaining information about Anishinaabe people; they saw Johnston and her siblings as fascinating sources of information about Anishinaabe people due to their fluency in Anishinaabemowin and familial connections to Anishinaabe leaders.

Johnston in particular faced probing questions and intense observation on the part of men and women eager to experience a taste of the "wilderness"—as they understood that concept by reading fiction by U.S. authors like James Fenimore Cooper, Henry Wadsworth Longfellow, and Washington Irving. The British writer Anna Brownell Jameson reported of her travels through Detroit and Bow-e-ting in 1838 that she was "amused every moment by the coincidence between what I see and what I have read [in Cooper, Irving, Charles Hoffman, and other novelists]," and she carefully inspected Johnston's body, features, and voice for evidence of her Anishinaabe familial ties.[34] Jameson sent Johnston a list of questions about Anishinaabe women after meeting her in 1837, and the Johnston sisters introduced Jameson to their mother and uncle Waishkey when she visited their home later that year, patiently answering her profuse questions about Anishinaabe life and history.[35] And just as Charlie McDonald "consummated" his relic hunting by "winning" possession of Christie in marriage in "A Red Girl's Reasoning," so several U.S. Army officials paired contributions to Johnston's album with demands on her affections. They even went so far as to try to discredit William McMurray after Johnston decided to marry him in early 1833. Charles Stitcher Frailey, who made the intricate paintings of roses in Johnston's Book, was likely one of these admirers; James Allen, who added detailed hand-drawn illustrations of Lake Superior, certainly was.[36]

This curiosity was shared and to some degree encouraged by Henry Rowe Schoolcraft, who touted the Johnstons as unique sources on Anishinaabe people and language. Schoolcraft himself relied heavily on the Johnstons' collaborations, given his limited knowledge of Anishinaabemowin and of kinship networks, but he downplayed or removed the Johnstons' labor from his ethnographic publications. Schoolcraft did describe these collaborations in his letters and autobiographical writings, explaining there that he queried the Native people with whom he interacted on "useful subjects of information during the day" and then repaired to the Johnston home in the evenings. There, he sought "to test my inquiries in the evening by reference to the Johnstons, who, being educated, and speaking at once both the English and Odjibwa [*sic*] correctly, offer a higher and more reliable standard than usual."[37] Schoolcraft imagined that the Johnstons would provide access to knowledge that he so eagerly desired in order to realize his ambitions of becoming a prominent government official and author. As he wrote breathlessly in his 1851 *Personal Memoirs*, "My connection with the Johnston family has thrown open to me the whole arcanum of the Indian's thoughts."[38] What the Johnstons established as a space of hospitality—a space created by and necessary to John's trading networks and Anishinaabe practices of reciprocity—also became through Henry's machinations and tourists' curiosity a site of extraction where settlers sought to take both objects and, sometimes, people as specimens for analysis and display.

In summer 1826, specimen making collided with compilation making in Johnston's poetic exchanges with several U.S. men, including Superintendent of Indian Affairs Thomas McKenney. That July, McKenney and the governor of Michigan Territory, Lewis Cass, stopped at Bow-e-ting for supplies before traveling west into Lake Superior. The Johnstons hosted McKenney and Cass for several dinners and a dance before the

officials went on to conduct treaty negotiations with Anishinaabe leaders at Waiekwakitchigami or Fond du Lac (currently Duluth, Minnesota).
The negotiations aimed to obtain those leaders' permission for the U.S. to
access mineral resources on their lands; Rowe Schoolcraft also hoped to
secure lands for the Johnston siblings (and by extension his own children).[39]
McKenney lodged at Fort Brady, erected at Bow-e-ting in 1822, as canoes
and supplies were prepared for the journey westward, a journey on which
Cass, Schoolcraft, George Johnston as translator, and the topographer and
illustrator James Otto Lewis also traveled.

During this stay, the Johnstons shared a song in Anishinaabemowin and
English prose and verse translations with McKenney, who transcribed the
song and recorded its title as "Ojibwe Maid." McKenney credited Johnston and Jane Johnston Schoolcraft with translating and performing the
song, writing that he "prevailed on [Charlotte Johnston] to sing this song
several times," which she did, he wrote, "with most enchanting effect."[40]
He added that "Charlotte has presented me with a version of it by Major
H. S——th, of the United States' army."[41] He published the song's musical notation and multiple versions in his epistolary travel narrative, *Sketches
of a Tour to the Lakes, of the Character and Customs of the Chippeway Indians, and of
Incidents Connected with the Treaty of Fond du Lac* (1827).

In that narrative, McKenney described the song as a flower he plucked
and sent home. He urged Secretary of War James Barbour, the imagined
recipient of the letters in *Sketches*, to circulate it:

> I hope to hear this pretty little song sung and played when I reach home. I
> wish you to introduce it into society. It is one of the wild flowers which I have
> gathered with great care—let it not "blush unseen," nor "waste" any of its
> "sweetness."[42]

McKenney framed his work as that of botanical collection, a process of
gathering flowers for arrangement and preservation in an album or case.
Flowers—in this case, the song—are aesthetic and ethnographic objects that colonists must display and consume to realize their sweetness
and beauty. Like the didactic images of flowers circulating in nineteenth-
century floral dictionaries and sentimental poetry, McKenney's flower
represents the transience of the present and the certainty of death.[43] But in
McKenney's case, the flower is also a figure for Indigenous women, who,

according to the metaphor's logic—and, as we will see, the song's—will soon fade and die.

McKenney was already casting Indigenous people as specimen before his travels to Anishinaabe territories (see chapter 2). The portraits in his Indian Gallery, including several of Anishinaabe men and women, constituted one project for transforming Indigenous people into objects. As a repository for McKenney's personal collection, the Indian Gallery also held what he called "relics," perhaps including the makaks he received as a gift from Ozhaawshkodewikwe, and "flowers," such as songs and "allegor[ies]" collected from the Johnstons.[44] And McKenney sought explicitly to turn Johnston into a relic or, as he called her, a "specimen." He described her as a living example of the *"character and customs of the Chippeway Indians"*:

> Here again, without the advantages of education to the same extent, or equal opportunities for improvement, but with no deficiencies in these matters, you have a beautiful specimen of a female of mixed blood. This interesting young lady has but little of the mother's complexion. She possesses charms which are only now and then seen in our more populous and polished circles. These are in the form and expression of a beautiful face, where the best and most amiable and cheerful of tempers—the loveliest and most captivating ornament of the sex—sits always with the sweetness of spring, and from whence the graces seem never to have departed even for a moment—and all this has imparted to it an additional interest in her own total unconsciousness of their presence, and of her powers to please. Her eyes are black, but soft in their expression, and between her lips, which I have never seen otherwise than half parted with a smile, is a beautiful set of ivory.[45]

McKenney dissected Johnston's body to classify her features, complexion, character, and behavior, much as a botanist might name each part of a flower. Categorizing Anishinaabe women according to their appearance and their quantity of "blood," he suggested that Johnston is all the more "interesting" because she is a "specimen" of "mixed blood," one who also has a "beautiful face," a sweet temper, and a lovely voice. And McKenney wished to "gather" her, much as he collected "wild flowers" or Anishinaabe songs, and to display her as an object for visual (and possibly sexual) consumption. He went so far as to invite Johnston to visit him in Washington, where he promised to introduce her to his social circle (John Johnston initially gave permission, but retracted it, seemingly concerned about the possible consequences of Johnston traveling alone to meet McKenney in Washington).[46] Just as McKenney hoped to introduce the song to display his collections of Anishinaabe "character and customs," so he seems to have hoped to introduce Johnston as a "specimen" of Anishinaabe beauty and talent so that she did not "blush unseen" in the supposedly remote locales of Anishinaabe country.

While Johnston rejected the proposal to travel to Washington, McKenney's concern that he not "waste" the song's sweetness framed the song—and Johnston herself—as specimen whose beauty and attraction were temporary and which must be observed before they faded. This anticipation of fading and death was ultimately grounded in the beliefs of McKenney and other colonial officials about Native peoples' relationship to time and the future, in particular their conviction that Indigenous life and sovereignty existed in the past and that colonists were witnessing its fading and foreclosure. McKenney explained in *Sketches* that he "glean[ed]"[47] "relics" from treaty negotiations because he believed that they would eventually replace Native peoples:

> I hope to take home with me some interesting relics from among these people, and some drawings, in addition to those which I am now and then putting aside for you, the better to illustrate my correspondence, and which are intended for the office in Washington, and to be preserved there for the inspection of the curious, and the information of future generations, and long after the Indians themselves will have been no more.[48]

For McKenney, objects like songs and relics stood in for Native people, who, like flowers, might bloom or prosper in the present only to wither away. Within the logic of this metaphor, Native people exist within a temporal category of short duration and certain withering.

Henry Rowe Schoolcraft dismissed McKenney's *Sketches* as the result of a "gossiping tour," perhaps hoping to secure an audience for his own publications on similar subjects.[49] Yet Schoolcraft was guided by the same anticipation of Native withering as McKenney, and like McKenney, he made Anishinaabe women and Anishinaabe literary practices figures for this supposedly imminent vanishing. Schoolcraft located in Anishinaabe literatures' form and modes of transmission evidence for his belief that

Indigenous peoples existed out of time. He argued in an article entitled "Indian Story Tellers" that acts of telling stories were in direct proportion to Native women's alleged disregard for time: "In the many waste hours of savage life, the mother often realizes the inconvenience of having to provide occupation for unemployed minds; and the story-teller is welcomed by her for the relief he brings."[50] Schoolcraft connected these "waste hours" to stitching in an essay on the "Indian" family, writing that Native women "set . . . little value on time, which is characteristic of all the race." Instead, Schoolcraft wrote, Native women spend their time in needlework: "She has no books to read. . . . What she does, is either very plain sewing, or some painstaking ornamental thing."[51] Needlework and listening to stories are once again paired, as they were in Schoolcraft's account of the Johnston sisters sewing while they listened to their brothers or father read. In his ethnographic commentary, both actions signal Indigenous women's failure to properly value and use time. Schoolcraft extended McKenney's metaphor of Indigenous women as fading flowers by citing Indigenous women's work—and specifically needlework—as a cause of this fated fading. Finally, he correlated his suppositions about labor and time with his analysis of Anishinaabe literary form to argue that Native stories have only "flash[es]" of ideas and that they are "imperfect, broken, or disjointed," characterized by repetition and transposition.[52] Schoolcraft read such characteristics as reflecting not Anishinaabe literary practices but what he viewed as shortcomings of language and a lack of "any sequence."[53] Like Indigenous women's supposed disregard for time, the lack of "sequence" in Anishinaabe literatures reflected Anishinaabe people's location outside time. From that position, Schoolcraft wrote, a powerful element of civilization will either "change, improve, undermine, or destroy them."[54]

It is no coincidence that McKenney and Schoolcraft made Indigenous women the focus of their predictions of Indigenous fading. By suggesting that Indigenous women must be displayed and admired before they eventually wither and die, they framed Indigenous women as rightful objects of colonial possession: as specimen, as objects of their own gazes, and as objects of sexual violence. As Indigenous Studies scholar Dian Million (Tanana Athabascan) has shown, violence against Indigenous women is a tactic of colonial power that is both, as Million puts it, "an attack on individuals, and . . . a mobile but durable feature of colonial power relations."[55]

The Michi Saagiig Nishnaabeg scholar Leanne Betasamosake Simpson furthers this point, writing that such attacks on Indigenous women and 2SQ people are direct attacks on Indigenous polities: "Heteropatriarchy is not a discrimination that has come with white supremacy and colonialism; it is a *foundational dispossession force* because it is a direct attack on Indigenous bodies as political orders, thought, agency, self-determination, and freedom."[56] McKenney's transformation of Johnston into a metaphor—the flower that is both ornament and specimen—acts as such a "dispossession force" by presenting Indigenous women as objects of colonial possession and imagining relations in which Indigenous women are exotic entities colonists can possess before they disappear. This certainty of fading, which Schoolcraft attributes to Indigenous women's labor and disregard for time, effaces, even as it justifies, the intertwined colonial violences of rape, objectification, and dispossession. McKenney's transcriptions of the "Ojibwe Maid" are, in this context, interactions through which he sought to transform Indigenous women's bodies into sites of dispossession and acts of sharing into extraction and consumption.

Answering the "Ojibwe Maid"

McKenney's manuscript notes and published book were not the only places the "Ojibwe Maid" song appeared, and examining its circulations into Johnston's albums illuminates other uses for and meanings of the song, which intervene in colonial specimen making. Johnston's albums contain multiple versions of the "Ojibwe Maid" poem, indicating that the song circulated in performance and manuscript on multiple occasions at Bow-e-ting. Johnston's acts of twining the different versions in her albums re-circulated the song without necessarily reiterating its content, and in some cases, she revised the song's content directly. In twining multiple versions, Johnston cast the song not as a flower or specimen to be plucked and displayed as a relic of the past, but as a shareable text that existed in multiple versions and to which there might be multiple responses. Her compilations establish alternate temporalities for Indigenous women and for Anishinaabe peoples' futures, rejecting settler nostalgia for supposedly vanishing Indigenous peoples and countering settler claims to Anishinaabe lands.

To examine these versions and their differences, we must begin with McKenney's transcriptions: the song he published in *Sketches* has three

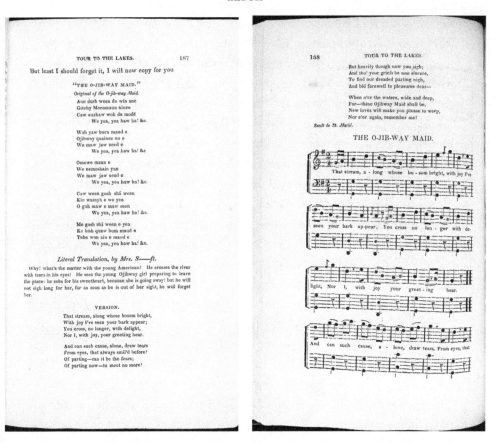

FIGURE 3.1. Thomas McKenney's versions of the "Ojibwe Maid" in *Sketches of a Tour to the Lakes* (1827). G 90 .538, Newberry Library, Chicago.

parts: first, he copied the five-stanza song that Johnston sang in Anishinaabemowin, in which each stanza ends with the phrase "We yea yea haw ha! &c." He credited Johnston Schoolcraft with a second version, a "literal translation" in prose.[57] This translation reads:

> Why! What's the matter with the young American? He crosses the river with tears in his eyes! He sees the young Ojibway girl preparing to leave the place: he sobs for his sweetheart, because she is going away! But he will not sigh long for her, for as soon as he is out of her sight, he will forget her.[58]

Finally, McKenney recorded an English-language version composed of four stanzas of iambic tetrameter in alternating rhyme (figure 3.1). In contrast to the prose translation's use of third person, the poem is in first person, spoken from the perspective of the Ojibwe maid. She laments that she will soon no longer see her beloved's "bark appear" on the water and fears that they are "parting now—to meet no more." She also predicts that "heavily though now you sigh; / And tho your griefs be now sincere," when "thine Ojibwe Maid" is far away, he will find new loves. The poem ends by predicting that he will "Nor e'er again, remember me!"[59]

Johnston's albums contain three additional versions of the poem. In Johnston's Book, a poem titled simply "Lines to ———" and transcribed in Rowe Schoolcraft's hand retells the Ojibwe maid's story, again from the perspective of the maid, and this time in rhyming couplets. However, "Lines to ———" takes place *after* the young man leaves, in this way revising the version McKenney transcribed, which anticipates the young man's departure and failure to remember the Ojibwe woman. In the second stanza, the young man "bid a sad adieu" and offered to ' "go with' " the woman. Her heart replied that she would go, but she remains silent: "on my tongue the answer died." The third and final stanza describes her "grief" and "pain of mind" upon being "left behind" and suggests that her grief "may kill" her. She still loves the young man, but he appears to have forgotten her, leaving her with emotions expressed in the couplets that conclude each stanza: "Oh the bitterness of mind / To be lov'd and left behind." The woman's inability to respond to the young man leaves her frozen in potentially fatal grief, left to contemplate "the bitterness of mind" at being "left behind."[60]

"Lines to ———" also appeared, absent the concluding refrain, in the eighth volume of the *Muzzeniegun / Literary Voyager*, where it is retitled "The Deserted Indian Maid." Its appearance in the magazine suggests that Rowe Schoolcraft may have transcribed this poem into Johnston's albums, or that Henry may have drawn on Johnston's albums for some materials for the magazine. He presented the poem as an ethnographic document that provided insight into Indigenous women, writing in an introduction:

> The affections of the Indian women are strong. Their love of their offspring is not surpassed in interest, or intensity by any nation. They are deeply attached to their friends, families, relatives and tribes. The following is a free version of a native song of a Chippewa girl, the original and literal translation of which, was put in our hands.[61]

Schoolcraft presented the poem not as an example of Anishinaabe literature but as a story about Native women's "affections" that he read to speculate about their attachments. And just as he concluded in "Indian Story Tellers" that Indigenous women failed to make use of their time, so "Lines to ——" and "The Deserted Indian Maid" envision a young Anishinaabe woman who is "left behind" by her beloved and by time itself due to her inability to accompany her young American, the vision of change and futurity.

These narratives of the young American and the Ojibwe maid evoke an old and ongoing story about Native women and European men, in which intimacy and intermarriage are a prelude to colonization and the assimilation and disappearance of Indigenous women. This is a story as old as the Powhatan girl Matoaka's/Pocahontas's rape, conversion, and baptism and as old as John Smith's (and other English colonial promoters') desire to use Native women's bodies to access Indigenous lands, literally and metaphorically.[62] As E. Pauline Johnson shows in "A Red Girl's Reasoning," this desire is ultimately about possession, a desire to incorporate Indigenous women—and their homelands—into U.S. or Canadian legal systems through marriage.[63] In Schoolcraft's and McKenney's hands, this story becomes one about absorption into U.S. political and temporal boundaries, demonstrating Million's and Simpson's point that attacking Indigenous women's bodies is also an attack on Indigenous communities and sovereignties. For them, Indigenous women embody the temporal incommensurability according to which Anishinaabe people could not exist in the same "now" as that of the "young American," and the maid's supposed desire and longing for the young man frames this as a tragic story of disappearance rather than a story of conquest.

Yet the additional versions of the song in Johnston's albums refuse to let these interpretations of the Ojibwe woman's affections and her tragic, lonely future stand unquestioned. In Johnston's Book, three pages after "Lines to ——" a song replying to "Ojibwe Maid" appears, signed by a man identified as McDonald and dated July 10, 1826. This date overlaps with McKenney's stay at Bow-e-ting, so McDonald likely heard Johnston's performance of the song and perhaps read its transcriptions. In contrast to McKenney's and Schoolcraft's versions, McDonald's poem takes the point of view of a "young American" who responds to the song Johnston sang, as signaled by the quotation marks McDonald places around the phrase "O-jeeb-wa Maid," which concludes the fourth line in each of the poem's three stanzas. The young man in this poem is a "wanderer from the land I loved." To the extent that "this land" represents the United States, his wandering may refer to the fact that while the United States had a presence at Bow-e-ting by 1826, Anishinaabe political power superseded that of both the U.S. and British Canada in the region. The youth wanders in this "strange" land, but he notes that he has rarely found pleasure like that "derived from 'thy 'O-jibwa Maid'" (line 4). He also praises the woman's simplicity and fairness in stanza 2 and in stanza 3 remarks on his imminent departure, noting, "The white sail on our bark is set." The concluding stanzas rewrite the end of the "Ojibwe Maid" as recorded by McKenney and Schoolcraft, for the young man ends by saying, "Then fare thee well I'll ne'er forget / The lovely, young 'O-jeeb-wa maid'" (figure 3.2).[64]

McDonald's poem writes back from the voice of the American, indicating that the impression the song and its singer made on him are so strong that he will remember them. Contributing the poem to Johnston's album enacted this promise, for the poem offered a material token of this remembrance. Moreover, this contribution understood Johnston's performance of the song differently from McKenney, by failing to frame it as a specimen to be plucked, pressed, and displayed as a token of transitory affections and peoples. Instead, the song stimulated further interaction, composition, exchange, and conversation. Johnston's acts of singing and transcribing the "Ojibwe Maid"—in spite of its content depicting a silent and lonely Ojibwe woman—in fact produced the opposite effect: that of stimulating social exchanges and acts of remembrance. And Johnston is not passive or nostalgic in these exchanges, for McDonald's reference to the song highlighted Johnston's active role, and his contribution to the albums located remembrance in acts of compiling rather than in fatal grief.

Johnston circulated the song once more, this time by transcribing it herself into the Ojibwa Book. "An Ojibway Song, Translated" is written in Johnston's hand, and although it largely follows the song she translated for McKenney, there are several differences. The version McKenney transcribed concludes its second stanza by noting that the fear of parting draws tears to the Ojibwe girl's eyes: "can it be the fears; / Of parting now—to meet no more."[65] Here, the "now" is the moment of parting, and the girl anticipates her grief upon the young man's departure and failure to remember her. In Johnston's version, she wrote: "can it be the

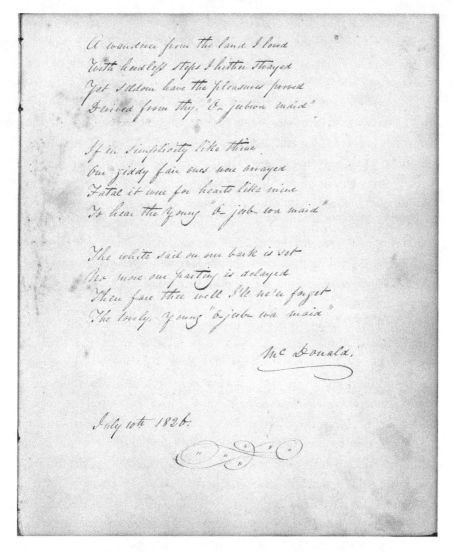

FIGURE 3.2. McDonald's response to the "Ojibwe Maid." Charlotte Johnston's Journal. Courtesy of the Judge Joseph H. Steere Room, Bayliss Public Library, Sault Ste. Marie, Michigan.

fears / Of parting, now to meet no more." The alternate punctuation—Johnston's movement of the comma to follow "parting" rather than McKenney's dash after "now"—revises the song's temporality. The Ojibwe maid is located in the "now" that follows parting, where she reflects on the young man's departure. Although this change might seem a minor one, Johnston's punctuation introduced a temporality in which Ojibwe women are active agents who remember and act in the present and into the future. This pause in the "now" revises the anticipatory logic of being "left behind" and of Native vanishing to which McKenney and Schoolcraft subscribed. Instead, Johnston's version imagined a future in which the Ojibwe woman is present—and present without the young American. She is not paralyzed by grief but actively speaks of her memories; she recalls the past even while existing in the present. Johnston's concluding line furthers this account of the Ojibwe woman's presence. While the Ojibwe maid in *Sketches* laments that the young man will find that "New loves will make you please to weep / Nor e'er again remember me," in Johnston's transcription, she revises the final line to read "And e'er again remember me." Here, the young man does depart, leaving the young woman to remember him fondly, but the poem ends by emphasizing his remembrance (figures 3.3 and 3.4).

The proliferating versions of "Ojibwe Maid" indicate that it would be a mistake to read the song solely as an expression of imperialist nostalgia, representing settlers' tears for what they have destroyed.[66] Such a reading would limit our focus to the poems' content and occlude their multiple circulations and versions. The "Ojibwe Maid" exists as a specimen or relic in McKenney's book and as an ethnographic specimen in the *Literary Voyager*, but those iterations do not exhaust or determine its meanings. Johnston's albums transform the "Ojibwe Maid" from a specimen into a text to be shared, revised, and retranscribed. The song was performed, heard, read, and written back to, carried among friends, and transcribed in new contexts, and in these circulations, it generated new meanings that were often in "excess" of its fatalistic content.[67] The girl's apparently plaintive call to "remember me" was answered, in actions, illustrations, and other responses transcribed in Johnston's books. Such acts of reciprocity are central to the "Ojibwe Maid," for the song's multiple versions question whether the relationship between the American man and Ojibwe woman would continue, and they pose several possible answers to that question. As the song—whether performed by Johnston or transcribed in her book—generated additional performances, collaborations, and compilations, it refused McKenney's and Schoolcraft's acts of gathering flowers or of assembling Anishinaabe stories like so many archaeological fragments.

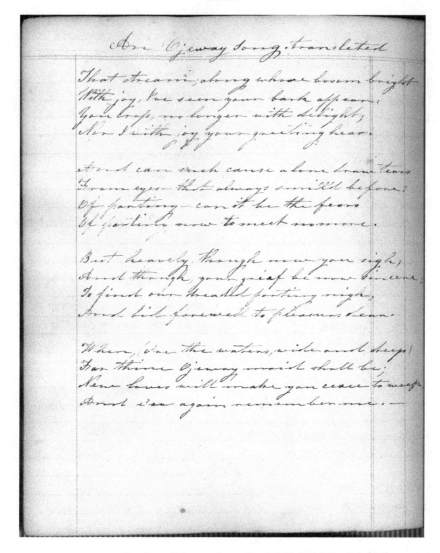

FIGURE 3.3. Charlotte Johnston's version of the "Ojibwe Maid."
Charlotte Johnston's Ojibwa Book. Courtesy of the Judge Joseph H.
Steere Room, Bayliss Public Library, Sault Ste. Marie, Michigan.

The exchange of poems and feelings in Johnston's albums creates what literary and gender studies scholar Naomi Greyser calls an "affective geography," a political and emotional common ground where Americans and Anishinaabe people might meet.[68] As Johnston found in her encounters with McKenney and other U.S. officials who wished to possess and

Lines to —
(In Johnston's Book)

"Ah, when remembrance brings to mind
The youth as brave as he was kind,
Love, hope and joy alternate start,
And wake a transport in my heart.
      Oh the bitterness of mind
        To be <u>lov'd and left</u> behind.

And when he bid a sad adieu,
He said, 'my love I'll go with you!'
'I'll go with you,' my heart replied,
But on my tongue the answer died.
      Oh the bitterness of mind
        To be lov'd and left behind

Alas, the grief__the pain of mind,
I felt when I was left behind
The kiss he gave__oh grief may kill,
Brave youth but I shall love thee still.
      Oh the bitterness of mind
        To be lov'd and left behind."

A version of this poem appears without the concluding refrain in *Literary Voyager*, no. 8, as "The Deserted Indian Maid."

Untitled Version
(In Johnston's Book)

A wanderer from the land I loved
Youth heedless steps I hither strayed
Yet seldom have the pleasures proved
Derived from thy, "O-jibwa maid"

If in simplicity like thine
Our giddy fair ones were arrayed
Fatal it were for hearts like mine
To hear the young "O-jeeb-wa maid"

The white sail on our bark is set
No more our parting is delayed
Then fare thee well I'll ne'er forget
The lovely, young "O-jeeb-wa maid"

McDonald

July 10, 1826

An Ojibway Song, Translated
(In Johnston's hand, in the
Ojibwa Book)

That stream, along whose bosom bright
With joy, I've seen your bark appear:
You cross, no longer with delight;
Nor I with joy your greeting hear.

And can such cause alone draw tears
From eyes—that always smil'd before?
Of parting—can it be the fears
Of parting, now to meet no more.

But heavily though now you sigh;
And though your grief be now sincere;
To find our dreaded parting nigh,
And bid farewell to pleasure dear.

When, (on the waters, wide and deep)
For thine Ojibway maid shall be;
New loves will make you cease to weep;
And e'er again remember me.

FIGURE 3.4. Three versions of the "Ojibwe Maid": "Lines to——,"
McDonald's version, and Johnston's version.

display her as a specimen, these affective grounds are sometimes produced by circulating and consuming images of Indigenous women, who become the very grounds for others' imagined intimacies. As Greyser writes, "Sentimentalism's dematerialization of differences in the name of togetherness has served projects of colonization, extraction, possession, and consumption; and it has underwritten projects of survivance, escape, stonewalling, and putting those who exploit in *their* place."[69] Johnston's recirculation of the "Ojibwe Maid" song in Johnston's Book and her rewriting of the song in the Ojibwa Book intervened in the temporalities that characterized settlers' imagined relations with Indigenous women, creating instead a space oriented by the "now" of the Ojibwe woman, a now that is not foreclosed by a U.S. future even as it recognizes the dangers the young American poses. Johnston took the supposed incommensurability between the young man's and the Ojibwe woman's temporalities and made this difference the foundation for articulating Anishinaabe temporalities that exist alongside, are at times entangled with, and yet are not absorbed by the young American. This is not an assimilation of difference but a marking of it. Johnston's twining of the song is a turn from colonial intimacy and all of the entanglements that it might entail.

Sharing Affections in the Ojibwa Book

If Johnston's Book was oriented toward interactions with visiting soldiers, officials, and tourists, in the Ojibwa Book Johnston gathered materials that generated and reflected affections she shared with other Anishinaabe people at Bow-e-ting and across the upper Great Lakes. She gathered most of the Ojibwa Book's entries between 1828 and 1833, when she was acting as a translator and when, for reasons I discuss in more detail below, Anishinaabe people were evincing increasing interest in Protestant religious practices. The Ojibwa Book's first four pages gather hymns and prayers in Anishinaabemowin, one transcribed by Johnston and three others contributed by the missionary George Henry and other Credit River Mississauga men who spent several summers at Bow-e-ting in the early 1830s to establish a congregation of Indigenous converts.

Along with Anishinaabe missionary John Sunday, these men traveled to Anishinaabe communities throughout the Great Lakes, bringing about what one white minister called a "revival, or rather a religious excitement among the Indians" and leading him to remark that "quite a number it is thought have become Christian."[70] Yet their presence at Bow-e-ting also fulfilled the Sauteur leader Shingwaukonse's request for a minister. Anishinaabe missionary Peter Jones noted that "in view of [Shingwaukonse's] application which he made to John Sunday some time since for a teacher to come and instruct his children, and to aid them in forming a settlement, we had now come."[71] White Baptist and Presbyterian ministers were furious at Sunday's success and the fact that people they viewed as their potential converts preferred to attend Sunday's sermons, and they attempted to prevent him from returning in subsequent years. Yet Jones made clear that Sunday came to Bow-e-ting not to compete with other ministers but in response to Shingwaukonse's "application." As Janet E. Chute has shown in her history of Shingwaukonse's life, missionaries like Jones and Sunday "gained widespread attention by promoting the idea of Native 'homelands' set apart from the pressures of frontier society, where Native people could seek spiritual solace, Christian fellowship, and material assistance."[72] Shingwaukonse strategically employed his community's adoption of Methodism and its relationship to ministers like Sunday and Johnston's husband William McMurray to seek U.S. and British Canadian recognition of Sauteur rights to their ancestral lands. What white ministers and officials viewed as a competition for converts was a process by which Anishinaabe people affirmed their belonging to place against pressure from settler nations to cede lands.

Johnston participated in this "revival," and the Ojibwa Book was central to her collaborations with both Anishinaabe and white missionaries. This album holds seventeen hymns in Anishinaabemowin which do not, as far as I have been able to determine, appear in any of the Anishinaabemowin hymnals printed in the early 1830s. Some of the Ojibwa Book's hymns share a line or two with translations in the first printed Anishinaabemowin hymnal or with some songs in Peter Jones's translations of hymns into Anishinaabemowin, *Tracts in the Chippeway and English* (1828) or *Collection of Hymns for the Use of Native Christians of the Iroquois* (1827) respectively. Otherwise, they depart from available published translations.[73] Rather than copied from a published hymnal, the hymns in the Ojibwa Book seem to have circulated through performance or manuscript exchange. These hymns entered a world in which "songs provided the currency of social relations. Songs served to mediate relations within Anishinaabe groups, as well as between Anishinaabeg and other native peoples."[74] The hymns were important not just as religious texts but also as social texts that made relations between Anishinaabe people. As religious studies scholar Michael McNally, echoing Craig Womack on Native writing, writes of Anishinaabe songs, "Songs fundamentally *did things* in the world of experience and survival."[75] Johnston and other interlocutors, such as her sisters, McMurray, and possibly other ministers, likely sang or read aloud the hymns in the Ojibwa Book; they may also have used the hymns in conversations or individual and communal reading.[76]

In a world in which song made and mediated relations among Anishinaabe people, singing hymns was one way Johnston articulated her relation to and feelings for other Anishinaabe people. Several white travelers described hearing Johnston "sing . . . most sweetly" in Anishinaabemowin, observing that she possessed a sweet voice and "correct ear."[77] She expressed a preference for singing in that language, saying, after a session singing hymns with the "Christian Indians"—that is, Sunday and his fellow Mississauga Ojibwe:

> "Why is it . . . that singing is so much better in Indian than in English"? this
> she uttered with her usual enthusiasm, & added, "There is no doubt but I
> am an Indian."[78]

For Johnston, singing was not just a pleasing activity at which she excelled or a talent on which she drew to perform songs like "Ojibwe Maid," but an act that expressed her belonging with other Anishinaabe people. The Presbyterian minister Jeremiah Porter observed that Johnston had a close bond with other Anishinaabeg, "speaking their language, having their affection, knowing their feelings."[79] Sharing and singing hymns seems to have been one avenue through which Johnston received other Anishinaabe people's affection. Porter commented that Sunday and the other Ojibwe Methodist ministers "sing sacred music in their own language delightfully. They are teaching others. They passed Saturday afternoon at Mrs Johnstons in singing."[80] In addition to Johnston, her mother, and sisters, these "others" likely included the Sauteurs and other Anishinaabe people at Bowe-ting for seasonal fishing with whom Johnston shared songs. Johnston's comment that there is "no doubt but that I am an Indian" speaks to affiliations constituted through actions like singing and a shared understanding of Anishinaabemowin.

These feelings were not distinct from Anishinaabe political formations or temporalities but generative of them, contrary to McKenney's and Schoolcraft's assessment of Anishinaabe women's affections. Johnston facilitated and participated in exchanges of affection, care, and comfort, and these exchanges constituted a "Native structure of feeling," which NAIS scholar Mark Rifkin glosses as "sensations of belonging to place and peoplehood excluded from settler governance but that remain present, most viscerally in the affective lives of Native people."[81] The structure of feeling shared among Anishinaabe people at Bow-e-ting is not outside the political or questions of sovereignty but central to and constitutive of them. Moreover, as these feelings are "excluded from settler governance," they also remain unmapped and unmappable by colonial political and epistemological systems that would constitute them as specimen or, in Rowe Schoolcraft's words, as "waste."[82] These feelings are traceable in ministers' and tourists' records of Johnston's work as a translator and minister's wife, where they often appear as moments of untranslatability, confusion, or even annoyance on the recorders' part. Reading those records alongside Johnston's albums can illuminate how the Ojibwa Book generated feelings that, even if they were unreadable to colonists—and perhaps precisely because they were unreadable—supported Anishinaabe people's belonging to place and to each other.

In addition to exchanging hymns with Anishinaabe ministers, Johnston translated sermons given by white ministers, and those translations were formative to the structures of feeling shared among Anishinaabe people. She translated the sermons of several U.S. ministers, beginning in 1827 with Congregationalist minister Alvin Coe and turning in 1828 to translate for Baptist Abel Bingham.[83] Johnston seems to have approached translation not only as a task of replicating or copying white ministers' words but also as a starting point for her own words to and relationships with Anishinaabe audiences. She received white ministers' sermons not as finished texts but as opportunities for sharing that remained beyond those ministers' comprehension. Ministers' journals attest to these creative acts: in his first journal entry to mention Johnston, Bingham wrote that she

composed hymns, which his congregation sang at the meeting he nomi-
nally led. He noted further that after translating the sermon, "Her mind
became so engaged that she continued, or provided with an address of
her own."[84] Johnston transformed the sermon's meaning and expanded
on its content to create her own text, one that was not in English and that
therefore remained illegible to Bingham. It was quickly evident that Bingham's converts preferred Johnston's "addresses," for when she returned to
translating after an illness, Bingham found to his "astonishment we had
about a housefull—those back in the woods having learnt that Miss J had
so far recovered her health as to be able to interpret."[85] The house full of
people to hear "Miss J" hints at Anishinaabe networks of communication
along which news of Johnston's recovered health traveled, attesting to the
ways that her addresses immersed Johnston in Anishinaabe social relations
extending "back into the woods."

The work of translating and addressing Anishinaabe people extended to
providing physical and spiritual care to those in need, and these exchanges,
like singing, generated shared feelings. Like Occom's recipes, which supported acts of healing that included conversations about feelings and in
turn supported Indigenous communities, so Johnston's books fostered relations of care that evaded colonial missionaries' oversight. Anishinaabe
men and women often came to the Johnstons seeking care, and Johnston
(and sometimes Johnston Schoolcraft) acted as their primary interlocutor
and caretaker, probably because she, unlike white ministers, could speak
directly with them. In early 1829, Bingham reported that a Métis man
named Thomas Shaw, in mourning from the recent deaths of two of his
children and in conflict with his wife, tragedies that had "led him to drink,
for the purpose of drowning his troubles . . . came in with Miss Johnston
our Interpreter [to?] relate to me the state of his mind."[86] As an ordained
minister, Bingham was authorized to provide spiritual guidance, but it
was to Johnston that Shaw came first, and she relayed the man's sorrow
to Bingham. Even when people approached Bingham directly, Johnston
facilitated conversations about their feelings, as in the case when several
Anishinaabe women brought Madam Cadotte (a trader's wife), who had
fallen ill, to Bingham's house. After the day's services were complete, "Miss
Johnston came in to see the sick woman—By her we were enabled to con-
verse with her—I [asked] About her love to Christ, she said it was very

strong, even greater than to her children—she express [*sic*] to her, the grateful feelings she cherished to us for the instructions we had given her, and our kind treatment to her."[87] Sometimes, people asked explicitly for Johnston, as when Jeremiah Porter noted that she "received a letter yesterday from Sophia Paro, a girl of Catholic parents, educated at Mr Ferry's, living in the opposite settlement. She expressed deep agony for sin. . . . Had no Christian friend to counsel her, not knowing Ms C's state, she begged Charlotte to go over & help her."[88] Johnston's singing and speaking "in Indian" allowed her to perform acts of material care that resulted in "grateful feelings." In this way, the albums exemplify and expand Creek literary scholar Craig Womack's comment that Native writing attempts to "*invoke* as much as *evoke*": in the case of Johnston's compilations, twining poetry and hymns was an act of invoking feelings that include and go beyond the compiled texts.[89]

After marrying William McMurray in 1833, these shared feelings continued to intersect with Anishinaabe political claims to belonging in their homelands. In 1834, McMurray and Johnston moved across the St. Mary's River, from lands claimed by the U.S. to those claimed by British Canada, into a house built by the trader Charles Oakes Ermatinger. Their move responded to Shingwaukonse's desire to seek recognition of his community's lands from British Canada rather than the U.S.[90] Shingwaukonse sought the community's move across the river because, as Indian subagent François Audrain wrote in 1833, the "whites built houses on the point caught their fish & destroyed the timber on Sugar Island."[91] He "sought out and followed McMurray," a relationship that, as Indigenous Studies scholar Karl S. Hele points out, entailed attending McMurray's sermons as well as enlisting him as an advocate for the community to British Canadian officials.[92] As Chute explains, Shingwaukonse used the relationship with McMurray to establish connections with what he perceived to be the "spiritual and political sources of white men's strength," in order to protect Anishinaabe lands and resources.[93]

The relationship among Shingwaukonse, the Sauteur community, and the McMurrays was built and sustained in part through acts of singing and hospitality. Johnston taught Anishinaabe women and children at her husband's mission to sing "pleasingly," and one observer wrote that "she says all the Indians are passionately fond of music, and that it is a very effective means of interesting and fixing their attention."[94] It is possible that the Ojibwa Book served as a guide for such singing and as a repository for hymns that Johnston learned or composed. She also welcomed other Anishinaabe women into her home. Anna Brownell Jameson complained that during the summer fishing season, the McMurrays' "rooms are crowded with [Anishinaabe people]; wherever there is an open door they come in" and that during less busy seasons, "the women especially, are always lounging in and out, coming to Mrs. MacMurray [*sic*] about every little trifle, and very frequently about nothing at all."[95] Jameson's disparaging complaint nonetheless provides a glimpse of the ways that Johnston's hospitality enabled her to know the feelings of her fellow Anishinaabe people and to receive their affection. Indeed, when the McMurrays left Bow-e-ting, after William failed to obtain Canadian permission for the community to stay on their homelands, Shingwaukonse's son, Augustine Shingwauk, wrote of William that he '"took Ogenebugokwa [Charlotte], one of our nation, for his wife; and we loved him still more, for we felt that he was now indeed become one of us.'"[96] If acts of singing arrested and directed Anishinaabe people's attention, Johnston acted in those exchanges in her capacity as one of "our nation." The networks of care in which Johnston participated emerged from and strengthened Anishinaabe political structures. These feelings and their material forms in the Ojibwa Book remain elusive in the textual record in part because ministers did not understand Anishinaabemowin and could not know what Johnston said to an audience or what she told other Anishinaabe women, and because exchanging care looked to British tourists like Jameson like lounging rather than sharing.

Johnston's and other Anishinaabe people's transcription, singing, and circulation of hymns attests to a "Native structure of feeling" that preexisted and remains apart from Canadian and U.S. boundaries, territorial, temporal, and ethnographic. Johnston circulated, expressed, and shared feelings that were not pinned to the page like a specimen but evoked and expressed in sharing and responding to songs. In fact, Johnston's own affections exist beyond the pages of the albums, located in a set of affective networks. Johnston's acts of compilation through twining and sharing to "act as one of our nation" indicates how those feelings participated in and supported Anishinaabe acts to remain on their territories. These feelings enact a commitment to making relations that continue into a future John-ston and other Anishinaabe people insistently imagined and enacted.

Conclusion

Johnston's albums continue to elicit additional versions of the songs re-corded on their pages, facilitating ongoing acts of compilation, translation, and relation as scholars study and engage with them today. The website ojibwe.net, facilitated by Anishinaabe literary scholar and poet Margaret Noodin, manifests one of these uses in a retranslation of the Ojibwa Book's first entry, Johnston's own translation of the Lord's Prayer into Anishinaa-bemowin (figure 3.5). A team of scholars, including Noodin, Kayla Gon-yon (then a student at the University of Michigan) and two instructors of Ojibwe-language classes at the University of Michigan, Howard Kimewon and Alphonse Pitawanakwat, translated the prayer into English and into contemporary orthographies. They explain that Johnston did not simply replicate the Lord's Prayer, instead taking the original as an invitation for creative revision. She titled the entry "Ah-nah-me-ah-win" (namewin, or prayer) in handwritten letters stylized to replicate block print. A note in Johnston's hand at the top of the page glosses the prayer as "The Lord's Prayer in Ojibway," and "Ah-nah-me-ah-win" does share some elements with the Lord's Prayer. But as the new translation on ojibwe.net makes clear, "Ah-nah-me-ah-win" offers an Anishinaabemowin version of the Christian prayer. Rather than the Protestant opening, "Our Father, who art in heaven, / Hallowed be thy name," Johnston's prayer begins:

> Ge-zha-mon-e-do! Wa-wo-se-me-go-yun, keen kah o-zhe-to-yun Ak-ke,
> Ge-zhig-ge-ge-zis, Tib-bik-ge-zis, Ah-nung-wug
> giya kok-kin-nuh ba-mah-de-ze-jig,
> keen gah-o-zhe-to-yun No-din-noan giya Je-an ne-me-ke-kahg.

The team of translators renders these lines in a contemporary Anishinaa-bemowin orthography and translates them into English:

> Creator! You made light for us you made Earth
> The daily sun, the nightly sun, the stars

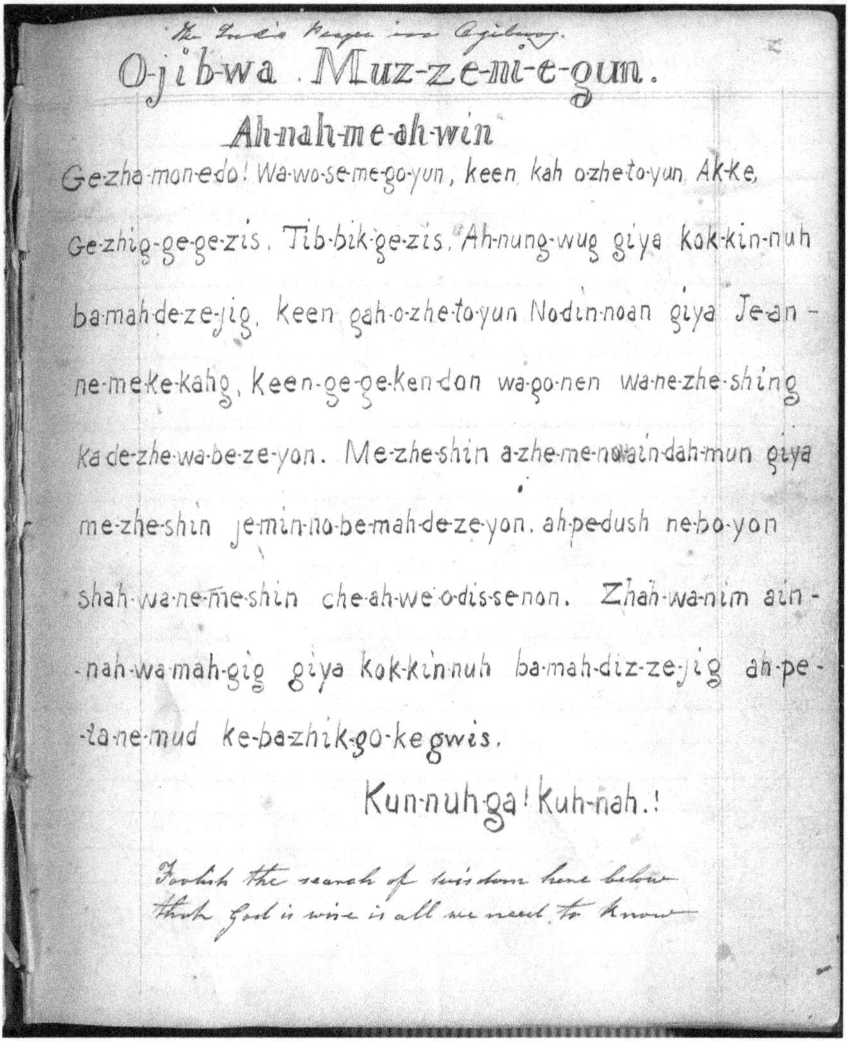

The Lord's Prayer in Ojibway.

Ojibwa Muz-ze-ni-e-gun.

Ah-nah-me-ah-win

Gezha-mon-edo! Wa-wo-se-me-go-yun, keen kah ozhe-to-yun Ak-ke,
Ge-zhig-ge-ge-zis. Tib-bik-ge-zis. Ah-nung-wug giya kok-kin-nuh
ba-mah-de-ze-jig, keen gah-o-zhe-to-yun Nodin-noan giya Je-an-
ne-me-ke-kahg, Keen-ge-ge-ken-don wa-go-nen wa-ne-zhe-shing
ka-de-zhe-wa-be-ze-yon. Me-zhe-shin a-zhe-me-nowain-dah-mun giya
me-zhe-shin je-min-no-be-mah-de-ze-yon. ah-pe-dush ne-bo-yon
shah-wa-ne-me-shin che-ah-we o-dis-se-non. Zhah-wa-nim ain-
-nah-wa-mah-gig giya kok-kin-nuh ba-mah-diz-ze-jig ah-pe-
-ta-ne-mud ke-ba-zhik-go-ke-gwis.

Kun-nuh-ga! Kuh-nah.!

Foolish the search of wisdom here below
that God is wise is all we need to know

FIGURE 3.5. Charlotte Johnston's translation of the Lord's Prayer into Anishinaabemowin. Charlotte Johnston's Ojibwa Book. Courtesy of the Judge Joseph H. Steere Room, Bayliss Public Library, Sault Ste. Marie, Michigan.

and all the ones living,
you made it the wind and thunderers.

And rather than going on to recognize human sinfulness and acknowledge divine "will," "Ah-nah-me-ah-win" emphasizes human goodness—"keen-ge-ge-ken-don wa-go-nen wa-ne-zhe shing ka-de-zhe-wa-be-ze-yon (you know it what will be beautiful in what we do)"—and requests help for "je-min-no-be-mah-de-ze-yon ([how] to live my life well)." Ending with a request for forgiveness for those who trespass and with an acknowledgment of "ah-pe-ta-ne-mud ke-ba-zhik-go-kegwis (how you respect that person [in the name of] your only son)," "Ah-nah-me-ah-win" emphasizes relationships among the speaker and the Creator, celestial and earthly realms, and with other people. A prayer for living a good life and for respecting the Creator, "Ah-nah-me-ah-win" lacks the sense of original sin and the danger of falling prey to "the evil one" present in the English-language prayer.[97]

The contemporary retranslation of Johnston's prayer on ojibwe.net recirculates the prayer in the orthography currently used for Anishinaabemowin, a translation that makes it legible to contemporary speakers. At the same time, the recent translation illuminates some of Johnston's decisions not simply to translate but to expand on original texts. She refused to orient the prayer with Christian categories of sin, deity, and human worth and dwelled instead in Anishinaabe understandings of powerful other-than-human beings and human relations. Finally, a digital recording gives the prayer voice, circulating it as Johnston might have sung or spoken it with other Anishinaabe people from Mississauga and Bow-e-ting, or as she translated part of a white minister's sermon. As the entries from the Ojibwa Book circulate along spoken and digital circuits, they continue to inspire acts of singing, sharing, and creating and the feelings those acts elicit.

Interlude

Jane Johnston Schoolcraft's Unfinished Scraps

Perhaps reflecting on her sister's albums, or on the many albums the Johnston siblings compiled, Jane Johnston Schoolcraft described album making in
an undated poem, held today within the Henry Rowe Schoolcraft Papers at the
Library of Congress. Written in Johnston Schoolcraft's elegant handwriting,
the five-line poem is metered in iambic tetrameter (lines of eight syllables, following an unstressed-stressed rhythm). Each line of the poem "Acrostic" offers
a description of an album, while also spelling "album" with the first letters of
each line.

> A thing of glitter, gleam, and gold,
> Loose thoughts, loose verse, unmeaning, old,
> Big words that sound a thousand fold;
> Unfinished scraps, conceit and cant,
> Mad stanzas, and a world of rant.[1]

At the level of the line, the acrostic suggests that albums are unfinished objects
that attract attention with their glittering, gleaming appearances but contain no
real content of importance. Formally, however, the poem enacts a very different

argument, by evoking and enacting the pleasure derived from compiling and reading albums. As the acrostic lists the elements placed within an album—loose thoughts, loose verse, scraps, stanzas—and arranges them within the letters A-L-B-U-M, the poem's assemblage of nouns and adjectives mirrors the ways albums compile diverse scraps and give them new meanings through their shared positions on the album's pages. Placing linguistic "scraps" within the poem's lines, like the act of transcribing poems or stories within an album, creates an object that might appear disjointed and thus symbolic of a "world of rant" but also brings those "loose thoughts" together in new combinations. A gold and purple flower sketched at the top of the page replicates the ways that albums gather both illustrations and poetry and highlights how albums are visual objects whose meanings are created through design as much as through the content of assembled poems. Like Indigenous compilations, this poem has a range of meanings that are only fully expressed when its linguistic content is read in relation to its form and materiality.

"Acrostic" resides today in one of the roughly one hundred boxes comprising the Henry Rowe Schoolcraft Papers, held at the Library of Congress. Its location in Washington, D.C., far from Johnston Schoolcraft's home and in a city to which she never traveled in her life, is in part a product of Henry's project to place Anishinaabe knowledge, stories, and words on paper to authenticate his own expertise. Henry filled many manuscript pages with his lists of Anishinaabemowin words, his own poetry, the Johnston siblings' translations of Anishinaabe stories, and his commentary on those translations. It was colonial ethnographers like himself, Henry held, who could reveal the true meaning and nature of Native literature by gathering, arranging, and editing stories, and he aimed to do just that with Johnston Schoolcraft's poetry and the Anishinaabe stories she and her family members shared with him. From publications such as *Algic Researches* (1839), in which Henry transcribed and commented on such stories, to his collections of Johnston Schoolcraft's manuscript poems, Henry gathered Anishinaabe literatures to try to determine their meaning.

But it is also the case that Johnston Schoolcraft decided to share stories and poetry with Henry, just as Charlotte Johnston shared versions of the "Ojibwe Maid" song with Superintendent of Indian Affairs Thomas McKenney. With these acts, the Johnstons do not seem to have imagined colonists' papers or publications as the final resting place for Anishinaabe songs or their own poetry, but one of several spaces into which their songs circulated, including spaces that remain separate from colonial archives. "Acrostic" and other poems by Johnston Schoolcraft thus require accounting for both the ways that Henry's archives have shaped interpretations of Johnston Schoolcraft's texts and the fact that her poem offers a reading of that archive. Rather than asking only how Henry's papers determine access to and interpretations of Johnston Schoolcraft's poems, we can ask as well how Henry's writings are shaped by their proximity to poems like "Acrostic."

As Johnston Schoolcraft watched and assisted her husband as he gathered materials for his studies, she may have viewed his albums as so many collections of "big words." The proximity of poems like "Acrostic" to papers describing Henry's theories of "Indian minds" and pasts raises questions about what exactly constitutes those theories, casting a bemused yet clear-eyed glance across the collection. Perhaps, just as William Apess compiled materials from colonial archives in the appendix to *Son of the Forest* to find the truths that gleamed through, so Johnston Schoolcraft saw albums as "thing[s] of glitter, gleam, and gold" that also contained some elements reflecting her knowledge and experiences. And the emphasis in "Acrostic" on forms characterized by "rant" and "conceit" anticipates how Johnston Schoolcraft's poetry and Anishinaabe stories were appropriated as inspiration by colonial poets. The Turtle Mountain Ojibwe poet Heid E. Erdrich describes this process as one in which Johnston Schoolcraft's poetry was "poured into a form from Europe with a misnamed hero [Henry Wadsworth Longfellow's 1855 *Hiawatha*]—a Native-inspired poem eventually memorialized by millions as *the* American poem. So very close to Native poetry, but no."[2] Just as Charlotte Johnston's albums gathered miscellaneous materials together and created new relations among them within the space of the blank book, so, if we see the archive as another space of relation, Johnston Schoolcraft's poems reflect on and are refracted by Henry's writings, with which they share archival space. Henry's propensity to "pour" some of those materials into European forms indicates the ways that this spatial relation could be used for appropriation and misinterpretation, even as we should not lose sight of the counter reading that Johnston Schoolcraft's poem makes possible.

After the mid-nineteenth century, Indigenous compilers began to use printed compilations to create critical reflections on archives, like Johnston Schoolcraft's "Acrostic," and simultaneously to send compilations on capacious circuits through their own nations. Within colonial archives, which government officials were then centralizing and bureaucratizing, Indigenous compilations disrupted the historical and geographic boundaries that colonial bureaucrats sought to place around Indigenous nations, forcing colonists to grapple with more complete and complex historical, linguistic, and pedagogical contexts. At the same time, within Indigenous communities, these printed compilations evoked uses that evaded and rejected the "forms" into which colonists were attempting to "pour" Indigenous peoples, literatures, and languages, instead generating collective uses that emphasized and sustained Indigenous communities' own understandings of themselves. The afterlives for these printed Indigenous compilations multiplied as well, as Indigenous people annotated, cared for, and bought and sold compilations in ways that carry forward into the present.

CHAPTER FOUR

LIST

Abenaki Histories and Linguistic Exchange

———————◆———————

Lists of Indigenous-language words are the compilation form that has garnered the most attention, from North American colonists in the seventeenth, eighteenth, and nineteenth centuries and from historians and literary scholars writing today. Colonists eagerly copied and compared word lists in printed books, in manuscript notebooks, on folio sheets printed with words in English and parallel columns of Indigenous-language words, on printed taxonomies designed especially for collecting words, and on scraps of paper. In colonists' hands, word lists could be an archival technology and a mechanism of dispossession, as we saw in the efforts of Albert Gallatin and James Barbour to use word lists to fix Indigenous nations in one place (see chapter 2). As Indian agents, treaty officials, soldiers, and travelers sought to obtain and translate words in Indigenous languages, their lists filled archives, from private collections like Gallatin's to government repositories.

In the twentieth and twenty-first centuries, scholars have read these word lists as texts significant to histories of science, race, religion, and literature. As I noted in the introduction, literary scholars and historians have examined word lists as historical documents that offer windows into "encounters with strangeness" and as documents with which colonists constructed theories of racial difference or found their cosmologies disrupted and challenged by the difficulties of translation. Scholars have acknowledged that Native people shaped representations of their languages in word lists and observed that some Native people assisted colonists as informants and translators. Yet in these readings, the word lists held in colonial archives are contained by and absorbed into U.S. and European conceptions of belief, knowledge, and difference.[1]

Vocabulary lists are certainly shaped by the institutional spaces in which they reside, and colonists from Thomas Jefferson to Henry Rowe Schoolcraft read lists of Indigenous-language words as evidence for their theories of Indigenous peoples' origins and histories. But, as the preceding interlude on Jane Johnston Schoolcraft's acrostic poem argues, colonial archives do not fully determine the meanings and uses for Indigenous compilations and other writings, for Indigenous compilations also offer critical perspectives on colonial archives, even while they serve purposes specific to Indigenous communities. In this chapter I follow the archival travels and uses of a book of Abenaki vocabulary lists, *New Familiar Abenakis and English Dialogues,* compiled by the Abenaki leader Joseph Laurent and published in 1884 in Quebec. The title page explained the book's status as "new" by noting that the vocabulary lists were the "first ever published on the grammatical system."[2] While French Jesuit priests created manuscript dictionaries of Abenaki in the seventeenth century, these materials lacked the *Dialogues*' "grammatical explanations" (title page). Laurent accomplished what European linguists and collectors had been unable to complete: a representation of the Abenaki language that made its grammatical and syntactical logics visible.

The book's cover also signals its "newness" by associating the *Dialogues* with attributes of the exotic and unfamiliar. The tan cloth cover is lined with a decorative border featuring Egyptian architectural imagery, including pyramids, sphinxes, and obelisks.[3] These images may have sought to harness public interest in the travels of about sixty Mohawk men from Haudenosaunee communities at Kahnawake, Kanesatake, and Awkwesasne, located near Laurent's community at Odanak, within Quebec. In 1884–85, the Mohawk men navigated the Nile River after they were conscripted to guide a British force tasked with rescuing a military leader taken captive in what is now Sudan. In the summer of 1884, Montreal newspapers carried news of the British government's request for Indigenous navigators to assist on the voyage and reported on the expedition with stories and illustrations.[4] The pyramids and palm trees on the cover of *Dialogues* also align with contemporaneous publishing practices of using typefaces and images to signal exotic difference for Native-authored books. E. Pauline Johnson's books published by William Briggs, including *The Moccasin Maker* (1913) and *The Shagganappi* (1913), featured cover lettering and images allusive of western stereotypes and conceptions of the foreign, often coded through Orientalizing images. Similarly, the cover of *Dialogues* presents the book as an exotic object by aligning it with western conceptions of "the East." Tiny versions of this imagery reappear on its spine, along with the book's title and date of publication, thus suggesting that the publisher sought to present the book as a collectible that would appeal to the eye on a library shelf and a table alike, an object whose value lay in both its material design and its contents.

Laurent put copies of *Dialogues* into circulation in ways that presented the book not as an exotic object but as a distinctive book whose lists disrupted readings of Indigenous books and words as collectibles that belonged in colonial archives. Shortly after the book's publication, Laurent sent a copy to Washington, D.C., directing it to James Pilling, a clerk at the Bureau of American Ethnology, which was founded in 1879 to centralize ethnographic collecting in government institutions devoted entirely to research (rather than pairing research and policy, as at the Interior Department, which relied on Indian agents like Henry Rowe Schoolcraft).[5] An envelope pasted onto the book's inside cover bears the traces of its travels to the Bureau (figure 4.1). The envelope, written in Laurent's hand, is addressed to the "Chief Clerk of the Smithsonian Institution Bureau of Ethnology" and indicates that the gift is from "Jos. Laurent."[6] Someone, probably Pilling, has written "Indian books" and "Samples" above the address, a phrase that may indicate how the book was categorized upon its arrival at the Bureau.[7]

In addition to managing bureaucratic tasks as the institution's clerk, Pilling created a voluminous archive of books in Indigenous languages by embarking on an immense project to collect and document vocabularies of Indigenous languages. This was a project of salvage bibliography, in

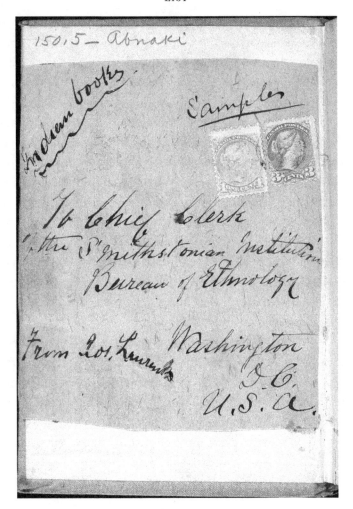

FIGURE 4.1. Envelope addressed to James Pilling, chief
clerk at the Bureau of American Ethnology, and pasted
inside the cover of the *Dialogues*. Joseph Laurent, *New
Familiar Abenakis and English Dialogues: The First Ever Published
on the Grammatical System* (1884). Ayer PM551 .L3 1884,
Newberry Library, Chicago.

which Pilling attempted to make an archive of Native books before supposedly authentic—which the Bureau defined as unchanged by western influence—Indigenous peoples vanished.[8] He processed word lists attained
from the Bureau's collectors, examined library and privately-held editions
of vocabulary books, and acquired vocabulary lists for the Bureau. One re-

sult of Pilling's project was a bibliography of North American Indigenous languages, which grew to such an unwieldy size (over a thousand pages) that it was eventually published piecemeal, as smaller, language family-specific bulletins.

Pilling's bibliographic project continued efforts across the nineteenth century to study, compare, and republish word lists. For colonists, the goal of such collecting and republishing was not speaking or learning languages but preservation. For example, an Abenaki language dictionary created by the Jesuit priest Sébastian Rasles was published in 1833 in the *Memoirs of the American Academy of Arts and Sciences,* where its editor presented the word list not as a resource for language learning but as a historical document. Rasles had studied the Abenaki language in the 1690s, while living with the Abenaki community at Norridgewock. Frustrated by his inability to learn Abenaki, Rasles lamented that "there are no books to teach these languages, and even though we had them, they would be quite useless; practice is the only master that is able to teach us."[9] Despite his sense that books were "useless" for learning the Abenaki language, Rasles made the manuscript dictionary, and it was this word list that the Academy printed in 1833. In the *Memoirs,* U.S. philologist John Pickering described the dictionary as "one of the most important memorials in the history of North American Languages"; its publication did not, Pickering insisted, include a "consideration of the use which may be made of this collection of philological materials."[10]

When Laurent created the *Dialogues* and sent a copy to Pilling, he put Abenaki word lists and dialogues into print and into circulation at a moment when colonists were gathering word lists in centralized ethnographic archives, like the Bureau, and printing word lists as historical documents or memorials. The travels of Laurent's book into institutional and private libraries gesture to his awareness of colonists' desires for "Indian books" and to the ways he made use of those desires to circulate copies of the *Dialogues* widely.[11] But Laurent's compilation did not, contrary to Pilling's work of salvage bibliography and Pickering's "memorial," cast word lists as historical documents or windows into the past. Laurent wrote in the preface that his goal was to "preserve the *uncultivated* Abenakis language from the gradual alterations which are continually occurring from want, of course, of some proper work showing the grammatical principles upon which it is dependent."[12] In contrast to the Bureau's view of preservation as salvage, Laurent did not position his work as an act of linguistic rescue or archival stabilization. It was the absence of an Abenaki grammar, Laurent argued—a grammar the *Dialogues* provides—that was responsible for linguistic alterations. And unlike Pickering's argument that Abenaki word lists offered "memorials" to be read as evidence of the past but not used, the *Dialogues* invites the *use* of the word lists to speak and circulate Abenaki words.

Like John Ridge's decision to send his letter to Albert Gallatin and Charlotte Johnston's decision to exchange poems with Thomas McKenney, Laurent made strategic decisions to place copies of the *Dialogues* within colonial archives and into ethnographers' hands. Yet unlike Indigenous compilations that circulated within their makers' own personal networks, such as Johnston's manuscript albums, print allowed Laurent to circulate multiple copies of the word lists, to send copies of the *Dialogues* into archives, and to *use* the book within Abenaki communities. I read the *Dialogues* and the books' travels as helping to constitute a Wabanaki network of compilation making and use, a network that encompasses colonial archives, supports the proliferation of Indigenous compilations in multiple copies and texts, and consequently rewrites colonial maps of Indigenous languages and territories. As the Abenaki scholar Lisa Brooks has observed in her analysis of Laurent's lists of place names, the word lists encode ways of "seeing and being in the land that is the Wabanaki 'world.'"[13] Building on this reading, I examine how Laurent embedded Abenaki histories in the word lists, such that reading and speaking the lists aloud was both a linguistic exercise and one that participated in and instigated acts of history telling. By locating the pathways along which several copies of the *Dialogues* traveled, I examine how Abenaki people used Indigenous compilations as an intellectual tool for surviving in a Wabanaki world shaped, but not ended, by colonialism.

Abenaki Linguistic Compilations

When Laurent published *New Familiar Abenakis and English Dialogues* in 1884, he built on a long history of linguistic translation, collaboration, and compilation across Wabanaki territories. In these cases, Abenaki translators answered colonists' interest in their language not simply by translating but also by transforming European words and concepts for use within Wabanaki worlds. As a result, the word lists they created are Indigenous compilations containing not just linguistic knowledge but cosmological, historical, and environmental knowledge as well. In the seventeenth century, Abenaki people advised Jesuit priests who sought to learn their language, directing the priests' attempts to learn to speak as well as their translations of theological texts. In letters reflecting on his struggle to learn Abenaki, Sébastian Rasles emphasized his reliance on Abenaki men at Norridgewock who patiently endured his questions and mispronunciations. Despite his best efforts (and his experience learning several Indigenous languages), Rasles wrote that: "it is not sufficient to study its terms and their signification, and to acquire a supply of words and phrases,—it is further necessary to know the turn and arrangement that the [Indigenous people] give them, which can hardly ever be caught except by familiar and frequent intercourse with these tribes."[14] Frustrated with his slow progress, he turned to spending as much time "in their cabins, hearing them talk" as he could, a task to which he had to devote his "utmost attention in order to connect what they said and to conjecture its meaning; sometimes I caught it exactly, but more often I was deceived,—because, not being accustomed to the trick of their guttural sounds, I repeated only half the word, and thereby gave them cause for laughter."[15]

After five months of such work, Rasles believed he had a working vocabulary, but he discovered that his teachers still found his knowledge insufficient. He did not yet:

> express myself to their satisfaction. I had still much progress to make before catching the form of expression and the spirit of the language, which are entirely different from the spirit and form of our European languages. In order to shorten the time, and thus enable me sooner to perform my duties, I selected a few [people] who had most intelligence, and who used the best language. I repeated to them in a clumsy manner some passages from the catechism, and they gave them to me again, with all the nicety of their language; I immediately wrote these down; and, by this means, in a reasonably short time I had made a dictionary, and also a Catechism which contained the precepts and Mysteries of Religion.[16]

If Rasles reported, with some relief, that he had at last completed a dictionary and catechism he and other priests could use to communicate with and convert Abenaki people, his comments also made clear that Abenaki people directed his translations. They determined when his knowledge was sufficient, thwarting his desire for mastery with their laughter at his failures to account for certain sounds in Abenaki. And they retranslated Rasles's halting attempts to translate passages from the catechism, rendering Catholic doctrine "with all the nicety of their language." This exchange made Rasles less a translator than a scribe for Abenaki peoples' linguistic and theological translation.

Over two hundred years later, Joseph Laurent's youngest son Stephen translated Rasles's catechism into English, finding a number of substitutions for Catholic ideas and French words that illuminate some details of the decisions these Abenaki translators made as they "gave" Rasles's passages to him "again." In notes for a speech, Stephen observed that the catechism substitutes the word "wigwam" for "manger," and translates "Palm Sunday" as the "day we spread Balsam boughs." He also observed that Rasles's dictionary spends the "greatest space (actually two and a half pages, double columned)" on words for "corn as the chief food." Stephen wrote, "From the dictionary we glean the process of clearing the land by fire or otherwise, the manner of planting and cultivating it, the process of its drying, grinding, and hulling." Rasles recorded three months of the year with names referring to corn: "April is 'when one sows corn'; May is 'when one covers the corn'; June, 'when one hills up the corn.'" This orientation around corn appears as well in the Abenaki version of the Lord's Prayer, where "daily bread" is translated as "daily corn cakes." Stephen's commentary underscores how Rasles's Abenaki collaborators rendered Catholic prayers and concepts in their own terms, maintaining corn's centrality as a life-sustaining plant and locating religious stories in wigwams rather than in mangers. The two and a half double-columned pages on corn in particular reflect the relations among plants, everyday activities, and sustenance that shaped Abenaki life: as Stephen wrote, "The amount of space devoted to expressions relating to certain phases of life is a measure of their importance."[17] Stephen observed that Rasles's dictionary and translations are oriented by Abenaki priorities and seasonal understandings of time, Rasles's intentions to introduce Catholic theology notwithstanding.

The work of the Norridgewock Abenaki translators continued in the north, at Laurent's community of Odanak, on the St. Francis River within the province of Quebec. Near the end of the seventeenth century, Abenaki people living in communities within their southern homelands, including at Norridgewock, traveled north to Odanak to escape expanding colonial settlements and colonial attacks, including throughout the Anglo-Abenaki Wars (1675–1760).[18] These movements north were sometimes temporary, as Abenaki people returned to their southern territories when violence subsided. In the 1690s, French priests built a mission at Odanak, offering protection from British forces to Abenaki people who attached themselves to the mission. Throughout these times of violence, displacement, and return, Abenaki people continued practices of observing, translating, and selectively using European languages and religious practices alongside Abenaki ones. Around 1715, the priest Joseph Aubery created an Abenaki-French dictionary while living at Odanak. A copy of the dictionary survived Rogers' Raid—a brutal 1759 British attack targeting Odanak, in which British soldiers killed Abenaki people and took several captives, while also forcing its inhabitants into temporary hiding; the dictionary is currently in the collections of the Musée des Abénakis at Odanak.[19] Aubery's and Rasles's dictionaries attest to the decisions Abenaki people made to circulate their linguistic knowledge in multiple media and in translation, in conversations and in French-language printed and manuscript texts. Despite Aubery's and Rasles's desires to convert Abenaki ways of life to resemble Catholic, European ones, Abenaki people directed linguistic translations and kept their own copies of the dictionaries to which they had contributed, even amidst colonial violence.[20]

Throughout the nineteenth century, Abenaki leaders from Odanak, including Laurent, Henry Masta, and Pierre Paul Wzokhilain, published their own translations.[21] In the 1830s and 1840s, Pierre Paul Wzokhilain wrote several instructional books in Abenaki, including a spelling book, translations of books of the Bible, and a hymnal.[22] Wzokhilain was one of several Abenaki young men who attended Dartmouth College in the early nineteenth century; he returned to Odanak in 1829 to teach at a Protestant church and school.[23] Several of Wzokhilain's books were published by Crocker and Brewster, the Boston-based printer for the American Board of Commissioners for Foreign Missions (ABCFM), including texts in Indigenous languages. Wzokhilain's collaboration with the ABCFM allowed him to circulate printed Abenaki language texts for students at Odanak, ensuring that children would learn both English and Abenaki.

As Wzokhilain circulated his translations within missionary publication networks and educational systems, he altered those systems to suit Abenaki linguistic contexts. He revised Crocker and Brewster's labels for their stock woodcuts, which appear without alteration across most of the firm's educational publications, despite the different Indigenous languages the woodcuts gloss. The images usually appeared with English subtitles, probably to aid non-Indigenous missionaries who had not yet learned the languages spoken by their prospective converts. In *Wobanaki kimzowi awighigan* (1830), Wzokhilain added an Abenaki caption above the existing English-language labels, using the word "kdakinna" to describe an image of the globe showing various climatic zones, from the Arctic to the Equator to the Antarctic (figure 4.2). While the English-language caption for this image reads "Circles," "kdakinna," as Lisa Brooks points out, is an inclusive word describing the land (or aki), so that the caption may be translated as ' "our earth,' 'our ground' . . . a land that contains all."[24] As the spelling book taught linguistic skills in English and Abenaki, it also reinforced understandings of the land as a place to which Abenaki people belong and for which they care. The spelling book translates words as well as the concepts they evoke; as Brooks writes, Abenaki-language books "were successful in translating cosmology, demonstrating the continuance of names and stories associated with particular places in communal memory, even for those families who lived in northern villages like Odanak, outside the original home territory."[25] Language, as Wzokhilain's caption demonstrates, is intertwined with "our ground," a space mapped through its capacity to contain all: people, plants like corn, and relationships that give life and sustenance. His translation of "circles" located a stock image—one that usually circulated without relation to specific contexts—within particular Abenaki places and understandings of the speakers' relation to those places embedded in language. Wzokhilain's decision to use "kdakinna" to represent the earth reminded Abenaki readers of the land or ground that "contains" them, situating Odanak within Wabanaki cartographies. In the 1830s and 1840s, Wzokhilain's decision to insist on understandings of the globe as

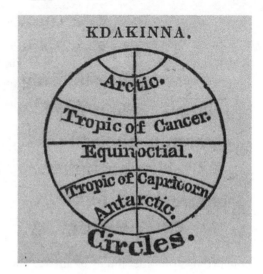

FIGURE 4.2. Pierre Paul Wzokhilain, revision of Crocker and Brewster's stock illustration "Circles." Pierre Paul Wzokhilain, *Wobanaki kimzowi awighigan* (1830). Ayer 3A 635, Newberry Library, Chicago.

"our land" countered nineteenth-century U.S. and Canadian policies of Indian removal and assimilation in ways that foreshadowed Laurent's circulation of the *Dialogues* later in the 1880s, as some U.S. officials were seeking to make language the foundation for drawing geographic and temporal boundaries across Indigenous homelands.

Linguistic Archives: Reading Indigenous Nations in Place

One center for this linguistic and geographic mapping was the very place Laurent sent a copy of the *Dialogues* in the 1880s: the Bureau of American Ethnology. In addition to Pilling's linguistic collecting, Bureau director John Wesley Powell hoped to make language the foundation from which settlers could classify Native people and determine their relations to the United States, relations that, for Powell, had biological, geographic, and political elements. He argued that:

> language alone served as a satisfactory basis for a practical classification of the Indians for use in grouping them on reservations, since clans of remote habitats speaking the same tongue soon find themselves dominated by a common or at least related law and religion constituting a self-evident bond of sympathy and ultimate union. Accordingly it was proposed to classify the American Indians for practical purposes on a linguistic basis, and on this basis they were grouped and from time to time assembled on reservations.[26]

For Powell, linguistic similarities and differences determined social and cultural characteristics, making language a guide to establishing boundaries among Indigenous nations and, ultimately, he hoped, to determining how to "group . . . and assemble [them] on reservations."[27] Just as Albert Gallatin and James Barbour imagined that linguistic collecting would illuminate language families and determine "to whom debatable country" belonged (see chapter 2), so Powell hoped to produce even more minute information with which to place Native people in geo-linguistic categories that would correspond to the plots of land on which the U.S. sought to confine them.[28]

Powell's "practical classification" rested on a set of imagined correspondences among language, cultural hierarchies, and place. Unlike Wzokhilain's use of "kdakinna" to invoke the relations between people and the land that contains them, the correspondences Powell sought were not contained within words and relations to place but were realized on paper. Powell distributed "schedules," or templates, consisting of lists of English-language words in a left-hand column, and in a right-hand column, blanks to be completed with Indigenous-language words (see figure I.5). He instructed officials to follow the schedules "*seriatim*," one after the other, in the order in which Powell arranged them.[29] That order moves from concepts of allegedly lesser to greater complexity, beginning with a person and body parts and then radiating outward to ways of living and food, on to colors and numbers, time and value, before encompassing the world around a person: social organization, government, and religion. Near the end of the schedules is the category "New Words," by which Powell referred to those adopted from European languages. He lamented the introduction of these new words because he believed they made it difficult to isolate and preserve words that reflect "primitive languages," even as the placement of this category at the end of the schedules suggests that imported, non-Indigenous-language words are evidence of an "advanced" level of linguistic and cultural organization.[30] A set of completed schedules would thus theoretically allow an observer to see at a glance the hierarchical social and cultural division in which the people speaking the language supposedly belonged.

Circulating Indigenous-language words within paper forms, from schedules to printed word lists, intensified their materiality, allowing collectors to place words into linguistic, temporal, and geographic categories that grew

increasingly stable, however shaky their foundation in Indigenous conceptions of place and language. The words' thickening materiality facilitated
their categorization by Bureau officials in frameworks that increasingly
relied on prior documents, not on spoken words. Powell drew on this archive in order to plot words onto place in his 1891 essay and accompanying map, "Indian Linguistic Families of America North of Mexico." In
the map, Powell represented Indigenous linguistic "stocks" and assigned
them each a "habitat," which he determined by synthesizing linguistic,
geographic, historical, and political information.[31] The map presents language families as spatialized categories, each of which are demarcated by
different colors and borders, foreshadowing the linguistic maps of North
America anthropologists would create decades later. Powell's language
families are represented as contained within settler geopolitical boundaries, for the color-coded "stocks" are bisected by lines delineating settler
states and territories, and Powell included English-language names for rivers, lakes, and mountain ranges throughout the map.[32] Indigenous linguistic and geographic borders exist in tension with the United States' (and
other settler nation's) presence and anticipated conquest of the continent.
Indeed, the map imagines that the Indigenous nations will be subsumed
within settler boundaries; it reflects cartographically Powell's anticipated
vision of assembling Indigenous peoples on reservations.

Powell's map is not a representation of tribal nations' ancestral homelands or of their shifting political relationships with other Indigenous nations, even if Powell made such claims for the document.[33] Instead, the
map represents where Indigenous peoples speaking different languages
were located when a colonial explorer or settler reported meeting them. It
is a map of past and contemporary relations between Indigenous and settler nations as reflected by the colonial historical record rather than a map
of Indigenous nations' relations to place.[34] As Powell explained in the essay
accompanying the map,

> The map undertakes to show the habitat of the linguistic families only, and
> this is for but a single period in their history, viz., at the time when the tribes
> composing them first became known to the European, or when they first
> appear on recorded history. As the dates when the different tribes became
> known vary, it follows as a matter of course that the periods represented by
> the colors in one portion of the map are not synchronous with those in other
> portions.[35]

The map's conflicting, inconsistent categories of time and place naturalize one another in order to represent linguistic information as timeless and to take settler nations' political boundaries as the basis for current and future relations with Indigenous nations. Imagining Indigenous nations as absorbed into settler geopolitical space laid a foundation for anticipating Indigenous peoples' incorporation into colonial histories, nations, and concepts of land ownership. In this sense, Powell's map visually represents the claims Indian officials like Thomas McKenney and Henry Rowe Schoolcraft had espoused fifty years earlier, that Native people were unable to exist within the future-oriented temporalities of the U.S. (see chapter 3). Powell's map demonstrates that assumptions about Indigenous time are deeply connected to claims to Indigenous land and that those assumptions are generated by reading colonial histories as indicative of Indigenous peoples' supposedly static relations to place.

When Laurent sent a copy of the *Dialogues* to Pilling at the Bureau, then, he circulated the book within an archive dedicated to attaching Indigenous words to colonial geographies made material on paper. The *Dialogues* entered an archive in which word lists were an engine for envisioning Native nations' containment within settler borders. Linguistic maps like Powell's added to the claims already circulating in both the U.S. and Canada that sought to limit the extent of Wabanaki homelands.[36] Yet Laurent followed in the footsteps of previous Abenaki leaders and linguistic compilers, who asserted maps of their relationship to the land and to each other in the face of policies and representations attempting to contain their communities within settler nation states. As a teacher in his community's school at Odanak and as a tribal leader, Laurent built on centuries of Abenaki compilation: linguistic collaboration, education, and publication that translated European ideas, temporalities, and words into Abenaki terms. The *Dialogues* gathered within its word lists stories and intellectual frameworks that refuse the boundaries in which Powell, Pilling, and other settlers sought to contain Indigenous languages and nations.

"Meteors, Ships, Etc.": Abenaki Histories of Colonization

Laurent's *Dialogues* invoke forms of reading that place the word lists in relation to Abenaki histories and that generate actions to circulate those histories. Like the Abenaki translators at Norridgewock who transformed Catholic religious principles so that they reflected the centrality of corn to Abenaki life, so Laurent used the list's capacity to assemble information in order to gather together elements of Abenaki histories and experiences of colonization. Assembling those pieces within word lists ensured that acts of reading and speaking the lists were also acts of language learning and of circulating Abenaki histories.

The *Dialogues* opens with word lists organized by categories for human and nonhuman entities: the vocabulary begins with the heading "Of God's Attributes," which includes translations for "God, The Great Spirit," "Deity," and "The Eternal," before continuing on to word lists for objects related to the heavens and the elements. The lists then extend to "Mankind, Kindred, Etc.," a list of kinship terms, "Parts of the Body," "Of the Table, Meals and Dishes," "Mechanical Arts," and humans' various relationships, habits, and activities. Yet if these categories seem to represent a spiritual and material hierarchy of being that might mirror the Bureau's schedules, Laurent's word lists quickly complicate that mode of organization. The word lists sometimes appear to mix words for different kinds of objects under the same heading. In particular, the category "Meteors, Ships, Etc." begins with the word "Wlôda" or heat, and "Tka" or cold, proceeding to "Pakwsatakisgad" and "Wdagkisgad," words for damp and dry weather (16–17). This list continues with "Pesgawan, Foggy it is," "Kladen, Frost; it is frozen," and "Nanamkiapoda, An earthquake; there is—" and "Padôgi, Thunder" (17). After "Petguelômsen, A whirlwind; there is," the list seems to shift registers, moving to "Ktolagw, A vessel; ship; frigate," and words for the parts of a ship and its crew (17). The *Dialogues* subsequently includes headings for the "Sea," the "Heavens," and the "Elements," headings that would seem to better fit the words for meteors and other celestial phenomena as well as for seafaring that are gathered together in "Meteors, Ships, Etc." Yet the existence of other relevant headings suggests that the words in "Meteors, Ships, Etc." are gathered together under a logic perhaps not immediately apparent to all. Reading this list and the *Dialogues* more broadly requires seeing the lists not as oriented by categories based on object types—as many colonial vocabularies were—but by Abenaki histories. In this case, the "Meteors, Ships, Etc." compilation invokes stories of a meteor-like ball of fire that preceded Europeans' arrival in Wabanaki homelands (figure 4.3).

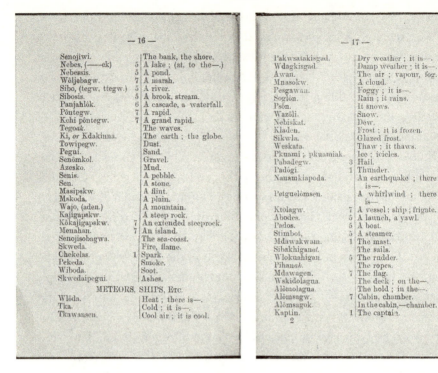

FIGURE 4.3. Laurent's word list for "Meteors, Ships, Etc." Joseph Laurent, *New Familiar Abenakis and English Dialogues: The First Ever Published on the Grammatical System* (1884). PM551 .L3 1884. Kim-Wait / Eisenberg Native American Literature Collection. Archives and Special Collections, Amherst College Library.

Penobscot Abenaki writer Joseph Nicolar placed one version of these histories into print in 1893, in his *Life and Traditions of the Red Man*. Nicolar began *Life and Traditions* by distinguishing his book from texts written by non-Native authors who purported to tell histories of colonization. *Life and Traditions*, he wrote, contains a "full account of all the pure traditions" handed down through many generations, a history that does not rely on any "historical works of the white man."[37] These traditions include stories of the peoples' origins and their meetings with Europeans along with lessons passed down for generations through oral histories. As Penobscot tribal historian James E. Francis explains, ways of telling these "pure traditions" can vary without the traditions themselves being altered.[38] For Nicolar, the separation between "pure traditions" and the "historical works of the white man" is necessary because "none of the studies nor the researches of the white man have ever penetrated—thereby dwelt upon [Penobscot histories]." Instead, Nicolar stated, these stories are "hidden things."[39] He described a "veil over the eyes and minds of the learned of these modern dates," which caused non-Native readers to inquire out of ignorance about Indigenous peoples, their origins, and their histories.[40] Nicolar presented his book as a corrective to these misguided researches and to the "veil" that shrouds and confuses white readers' eyes and minds. He accordingly established a history for Penobscot interactions with colonists by relating an Abenaki timeline for and interpretation of the events that preceded Europeans.

Nicolar's book describes how Penobscot people developed new practices and political alliances to confront the changes brought by Europeans. In *Life and Traditions,* Penobscot people learn about Europeans from their teacher and the "first person,"[41] Klose-kur-beh, who explained that white men "want[ed] the power over all the earth," so the Great Spirit "sent him to chase the sun," with the result that he eventually reached North America.[42] Klose-kur-beh said that the first sign of the white people will be a swan and that they could call for and receive help when they see such portents. Accordingly, the people looked to the east, expecting the "appearance of other people in that direction, which proved to them afterwards that their belief was a true one."[43] In chapter 5, Penobscot people observed strange tracks in the sand and read them as a sign of the white men, after which they began to prepare for the "change [that] must follow his coming."[44] Then, a thick fog covered all of the country so that no one could find fish, and as a result, famine ensued. Before the people could starve, they called for help, and the loon who took the form of an elderly woman appeared. She brought a wind that cleared away the fog, and she warned that the people would be happy until they fell into the ways of the Europeans, who were then floating on the ocean, on their way to North America: '"If the power that is in you has not the force to overcome [the spiritual power in the Europeans], woe unto you.'"[45] The elderly woman transformed herself back into a white loon, called Mata-we-leh in the text. She threw a spear at the swan that was carrying the Europeans across the ocean, in an attempt to turn it away and to capture the men. But she only delayed the colonists, who continued their voyage and eventually landed in America. Before they reached the shore, however, the loon "turned itself into a great ball of fire, and fell swiftly down to the water; and when it struck the water, the earth shook and the roar of it was great."[46] The impact of the ball of fire brought back the fog, but it also left fragments of stone for the people. Following Mata-we-leh's advice, they made these fragments into tools for catching fish, thus avoiding the threat of another famine. The stone fragments also signified contact and conflict between the Penobscots and the Europeans, for the stones, she instructed, were ' "the fragment of the first contention between you and the strange people." '[47]

When the lists in Laurent's *Dialogues* are read alongside Nicolar's history, the heading "Meteors, Ships, Etc." figures less as a prescriptive title or category that defines the content of the lists than as an element connecting the list to Abenaki narratives of colonization. Rather than denoting only material referents, the words in Laurent's *Dialogues* also invoke intellectual frameworks that Abenaki people employed to face a world altered by colonization. "Meteors, Ships, Etc." and the compilation of Abenaki words under that heading invoke Abenaki histories in which meteors precede ships and, eventually, Europeans' arrival. In the story recorded by Nicolar, the appearance of Europeans was preceded by a "snow and ice period"[48] and in Laurent's list, "Wazôli, Snow"; "Kladen, Frost; it is frozen"; "Sik-wla, Glazed frost"; "Weskata, Thaw; it thaws"; and "Pkuami; pkuamiak, Ice; icicles" precede "Ktolagw, a vessel; ship; frigate" (17). Such words as "Pesgawan, foggy" and "Nanamkiapoda, an earthquake" (17) correspond to the "dense fog [that] came over the whole country" and that created a famine and to the earthquake that the ball of fire caused when it struck the water.[49] Similarly, Laurent's representation of "Padôgi, thunder" in the list glosses Abenaki histories of colonization. In his account, Nicolar described the ball of fire as roaring as it struck the ground, making it possible that padôgi in Laurent's text references this noise.[50] The word "padôgi" (also spelled "badôgi") may be translated as "he who thunders," thus invoking not simply the natural phenomenon that follows lightning but a nonhuman being or entity known in northeastern cosmologies as a Thunder Bird or Being.[51] By including nonhuman beings in a list of apparently inanimate objects, "padôgi" also references the spiritual disorder that preceded and followed Europeans' arrival and, possibly, the intervention of beings like Mata-we-leh on the Abenakis' behalf.

Laurent's word lists are compilations of intellectual frameworks and responses to colonialism, pointing, as Nicolar's descriptions of fog and vapor do, to the far-reaching repercussions of Europeans' arrival on Abenaki communities and everyday life. In both texts, the blazing star or meteor is linked to cosmological, social, and environmental shifts: relationships tipped out of balance, usual food sources exhausted or altered, frost and snow, earthquakes, and whirlwinds. In Nicolar's text, Abenaki people prepared for these new challenges by consulting their "spiritual men," who heard "voices of men on the sea in the direction where the sun rises."[52] In an episode related earlier in *Life and Traditions*, these men have a vision in which they can see to the east and hear sounds "like those made by man."[53] But the men cannot determine who is making the sounds, for "upon looking in the direction where the sun rises there was a thick vapor standing in the middle of the ocean beyond which they could see nothing."[54] This vapor is similar to the "very dense fog [that] came over the whole country and remained seven moons" before the Europeans are seen.[55] Both fog and vapor prevented Abenaki people from fully "seeing" Europeans, that is, from literally observing them and from understanding their desires and the full implications of their presence. The fog seems to describe a natural phenomenon and a state in which interpretations are difficult, in which Abenaki people attempted to determine how to respond to the Europeans, whom they knew could be problematic given their desire for power over the whole earth.[56] The fog casts Europeans' intentions as perplexing—obscured, murky, and unclear. At the same time, the fog hindered Abenaki people from finding food, so that Europeans' actions are associated with challenges to finding sustenance and, by extension, to kinship networks linking people and the nonhuman world.

Rather than presage the end of Abenaki ways of life or communities, which the Bureau's salvage bibliography and linguistic mapping posited as outcomes of Europeans' arrival, the blazing star generated strategies of survival for Abenaki people to navigate a strange world, shaped by colonialism.[57] In *Life and Traditions*, the ball of fire changed how the people use natural resources: they developed new ways to find and prepare food thanks to the stone fragments they used to catch fish. These resources come from within the community rather than from European technologies or religious practices, even as the tools prepared the Penobscots for "contention" with people from across the sea.[58] This contention has multiple repercussions, for the Penobscots' interactions with nonhuman beings like the loon woman and fish, on whom the people relied for their survival and health, position questions of well-being and nourishment as intimately affected by Europeans.[59] For example, the famine in Nicolar's history points to the ways that colonization upset Abenaki peoples' use of resources, an event with multiple aftershocks. These stories make no division between the natural and supernatural origins and repercussions of such events, for the comets that preceded Europeans' arrival in *Life and Traditions* were sent by or linked to such other-than-human entities as loons. Famine resulted from imbalances between spiritual or human entities, with causes and consequences in the natural and supernatural worlds. Physical hardship certainly followed the ball of fire, but spiritual, social, and political changes came as well, as indicated by the appearance of new means of sustenance, new spiritual relations, and new alliances among peoples.

The words in Laurent's lists act as pieces that, when arranged together, constitute "useful implements," similar to the fragments of stone that the ball of fire created when it struck the water and that symbolized the "fragment of the first contention between you and the strange people."[60] By assembling the words in the lists, Laurent presented them as linguistic and cultural tools for Abenaki people, "useful implements" for survival. The list elicited a participatory relationship with readers, a relationship that relies on actions of reading, speaking, and repeating individual words. By speaking both Abenaki and English in studying the *Dialogues,* people would retell and contemplate the environmental, biological, social, and spiritual crises that colonization continues to precipitate. As the word lists invite readers to participate in the recounting of Abenaki histories, they make the act of removing the fog covering Europeans' actions and intentions a collective one that simultaneously strengthens relations among Abenaki people as they speak to one another. These practices of actively telling histories align with Lisa Brooks's discussion of the "work of history, which in the Abenaki language is called '*ôjmowôgan,*' a cyclical activity of recalling and relaying in which we are collectively engaged."[61] The *Dialogues* locates histories in word lists and in speakers' actions, as Laurent used words as intellectual tools for continued living in a world made foggy and strange by Europeans' arrival. Moreover, the word lists elicit exchanges that circulate the kinds of knowledge—linguistic, historical, environmental, political—compiled within the *Dialogues*; using the lists brings their content fully into play and places it into motion among speakers.

Sending copies of the *Dialogues* into colonial archives, as Laurent did when he sent Pilling a copy, aligned the intellectual implements present in the lists' content and arrangement with the book's circulation. Laurent's decision to place a copy of the *Dialogues* at the Bureau was an act that used the book as a linguistic tool to dispel the fog that colonists' linguistic archives cast over Abenaki histories and homelands. Laurent's gift to the Bureau did not accede to salvage bibliography, for the *Dialogues* evoked actions that intervened in the assumptions embedded in the word lists, maps, and bibliographies with which it shared shelf space at the Bureau. In this way, the *Dialogues* demonstrates how circulating Indigenous compilations could amplify and extend the meanings created on the page. This relation between assemblage and circulation exemplifies the capacious uses that Indigenous compilations evoked, while also requiring a reconsideration of the effects that circulation through social space has on those compilations.

As the *Dialogues* traveled into archival "domains" at the Bureau, or what book historian Adrian Johns identifies as "dynamic localities defined by physical environment, work, and sociability" and associated with specific behaviors, values, and practices, some of the book's meanings were shaped by the norms specific to institutions like the Bureau.[62] At times, those norms certainly conflicted with the lists' content and the meanings the book held within Abenaki communities. But this influence did not move in one direction, for the *Dialogues*' content and its mobility also charted out different linguistic, geographic, authorial, and readerly categories with which to orient its uses. Even when colonists saw the book as an ethno-bibliographical object, the book invoked other uses, which refused attempts to arrange words in hierarchical orders or on a map. As the following section details, several copies of the *Dialogues* traveled through ethnographic spaces, and circulating and reading from the book located those archival domains within the circles Wzokhilain described as "kdakinna," that is, within the Wabanaki world.

Remapping Colonial Geographies

The *Dialogues'* late nineteenth- and twentieth-century travels generated acts of speaking and translating that, like the word lists themselves, re-mapped colonial visions of Wabanaki lands and expectations of Abenaki disappearance. I draw here on Seneca literary scholar Mishuana Goe-man's discussion of Indigenous remapping as a creative act that intervenes in colonial spatializing, which defines lands, bodies, and ways of being ac-cording to western concepts of ownership, gender, and labor. Remapping, for Goeman, does not seek a return to an authentic or original moment (such as the one Powell's schedules invented by separating "new" from allegedly "primitive" words) but rather "conceiv[es] of Native spaces that encourage the dismantling of boxed geographies."[63] For Goeman, colonial mapping affects not just place but also bodies, territories, relationships, and belonging, encompassing colonists' attempts not just to gain access to Native lands but to reconfigure Native peoples' place-based relationships and forms of belonging.[64] Against such maps, Laurent's circulations of the *Dialogues* remapped space and belonging by linking Abenaki people across their homelands and by generating relationships grounded in speaking Abenaki to one another.

A postcard pasted inside the front cover of a copy of the *Dialogues* now residing in the Amherst College Special Collections limns some of these circulations (figure 4.4).[65] The postcard advertises a summer camp at Pe-quaket (or what settlers call the village of Intervale, near what is currently Conway, New Hampshire), established the same year the *Dialogues* was pub-lished. The White Mountains had become a popular tourist destination for people seeking a summer retreat; hotels and other lodging sprang up in the small town of Conway, creating a thriving regional summer industry. Lau-rent and other Abenaki people sold baskets and other hand-crafted items at the summer camp.[66] For the next several decades, Laurent's family and other Odanak families went south to spend summer months at Pequaket, living at the camp and selling "Indian wares," which the postcard adver-tises as including baskets, fans, canoes, bows and arrows, and pipes. The postcard indicates that Laurent himself would fulfill orders: "Order taken and promptly attended to by Chief Joseph Laurent, alias Lawrence, of the Abenaki Indian Tribe of St. Francis." The camp provided Abenaki people

FIGURE 4.4. Postcard advertising the "Indian Camps" at Pequaket, pasted to inside cover of *Dialogues.* Joseph Laurent, *New Familiar Abenakis and English Dialogues: The First Ever Published on the Grammatical System* (Quebec, 1884). PM551 .L3 1884. Kim-Wait / Eisenberg Native American Literature Collection. Archives and Special Collections, Amherst College Library.

with a rationale for continuing seasonal labor and other practices that the U.S. and Canada sought to eliminate and replace with western modes of sustenance.[67]

The *Dialogues* traveled with Abenaki families on these circuits, supporting the circulation of linguistic knowledge along pedagogical, ethnographic, and touristic routes. The Amherst copy bears the marks of some of the ways Abenaki people may have used the book on these travels: it is inscribed on one of the flysheets by Laurent's daughter, who wrote her name as "Octavie Laurent."[68] Marie-Cecile Octavie Laurent was eight when Laurent established the camp, and her signature, placed just a few pages after the postcard advertising the camp, suggests that she may have carried the book to and from Odanak and Pequaket, perhaps consulting it for lessons in between selling goods to tourists or assisting with basket making. In this capacity, the *Dialogues* complemented materials in Abenaki, English, and French available to students attending Odanak's schools, and the book would have fulfilled Laurent's stated goal of teaching Abenaki children English, a language useful both at Octavie's home in Odanak and in exchanges with U.S. tourists at the Pequaket camp. At the same time, the *Dialogues* would also have ensured that children would learn Abenaki, supporting the language lessons they were already receiving from their families. As Octavie and other children learned vocabulary words and practiced exchanges in Abenaki, they also circulated the elements of Abenaki stories of colonialism and survival, ensuring their longevity and use as tools for navigating a world shaped by colonists' hunger for power and land.

The travels of Abenaki families between Odanak and Pequaket remapped the boundaries colonists drew to claim lands in their quest for, as Nicolar put it, "power over all the earth."[69] The southern summer routes Abenaki people followed to participate in the tourist trade at Pequaket allowed them to visit relatives in southern homelands and to demonstrate through their movements the expanse of those homelands. As Gary W. Hume observes, the camp "made possible a return to ancestral Abenaki land" for Laurent's community, and it served as an "early center of Abenaki identity" from which to carry on linguistic and cultural education.[70] Despite the fact that colonial wars and violence had separated Abenaki communities, the camp offered the opportunity to "return . . . to Wôbanakik during the summer to sell their wares or during other times of the year to hunt or visit relatives in New England."[71] At a time when the United States and British Canada sought to determine the legal status of Indigenous lands and to demarcate boundaries between their nation-states and tribal nations, by grouping and confining Native peoples on reservations and by questioning Native peoples' title to their lands, Laurent and other Odanak Abenakis enacted a different set of geographic orientations, shaped by Abenaki territorial knowledge and memory. Their travels across colonial borders also rewrote the political and temporal boundaries on maps like Powell's, boundaries that aimed to contain Wabanaki lands within settler national and state borders. Just as Laurent's list of place names in the *Dialogues* represented those places as sites "where Abenaki people live, as continuing Abenaki space, as part of a conceptual map of the territory that continued in the language long after Americans claimed these spaces as their own," so the travels of Laurent and his family south to the "original home territory" asserted these spaces as part of Wabanaki homelands.[72]

The camp fostered a space for circulating compilations into colonial archives as well: as Stephen Laurent put it, the camp "became a nucleus as well for Indian scholars seeking out the Chief whose published grammar-dictionary had become known."[73] Tourism and ethnography met and mingled at the camp, as Joseph Laurent engaged both vacationers looking for a memento of their visit to the mountains and a growing number of university-trained anthropologists, who often brought their families along for a summer vacation while they worked. In an unpublished paper on Abenaki peoples' presence in Intervale, Stephen listed some of these "Indian scholars," who sought out his father, and he links the camp's status as a site for ethnographic discussion and collection to Laurent's decision to exercise his rights as an Abenaki man to cross U.S.-Canadian boundary lines:

> Dr. Frank Speck, of the University of Pennsylvania, spent several summers in the little Abenaki settlement, living among the Indians and studying their language and traditions first hand. Others who visited the Indians in Intervale were Dr. A. Irving Hallowell of the University of Chicago, and Dr. Montague Chamberlain of Harvard University. The Chief [Laurent] had letters from Prime Ministers Sir John Macdonald and Sir Wilfrid Laurier of Canada, and one from President Theodore Roosevelt on the subject of Article III of the Jay Treaty, which recognized the rights of the American Indians to travel unmolested and duty-free across the international boundary between the United States and Canada.[74]

The summer camp materialized Indigenous geographies that exceed and preexist settler nation-state borders, as Laurent insisted that the U.S. and Canada fulfill their promise to allow Indigenous peoples free travel throughout their own homelands. The presence of the summer camp and of Abenaki people from Odanak within the state of New Hampshire illuminated the inaccuracy of maps and other documents that asserted Abenaki people's disappearance or confined them within settler borders. The camp also influenced how university anthropologists described Abenaki histories: for example, Speck identified the Abenaki networks stretching across the U.S.-Canadian border in an article published in 1945 in the *International Journal of American Linguistics*. He wrote that one of his sources was Eli Nolet, an Odanak man who "was accustomed to return to the White Mountain region of New Hampshire with his family to enjoy the associations of the home land from which his Abenaki ancestors had migrated by the middle of the 18th century."[75]

The geographic remapping that Laurent's travels to and from Pequaket accomplished also facilitated a remapping of the categories in which ethnographers like Speck sought to place Abenaki people. According to one of Stephen's talks on Abenaki history, Speck attempted to use conversations with Laurent to collate linguistic and cultural information that would allow him to generate and populate "ethnic" categories.[76] Yet Speck repeatedly revised those categorizations, prompting an exchange in which Laurent "smiled and said: 'Well, Dr. Speck, I hope that I'll live long enough to find out before I die just what kind of Indian I am!'"[77] Speck's revisions to his own work show how, decades after Powell directed the creation of the Bureau's linguistic maps, anthropologists continued to try to link language and place to create categories in which they could contain Indigenous peoples. Laurent's teasing remark might suggest his familiarity with such categorizations, a familiarity that interacting with tourists and ethnographers at the camp would certainly have provided. His response might also suggest his knowledge of alternate ways of understanding and representing the relations between language and place, those expressed by the word "kdakinna" rather than by Speck's "ethnic" categories. As Stephen explains in his own corrective to Speck, names for Abenaki communities were "geographical rather than racial," corresponding to the "names of the regions, rivers and lakes near which they lived."[78] Speck missed the point by trying to correlate language and "racial" categories. By contrast, lists of place names within Wabanaki territory found in the *Dialogues* offer not only a map of geographic space but also a compilation that represented and supported relations among Abenaki people across those homelands.[79] Speck's conversations with Laurent likewise indicate the active interventions Laurent made into ethnographic assumptions, and we can understand his decision to send Pilling a copy of the *Dialogues* as part of these remappings.

Using and circulating *Dialogues* produced additional compilations of Abenaki language and history throughout the twentieth century when Stephen took up his father's practice of engaging with settler scholars and tourists. He corresponded about Abenaki history and linguistics with the ethnohistorian Gordon M. Day and gave speeches about Abenaki people to northeastern historical societies and social organizations.[80] Drafts and copies of those speeches now reside at the American Philosophical Society

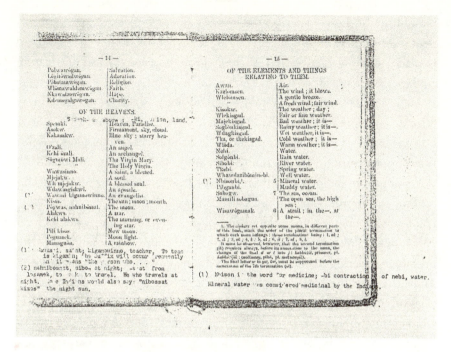

FIGURE 4.5. Stephen Laurent's annotations on a Xeroxed page from *New Familiar Abenakis and English Dialogues*. Stephen Laurent Papers, American Philosophical Society, Philadelphia.

in Philadelphia, along with Stephen's own compilations. He annotated by hand a Xeroxed copy of Sébastian Rasles's dictionary, adding English words alongside the French and Abenaki ones. Then, working with a Xeroxed copy of the *Dialogues,* he typed notes in the page margins and footers, adding additional translations to Joseph Laurent's word lists (figure 4.5). Stephen described his method as one of excerpting and insertion: "What I had done was to take every word found in my father's book and insert it in its proper place in the English part of the [French-English] dictionary [Rasles's], that being the second part of the book, English-French. I did the same with the words found in Masta's ABENAKI INDIAN LEGENDS, GRAMMAR & PLACE NAMES, and with other words picked up through conversing with old Indians in the village."[81] As Stephen translated across three languages, he continued his father's practice of compilation, this time by reading across and expanding existing word lists. He used this process of compilation as accretion on maps as well, annotating a copy of a French map of the St. Lawrence river valley with Abenaki place names. Stephen penciled numbers on the page, creating a key whose numbers correspond to place names in English and Abenaki. Perhaps using the lists of words in *Dialogues*, Stephen added words for Abenaki villages, rivers, and lakes to the French map, literally remapping French visions of space by bringing them into Wabanaki cartographies.[82] He made French maps and dictionaries into the surfaces for new compilations, in the process remapping not just their representation of space but their relation to Wabanaki homelands.

Making compilations, for Stephen as for Joseph Laurent, entailed proliferating and reproducing copies, correcting colonists' lists, and remapping colonial conceptions of language and place. Stephen's compilations indicate how the *Dialogues* continue to spur interventions into colonial archives and their ordering forms, from ethnographic categories to dictionaries to maps. He used the *Dialogues* as an engine and a surface for additional compilation and translation, acts that drew existing publications and sources from ethnographers, priests, and cartographers into Abenaki networks of language, history, and place. Rather than transforming word lists into paper objects that could be arranged to create geographic and cultural categories, as the Bureau's staff and other ethnographers hoped to do, the Laurents used word lists to represent capacious, interrelated repositories of memory.

social scientist
who studies and describes
human societies and
cultures

Conclusion

The compilations Joseph and Stephen Laurent made on the page continue to shape how scholars and the public understand Abenaki homelands and history. Stephen and his brother Emmanuel took over the care of the summer camp after their father's death in 1917. Born at Odanak, Stephen lived for more than sixty years at Pequaket, and after retiring from his job as a postal employee, he dedicated his time to running the camp as a shop for "Indian wares," including the *Dialogues* and other books, and to writing and speaking about Abenaki history.[83] As a result of the Laurents' work, Conway, New Hampshire, recognized Odanak Abenaki families as part of the region's history and future, departing, at least in this case, from the claims made by surrounding states and towns that Abenaki and other Native people had disappeared from the northeast. The Laurent sons and other Odanak families helped organize commemorative events and physical memorials to Joseph Laurent. In 1959, the Laurents and other Odanak families participated in a ceremony to unveil a plaque for him at Pequaket, a plaque that also visibly marked Abenaki presence. A program for the event indicates that Gordon M. Day gave a talk, and Odanak Abenaki people recited the Lord's Prayer and sang hymns in Abenaki. Abenaki community members Elvine Obamsawin Royce and Ambrose Obomsawin engaged in an "Abenaki Dialogue," performatively enacting in speech the kinds of exchanges that Laurent committed to the page in the *Dialogues*.[84] The ceremony demonstrated the ongoing ties between Abenaki people separated by settler-national borders and attests to several occasions on which people from Odanak continued to visit their relatives in the south. The fact that Stephen reported that the marker had been vandalized and stolen a few years later might evidence ongoing hostility toward Abenaki people on the part of northeastern settlers who hoped to secure the region as a U.S. one, both politically and historically. Nonetheless, Odanak Abenakis visited the camp again to celebrate its centennial in 1984.

Circulating and reading copies of the *Dialogues* likewise still support interactions across Wabanaki homelands. Octavie Laurent's copy of the *Dialogues* traveled along Wabanaki networks in its route to Amherst College Library's Younghee Kim-Wait/Pablo Eisenberg Native American Literature Collection. In 2014, Rhonda Besaw, an Abenaki beader, sold Octavie's copy to Amherst after obtaining the book from artist Gerry Biron, in exchange for some beaded purses (in turn, Amherst bought the book for the value of the beadwork Besaw had traded with Biron). As Besaw explained to me, Biron had purchased the book from a rare book dealer.[85] Besaw decided that Amherst's collections were a good place for the book because, as she wrote, "I felt a responsibility as an Abenaki to receive and take care of this book in a good way."[86] She further explained that she wanted the "book to stay close to home" and to go to "someone or somewhere where it would be loved."[87]

Besaw's decision to send the book to the Native American Literature Collection at Amherst, similar to Laurent's decision to send a copy of the *Dialogues* to Pilling at the Bureau of American Ethnology, places Octavie Laurent's copy into a collection which it shapes and by which it is shaped.

In the case of Amherst's collection, the *Dialogues* shares space with other books published by Native writers in the nineteenth century, from Pequot William Apess's *Son of the Forest* (1829) to Ojibwe Peter Jones's *Collection of Chippeway and English Hymns* (1847), Mohawk E. Pauline Johnson's books, and many others. The copy of the *Dialogues* at Amherst resides in a collection dedicated to making accessible the vast printed materials created by Native people. The book figures within Amherst's collections as part of the literary and political work Native people took up throughout the nineteenth century to translate and publish their languages and stories and to insist on their rights to their homelands in the face of colonial violence and paper claims of disappearance. Finally, Amherst's commitment to making the collection accessible to Native communities helps ensure that the *Dialogues* will be used by Abenaki people as well as by Native and non-Native scholars. Significantly, only one of those uses is reading; as Besaw notes, she wanted the book to go where it would be "loved."[88]

In its content and its circulations, *New Familiar Abenakis and English Dialogues* generates uses for and orientations to itself that center Abenaki histories and homelands. Joseph, Stephen, and Octavie Laurent—and other Abenaki families—intervened into the archival, ethnographic, and colonizing projects of the U.S. by strategically circulating the book—and by themselves traveling—in ways that remapped U.S. and Canadian efforts to preserve Abenaki linguistic knowledge and to contain Abenaki people in static geographic and cultural categories. The *Dialogues* accomplished these ends by functioning as an object that people read as well as one that they used to speak Abenaki, gave as gifts, sent to collectors, and loved. The copies of the *Dialogues* I have followed in this chapter show that the books moved throughout Wabanaki lands as tools for reading and language learning and as objects that generated Abenaki relations across time and place.

Interlude

Carlos Montezuma's Famous Indians

The Yavapai Apache physician Carlos Montezuma kept a scrapbook in the early twentieth century (see figure I.4). Reusing a notebook whose pages were first devoted to Latin homework, Montezuma pasted clippings from Albert Payton Terhune's series "50 Famous American Indians" (published between 1905 and about 1914). Each installment in the series tells the story of a "famous" Native person, often leaders well known for resisting colonialism, from the Wampanoag King Philip and Shawnee Tecumseh to the Ute Ouray and Mohawk Joseph Brant. Terhune framed each story with a commentary on Native histories and possible futures, beginning with a statement placing Native people in relation to "the history of America" and reminding his readers of their anticipated vanishing:

> The American Indian of today is a broken, fast-vanishing descendant of the great red men who once ruled this country and who fought with desperate fury against the white man's march of progress. The history of those savage warriors and statesmen is woven closely into the history of America itself. Their deeds were as thrilling and their fate as dramatic as any dime-novel hero's. In this series the stirring life stories of fifty of the greatest American Indians will be related.[1]

Each installment in Terhune's series discusses the significant actions and defining characteristics of a famous "Indian," and each story attempts to realize
Terhune's anticipation of Native vanishing by concluding with the individual's
death. Philip, for example, "had tried to stand against the march of Progress.
With his life he had paid the penalty." Meanwhile, Tecumseh's brother "Ellskwa-
tawa" (Terhune probably refers to the Shawnee spiritual leader Tenskwatawa)
has a death "shrouded in mystery. It is thought by some that he 'vanished' in
order to keep up his reputation for supernatural power."[2]

Terhune's series provided a weekly disappearance, casting Indigenous peoples as existing only in history and in the imaginations of consumers of mass
media, including the newspapers in which the series appeared. At a time when
the U.S. was saturated with cheap, easily accessible serial media such as newspapers and magazines, an early version of our current media culture defined by
accelerated news cycles and ever-increasing amounts of information, "Famous
Indians" constituted a recurring image that readers could trace across multiple
issues. Both the same—"Famous Indians" are always exceptional, and they always die or disappear—and unique—each person gets his or her own story—the
stories train readers to expect certain actions of "Indians."

Echoing the compilations made by John Ridge and Charlotte Johnston,
Montezuma's act of arranging the articles into a notebook removed them from
the periodicals in which they originally appeared and recontextualized them by
placing them next to each other in the scrapbook. His compilation made possible multiple, alternate routes through the series. The scrapbook collapses the
space and time separating serial publications by placing the images on consecu-
tive pages, in the process creating new ways to interact with them. No longer
mediated by the pace of print publication, as items in Montezuma's scrapbooks,
the excerpts may now be read as a collective, straight through from beginning to
end, or they may be perused nonsequentially, as readers chose different routes
through the scrapbook. Montezuma seems to have used the notebook to track
not Indigenous histories but U.S. visions of Native people, one of his persis-
tent interests. As a practicing physician with an office on State Street, in Chicago, Montezuma knew that his vocation and even his very person disrupted
settler expectations for Native peoples. In his notes for a speech, he included an
ironic commentary on the contrast an "educated, cultured, and refined [Native]
gentleman" posed to these expectations, writing, "the white man experiences
a sad disappointment, because this Indian gentleman is not painted and feath-

ered from scalp lock to moccasins."[3] As he arranged episodes of "50 Famous American Indians," Montezuma would have seen representations of Native people who appeared "painted and feathered from scalp lock to moccasins" and perhaps considered the repercussions of such images for living Native peoples. He identified these consequences, writing, "Misrepresent the Indian and you will cause him to be misunderstood. That is what Buffalo Bill and many Indian novels have accomplished."[4] He went on to explain in a 1915 speech: "Keep in mind that Indian Bureau, Indian Reservations, Indian Schools, Indian College, Indian Art, Indian Novels, Indian Music, Indian Shows, Indian Movies, and Indian Everything create prejudice and do not help our race."[5] Montezuma linked misrepresentations—in wild west shows, in novels, films, music, and art—with the colonial policies and bureaucracy dedicated to bringing about the "vanishing" that Terhune imagined. Montezuma's speech made visible how U.S. mass media circulated visions of Native people that "create prejudice," holding hands with the government offices dedicated to managing the assimilation, confinement, and elimination of Native people.

When Montezuma compiled the "50 Famous American Indians" series in his scrapbook, he tracked these misrepresentations, prejudices, and policies. The scrapbook provided a space in which Montezuma constructed a perspective from which to see and criticize prejudicial images. The perspective he cultivated, as his notes indicate, reads across multiple images to make an argument about their collective effect. Montezuma's scrapbook presents a view of this system of misrepresentation as a whole while allowing him to look at individual representations and compare them with others, in novels, films, and pageants, in order to ask what kinds of "Indians" he saw looking back at him. He used this critical perspective to expose associations between mass media representations of Native people and the dispossession of Native lands and scarcity of resources for Native people. The scrapbook made possible a viewpoint that looked at U.S. history and saw not vanishing Indians but the mechanisms the U.S. employed, from "government bullets" to "government red tape," to try to kill them. Montezuma's compilation participated in a long history of Indigenous compilations that read colonial representations critically, from William Apess's extracts of newspaper clippings about the 1833 Mashpee Revolt to Charlotte Johnston's compilation of "Ojibwe Maid" versions and, more recently, to Cheyenne and Arapaho novelist Tommy Orange's 2018 account of the "copy of a copy of the image of an Indian" in textbooks, films, TV programs, advertisements, and mascots.[6] At the end of the nineteenth century, as U.S. mass media churned out representations of Indigenous people as alternately heroic, degraded, vanished, and threatening, Indigenous writers assembled and circulated compilations. This moment at the turn of the century saw a proliferation of Indigenous compilations, which included sending multiple copies into colonial archives and other spaces of knowledge production, as Joseph Laurent did with the *Dialogues*, as well as transforming material texts into genres and critical perspectives that provided orientations to settler representations, as Carlos Montezuma and Simon Pokagon did.

CHAPTER FIVE

ACCOUNT

Reading Colonialism at the 1893 World's Columbian Exposition

———◆———

Indigenous compilation confronted colonial archives at the Columbian Exposition and World's Fair, held in Chicago from May to the end of October 1893. A celebration of Columbus's so-called discovery of the Americas and a vast, performative demonstration of western "progress," the fair's displays sprawled over 600 acres on the city's south side; 27 million visitors attended from across the United States and the world, and historians, anthropologists, and activists held formative meetings that shaped newly emerging disciplines over the next century. The historian Frederick Jackson Turner delivered his influential argument about the closing of the frontier, inaugurating a vision of American exceptionalism that remained influential for decades in such disciplines as history, American studies, and literary studies. The activists Ida B. Wells and Frederick Douglass distributed the pamphlet Wells edited, *The Reason Why the Colored American Is Not in the World's Columbian Exposition*, foreshadowing W. E. B. Du Bois's sociological studies and "data portraits" of Black experience, presented at the 1900 Paris Exposition.[1] Meanwhile, in one of the buildings dedicated to ethnographic collections, anthropologist Franz Boas demonstrated his argument for studies of specific environmental, historical, and cultural contexts by constructing life groups of Indigenous peoples, displays of mannikins engaged in culturally specific activities. Boas's approach would orient the Department of Anthropology he later headed at Columbia University and the discipline of anthropology as it took shape within universities in the early twentieth century.[2] Finally, the fair's exhibits live on in Chicago: the materials collected and displayed in the ethnological exhibits were repurposed as the formative collection for Chicago's Field Museum of Natural History, which opened in 1894.

But when seen from the perspective of the people who supposedly constituted the objects of display and science, the fair looks less like a turning point in the history of multiple disciplines than a continuation—and amplification—of the practices that framed Native people within settler temporal and geographic boundaries. Simon Pokagon, a leader of the Pokagon Band of Potawatomi Indians in what is currently Michigan and Indiana, visited the fair in October 1893. Earlier that year, he wrote a critique of the fair's collections and claims, its celebration of Columbus, and its strategies for representing Native peoples. Pokagon printed this critique on birchbark pages and sold the pamphlet at the fair under two titles, *The Red Man's Greeting* and *The Red Man's Rebuke* (figure 5.1).[3] The birchbark pamphlet was available for sale on the Midway Plaisance, the thoroughfare lined with replica villages where fairgoers could encounter people from across the world.[4]

As Pokagon circulated his birchbark pamphlet throughout the fair's exhibits and buildings, fairgoers interpreted it as a souvenir, prizing its birchbark pages and what they saw as the novelty of printing on birchbark. The fair brought together the tourist and ethnographic networks that Abenaki leader Joseph Laurent had engaged by sending a copy of *New Familiar Abenakis and English Dialogues* to the Bureau of Ethnology and by holding conversations with anthropologists at the Pequaket camp (see chapter 4). In 1893, Pokagon sent copies of the *Rebuke/Greeting* through a space where the scientific, touristic, and carnivalesque were difficult to distinguish. Indigenous people, objects, and representations circulated as souvenirs through what historian Boyd Cothran characterizes as "marketplaces of remembering": "networks of exchange and commodification. . . through which we access the past" and that define how "we use the past in the present."[5] In its displays, floats, and consumption of the *Rebuke/*

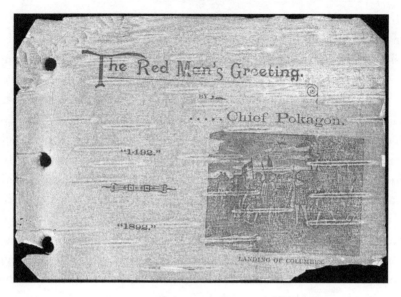

FIGURE 5.1. Simon Pokagon, *The Red Man's Greeting* (Hartford, MI, 1893).
Ayer 251 .P651 P7 1893, Newberry Library, Chicago.

Greeting, the fair placed Pokagon and his pamphlet into marketplaces of remembering that aimed to define how Chicago's Indigenous past signified in the present.

The fair's marketplaces of remembering framed—and still orient—readings of the *Rebuke/Greeting.* The text continued to generate interest as a souvenir after the fair: C. H. Engle, the Hartford, Michigan, lawyer who was Pokagon's publisher, referenced the *Rebuke/Greeting* in the prefatory materials for *O-gî-mäw-kwĕ Mit-i-gwä-kî (Queen of the Woods),* Pokagon's 1899 posthumously published novel. This reference suggests that the pamphlet was sufficiently well known to serve as promotional material for Pokagon's other publications. The pamphlet soon became a collector's item, with its birchbark pages and illustrations drawing book collectors' interest.[6] Literary scholars have largely maintained this focus on the pamphlet's materiality, remaining fascinated by its birchbark pages, which they connect to histories of Indigenous writing practices. Yet this interest in the pamphlet's materiality has been in inverse proportion to readings of its content. Collectors' and scholars' interest in Pokagon's birchbark pages have solidified approaches to the *Rebuke/Greeting* that value it for its materiality rather than for its subject matter.[7]

In this chapter I make two principal interventions. The first argues that the *Rebuke/Greeting* is a compilation. By reading the pamphlet's content, I show that Pokagon excerpted extensively from Washington Irving's nineteenth-century history of Christopher Columbus's so-called discovery of America, by placing materials from Irving's text throughout the pamphlet. But Pokagon did not merely replicate Irving's words: instead, the *Rebuke/Greeting* assembled the excerpts to make an account book of colonialism, or a tally of colonial depredations. In a space in which fair organizers and attendees circulated images of Native peoples that created a "transit," or what Chickasaw literary scholar Jodi A. Byrd has identified as a "site through which U.S. empire orients and replicates itself," Pokagon rearranged the materials of U.S. empire and national literary histories to insist on very different readings of those materials.[8] His compilation created perspectives that were rooted in place and that participated in the communication networks through which Indigenous knowledge about colonization traveled. Reading the *Rebuke/Greeting* as an Indigenous compilation shows that the pamphlet generated critical readings of colonial archives.

Second, I argue that Pokagon's reading of colonial archives emerges from Anishinaabe historiographical practices, and I read his compilation within these Great Lakes Indigenous literary histories. The *Rebuke/Greeting* is not solely a book created for the fair and oriented to its displays, but a literary and material object shaped by Anishinaabe, and specifically Neshnabek, understandings of history and of the relations between Potawatomi people and their homelands.[9] Pokagon used compilation to create ways of reading colonialism's effects on Native peoples across time and place.

The *Rebuke/Greeting* marks a moment when Indigenous compilation is thematized, transformed into a literary form and practice of reading. Accounting for the content of *Rebuke/Greeting* and its materiality exposes Pokagon's own careful reading of nineteenth-century ethnographic and literary forms and the pamphlet's status as an object that trains its interlocutors how to see Potawatomi histories and futures while remaining cognizant of the colonial origins of American literature and history. Pokagon addressed colonists' reading practices as they manifested in multiple spaces, including archives, histories, and visual displays. This attention to colonial archives and reading prefigures one shape that Indigenous interventions into colonial archives took in the early twentieth century, when Indigenous writers such as Gertrude Bonnin (Zitkála-Šá, Yankton Dakota), Carlos Montezuma (Yavapai Apache), and Charles Eastman (Dakota) extended Pokagon's critique of the fair to expose the false claims of colonial archives.

Object Lessons and Origin Stories of Chicago

When Pokagon attended the World's Fair in October 1893, he entered into a space dedicated to teaching viewers how to place objects (including Pokagon himself) in relation to one another. Within this space, he was both on display and an object fairgoers read against and alongside other collections. Curators aimed for the fair's displays of Native peoples and materials to tutor fairgoers in modes of seeing oriented by seriality, which functioned as a set of practices, a principle of arrangement, and a visual aesthetic "that pose[d] a set of pervasive and prominent questions about continuity versus discontinuity, the play of difference through standardized objects, and the sequential display versus the array that could be seen at a glance."[10] Many fairgoers were already familiar with serial forms of labor, visual presentation, and consumption, for seriality permeated everyday life in the U.S. at the end of the nineteenth century. The proliferation of mass culture made possible through increased printing speeds and inexpensive paper brought periodicals and serialized narratives to a large and diverse audience. Bureaucratic forms like timetables and modes of labor like the factory and assembly line trained bodies and eyes to order work, time, and information in serial forms.[11] Seriality shaped people's labor, leisure, and understandings of the past. And world's fairs were, as historians of science Nicholas Hopwood, Simon Schaffer, and Jim Secord observe, a "great symbol of serial practice."[12]

Given existing histories of the fair, which have highlighted its importance for disciplinary emergence and methodological debates among anthropologists, my argument that the fair was a space of serial display and reading might seem to gloss over important methodological differences. Historians of science cite the fair as a site of contests between the Smithsonian Institution's proponents of "evolutionary typology"—series of decontextualized objects, each representing a stage from "primitive" to "complex"—and the Peabody Museum's advocates of "tribal arrangement[s]," objects represented in their milieu in displays called life groups that sought to depict people in their historical and sociological specificity.[13] These differences certainly existed, but curators were united in a desire to train fairgoers in forms of serial reading.

Curators and commentators across a spectrum of anthropological methods imagined the fair not just as a set of separate, themed departments but as displays that should be read collectively and serially, with the goal of locating Indigenous peoples in ethnological and historical categories. As the collector Hubert Howe Bancroft noted in his report on Department M, "The general plan, however, is to illustrate in a series of object lessons the development of various phases and adjuncts of civilization, as architecture, household conveniences, appliances and methods for the saving of life and labor, for the discipline and reform of criminals, for the cure of the sick and the relief of those who are in need."[14] For curators, Native peoples and their histories, belongings, and remains constituted a foundation for series reflecting the supposed phases of "civilization." Frederic Ward Putnam, a Peabody Museum curator for Department M, the fair's official ethnology department, remarked that the "great object lesson" of the fair could not be completed without Native peoples "being present," writing that "without them the Exposition will have no base. It will show the material prosperity and the development of our race in the arts and in culture, but it will have no beginning; it will be a monument standing upon nothing, so far as concerns America of 400 years ago; for it will be showing simply America of today."[15] Putnam imagined fairgoers reading across the exhibits, linking displays of objects to those featuring living people in a series oriented by time and cultural hierarchies. Putnam's employee and fellow curator Franz Boas indicated that the curators expected visitors to read the different displays in relation to each other and to living Indigenous peoples: he wrote that the "meaning of the ethnographical specimens is made clearer by the presence of a small colony of Indians, who live in their native habitations near the Anthropological building."[16]

Far from seeking a single interpretation, curators encouraged experimental reading by arranging exhibits to support several possible interpretations. As Smithsonian curator Otis T. Mason explained of the Smithsonian's ethnological exhibit, he "arranged the costumes and art productions of these [language] families in separate alcoves, so that the student taking his position in one of them may have before his eye practical solution of some of the theoretical questions which have recently arisen concerning the connection between race and language and industries and philosophies."[17] Mason encouraged viewers to experiment with creating multiple perspectives through which to elucidate answers to questions of race and language, continuing: "In order to afford the student another point of view from which to look at the same set of phenomena, a few alcoves have been arranged upon another plan, in which a typical industry is made the primary classific concept, tribe or nationality the second concept, and linguistic affinities the third concept."[18] While the government exhibit (curated by Mason) and the ethnological exhibit (or Department M, curated by Putnam) each emphasized different "theoretical questions,"[19] they were united in aiming to train attendees in practices of piecing Indigenous peoples and belongings together into "object lessons."[20] The exhibits presented materials for viewers to practice arranging into series that reflected histories, racial categories, and theories of civilization.

For their part, fairgoers experienced the exhibits not through clearly identifiable disciplinary or methodological divisions but through their own experiences in reading. Exhibits jostled for space across the fair, eliciting strange juxtapositions and repetitions, rather than coherent conclusions (figure 5.2). Reviewers described "collections of contemporaneous Indian implements, arms, dress and household articles, one collection being nearly like another, at least to casual observers."[21] Similarly, the Indigenous peoples who traveled or were taken to the fair and who lived during much of its duration in the simulated villages near the Manufactures and Liberal Arts Building or on the Midway Plaisance found a strange double in displays of mannikins depicting tribal groups.[22] Such repetitions created confusion and uncertainty, as commentators complained that many departments left visitors to "grope their way, with the aid of an incomplete and faulty catalogue."[23]

Yet this confusion nonetheless did generate serial readings of Indigenous peoples. For example, Department M was situated immediately next to a section on "Sanitary and Reformatory Measures," which included exhibits on hospitals, charities, and penal institutions, including an electric chair from the Auburn Penitentiary. As one observer wrote, "It was probably only accidental that these symbols of mercy and benevolence were placed so close to the Mexican altar on which human victims were butchered with

SECTION OF THE ETHNOLOGICAL DEPARTMENT

FIGURE 5.2. Ethnological Department at 1893 World's Columbian Exposition and Chicago World's Fair, showing crowded exhibit spaces. Hubert Howe Bancroft, *The Book of the Fair: An Historical and Descriptive Presentation of the World's Science, Art, and Industry, As Viewed through the Columbian Exposition at Chicago in 1893* (Chicago, 1893). Case oversize R 1832 .07, Newberry Library, Chicago.

flint knives 300 years ago."[24] Unexpected or disorienting juxtapositions did not detract from curators' object lessons; instead, the proximity of exhibits on reform and on ethnology allowed viewers to consider the methods of care and punishment that so-called civilized nations developed alongside cases that lacked such institutional tools of correction. Placing these exhibits next to one another encouraged fairgoers to see progressive forms of social order thought to be exhibited by cultures at allegedly varying stages of civilization.

Accounts of Pokagon's visits to the fair make clear the consequences of serial reading for Indigenous peoples and nations. The fair's seriality positioned Indigenous peoples in a past outside of "authentic history"—defined at the fair as settler history—and disconnected from place and thus from Indigenous homelands.[25] Newspapers presented Pokagon as a bridge between past and present: they described him as looking like a "typical Indian on the war path" and "standing as a historic figure between the Chicago of yesterday and the Chicago of to-day."[26] On October 9 (designated Chicago Day), Pokagon ceremonially delivered to Chicago mayor Carter Harrison, Sr., a duplicate of the 1833 Treaty of Chicago, in which Ojibwe, Odawa, and Potawatomi leaders had ceded the land Chicago now occupies. The *Tribune* presented this moment as reenacting the original land cessions and justifying settler occupation, writing that Pokagon's "father [had] conveyed Chicago and the Fair grounds, together with the surrounding country, to the United States" and that the mayor responded that he was "happy to receive this gift free from the band of one worthy to bestow it."[27] The paper presented Leopold Pokagon as a representative, singular leader capable of approving the land cession (erasing the fact that he was a signatory to the treaty's subarticles pertaining to his community).[28] Similarly, as Pokagon Potawatomi historian Michael Zimmerman, Jr., emphasizes, the fair's performances obfuscated the many Indigenous leaders who negotiated the treaty, the violent removal of many Potawatomi people from Indiana and Michigan in 1838 as a result of the treaty, and the fact that many Potawatomi people (and those from other tribal nations) remain in the region, notwithstanding the cession and removal.[29]

The desire to view Pokagon as a temporal bridge between past and present was further enacted by the float on which he rode during the Chicago Day parade. The parade represented moments in the history of Chicago and the Americas, from a float depicting the 1871 Chicago fire to floats entitled "Columbus at the Court of Isabella," and "The Early Discoverers and First Settlers." Pokagon rode on the third float, titled "Chicago in 1812—A Trading Post—Massacre!" This float created a living representation of the moment U.S. settlers still claim as Chicago's founding event, by representing the battle, part of the War of 1812, between U.S. and Potawatomi soldiers near the U.S. Fort Dearborn. While the U.S. lost the battle, colonists reimagined the event as a massacre in which Potawatomi men attacked settler women and children, and settlers framed their own violence as an example of the qualities of courage and brave defense supposedly characterizing the city's non-Native occupants. The float featured a platform surrounded by what the *Tribune* described as "pictures . . . representing the old Fort Dearborn and [Quebec-born trader] Mr. Kinzie's house [and] a group representing the famous [Potawatomi man] Black Partridge in the act of rescuing a white woman from the savage Pottawawtomie's tomahawk." Pokagon and other people were to make the float come alive, even as they represented not themselves but historical figures. At the float's rear, the newspaper explained, rode a "picturesque group of Indian traders, and a priest as well as singing maidens [which] give a peaceful aspect in pleasing contrast to the more sanguinary scenes." Finally, the float "was furnished with native American Indians of historical prominence," including Pokagon and three Cherokee "maidens, Misses Rose, Rena and Carrie Bluejacket." Together, these groups formed a "most unique and authentic historical display."[30]

The "Chicago in 1812" float and Pokagon's ceremonial presentation of the treaty of 1833 partially acknowledged Chicago as the homelands of Potawatomi and other Native nations, even as the float cited 1812 and 1833 as the founding dates for the city's "authentic history." The Chicago Day events connected founding moments in this "authentic history" with the removal of Indigenous peoples from their lands and, by extension, from settler colonial memory.[31] For fair organizers, Pokagon represented the historical moments of battle and land cession in which some Potawatomi communities participated, thus symbolically placing Indigenous peoples at the moment of Chicago's origin, but only at that moment.[32] From this point of view, Pokagon's body acted as a living version of the mannikins and objects displayed in the exhibit halls as evidence of presumably vanished peoples against which Chicago's imagined "progress" could be seen.

Across the fair's exhibits and events, Indigenous land was invoked at the scene of temporal classification even as seriality's lateral gaze simultaneously effaced Indigenous histories and relations to those lands. In part, this separation of place and time is a function of seriality, for seriality creates a horizontal line of sight, a perspective that moves across the surface of exhibits, placing objects in relations in which moving from one point to another represents change or difference. Whereas Pokagon's appearance at the fair might seem to constitute an acknowledgment of Indigenous peoples and histories and while some newspaper accounts might attest to Potawatomi peoples' survival and resistance, the displays presented Indigenous peoples as marking singular, "pre-historic" moments in time, not ongoing and historical relations to place. Representing Pokagon's relation to Chicago as confined to the past obfuscated Leopold Pokagon's and the Pokagon Band's effective advocacy to remain on their lands within the state of Michigan. Moreover, locating Pokagon and displays of Indigenous peoples in prehistoric time removed them symbolically and materially from both place and contemporary time. This geographic dislocation cast Indigenous dispossession as already complete.[33]

But despite the fair's serial reading of Native peoples out of place and present time, the 1833 treaty remained a powerful, active document with which the Pokagon Band insisted on their relationship to their homelands in Chicago. The Pokagon Band of Potawatomis successfully petitioned the United States to acknowledge the agreements stipulated in the 1833 Treaty of Chicago and other treaties, including the responsibility to compensate the tribe for land cessions. As a result of decades of appeals in Michigan and Washington, D.C., by Pokagon Potawatomi leaders and community members and advocacy by the tribe's business committee, the Band had recently been awarded a settlement of just over $100,000 as compensation for unpaid annuities dating to treaties made in the early nineteenth century.[34] Although tribal members did not receive the payments until 1896, stories about the decision circulated several years before the fair in newspapers throughout the Midwest and East Coast.[35] An 1891 Nebraska newspaper article noted that the Pokagon Potawatomis "successfully resisted removal to Kansas in 1833, but claimed the annuity promised at that time. They received a small sum in 1866, since which time the present claim has been prosecuted."[36] Some articles acknowledged that, in addition to remaining on their lands, Potawatomi people "still maintain their ancient tribal relations."[37] Viewed through this history of insistence on Potawatomi relations to their homelands, Pokagon's appearance at the fair was the most recent manifestation of the Pokagon Band's strategic actions to remind U.S. settlers of the treaties stipulating Potawatomi peoples' rights to their ancestral lands and of their ongoing presence in those homelands.

The Red Man's Greeting and Great Lakes Native Histories

Just as his father had participated in treaty-making processes even while insisting on different outcomes for those processes than U.S. officials envisioned, so Pokagon visited the fair even while reading its displays and performances in ways that interrupted their serial logics. He began the *Rebuke/Greeting* by critiquing the very purpose of the fair from the perspective of Native people. He declared that "we have no spirit to celebrate with you the great Columbian Fair now being held in this Chicago city, the wonder of the world" (1). Pokagon amplified this statement by opening with a story that established the viewpoint or perspective for *Rebuke/Greeting*. Pokagon calls this story a "tradition"; as Zimmerman, Jr., explained to me, it does not appear to be a Potawatomi traditional story but rather one Pokagon created to describe colonialism's effects.[38] Pokagon's story participates in an extensive Anishinaabe historiography grounded in linguistic and material understandings of stories.

In the story, a Native man has a vision of colonialism and its meaning for Native peoples:

> "A crippled, grey-haired sire told his tribe that in the visions of the night he was lifted high above the earth, and in great wonder beheld a vast spider-web spread out over the land from the Atlantic Ocean toward the setting sun. Its net-work was made of rods of iron; along its lines in all directions rushed monstrous spiders; greater in strength, and larger far than any beast of earth, clad in brass and iron, dragging after them long rows of wigwams with families therein, outstripping in their course the flight of birds that fled before them. Hissing from their nostrils came forth fire and smoke, striking terror to both fowl and beast." (3–4)

The man's dream offers a glimpse into what for him is future time, allowing him to foresee the hardships his people will face. The vision also establishes a viewpoint that sees laterally—across multiple temporal periods, not unlike the serial reading at the fair. But in contrast to serial logics, the elderly man's perspective also reads vertically, as he looks at the layered histories in one place and their effect on that place. For example, he sees what preceded and will follow the railroad. His bird's-eye view allows him both to see into a future in which the U.S. has built railroads across North America and to survey the entire geographic space throughout which that railroad and its violence extends. Significantly, the man's transtemporal vision derives from his position in place: he is lifted up above the earth and sees not only the passage of time but also the entirety of North America. His vision creates narratives of colonialism that are grounded in place and account for multiple temporalities—he might look into the future, only to return to consider the past or the present, or he might compare the future moment characterized by the network of rods and iron with his own time.

Pokagon's story of the man's place-based perspective aligns with the historiographical structures employed by contemporaneous Anishinaabe historians, and close readings of the *Rebuke/Greeting* must position the pamphlet within this literary history. Throughout the nineteenth century, Ojibwe, Odawa, and Potawatomi men began to seek out their peoples' histories and place them into print. From the Anishinaabe men George Copway and William Whipple Warren to Pokagon's Odawa friend and classmate Andrew J. Blackbird, these men wrote out of the knowledge that colonial archives already contained reams of paper dedicated to telling Native histories, books in which they and their families might appear but that often remained inaccurate and inaccessible.[39]

As I explained in the introduction, William Whipple Warren wrote his history after rejecting colonists' practices of collecting and organizing knowledge about Ojibwe people. Instead, he turned to acts of "sifting and procuring testimony" from Ojibwe elders and to such Ojibwe material and historiographical practices as quillwork and pictographic records.[40] These practices align his history with Anishinaabe historiographic practices embedded in Anishinaabemowin words used to describe history keeping or telling. As Ojibwe literary scholar and poet Margaret Noodin points out, the Anishinaabemowin word for story is "dibaajimowinan" or "aadizokaanag." English translations of these words cannot convey their full meanings, but Noodin offers an approximate literal translation that connects "dibaajimowinan" to "dibaajimo": "the act of collecting and redistributing the truth that you've heard."[41] Drawing on this view of history telling as collecting and redistributing stories, mid-nineteenth-century Anishinaabe writers like Warren experimented with how to collect, sift, and redistribute Anishinaabe histories and narratives.[42] In doing so, these writers participated in what Noodin calls an "Anishinaabe tradition of studying ideas across time and dimension, creating cycles of ideas instead of chronologies."[43]

These historiographic practices are evident in the structure of Warren's text: *History of the Ojibways* is organized around the accounts of Ojibwe storytellers, sixteen of whom Warren named in the text. Warren's *History* was posthumously published in the *Collections of the Minnesota Historical Society* in 1885, thirty years after his death. One of the society's editors, Edward D. Neill, may have arranged the chapters to adhere to a chronological order, but the individual chapters are anchored not by time but by the storytellers and their stories, which generate each chapter's form and organization. Chapters are also structured around key subjects, from Ojibwe origin stories, to doodems (or clans), migrations from the east, religion, and so on. Warren usually began the chapters by describing his own knowledge of the subject. He then related the storytellers' accounts, in this way drawing out the subject's history and significance from several perspectives. Warren often introduced his speaker formally, citing their name and tribal or clan affiliation; at other times, he noted merely that "an anecdote is told" or used quotation marks. At times, the chapters do proceed chronologically, for example, by noting the sequence of events by which a village was evacuated of people, but they often then shift to offer multiple "annals" on this event, which do not move forward in time but provide a thick description of a single event from multiple vantage points.[44]

Two years after Warren's book was published, Andrew J. Blackbird also compiled histories: personal, familial, tribal, and those dealing with both human and nonhuman entities. In *History of the Ottawa and Chippewa Indians of Michigan: A Grammar of Their Language, and Personal and Family History of the Author* (1887), Blackbird centered his narrative in places in Odawa homelands and in what he, like Pokagon, called traditions. In Blackbird's text, these traditions are Odawa stories about the past, whether stories gleaned from recent memory or accounts of the world's beginning and its human and nonhuman beings. Blackbird often began a chapter with one event or place, only to turn to an earlier moment to elucidate that moment or place further. As a result, individual stories factor not as points in a chronology but as elements that clarify the tribe's or Blackbird's own relation to a place. For example, an account of how the Odawas and Ojibwes resolved intertribal murders not only relates information about a particular murder but ultimately explains why some Ojibwes live in the Grand Traverse region within what is currently the state of Michigan.[45] Similarly, Blackbird related information about norms for punishing murder and about marriage practices to relay the rules and guidelines that determined how Odawa and Ojibwe people interacted with one another as they defined their geographic and political relations. An account of murder thus spirals out into concerns about intertribal relations, stories of tensions between the two nations in the recent and what Blackbird called the "primitive" past, and the negative influence of white settlers on justice in Odawa communities.[46] Finally, one story explains why a place is named Pe-wa-na-go-ing (or flinty point), noting that the name originated with the "great rocks of flint lying near the lake shore."[47] These flint rocks are the carcass of a monster, Blackbird noted, who was the brother of Nanabozhoo and who traveled over the continent in human and sometimes in animal form, leaving tracks in the rock along the way. The chapter continues with stories about Nanabozhoo and the origins of the world, ultimately grounding these stories in the places that bear the marks of these ancient events. Like Warren's history, Blackbird's account moves back and forth throughout time to relate "cycles of ideas," doing so to explicate people's relations to place.[48]

These Anishinaabe historical compilations, created by sifting and procuring stories, generate a point of view that is rooted in place and looks in multiple spatial and temporal directions. These histories are not structured by chronology or even necessarily by time but by the network of stories explaining an event or place, or by what Noodin, in a comment about Pokagon's writing, describes as acts of "identifying central relationships and building spiraled levels of knowledge outward from a core meaning."[49] Such practices produce materially and textually what Noodin calls the "narrative anarchy with a geographic center" that characterizes Anishinaabe literature.[50] These compilations "feed the need to see in all directions at once" by describing stories about beings who move between human and nonhuman states, life and death, past and present, and by making "equations of word and meaning that connect all possible interpretations of the place. This paradigm offers an alternative to linear chronologies, binary comparisons, and hierarchical readings."[51] The stories that Anishinaabe historians collected and sifted eschew single narratives to offer multiple stories about a place, thereby relating the deep, place-based histories of an event or person.

The elderly man in Pokagon's story adopts a perspective that looks in multiple directions in order to understand a phenomenon, in this case, colonialism, its processes, and its effects on a particular place. Like Anishinaabe historians, the elderly man sees "in all directions at once," and Pokagon created spiraling story structures throughout the *Rebuke/Greeting* that build on the elderly man's view of colonialism and its far-reaching effects. Like Warren, Pokagon considered the practices of archiving and reading through which colonists made claims about Indigenous peoples, and Pokagon excerpted and reassembled those claims within Indigenous histories and experiences of colonialism. Like Warren and Blackbird, he sought the "truth" in these stories by viewing colonial texts from different angles and in multiple historical moments.[52] In the *Rebuke/Greeting*, Pokagon created an account of European colonialism and its aftermath organized not by timelines of progress but by its effects on Native peoples' lives at different moments and places. In this way, he insisted that the pamphlet's readers adopt a perspective that sees colonialism in light of its far-reaching consequences.

Reading the Archives of Colonialism

Pokagon developed this reading practice by taking excerpts from the U.S. writer Washington Irving's *History of the Life and Voyages of Christopher Columbus* (first published in 1828) and compiling them in *Rebuke/Greeting*. In the pamphlet, the excerpts serve as a record both of Columbus's voyage itself and, due to their origin in Irving's *History*, of the ways that U.S. settlers were currently representing those histories, constituting colonial archives, and formulating American literary histories. It is particularly significant that Pokagon selected excerpts from Irving's *History*, given Irving's reputation as one of the first internationally recognized U.S. writers and the centrality of his work in the 1890s to the nationalist literary histories that editors were formulating in anthologies and serialized magazines.[53] As book historian Lindsay diCuirci explains in her study of nineteenth-century republications of early colonial histories, *History of the Life* was the product of Irving's research in the 1820s, in recently accessible Spanish archives, and his *History* made Columbus newly visible and newly Americanized as a symbol of discovery.[54] Pokagon's excerpting of Irving thus allowed him to read the archival documents and methods that constructed theories of Columbus's so-called discovery, in the process creating a perspective for reading claims to the continent's past and future. Pokagon's compilation, in other words, addressed not just Irving's *History* and its popularity at the end of the nineteenth century, but the host of archiving, reading, and publishing practices through which U.S. writers were producing histories of the Americas.

Pokagon selected quotations from Irving's *History* that describe the kindness of Indigenous people, their practice of holding land in common, and the prosperity and peace that characterized their communities when he arrived in the Americas. But Pokagon did not read these quotations straightforwardly, as representations of the past. Instead, he illuminated the archival practices through which settlers constructed histories of Columbus and colonialism. In a move that effaced his reliance on Irving's text, Pokagon urged his audience to "read the following, left on record by Peter Martyr, who visited our forefathers in the day of Columbus" and wrote that "your own histories show that Columbus on his first visit to our shores, in a message to the king and queen of Spain, paid our forefathers this beautiful tribute" (8). Here Pokagon altered Irving's text by suggesting that Martyr visited America himself; as Irving correctly notes, Martyr gathered information from "conversations of the admiral."[55] By detaching Irving's name as author from the *History* and suggesting that Martyr traveled to the Americas, Pokagon invented archival genealogies, in this way unmooring his account from European and U.S. historians' obsession with Columbus's journals and the other archival documents they took as capable of reconstructing accurate histories of colonialism. The archive of Columbus's writings and experiences was from the beginning one composed of multiple accounts from priests and historians. Pokagon thus excerpted from an already diffuse and proliferating archive, and he read those accounts in ways that attended to the consequences of conquest for Indigenous peoples.[56]

Pokagon accomplished this recontextualization by rewriting Irving's text, in particular the excerpts from Irving's book 8, chapter 7, which

Irving titles "Subjugation of the natives—Imposition of tribute." Irving wrote that Indigenous people grew filled with "despair . . . when they found a perpetual task inflicted upon them, enforced at stated and frequently recurring periods. Weak and indolent by nature, unused to labour of any kind, and brought up in the untaxed idleness of their soft climate, and their fruitful groves, death itself seemed preferable to a life of toil and anxiety."[57] As a consequence, Irving explained, they decided to withhold food from the Spanish colonists and to withdraw to the hills, where many of them died, he claimed, "through famine, fatigue, terror, and various contagious maladies engendered by their sufferings."[58]

Pokagon described this history quite differently, departing from his source even while still claiming that he was quoting from a colonial history. He commented that "your historians left to be perused with shame, the following facts," namely, that the Spanish

> most treacherously seized and bound in chains the unsuspecting natives; and as a ransom for their release demanded large sums of gold, which were soon given by their subjects. But instead of granting them freedom as promised, they were put to death in a most shocking manner. Their subjects were then hunted down like wild beasts, with blood-hounds, robbed and enslaved; while under pretext to convert them to Christianity, the rack, the scourge, and the fagot were used. Some were burned alive in their thickets and fastnesses for refusing to work the mines as slaves. (8–9)

Rather than attribute Indigenous deaths to a refusal to work and to their "weak" nature, as Irving's *History* and many other colonial histories do, Pokagon identified enslavement, deception, and torture as responsible for the loss of Indigenous lives and homelands. Moreover, he assembled the descriptions of Indigenous peoples in the fifteenth century without the laudatory accounts of Spanish "discovery" with which they appeared in Irving's and Martyr's histories or in the fair's celebrations of Columbus.

Pokagon's recontextualization of Spanish archives of discovery and their manifestations in American literary histories opened up space for Indigenous accounts of colonialism. He imagined Indigenous peoples across the hemisphere as communicating news to one another of the violent actions of Columbus and other Spanish colonists. He described these networks in a piece published in 1897, in which he imagined Indigenous people from the Caribbean traveling to North America to warn people farther north of Spanish colonists. In this piece, he glossed another archive on Columbus, this one a set of Indigenous responses and warnings about colonists' intentions and actions. He wrote:

> Certain it is that in those days, which tried the souls of the Carib race, some fled from the lust and lash of their oppressors by sea to the coast of Florida, and reported to the natives there that Wau-be-au'-ne-ne-og' (white men), who fought with Awsh-kon-tay' Au-ne-me-kee' (thunder and lightning), who were cruel, vindictive, and without love, except a thirsty greed for gold, have come from the other side of Kons-ke-tchi-saw-me' (the ocean) and made slaves of Mis-ko-au-ne-ne-og' (the red man) of the islands, which was reported from tribe to tribe across the continent.[59]

Pokagon's vision of Indigenous communication across the hemisphere countered archival and publishing networks that disseminated misleading histories. Moreover, by reading the fair and its celebration of Columbus through a perspective that saw far to the south and attended to the experiences of Indigenous peoples in the Caribbean, Pokagon linked the fair's displays and reading practices to archival and historiographic practices that produced misrepresentations of Indigenous peoples. Like the Ojibwe and Odawa histories compiled by Blackbird and Warren, the *Rebuke/Greeting* is structured by "central relationships" among texts and an ability to see in multiple directions at once.[60] Pokagon's historical compilation moves capaciously across time and space, from Potawatomi, Ojibwe, and Odawa lands to Kalingo (Carib) territories in the Caribbean, and it illuminates Indigenous peoples' experiences in these places at different historical moments.

Like John Ridge's letters, William Apess's appendix, and Charlotte Johnston's albums, Pokagon's compilation of excerpts from Irving's *History* both commented on and revised colonial histories. In the case of the *Rebuke/Greeting*, Pokagon staged this intervention at the level of the colonial archive itself. He excerpted and compiled the printed versions of that archive available in the Americas, while upsetting its claims to truth and origin with his "inaccurate" citations. In doing so, Pokagon asked readers of the *Rebuke/Greeting* to view settler histories of "discovery" and conquest from a different vantage point: one oriented by hemispheric Indigenous networks and experiences of colonialism.

Attending to Pokagon's excerpting from histories of Columbus shows that, despite the ways in which it has been circulated, catalogued, and read as a souvenir, the *Rebuke/Greeting* is a compilation that models alternate ways of seeing colonialism, U.S. literary histories, and their consequences for Native peoples. The *Rebuke/Greeting* is assembled in part out of the materials with which settlers represented Indigenous peoples, and it is an Indigenous compilation informed by Anishinaabe historiography and invested in how people read the archives of colonialism. Pokagon created an intertextual archive in *Rebuke/Greeting* that exposed how settler practices of archiving and publishing circulated inaccurate histories of Indigenous peoples and colonialism. In doing so, he positioned Native peoples not as a background or as evidence of ancient, primitive historical stages against which modernity may be contrasted, but as peoples who historically possessed and defended—and continue to defend—their lands from colonial encroachments. These compilations require readers to approach the archives of colonialism, ethnography, and national literary history from a different perspective, one that is rooted in place and can see across time and the continent. Pokagon's compilations enacted this form of reading by producing his own object lesson for reading colonial archives.

Birchbark Accounting

Pokagon elaborated the *Rebuke/Greeting*'s status as an object that trains its readers in new reading practices in its last section, where he described the pamphlet as an account book. This generic claim might seem strange, as the *Rebuke/Greeting* does not feature the lines of debits and credits or the numerical tallies that typically characterize account books. But Pokagon referenced account books throughout his writings, where he described them as tabulating not just financial debts but the costs of colonialism on Indigenous peoples' lives. Modeled after the elderly man's perspective that is grounded in place and can see in multiple directions, Pokagon's account books demonstrate forms of reading that are place-based and attentive to multiple temporal dimensions.

At the end of *Rebuke/Greeting*, Pokagon imagined a scene in which the Great Spirit summons everyone before him to be judged, dividing them into "pale-faced" and "red spirits" (13). The Great Spirit turns to the "red

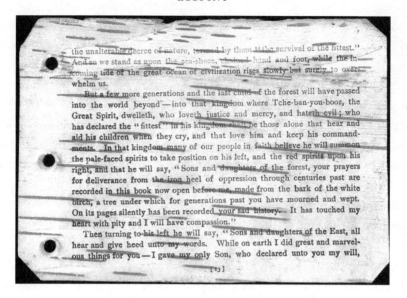

FIGURE 5.3. Pokagon's account book of colonialism.
Simon Pokagon, *The Red Man's Greeting* (1893). Ayer 251.
P651 P7 1893, Newberry Library, Chicago.

spirits" first, comforting them with the assurance that their ' "prayers for deliverance from the iron heel of oppression through centuries past are recorded in this book now open before me, made from the bark of the white birch, a tree under which for generations past you have mourned and wept. On its pages silently has been recorded your sad history. It has touched my heart with pity and I will have compassion' " (13). This scene suggests that the Great Spirit reads from the very book readers presently hold in their hands, the book made from the "bark of the white birch" and that contains accounts attesting to Native people's "sad history," that is, the *Rebuke/Greeting* (figure 5.3).

The excerpts from colonial histories that Pokagon includes in the *Rebuke/ Greeting* constitute entries in an account book that operated in multiple dimensions, spiritual and human; in the fifteenth century, the nineteenth, and the future; in the Caribbean and in the Midwest. The Great Spirit enumerates with a "voice of thunder to the shame-faced multitude" of "pale-faced spirits" the acts of which they are guilty: "the wholesale butchery of their game and fish"; using tobacco to create "unhealthy, filthy habits"; tricking Native peoples out of their homes, liberty, lands, money, and goods;

and introducing liquor into Native communities (14-15). He concludes this section by stating, "Neither shall you with gatling [*sic*] gun or otherwise disturb or break up their prayer-meetings in camp any more" (16).[61]

Pokagon referenced account books often in his writings, defining them both as "relics" of colonialism and objects that can ground Native readings of colonial histories. Shortly after his second visit to the fair, in one of several newspaper articles reflecting on the Fort Dearborn float, Pokagon presented account books as an alternate source for histories of the battle. In an October 20, 1893, article printed in the *Chicago Inter Ocean* newspaper, Pokagon described seeing the Astor account books (from the American Fur Company), noting that they feature the "finest" writing "I ever saw. While examining them my heart whispered, 'If these books come up in evidence in the world beyond no expert will be necessary to read them.'"[62] He returned to this description six years later, in his novel *O-gî-mäw-kwĕ Mit-i-gwä-kî (Queen of the Woods)*, writing that on a trip to Mackinac Island he had stayed

> all night at the old Astor house on the island, which is now run for a hotel.
>
> The old Astor books are still kept there as relics of early days. In the books of 1817 and 1818 and so on, I found the invoice for whisky [*sic*] exceeded that of all other goods. The handwriting is the plainest I ever saw.
>
> As I was examining them, I thought in my heart, if these books are ever required in the supreme court of Heaven as evidence against the white man for dealing out "ish-kot-e-waw-bo" to the red man, no experts will be necessary to read them.[63]

By arguing that the meaning of the account books should be clear to anyone who read them, Pokagon does not necessarily mean that they are transparent or that their meaning is explicit. Instead, the account books, much like the colonial histories he excerpted in the *Rebuke/Greeting*, will generate reading practices capable of seeing the stark effects of dispossession and settlement.

Pokagon expanded on the account books' "plain" and "fine" writing and the forms of reading it elicited in *O-gî-mäw-kwĕ Mit-i-gwä-kî*. He included the story of an "object-lesson" (perhaps a rewriting of the fair's own object lessons), which in the novel is provided by an Odawa woman, Ashtaw, who is known as a "temperance worker."[64] Ashtaw appears within a story told by an elderly Odawa man whom Pokagon calls Uncle Kaw-be-naw, a story about the connections between whiskey and trading on Mackinac Island, Michigan, "where Astor got rich, and we very poor."[65] Pokagon embedded a longer story about Ashtaw in a note to the elderly man's narrative, in which he explained that Ashtaw gives "object-lessons" to the children she met on her travels:

> She always managed to keep on hand a stock of snakes' eggs. She would hold her meetings at such times as some of the egg litters were about to hatch. She stained them a beautiful red color, placing them on green moss in "wig-was-si ma-kak-ogans (small, white birch-bark boxes)" so as to have them appear to the children as charming as possible. After the children were assembled, she called them about her; then opened the boxes one by one in their presence; and when their admiration was sufficiently excited so they all began to inquire what kind of eggs they were, she would make reply, "these are ish-kot-e-waw-bo wän-än-og (whisky eggs);" then she would add, "Would you like to take some of them?" She would then carefully put into each extended hand some of the charming-colored little eggs.[66]

The children were entranced by the "little beauties" and held the eggs delicately, only to have the egg shells "crumble away, and from each come forth a little snake squirming and wriggling in their hands. Then with a shriek of horror they would let the young retiles drop, and scatter like leaves in a whirlwind." This object lesson impresses the children's minds with "such a loathsome hate against ish-kot-e-waw-bo that their very souls ever after would revolt at the sight, smell, or even thought of the deceptive curse." Ashtaw then follows the "strong object-lesson" with a discussion of the dangers of alcohol and the torments of "'mi-chi-gin-e-big' (great big snakes)."[67]

Ashtaw's object lesson is not simply a warning about the dangers of alcohol and its apparently enjoyable qualities but dangerous hidden effects; it is also a lesson about how to see. She teaches the children to analyze the eggs by looking not only at their beautiful exterior designs but also by anticipating their interiors. That is, the children must look not only at and across surfaces but also at interiors and what is hidden in them. The object lesson trains the students in the mechanisms of colonialism, the ways its seemingly straightforward promises obfuscate an ugly, violent core. Colonialism, the story suggests, is composed of dangerous elements that root themselves into communities and individuals, with effects that long outlast their initial appearance. Ashtaw's lesson teaches the children how to see surfaces and their interiors, how to anticipate future implications or consequences, and how to respond to them. This object lesson furthers the forms of seeing modeled by the elderly man in *Rebuke/Greeting* and by Ojibwe and Odawa histories, for the egg's meaning is found not through an observation of its surface or its status in a collection of many beautiful eggs. Instead, the egg's hidden nature must be understood by seeing past surface appearances and by considering multiple temporal dimensions: not only the present moment of a charming object but also its future consequences.

Like Ashtaw's object lesson, Pokagon's account book of colonialism in the *Rebuke/Greeting* elicited forms of visual literacy that can see in multiple directions and dimensions. He applied these forms of seeing to read colonial archives. After compiling the excerpts from Irving's *History*, he asked readers to "pause here, close your eyes, shut out from your heart all prejudice against our race, and honestly consider the above records penned by the pale-faced historians centuries ago; and tell us in the name of eternal truth, and by all that is sacred and dear to mankind, was there ever a peopl [*sic*] without the slightest reason of offense, more treacherously imprisoned and scouraged [*sic*] than we have been" (9). In Pokagon's model of visual literacy, readers must "pause" and "close [their] eyes." They must refuse to place colonial records in a temporal series moving from past to present but close their eyes to those forms of organizing and producing knowledge. Closing their eyes allows readers to examine the account book of colonialism from multiple viewpoints and in several dimensions, to study both the future and past implications of colonists' actions. This account book requires readers to see the future repercussions of an object that appears innocuous, adopting a panoramic perspective very much like that modeled by the elderly man at the opening of *Rebuke/Greeting*. Pokagon's account book considers colonists' actions not as points in a historical narrative of linear, progressive time but as events with far-reaching, past and present, ethical and material implications for both Native people and U.S. settlers. The forms of reading evoked in the account book require audiences to account for long histories of colonialism and empire and to analyze Columbus's writings and actions—and the methods of knowing circulating at the fair—within those histories. Pokagon's compilation of colonial histories into an account book generated new readings of those sources and of the past.

These forms of reading are intimately tied to the pamphlet's materiality and through that materiality to Potawatomi homelands. Like Joseph Laurent's placement of Abenaki histories into a list form that facilitated their circulation as people read and spoke the words in the list (chapter 4), so Pokagon's compilation in the *Rebuke* extended from the account book form to the birchbark pages on which he printed the pamphlet and to Potawatomi practices for using birchbark. Pokagon described some of these practices a few years after he published the *Rebuke/Greeting*, in an article published in the February 1898 issue of *The Chautauquan*, where he designated birchbark as a foundation for Neshnabek modes of reading. In an article titled "Indian Native Skill," Pokagon praised the objects that Neshnabek people create out of birchbark, from baskets to canoes. He wrote that the "thin, tough, paper-like" bark is useful for making hats, caps, dishes, kettles, canoes, and wigwams, in this way supporting ceremonies, securing marriages, and cementing social relationships among communities.[68] He concluded with an anecdote in which a birchbark canoe piloted by a Native man beats a white man's boat in a race, thus proving the superiority of "Indian Native Skill." Pokagon's decision to describe birchbark and its uses emerged, he explained, from his observation of U.S. science, namely his

> consideration of the fact that the burial-places of our fathers in times past have been laid waste by the dominant race, and their graves robbed of their bones and those implements which were buried with them according to our ancient custom. The only excuse, outside of curiosity, yet given by white men for such acts of inhumanity has been the desire that they may better understand the physical development of our forefathers and their ancient history, claiming they were able to read in the battle-axe and spear of stone and in the arrow-head and knife of flint found in our burial-places that we were savages from the beginning.[69]

Perhaps recalling the ethnographic displays he observed at the World's Fair, which trained viewers to generate cultural and racial hierarchies by reading spears, arrowheads, and knives taken from burial places, Pokagon called such grave robbing in the name of science "wanton acts of inhumanity."

Instead, he posited a form of reading that rerouted these temporal series and that emerged instead from material practices for using birchbark. Pokagon explained that baskets and other birchbark objects demonstrate what "our people are now and what they may become."[70] Birchbark locates acts of reading in Potawatomi homelands—the places where birch trees grow—and orients those readings to Potawatomi futures, or what the people may become. Pokagon's observations in "Indian Native Skill" connected place and time in a vision that sees colonialism's effects even as it envisions futures for Native people that elude colonists' marketplaces of remembering and ethnographic displays.[71] The archives for those futures exist on birchbark, Pokagon suggested, and in Potawatomi peoples' use of birchbark as an object for everyday and ceremonial events.

Likewise, in *Rebuke/Greeting*, Pokagon explicitly linked Potawatomi forms of seeing to birchbark. In the account book of colonialism, the Great Spirit comments that the "white birch" produces bark for "pages [on which] has been recorded your sad history"; the birch tree is also a place "under which for generations past you have mourned and wept" (13). Lands and trees are the surfaces on which Potawatomi histories are inscribed, meaning that the account book of colonial depredations is literally located on Potawatomi homelands. And as the pages for Pokagon's account book, birchbark rewrites the fair's serial histories by visually and materially linking that accounting to Indigenous homelands that still exist and are still held by Indigenous nations like the Pokagon Band.

Pokagon demonstrated how this birchbark-oriented reading might revise the fair's forms of serial reading by placing a map, "Chicago in my Grandfather's Day's," in the opening pages of *Rebuke/Greeting*. The map recontextualized an earlier, settler map, "Chicago in 1812," that appeared in Juliette Kinzie's *Narrative of the Massacre at Chicago* (1844), a narrative that historian Ann Durkin Keating calls a "fanciful tale" of the battle at Fort Dearborn by the woman who married John H. Kinzie (son of the trader who participated in the battle between Potawatomi and U.S. soldiers in August 1812).[72] The "Chicago in 1812" map, subsequently republished many times as a representation of early Chicago, represents a handful of Native homes near Fort Dearborn as well as homes marked by settlers' names: Lee's Place, Burns', Ouilmett's, Kinzie's. Both "Chicago in 1812" and "Chicago in my Grandfather's Day" include the distinctive T of the

Chicago River's north and south branches. In the "Chicago in 1812" map, the river stretches away to a large blank area labeled "Prairie," signaling the possibility for further settler navigation and agriculture and imagining the disappearance of Indigenous peoples. This vision of empty space and colonial settlement as forming Chicago's origins was taken up in the fair's displays and floats and is reiterated in Chicago's monuments to its "first" settlers and the Fort Dearborn "massacre." In contrast, in Pokagon's map Native peoples' houses cluster along the river's main channel and both branches, and Native people in canoes travel along the river and lake: it is a busy, urban, Native space connected by rivers and lakes not to empty expanses but to known homelands. Pokagon's map insistently represents Chicago as a Native space, and Pokagon's recontextualization of Kinzie's map required readers of the *Greeting/Rebuke* to see familiar representations of the city through Potawatomi histories and presences (figures 5.4 and 5.5).

In his revision of "Chicago in 1812," Pokagon drew on long-standing practices of using birchbark messages to locate one's self in multiple dimensions, including place, time, and kin networks. Native and European accounts document birchbark messages left as guides or letters for subsequent travelers. For example, the white captive and adopted Ojibwe man John Tanner noted in his 1830 narrative: "Here we saw, as we were passing, some little stakes in the ground, with pieces of birch bark attached to them, and on two of these the figure of a bear, and on the others, those of two other animals."[73] Tanner explained the significance of the messages: "This was left for my information, and I learned from it, that Wa-me-gon-a-biew, whose totem was She-she-gwah, the rattlesnake, had killed a man whose totem was Muk-kwah, the bear."[74]

Birchbark messages serve as a map to multiple dimensions: they locate people in place—geographically and socially—and in time—by indicating how much time has passed since the person traveled through. Historian Heidi Bohaker argues that these "notational practices" were ways of making one's self legible or readable in a world defined by kinship relations, allowing one to be identified at a glance and from a distance.[75] As she writes: "This was not a world of bounded spaces but one of webs, of networks, of interaction. And in this world, the public and immediately visible communication of political identity was paramount. It was vitally important in this region to achieve 'at-a-glance' and 'from-a-distance'

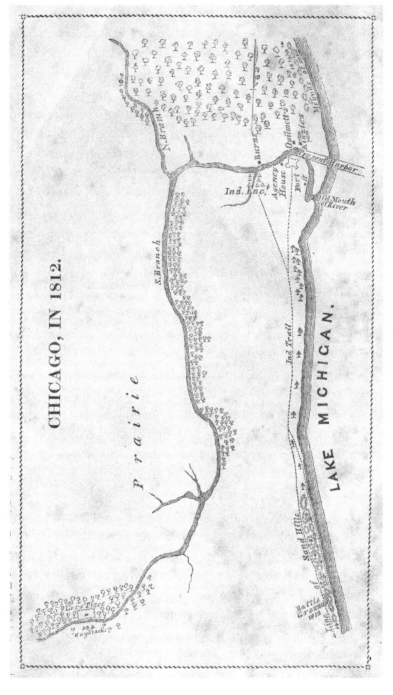

FIGURE 5.4. "Chicago, in 1812," from Juliette Kinzie, *Narrative of the Massacre at Chicago, August 15, 1812, and of Some Preceding Events* (Chicago, 1844). VAULT Ruggles 209, Newberry Library, Chicago.

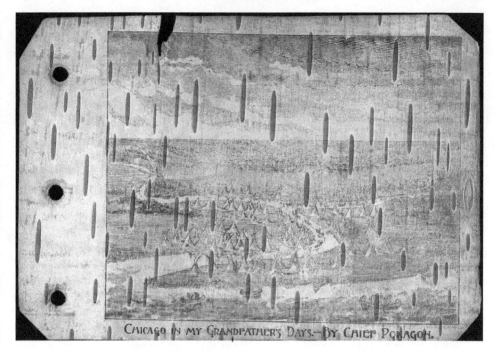

FIGURE 5.5. "Chicago in my Grandfather's Days.—By Chief Pokagon."
Simon Pokagon, *The Red Man's Greeting* (1893). Ayer 251 .P651 P7 1893,
Newberry Library, Chicago.

recognition of just whom one was meeting: friend, family, or enemy."[76]
In this context, the *Rebuke/Greeting* figures as a marker that locates the Pokagon Potawatomi and other Potawatomi communities in both time and place, demarcating their relationship to other Indigenous people throughout the Americas who have experienced colonization and to settler newcomers at the fair who brought different ways of analyzing the world. As *Rebuke/Greeting* compiled colonial histories to intervene in ethnographic displays and archival formations, the pamphlet also established a critical perspective that orients readers to Neshnabek temporal, geographic, and relational networks.

This critical perspective results, as Pokagon's many engagements with influential U.S. literary and ethnographic representations suggest, not in an expanded canon of American literature or reconfigured archives or displays, but in different ways of reading, using, and interacting with texts. Pokagon's compilations imagined Native literature's relation to American national literary histories as one in which Native literary practices and material forms recontextualized colonial archives, genres, and texts. But rather than positing another discipline or field that would counter or rival that of American literature, history, or anthropology, Pokagon's compilation exists as a capacious practice of mixing and recontextualizing that remains outside colonial archives and disciplines. Pokagon's compilation did not generate disciplinary formations or methods but made available a critical perspective for analyzing those formations and their effects on Indigenous peoples.

Conclusion

The forms of critical reading Pokagon enacted in the *Rebuke/Greeting* set the stage for one of the twentieth-century afterlives we can trace for Indigenous compilations, in which Native American writers repurposed Indigenous compilations' material juxtapositions and interventions as a narrative device. In the early twentieth century, the Yankton Dakota writer Gertrude Bonnin (Zitkála-Šá) extended Pokagon's attention to material forms—the account books, paperwork, display cases, newspapers, mass media, and archival arrangements—that produced knowledge about Native peoples by making these forms central elements in her short stories. In several narratives published in *American Indian Stories* (1921), Bonnin describes Indigenous women and children who grapple with and reject the increasingly centralized and bureaucratized frameworks within which settlers sought to contain and study their lives, beliefs, and relationships. Bonnin not only continued Pokagon's attention to the reading practices with which Indigenous peoples might approach colonial archives, she also linked those archives to government bureaucracies, showing how both institutions claimed power to determine Indigenous peoples' relation to the United States and to the representational forms within which settlers represented them.

In "The Widespread Enigma of Blue-Star Woman," Bonnin describes a woman who is consumed by a question— "'Who am I?'"—that "had become the obsessing riddle of her life."[77] She considered this question because government officials had made it central to her tribal membership and share in tribal lands and because the "Indian Bureau" required

Indigenous peoples to account for themselves within its frameworks of genealogy and citizenship. Bonnin's story probes how those policies required Indigenous people to give accounts of themselves in ways that proved detrimental to kinship relations, as evidenced by the two "Sioux" men who inquire after Blue-Star Woman, seeking not her well-being but her land and consuming the last of her food. These young men are the "by-product of an unwieldy bureaucracy over the nation's wards," one that corrupted relationships and responsibilities into desires for land that ultimately served the Bureau.[78]

Against this bureaucracy and its forms of control, Bonnin imagined a spectrum of responses that, like Pokagon's critical reading of the account book of colonialism, insists on interpretations of and uses for colonial books, archives, and paperwork that reckon materially with their inaccuracies and consequences. In "The School Days of an Indian Girl" (first published in the *Atlantic Monthly* in 1900) Bonnin writes of a girl at an Indian boarding school who scratches out an image of the devil in a Bible in order to resist his ability to punish "little girls who disobeyed school regulations."[79] Bonnin writes of the girl: "With a broken slate pencil I carried in my apron pocket, I began by scratching out his wicked eyes. A few moments later, when I was ready to leave the room, there was a ragged hole in the page where the picture of the devil had once been."[80] The girl's attention to the page as the site of the devil's authority over her and her act to scratch out the devil's "wicked eyes" echoes Pokagon's call for his readers to close their eyes in order to interrupt the narratives told in display cases and histories of Columbus. For Bonnin, this intervention happens in books themselves, as the girl refuses the regulations and moralistic rules the school imposed on Indigenous children by physically altering the book.

We might juxtapose the scene in "School Days" with one in "A Dream of Her Grandfather," in which Indigenous relationships and material objects support alternate forms of reading and use. In "A Dream," a young "Sioux" woman is working in Washington, D.C., "the very seat of government," where she seeks to "carry on his [her grandfather's] humanitarian work."[81] She has a dream in which she sees a large cedar chest sent from her grandfather. She opens it, imagining that she will see bags embroidered with porcupine quills and other materials that settlers treated as "relics."[82] Instead, she sees not material objects but "a vision! A picture of an Indian camp, not painted on canvas nor yet written." In the vision, a man speaks words of encouragement to the people in Dakota, calling them to look to the "new day dawning."[83] In Bonnin's stories, lessons in how to read or see, much like Pokagon's object lessons, juxtapose colonial bureaucracy, books, and relics with Indigenous relationships and ways of seeing that account for but are not reducible to those books and relics. Building on Pokagon's refusal of settlers' attempt to locate Potawatomi and other Indigenous peoples in the past, Bonnin orients her stories around Indigenous women's refusal of the constraining categories of time, religion, and identity imposed by the U.S. Bonnin, like Pokagon and other Indigenous compilers, uses these forms of seeing and reading to insist on Indigenous archives for Indigenous peoples that are conscious of but not contained by settler bureaucracy and books. The critical perspective that Pokagon and Montezuma worked to generate in their compilations reemerges and proliferates in Bonnin's stories and in twentieth-century Native American fiction more generally as a narrative device, a turning point or set of actions in which Indigenous characters decide to reject settlers' intended uses for books or material objects and turn instead to pursue other ways of knowing, communicating, and interacting with Indigenous communities and Indigenous archives.

EPILOGUE

Compilation's Afterlives

———————

Over a century after Simon Pokagon compiled an account book of colonial depredations and circulated it at the 1893 Columbian Exposition, the Dakota writer Susan Power wrote a short story set at the Field Museum, "Museum Indians" (2002). Founded a year after Pokagon published *The Red Man's Rebuke/Greeting,* the Field Museum was born out of the fair's exhibits, for curators and promoters relocated many items from the fairgrounds to the museum. The museum's displays feature centrally in "Museum Indians," which follows a young girl and her mother through Chicago "on foot, on buses," from the Chicago Historical Society (now the Chicago History Museum) to the Art Institute of Chicago (its building also erected for the fair) and the Field.[1] At the museum, they walk through its halls until they find a buckskin dress belonging to the girl's great-grandmother, pausing before the headless mannikins the girl calls "dead Indians." She imagines the dress's weight and her great-grandmother's work to bead the designs: "The yoke is completely beaded—I know the garment must be heavy to wear. My great-grandmother used blue beads as a background for the geometrical design, and I point to the azure expanse." They "stand before the glass case as we would before a grave," and her mother laments that she doesn't " 'know how this got out of the family.' "[2]

The glass cases displaying dresses and other belongings at the Field Museum participate in a monumental landscape constructed across Chicago in the late nineteenth and early twentieth centuries, when city officials, donors, and curators repurposed materials displayed at the fair into public art. These relocated objects include two bronze bison, now in Humboldt Park; *Signal of Peace*, a sculpture representing a head-dressed Indian on a horse, which sits along Lake Michigan; and *End of the Trail*, another bronze sculpture first cast for the 1893 Exposition (a copy sits in the Art Institute).[3] Redistributed, the objects from the fair now take the city itself as a frame, providing a counterpoint to the modernist skyscrapers and the neoclassical buildings housing cultural institutions. The objects are conscripted as signposts for settlers to read Indigenous peoples in relation to Chicago and the United States, representing settler claims about what Power calls "dead Indians," who are represented as out of place and time in Chicago and the twenty-first century. The claims colonial archives and exhibits made in the nineteenth century remain present in the urban landscapes, where they still function to produce Indigenous peoples as invisible and to justify settler colonialism.

But "Museum Indians" does not stop at illuminating the lasting consequences of the fair's object lessons and serial reading practices, for Power's story echoes Pokagon's turn from the fair's displays to Indigenous homelands and relations. Before the girl and her mother leave the museum, they greet a "little buffalo across the hall, stuffed and staring." The mother speaks to him, saying, " 'You don't belong here. . . . It makes me angry to see you like this. . . . We should be in the Dakotas, somewhere a little bit east of the Missouri River. This crazy city is not a fit home for buffalo or Dakotas.' "[4] The mother's statement does not cast indigeneity and urbanity as mutually exclusive, nor does it suggest that, as the fair's exhibits would have it, cities represent modern time in which Indigenous people do not live. "Museum Indians" rejects such conclusions, for the mother and daughter traverse the city, marking out routes by foot and bus, inventing stories about Picasso, attending protests, and "wrestling with the Chicago police."[5] Their itineraries map Chicago as Indigenous homelands while maintaining relations with family belongings and histories even if they have been taken to settler institutions like the Field. In a moment that echoes Pokagon's critical perspective on colonial archives, the girl leads her mother outside the museum, where they "can see Lake Shore Drive spill ahead of us, and I sweep my arm to the side as if I were responsible for this view. I introduce my mother to the city she gave me. I call her home."[6] The girl's turn away from display cases and mannikins to face Lake Shore Drive curving along the lake creates a viewpoint that emerges from the home the girl and her mother have made in the city. They echo Pokagon's insistence on seeing Chicago as Native homelands in the past *and* the present by making the city a place Dakota women call home.

Like the girl in "Museum Indians," who turns from the display cases to insist on alternate relations to the city and to her family than those marked by loss, plunder, and disappearance, Indigenous compilations interact with but are not assimilated by colonial archives and archival forms. Sending a compilation into an archive could be an act of strategically taking up colonists' lists and categories in order to put them under analysis and expose the faulty assumptions on which they rested, as John Ridge extracted Albert Gallatin's and other colonists' own words to expose their inaccuracies and reject their logic. Or, as we saw with Charlotte Johnston's acts to gather versions of the "Ojibwe Maid" song in her albums and with Joseph Laurent's decision to send a copy of *New Familiar Abenakis and English Dialogues* to James Pilling at the Bureau of American Ethnology, Indigenous compilations' circulations could pointedly disrupt archival projects and the political boundaries of the nation-state those projects sought to construct and solidify. When Simon Pokagon used Indigenous compilation to model critical readings of colonial archives and the claims to place and history they produced across Chicago, he demonstrated how this history of archival interventions required approaches to colonial archives that could see the past, present, and future repercussions of colonialism. He called for readers who would close our eyes to the claims to authority and knowledge produced as natural and familiar in colonial archives and who would instead read in Indigenous literatures the stories of Indigenous pasts and futures, of what the people "may become."[7]

As Pokagon's attention to these networks suggests, Indigenous compilations also had distinct uses within Indigenous communities, as texts that Native people read and took up in ways they found worthwhile. Sometimes these uses overlapped with compilations' circulations into archives, as in Occom's sale of his copy of *Up-Biblum God* and possibly the "Herbs & Roots" booklet to Thomas Shaw, which may have helped provide for his family and fund the Brothertown emigration, or when Ridge's letters to Gallatin called for the U.S. to acknowledge Cherokee sovereignty. And sometimes, compilations' uses in Indigenous communities aligned with their archival interventions, as in the copies of Laurent's *Dialogues* that he sent to the Bureau of American Ethnology and used to encourage both language learning and collaborative history telling in Abenaki communities at Odanak and Pequaket. Other uses for Indigenous compilations remained separate from colonial archives and forms of interpretation, as in the acts of medical care Occom provided to northeastern Native communities who were gathering to found Brothertown, or the personal archives in the Cherokee syllabary that Ridge referenced in his letter. These uses extend as well to the acts of translation with which Charlotte Johnston addressed Ojibwe people who assembled not to hear a minister's message but to listen to her, and to the hospitality and songs she shared with other Ojibwe people and that provided a foundation from which she and William McMurray supported Sauteur efforts to protect their homelands from U.S. and Canadian encroachment. Indigenous compilations were not simply responses to or counteractions against colonial archives but texts that affirmed and extended alliances among Indigenous communities, as shown by Johnston's use of her Ojibwa Book to exchange hymns with Ojibwe missionaries and Octavie Laurent's copy of the *Dialogues* renewing relations with Abenaki relatives as the Laurents traveled to Pequaket. The making, uses for, and circulations of Indigenous compilations expand our understandings of the hands that made early Native literatures, allowing us to recognize the relations among people already familiar in literary histories and those usually absent from such narratives but significant as requestors of healing, senders and readers of letters, singers of hymns, sewers of makaks, speakers of dialogues in an Indigenous language, and tellers of histories.

In this book I have traced compilations' travels within Indigenous communities and colonial archives, but copies of Indigenous compilations also found physical homes within tribal archives, which keep, arrange, and interpret Indigenous literatures and histories on tribal nations' own terms. In Chicago, the site of Pokagon's and Power's critical readings, these tribal archives take the form of transnational community archives that represent the history of an urban Native American community. I consider here one such community archive alongside literary and artistic interventions in Chicago's representations of Indigenous peoples, in order to trace some of the place-specific legacies of Indigenous compilations' circulation into colonial archives. By concluding in Chicago I am able to locate myself in some of these stories as a non-Native observer of and sometimes participant in these contemporary acts of archival making and use and to recognize their influence on my own scholarly practices.

In the mid-1950s, Chicago was named as a relocation site in the federal program that sought to reconfigure yet again the relationship among Native nations, their homelands, and the United States. With the Indian Relocation Act of 1956, the U.S. sought to sever the relation between Native nations and their homelands by moving Native people to cities, where government officials assumed that assimilation into U.S. gender, political, and economic structures would be more easily accomplished. A transnational Native community in Chicago grew as people from reservations in surrounding and more distant states traveled to the city for jobs offered by the relocation program or to join family members already in the city. Native people and non-Native collaborators founded a host of institutions—the American Indian Center of Chicago (AIC), the Anawim Center (now the Kateri Center), and the American Indian Association of Illinois, among others—all of which served the growing urban community and created distinct spaces for Native people within the city.[8]

Throughout its existence, the American Indian Center has maintained an archive of organizational records and photographs that document the center's history and its service to Chicago's Native American community. In 2018, a group consisting of AIC staff, interns from the community, and Northwestern University faculty and staff (of which I was one) received an NEH Common Heritage grant to digitize some of the photographs in the archive and create a digital archive, build AIC's archival infrastructure, and host a culminating exhibition at AIC's First Voice Gallery, "Urban Sovereignty at the Center."[9] The project deliberately reoriented received narratives about archives and "heritage," for we were not seeking to rescue archival materials from loss. The AIC already holds and curates the stories of its community; if anything, it is non-Native people in Chicago who do not know—or refuse to know—the history of Native American peoples in Chicago and elsewhere. Moreover, unlike colonial archives, the AIC does not hold materials that have been taken from the community but rather materials created by and for the community. Instead of working against narratives of fragility and loss, the group sought to establish ways for AIC members to access archival materials more easily, to bring community members' knowledge of the center's histories together with photographs in the archive, and to create spaces for sharing some of those materials with broader publics when appropriate.

In addition to revising narratives of archival loss, the project made me —as one of the non-Native members of the grant—reconsider my own conceptions of archives and my understanding of the archival institutions where I was conducting the research for this book. Working with AIC staff and the project interns taught me that archives are physical places and collections, and they are sets of relationships. In the case of the AIC's archive, those relations extended to the group members, the interns, the people in the photographs we were digitizing, Native American organizations and Native homelands, and finally, the city of Chicago. One of my roles was to learn how to be a good participant in those relationships, whether that meant trying to redirect financial and social capital from the university to the AIC or assisting in discussions about the digital archive. Being a good participant also meant taking up the responsibility to challenge my own assumptions about what is useful or which materials have significance to community members (an ongoing process, to be sure). These lessons bear as well on my scholarship in early American studies, which might appear to some readers to be far afield from a collaborative project formed around a contemporary community archive. But if scholars take seriously the fact that colonial archives exist on Native homelands and, due to Indigenous writers' and tribal members' own actions, in relation to Native communities, we also need to see that those relations entail responsibilities for non-Native scholars working in and with national archives and community archives alike.

I conclude with a final story about archival interventions in Chicago, an intervention that addressed the legacies of collecting at the Field Museum. From November 2016 to January 2019, the Field hosted an exhibition by the artist Chis Pappan (Kaw/Osage, Lakota) that invited viewers to see the museum's displays differently. Preceding a wholesale renovation of the Native American Hall that began in 2018, *Drawing on Tradition: Kanza Artist Chris Pappan* peopled the hall of what Power calls "dead Indians" with images of Native people who are located in tribal homelands and particular moments, including the present.[10] The exhibition features Pappan's drawings of Indigenous people who are often juxtaposed against historic maps or ledger paper, a contemporary continuation of nineteenth-century ledger art (drawings or paintings on repurposed ledger or account book paper). A stand-alone case featuring Vans shoes hand-painted with two portraits, of Osage Chief Bacon Rind and Kanza Chief Washunga, required visitors to alter their routes through the hall and thus to encounter the older cases from new directions and in different contexts. Pappan placed transparent overlays on the glass cases erected in the 1950s, the same cases that the girl and her mother visit in Power's story. In one overlay, Indigenous people holding umbrellas look into a case containing a diorama of tiny tipis representing a "Plains Indian Village." Pappan created this and other overlays by working from the Field's collections of ledger art, in this way recontextualizing the museum's own collections to imagine Indigenous audiences looking at, not out of, its exhibits.[11]

These overlays also intervened in viewers' interactions with the "museum Indians" behind glass. One overlay on a display case features a map of Indian Territory, thus referencing Indian Removal and the ongoing attempts by the U.S. to limit Native sovereignty and suggesting that the faceless mannikins behind glass must be read not as representative types but as objects produced by ongoing processes of conquest and dispossession. Pappan's drawings of contemporary Native people juxtaposed with the museum's static mannikins question the displays' claims of Indigenous vanishing and activate temporal categories that do not end in the nineteenth century, the only date identified within the cases. And on the case containing the "little buffalo," Pappan installs an overlay featuring a buffalo running against a background of a map. The overlay places the buffalo into motion, locating it outside the city and imagining it free from the museum. These artistic interventions are furthered by the work of Indigenous staff and curators, as well as allies, at the museum, who are reconnecting Native American community members with their tribal nations' belongings at the Field and taking part in the renovation of the Native American Hall.

Pappan's installation, like Power's story and the AIC's archives, demonstrates the wide-ranging afterlives for Indigenous compilations: stories, art, photographs, and archival projects remix and recontextualize colonial archives and museums to foster a critical perspective on those institutions and to create artistic and archival objects that center Indigenous perspectives, experiences, and knowledge. Like these recent interventions, the Indigenous compilations this book has brought together tell a story of making and continuing relations among texts and with people. These relations are made, as the chapters gathered here have shown, as people make and use compilations, as compilations travel across colonial boundaries and throughout Native communities, and as their makers send them into or remove them from archival and anthropological collections. Indigenous compilation is a practice of making and using texts that create relations among texts and institutions, among people, and with place. And Indigenous compilations' afterlives call for research methodologies that acknowledge, build on, and sit in relation to compilations' capacious archives, textual forms and circulations, their seemingly quotidian uses, and the critical perspectives they foster.

NOTES

Introduction

1. William Whipple Warren, *History of the Ojibways, Based upon Traditions and Oral Statements* (St. Paul: Minnesota Historical Society, 1885), 298.

2. Warren, *History,* 298.

3. Warren, *History,* 57 and 77.

4. Warren, *History,* 89, 173, and 62.

5. Warren, *History,* 24.

6. John Ridge, "Strictures on 'The Report of the Joint Committee on the State of the Republic,' in the Legislature of Georgia, on the subject of the Cherokee Lands; purporting to prove the absolute jurisdictional right of the said state to the same," *Cherokee Phoenix,* March 13, 1828, 2; Charlotte Johnston, "Journal," George Johnston Papers, Judge Joseph H. Steere Room, Bayliss Public Library, Sault Ste. Marie, MI; William Apess, *Indian Nullification of the Unconstitutional Laws of Massachusetts Relative to the Marshpee Tribe: or, The Pretended Riot Explained* (Boston: Jonathan Howe, 1835), 48.

7. I'm indebted in my thinking about compilations as literary technologies of relation to Dahlia Porter's work on the poetics of inventory and on reanimation and vitality in botanical taxonomies. See Dahlia Porter, "Specimen Poetics: Botany, Reanimation, and the Romantic Collection," *Representations* 139 (Summer 2017): 60 –94. See

also James Delbourgo's and Staffan Müller-Wille's discussion of lists as "conceptual propinquity engines" in their "Introduction: Listmania," *Isis* 103, no. 4 (2012): 711.

8. On this etymology, see "compile, v." OED Online. Oxford University Press, June 2020 (accessed July 13, 2020), especially I.1–2 and II.5–6. The French "compiler" refers to acts of putting together or collecting; the Latin *compilāre* references plundering and stealing.

9. In my focus on "doing," I follow Ojibwe literary scholar Scott Richard Lyons, who argues for scholars to complicate "conceptions of Indians as 'things'" and to embrace a "deeper analysis of Indians as human beings who *do* things—things like asserting identity, defining identity, contesting identity, and so forth—under given historical conditions." Lyons, *X-Marks: Native Signatures of Assent* (Minneapolis: University of Minnesota Press, 2010), 59. See also the Osage literary scholar Robert Warrior's discussion of experience. Warrior, *The People and the Word: Reading Native Nonfiction* (Minneapolis: University of Minnesota Press, 2005), xxix.

10. Contemporary editions of early Native literatures have been essential to shifting these conversations, including LaVonne Ruoff Brown's editions of George Copway and Charles Eastman (among many others at University of Nebraska Press), Barry O'Connell's edition of William Apess's writing, Joanna Brooks's edition of Samson Occom's collected writing, Laura Murray's edition of Joseph Johnson's journals, Theresa Gaul's editions of the work of Cherokee writers Elias Boudinot and Catherine Brown, Robert Dale Parker's edition of Jane Johnston Schoolcraft's poetry, and collections of Native writing from the Northeast edited by Kristina Bross and Hilary Wyss and by Siobhan Senier. For scholarly works, see in chronological order, Hilary E. Wyss, *Writing Indians: Literacy, Christianity, and Native Community in Early America* (Amherst: University of Massachusetts Press, 2000); Robert Warrior, *People and the Word;* Daniel Heath Justice, *Our Fire Survives the Storm: A Cherokee Literary History* (Minneapolis: University of Minnesota Press, 2006); Lisa Brooks, *The Common Pot: The Recovery of Native Space in the Northeast* (Minneapolis: University of Minnesota Press, 2008); Phillip H. Round, *Removable Type: Histories of the Book in Indian Country, 1663–1880* (Chapel Hill: University of North Carolina Press, 2010); Drew Lopenzina, *Red Ink: Native Americans Picking Up the Pen in the Colonial Period* (Albany: SUNY Press, 2012); Birgit Brander Rasmussen, *Queequeg's Coffin: Indigenous Literacies and Early American Literature* (Durham: Duke University Press, 2012); Wyss, *English Letters and Indian Literacies: Reading, Writing, and New England Missionary Schools, 1750–1830* (Philadelphia: University of Pennsylvania Press, 2012); Matt Cohen and Jeffrey Glover, eds., *Colonial Mediascapes: Sensory Worlds of the Early Americas* (Lincoln: University of Nebraska Press, 2014); Kiara M. Vigil, *Indigenous Intellectuals: Sovereignty, Citizenship, and the American Imagination, 1880–1930* (New York: Oxford University Press, 2015); Caroline Wigginton, *In the Neighborhood: Women's Publication in Early America* (Amherst: University of Massachusetts Press, 2016), chap. 1; Adam Spry, *Our War Paint Is Writers' Ink: Anishinaabe Literary Transnationalism* (Albany:

SUNY Press, 2018); Angela Calcaterra, *Literary Indians: Aesthetics and Encounter in American Literature to 1920* (Chapel Hill: University of North Carolina Press, 2018); Frank Kelderman, *Authorized Agents: Publication and Diplomacy in the Era of Indian Removal* (Albany: SUNY Press, 2019). See also several recently completed dissertations in early Native studies: Alanna Hickey, "The Forms of National Belonging: The Politics of Nineteenth-Century Native American Poetry" (PhD diss., Northwestern University, 2016); Daniel M. Radus, "Writing Native Pasts in the Nineteenth Century" (PhD diss., Cornell University, 2017); Marie Balsley Taylor, "Diplomatic Conversions: Recovering Sachem Influence in Seventeenth-Century New England Missionary Writings" (PhD diss., Purdue University, 2017); and Amy Gore, "Material Matters: Paratextual Bodies in Nineteenth-Century Indigenous Book History" (PhD diss., University of New Mexico, 2019).

11. James Rosier, *A True Relation of the most prosperous voyage made this present yeere 1605, by Captaine George Waymouth, in the discovery of the land of Virginia*, in *The English New England Voyages, 1602–1608* (London, 1605), ed. David B. Quinn and Alison M. Quinn (London: Hakluyt Society 1983), 250–311; Experience Mayhew, *Indian Converts: Or, Some Account of the Lives and Dying Speeches of a considerable Number of the Christianized Indians of Martha's Vineyard, in New-England* (London: Samuel Gerrish, 1727), x; for some of the Dawes Rolls, see the online records at the National Archives, https://www.archives.gov/research/native-americans/dawes/tutorial/intro.html; and for examples of Carlisle Indian School student records written on blank forms, see http://carlisleindian.dickinson.edu/student-files.

12. Henry Rowe Schoolcraft, *Historical and Statistical Information Respecting the History, Condition, and Prospects of the Indian Tribes of the United States* (Philadelphia: Lippincott, Grambo, 1851), vol. 1, 344. Six volumes of *Historical and Statistical Information* were published between 1851 and 1857.

13. For two such studies, see Sean Harvey, *Native Tongues: Colonialism and Race from Encounter to the Reservation* (Cambridge: Harvard University Press, 2015) and Sarah Rivett, *Unscripted Americas: Indigenous Languages and the Origins of a Literary Nation* (Oxford: Oxford University Press, 2017).

14. Laura J. Murray, "Vocabularies of Native American Languages: A Literary and Historical Approach to an Elusive Genre," *American Quarterly* 53, no. 4 (2001): 590–623 (quotations on 594 and 613).

15. See Roger Chartier, who writes, "Reading is not uniquely an abstract operation of the intellect: it brings the body into play, it is inscribed in a space and a relationship with oneself or with others." Chartier, *The Order of Books: Readers, Authors, and Libraries in Europe between the 14th and 18th Centuries* (Stanford: Stanford University Press, 1994), 8. Building on Chartier's work, historians of the book have advanced methods for studying "book use." For example, Leah Price examines nineteenth-century Victorian representations of books and their circulation with particular attention to the "relations

among three operations: reading (doing something with the words), handling (doing something with the object), and circulating (doing something to, or with, other persons by means of the book)." See Leah Price, *How to Do Things with Books in Victorian England* (Princeton: Princeton University Press, 2012), 5. See also Michael C. Cohen, *The Social Lives of Poems in Nineteenth-Century America* (Philadelphia: University of Pennsylvania Press, 2015); William H. Sherman, *Used Books: Marking Readers in Renaissance England* (Philadelphia: University of Pennsylvania Press, 2008), esp. the introduction; and Wendy Wall, *Recipes for Thought: Knowledge and Taste in the Early Modern English Kitchen* (Philadelphia: University of Pennsylvania Press, 2016).

In addition to being texts that generated readings in the eighteenth and nineteenth centuries, Indigenous compilations require multiple modes of scholarly reading in order to grasp the full scope of their lives, interlocutors, and meanings, including close reading (reading the page), bibliographic reading (tracing the origins for assembled materials), and relational reading (following compilation's circulations and the relations they make). Compilations therefore complicate recent scholarly debates about reading, from distant reading's use of computational methods to track textual networks to surface reading's critique of suspicion. Relying solely on one of these forms of reading will produce misreadings of compilations, missing, for example, how an excerpted text does not necessarily reflect the author's own viewpoint (a point I take up in more detail in chapter 2). On surface reading, see Stephen Best and Sharon Marcus, "Surface Reading: An Introduction," *Representations* 108, no. 1 (2009): 1–21; on computational methods, see Franco Moretti, *Distant Reading* (London: Verso, 2013).

16. Jeffrey Todd Knight, *Bound to Read: Compilations, Collections, and the Making of Renaissance Literature* (Philadelphia: University of Pennsylvania Press, 2013) and Ellen Gruber Garvey, *Writing with Scissors: American Scrapbooks from the Civil War to the Harlem Renaissance* (New York: Oxford University Press, 2013). On compilations as a form of early modern information management, see also Ann M. Blair, *Too Much to Know: Managing Scholarly Information before the Modern Age* (New Haven: Yale University Press, 2011).

17. Lisa Gitelman, *Paper Knowledge: Toward a Media History of Documents* (Durham: Duke University Press, 2014), 22. On blanks, see also Peter Stallybrass, "Little Jobs: Broadsides and the Printing Revolution," in *Agent of Change: Print Culture Studies after Elizabeth L. Eisenstein,* ed. Sabrina Alcorn Baron, Eric N. Lindquist, Eleanor F. Shevlin (Amherst: University of Massachusetts Press, 2008): 315–41. Matthew P. Brown has countered Gitelman's argument that blanks (and other documentary forms) lack "readerly subjectivities" (Gitelman, *Paper Knowledge,* 31). Brown resists Gitelman's (and other scholars') move to contrast "'function' and 'use' to 'reading,'" and argues instead that documentary forms can reflect the "norms of personhood." He finds a "theater of literacy structured by the blank artifact" that offers a window into the various forms personhood might take. See Brown, "Blanks: Data, Method, and the British American Print Shop," *American Literary History* 29, no. 2 (2017): 229. There is valuable

work to be done in considering the ways that Native "subjectivities"—to use Brown's term—might be present within colonial paperwork. Laura J. Murray's work is a crucial starting point for such studies; see Murray, "Vocabularies of Native American Languages." I've also briefly considered these questions in "Encounters, Objects, and Commodity Lists in Early English Travel Narratives," *Studies in Travel Writing* 17, no. 3 (2013): 264–80.

18. Stallybrass, "Little Jobs," 340, and Gitelman, *Paper Knowledge,* 11 and chap. 1.

19. Gitelman, *Paper Knowledge,* 31.

20. Michel de Certeau, *The Practice of Everyday Life* (Berkeley: University of California Press, 2011), 35. Certeau describes these acts of making do as reading, using, poaching, and walking. They operate within received structures, but, he writes, "although they remain subordinated to the prescribed syntactical forms (temporal modes of schedules, paradigmatic orders of spaces, etc.), the trajectories trace out the ruses of other interests and desires that are neither determined nor captured by the systems in which they develop" (xviii). He takes as a key example of these tactics the ways that Indigenous people "made something else" out of the order colonists imposed on them (32). For scholars who have applied Certeau's work in Indigenous and African American Studies contexts, respectively, see Nicole Tonkovich, *The Allotment Plot: Alice C. Fletcher, E. Jane Gay, and Nez Perce Survivance* (Lincoln: University of Nebraska Press, 2012), esp. chap. 10, and Saidiya V. Hartman, *Scenes of Subjection: Terror, Slavery, and Self-Making in Nineteenth-Century America* (New York: Oxford University Press, 1997), 11.

21. Karen A. Weyler, *Empowering Words: Outsiders and Authorship in Early America* (Athens: University of Georgia Press, 2013), 16. Weyler's study details how people with varying levels of literacy participated in print culture; I expand her focus on literacy and print by considering manuscript and other inscriptive forms. I'm grateful to Michael Kelly and Kiara Vigil for a discussion of functional literacy and Native books at a summer 2018 Rare Book School class.

22. Thanks to Wendy Wall for a comment that helped distill these functions.

23. On colonists' descriptions of Native book use as signs not of illiteracy but of Indigenous peoples' familiarity with colonists' "literacy practices," see Andrew Newman, *Allegories of Encounter: Colonial Literacy and Indian Captives* (Chapel Hill: University of North Carolina Press, 2019). On ministers' desires for "readerly Indians," who would passively imbibe texts and enact missionary fantasies of docile converts, see Wyss, *English Letters,* esp. the introduction and chap. 1. On devotional reading, see Round, *Removable Type,* chap. 2. Other early American studies scholars have approached questions of literacy by defining publication as performative and embodied, showing how "publication events" and "relational publication" constituted complex systems of communication in which Native people and colonists exchanged information. Those publication events ultimately shaped the material form and content of works authored by colonists. See Matt Cohen, *The Networked Wilderness: Communicating in Early New England*

(Minneapolis: University of Minnesota Press, 2010) (publication events) and Caroline Wigginton, *In the Neighborhood* (relational publication).

24. Craig Womack, *Red on Red: Native American Literary Separatism* (Minneapolis: University of Minnesota Press, 1999), 16. On Native stories as invoking actions that include and exceed reading, see also Julie Cruikshank, "Oral History, Narrative Strategies, and Native American Historiography: Perspectives from the Yukon Territory, Canada," in *Clearing a Path: Theorizing the Past in Native American Studies,* ed. Nancy Shoemaker (New York: Routledge, 2002): 3–28 (esp. 3 and 11) and Phillip H. Round, "Early Native Literature as Social Practice," in *The Oxford Handbook of Native American Literature,* ed. James H. Cox and Daniel Heath Justice (Oxford: Oxford University Press, 2014), 65–80.

25. Bradin Cormack and Carla Mazzio, *Book Use, Book Theory: 1500–1700* (Chicago: University of Chicago Press, 2005), 4.

26. Lindsay diCuirci, *Colonial Revivals: The Nineteenth-Century Lives of Early American Books* (Philadelphia: University of Pennsylvania Press, 2019), 3.

27. Jacques Derrida, "Archive Fever: A Freudian Impression," *Diacritics* 25, no. 2 (1995): 9–63.

28. For a few examples, see Stephen Long, *Account of An Expedition from Pittsburgh to the Rocky Mountains, Performed in the Years 1819 and '20, by order of the Hon. J. C. Calhoun, Sec'y of War, under the command of Major Stephen H. Long, from the Notes of Major Long, Mr. T. Say, and other Gentlemen of the Exploration Party. Compiled by Edwin James, Botanist and Geologist for the Expedition,* vol. 1 (Philadelphia, 1823), 202; Henry R. Schoolcraft, *Personal Memoirs of a Residence of Thirty Years with the Indian Tribes on the American Frontiers* (Philadelphia, 1851), 133.

29. Ellen Cushman, "Wampum, Sequoyan, and Story: Decolonizing the Digital Archive," *College English* 76, no. 2 (2013): 119. See also Malea Powell, "Dreaming Charles Eastman: Cultural Memory, Autobiography, and Geography in Indigenous Rhetorical Histories," in *Beyond the Archives: Research as a Lived Process,* ed. Gesa E. Kirsch and Liz Rohan (Carbondale: Southern Illinois University Press, 2008), 115–27; Timothy B. Powell, William Weems, and Freeman Owle, "Native/American Digital Storytelling: Situating the Cherokee Oral Tradition within American Literary History," *Literature Compass* 4, no. 1 (2007): 1–23; and Ivy Schweitzer and Gordon Henry, eds., *Afterlives of Indigenous Archives: Essays in Honor of the* Occom Circle (Hanover: Dartmouth College Press, 2019). On the ways that the settler archive perpetuates the "righteous fiction of the nation-state and its fundamental desire to disavow the existence and rights of indigenous peoples and communities," see Melissa Adams-Campbell, Ashley Glassburn Falzetti, and Courtney Rivard, "Introduction: Indigeneity and the Work of Settler Archives," *Settler Colonial Studies* 5, no. 2 (2015): 109–16 (quotation on 110). My analysis of colonial archives is also indebted to scholars of slavery, especially Marisa Fuentes's call to "read . . . along the bias grain" in ways that make visible the violence mediating rep-

resentations of enslaved people and Saidiya Hartman's use of the archive to produce counternarratives that compromise "the status of the event." Marisa Fuentes, *Dispossessed Lives: Enslaved Women, Violence, and the Archive* (Philadelphia: University of Pennsylvania Press, 2016), "bias grain" quotation on 143; Saidiya V. Hartman, "Venus in Two Acts," *Small Axe* 12, no. 2 (2008): 1–14, "status of the event" quotation on 12. See also Jennifer L. Morgan, "Archives and Histories of Racial Capitalism: An Afterword," *Social Text* 33, no. 4 (2018): 153–61; Britt Rusert, "Disappointment in the Archives of Black Freedom," *Social Text* 33, no. 4 (2018): 19–33; Stephanie E. Smallwood, *Saltwater Slavery: A Middle Passage from Africa to American Diaspora* (Cambridge: Harvard University Press, 2008); Deborah A. Thomas, "Caribbean Studies, Archive Building, and the Problem of Violence," *Small Axe* 17, no. 2 (2013): 27–42; and Dana A. Williams and Marissa K. López, "More Than a Fever: Toward a Theory of the Ethnic Archive," *PMLA* 127, no. 2 (2012): 357–59. On reading along the grain, see Ann Laura Stoler, *Along the Archival Grain: Epistemic Anxieties and Colonial Common Sense* (Princeton: Princeton University Press, 2010).

30. Audra Simpson, *Mohawk Interruptus: Political Life across the Borders of Settler States* (Durham: Duke University Press, 2014), 102. Simpson examines the relations between land dispossession and knowledge production in the making of anthropology, particularly "Iroquois Studies." She argues that scholarship "on the Iroquois is a realization of early anthropological desire—a desire for order, for purity, for fixity, and for cultural perfection that at once imagined an imminent disappearance immediately after or just within actual land dispossession." Simpson, *Mohawk Interruptus*, 70. Likewise, Jodi A. Byrd has shown how critical theory remains indebted to "traces of 'Indianness' which are vitally important to understanding how power and domination have been articulated and practiced by empire, and yet because they are traces, they have often remained deactivated as a point of critical inquiry as theory has transited across disciplines and schools." Byrd, *The Transit of Empire: Indigenous Critiques of Colonialism* (Minneapolis: University of Minnesota Press, 2011), xvii–xviii.

31. See Thomas Jefferson, *Notes on the State of Virginia*, ed. Frank Shuffelton (New York: Penguin, 1999), 107–8.

32. Kevin Bruyneel, *The Third Space of Sovereignty: The Postcolonial Politics of U.S.-Indigenous Relations* (Minneapolis: University of Minnesota Press, 2007), 10. Bruyneel shows that the U.S. imposed "political boundaries" on Native nations, including the "spatial boundaries around territory and legal and political institutions and the temporal boundaries around the narratives of economic and political development, cultural progress, and modernity." Bruyneel, *Third Space*, xiii.

33. Simpson, *Mohawk Interruptus*, 102.

34. Warrior, *The People and the Word*, 181.

35. Arjun Appadurai observes that things accrue meanings through circulation and use, writing, "We have to follow the things themselves, for their meanings are

inscribed in their forms, their uses, their trajectories." See Arjun Appadurai, "Introduction: Commodities and the Politics of Value," in *The Social Life of Things,* ed. Arjun Appadurai (Cambridge: Cambridge University Press, 1986), 3–63 (quotation on 5, and see also 16–17, 28–29).

36. Here I follow Ellen Cushman's work on decolonizing archives, which argues that the stories books and their journeys tell are incomplete without the stories of the people who sent them into motion and used them. See Ellen Cushman, "Wampum, Sequoyan, and Story."

37. Bruyneel, *Third Space,* 221.

38. Bruyneel, *Third Space,* xvii.

39. Lisa Brooks, "Turning the Looking Glass on King Philip's War: Locating American Literature in Native Space," *American Literary History* 25, no. 4 (2013): 729. Brooks draws the formulation of foreign/familiar from Yael Ben-Zvi's "Ethnography and the Production of Foreignness in Indian Captivity Narratives," *American Indian Quarterly* 32, no. 1 (2008): 5–32.

40. On decolonizing museums, see Amy Lonetree, *Decolonizing Museums: Representing Native America in National and Tribal Museums* (Chapel Hill: University of North Carolina Press, 2012), and on digital repatriation, see Kimberly Christen, "Opening Archives: Respectful Repatriation," *American Archivist* 74 (2011): 185–210; Kim Christen and Jane Anderson, "Toward Slow Archives," *Archival Science* 19 (2019): 87–116; and Jane Anderson and James Eric Francis, Sr., "Decolonial Futures of Sharing: 'Protecting Our Voice,' Intellectual Property and Penobscot Language Materials," in *Indigenous Languages and the Promise of Archives,* ed. Adrianna Link, Abigail Shelton, and Patrick Spero (Nebraska: University of Nebraska Press, 2021). Many librarians and archivists have been leaders in the process of considering archives' colonial histories and legacies by thinking critically about questions of access, classification, and ownership within collections. The 2007 publication of "Protocols for Native American Archival Materials" has been crucial to this work (see http://www2.nau.edu/libnap-p/index.html). For just a few of many archives seeking to build relations with Native communities and with Native American collections, see the American Philosophical Society's Center for Native American and Indigenous Research and its digital repatriation projects (founded by Timothy Powell and carried on, as of this writing, by Brian Carpenter and Alyssa Mt. Pleasant); Amherst College Special Collections, Digital Atlas of Native American Intellectual Traditions (as of this writing, headed up by Michael Kelly); and the Newberry Library's D'Arcy McNickle Center for American Indian and Indigenous Studies (directed by Rose Miron as of this writing) and the Newberry's Ayer Librarian for Native American and Indigenous Studies (as of this writing, Analú Maria López).

41. See, for example, the American Antiquarian Society's "Indigenous Cultures of Print in Early America" History of the Book seminar in 2013 (taught by Phillip

Round); the Rare Book School class at Amherst College Special Collections, "A History of Native American Books and Indigenous Sovereignty" in 2018 (taught by Michael Kelly and Kiara Vigil); and Newberry Library's long-standing, annual summer institute for graduate student members of the Newberry Consortium on American Indian and Indigenous Studies.

42. Margaret M. Bruchac, *Savage Kin: Indigenous Informants and American Anthropologists* (Tucson: University of Arizona Press, 2018) and Vigil, *Indigenous Intellectuals.*

43. Bruchac, *Savage Kin,* 17, and see Vigil's *Indigenous Intellectuals,* esp. 22.

Chapter One. Recipe

1. Samson Occom, "Autobiographical Narrative, Second Draft (September 17, 1768)," *The Collected Writings of Samson Occom, Mohegan: Leadership and Literature in Eighteenth-Century America,* ed. Joanna Brooks (Oxford: Oxford University Press, 2006), 53. On the relations of Occom and other Mohegans to northeastern Native communities, including Montaukett people, see Melissa Tantaquidgeon Zobel, *The Lasting of the Mohegans* (Mohegan, CT: Little People Publications, 1995) and Lisa Brooks, *The Common Pot: The Recovery of Native Space in the Northeast* (Minneapolis: University of Minnesota Press, 2008), chap. 2.

2. All citations in this paragraph are from Occom, "Autobiographical Narrative," 56.

3. Scholars have read this scene as a moment of entry into the disciplinary functions of English literacy. Phillip H. Round argues that Occom " 'embodied' literacy by making the letters of the alphabet tactile, thus bringing Native bodies into play with the alphabet quite literally." See Phillip H. Round, *Removable Type: Histories of the Book in Indian Country, 1663–1880* (Chapel Hill: University of North Carolina Press, 2010), 57. On the arbitrary arrangement of the alphabet, see Patricia Crain, *The Story of A: The Alphabetization of America from* The New England Primer *to* The Scarlet Letter (Stanford: Stanford University Press, 2000), esp. chap. 2. For more on the intersections among colonialism, reading, and writing, see Ellen Cushman, *The Cherokee Syllabary: Writing the People's Persistence* (Norman: University of Oklahoma Press, 2011); E. Jennifer Monaghan, *Learning to Read and Write in Colonial America* (Amherst: University of Massachusetts Press, 2007), chaps. 2, 5, and 10; and Hilary E. Wyss, *English Letters and Indian Literacies: Reading, Writing, and New England Missionary Schools, 1750–1830* (Philadelphia: University of Pennsylvania Press, 2012), chap. 1.

4. Occom, "Herbs & Roots," New London County Historical Society, New London, CT, and "Samson Occom, herbal remedies and letter fragment," Rauner DC History, Rauner Library Special Collections, Dartmouth College Library, Hanover, NH. ("Sore eyes" is in the Rauner booklet.) Occom identifies the plants and the malady they are "good for" throughout the booklets.

While I've elsewhere called Occom's medicinal booklets an herbal, I revise that categorization here by arguing that they better fit the genre of the recipe book. Seventeenth- and eighteenth-century recipe collections, similar to Occom's booklets, featured "a title-page or declaration of ownership; recipes with titles separated from the main body of the text in some way; 'author' or donor names attached to some recipes; numbering (either page or entry or both); indexing or other information-retrieval apparatus." Michelle DiMeo and Sara Pennell, "Introduction," in *Reading and Writing Recipe Books, 1550–1800*, ed. Michelle DiMeo and Sara Pennell (Manchester: Manchester University Press, 2013), 9. By contrast, seventeenth- and eighteenth-century herbals are characterized by descriptions of plants that draw together classical, literary, and experiential knowledge. The short, second-person entries in Occom's "Herbs & Roots" do not offer an herbal's detailed descriptions and histories for plants; instead, like recipes, they record technical information for transforming plants into a medical concoction.

5. See Sara Pennell, "Perfecting Practice?: Women, Manuscript Recipes and Knowledge in Early Modern England," in *Early Modern Women's Manuscript Writing: Selected Papers from the Trinity/Trent Colloquium*, ed. Victoria E. Burke and Jonathan Gibson (Burlington, VT: Ashgate, 2004), 237–55 (quotation on 249), and Wendy Wall, *Recipes for Thought: Knowledge and Taste in the Early Modern English Kitchen* (Philadelphia: University of Pennsylvania Press, 2016).

6. On the place of Occom's autobiography in anthologies, see Robert Warrior, "Foreword," *The Collected Writings of Samson Occom, Mohegan: Literature and Leadership in Eighteenth-Century Native America*, ed. Joanna Brooks (New York: Oxford University Press, 2006), v, and Warrior, *Tribal Secrets: Recovering American Indian Intellectual Traditions* (Minneapolis: University of Minnesota Press, 1995), 3. On Occom's autobiography more generally, see also Jace Weaver, *That the People Might Live: Native American Literatures and Native American Community* (New York: Oxford University Press, 1997), 49–53, and Arnold Krupat, ed., *Native American Autobiography: An Anthology* (Madison: University of Wisconsin Press, 1994), 105–13.

7. Occom, "Samson Occom, herbal remedies and letter fragment," 1754–56, Rauner DC History, Rauner Library, Dartmouth College. Occom numbered recipes rather than pages.

8. Siobhan Senier, "'Traditionally, Disability Was Not Seen as Such': Writing and Healing in the Work of Mohegan Medicine People," *Journal of Literary & Cultural Disability Studies* 7, no. 2 (2013): 217. See also Siobhan Senier, "Commentary: Sovereignty and Sustainability in Mohegan Ethnobotanical Literature," *Journal of Ecocriticism* 6, no. 1 (Spring 2014): 1–15, and Jason Mancini, "Whose Medicine?: Observations on the Transformation of Native American Medicinal Practices in the Context of European-American Medical Theory, Religion, and Law," paper presented at the 3rd Mashantucket Pequot History Conference, September 20, 2002. I'm grateful to Jason

Mancini for sharing this paper with me and for a conversation about Occom and medical knowledge in 2018.

9. See Occom, *Collected Writings*, 44–47. The Dartmouth booklet is digitized and may be viewed at https://www.dartmouth.edu/occom/.

10. Brooks moves the first recipe in the NLCHS booklet ("Take some Weecup") to the middle of the list and moves Occom's citation of his payment to Ocus to the very end of the list, despite its location in the NLCHS booklet following the recipe beginning "Take some Speccle Alder." See "Herbs & Roots," *Collected Writings*, 45 and 47.

11. My analysis of these relations is informed by scholarship on Mohegan medicinal knowledge by Mohegan scholars and by non-Native scholars who have worked closely with Mohegan knowledge keepers. I rely on works published by Mohegan scholars, while recognizing that much medicinal knowledge remains unpublished and is not shared with individuals who are not tribal members. See Gladys Tantaquidgeon's *Folk Medicine of the Delaware and Related Algonkian Indians* (Harrisburg: Pennsylvania Historical and Museum Commission, 1972) and Melissa Jayne Fawcett's *Medicine Trail: The Life and Lessons of Gladys Tantaquidgeon* (Tucson: University of Arizona Press, 2000).

12. See Brooks, *Common Pot*, chap. 2, and Wyss, *English Letters*, chap. 1.

13. In the 1720s, the colony appropriated a vast portion of Mohegan hunting and planting lands—called the "sequestered lands"—by claiming that the Mohegans had never rightly possessed the lands in the first place and calling into question Uncas's legitimacy as a sachem after the Mohegans and Pequots split in the seventeenth century. Refusing to comply with the crown's 1705 confirmation of Mohegan rights to the sequestered lands, the colony continued to circulate narratives of illegitimacy and extinction about the Mohegans. See Amy E. Den Ouden, *Beyond Conquest: Native Peoples and the Struggle for History in New England* (Lincoln: University of Nebraska Press, 2005), 91–119. On Occom's work on the Mohegan land case, see Brooks, *Common Pot*, 90–105, and on the Mohegan Tribe's long-standing resistance to colonial incursions on their lands, see Melissa Jayne Fawcett, *The Lasting of the Mohegans: Part I, The Story of the Wolf People* (Uncasville, CT: Mohegan Tribe and Pequot Printing, 1995), 6–34.

14. Brooks, *Common Pot*, 87.

15. Brooks, *Common Pot*, 86.

16. Occom, December 6, 1743, in *Collected Writings*, 248.

17. As Lisa Brooks shows in *The Common Pot*, Occom's journals are a "rich source for understanding the relationships between people and places" (226), and she reads those journals as reflecting Occom's "keen understanding of geographic and social ties" (227). See Brooks's map of these journeys at https://lbrooks.people.amherst.edu/thecommonpot/map9.html.

18. Brooks, *Common Pot*, 226–27. See also Jace Weaver's analysis of Occom's writing in terms of communitism, or Native literature's "proactive commitment to Native community." Weaver, *That the People Might Live*, 43–45 (quotation on 43) and 49–53.

19. On Mohegan's centrality throughout Occom's life, see Brooks, *Common Pot,* 227.

20. Occom, September 7, 1745, in *Collected Writings,* 249. Occom spells the name of the community as "Brotherton"; I use the spelling now employed by the Brothertown Indian Nation, to indicate the nation's unbroken continuation. Thanks to Courtney Cottrell, PhD, Brothertown tribal historic preservation officer, for her consultation on this and other questions.

21. Occom, November 29, 1748, in *Collected Writings,* 251.

22. Occom, June 21, 1750, in *Collected Writings,* 251. Lisa Brooks observes that Occom often traveled with "his relations, including Robert Ashpo, Joseph Johnson, and his brother-in-law David Fowler, building and maintaining connections between coastal communities." Brooks, *Common Pot,* 86.

23. *Collected Writings,* 54, n. 34.

24. Occom, September 7, 1745, in *Collected Writings,* 249.

25. Occom, "4 October 1750," in *Collected Writings,* 252.

26. See Joanna Brooks, "'This Indian World': An Introduction to the Writings of Samson Occom," in *Collected Writings,* 12 and 252, n. 11, and Den Ouden, *Beyond Conquest,* 23.

27. On Montaukett history and resistance to colonial dispossession in particular, see John Strong, "How the Montauk Lost Their Land," in *History and Archaeology of the Montauk,* ed. Gaynell Stone, vol. 3, 2nd ed. (Suffolk County Archaeological Association, 1993), 77–120.

28. See John Strong, "Azariah Horton's Mission to the Montauk, 1741–44," in *History and Archaeology of the Montauk,* 193.

29. Trudi Lamb Richmond "'Put Your Ear to the Ground and Listen': The Wigwam Festival is the Green Corn Ceremony," *Artifacts* 17, no. 4 (1989), 25.

30. Solomon Williams to Samson Occom, September 7, 1749, the Occom Circle, https://collections.dartmouth.edu/occom/html/diplomatic/749507-diplomatic .html (accessed April 3, 2018).

31. Montaukett people experienced an epidemic in the early 1740s, as the journal of the minister Azariah Horton records. Reports of dysentery outbreaks on other parts of Long Island during this time suggest that Montaukett people may also have suffered from this disease. As Horton wrote in June 1842: "Many among them are now sick; and it has been a Time of distressing Sickness fr some Months past" (206). Horton wrote later that year that he hoped the illness would be a means of converting Montaukett people (202). See "Second Journal of Mr Azariah Horton, Missionary in the Province of New York, from 22nd November 1741, to 16th May 1742," in *History and Archaeology of the Montauk,* vol. 3, 2nd ed. (Suffolk County Archaeological Association, 1993), 198–205.

32. Occom, "Autobiographical Narrative," 55.

33. Occom, "Autobiographical Narrative," 55.

34. Occom, "Samson Occom, herbal remedies and letter fragment," 1754–56, Rauner DC History, Rauner Library, Dartmouth College.

35. Margaret M. Bruchac, *Savage Kin: Indigenous Informants and American Anthropologists* (Tucson: University of Arizona Press, 2018), 141. Bruchac discusses Speck's relations with Mohegan people and Tantaquidgeon's life in *Savage Kin,* chap. 6.

36. Frank G. Speck, "Medicine Practices of the Northeastern Algonquians," *Proceedings of the 19th International Congress of Americanists* (Washington, DC, 1917), 305.

37. Speck writes, "The uses of all these [plants] are determined from their appearance." Speck, "Medicine Practices of the Northeastern Algonquians," 305.

38. Gladys Tantaquidgeon, "Mohegan Medicinal Practices, Weather-Lore and Superstition," in *Annual Report of the Bureau of American Ethnology to the Secretary of the Smithsonian Institution, 1925–1926* (Washington, DC, 1926), 264 and 265.

39. Speck, "Medicine Practices of the Northeastern Algonquians," 306.

40. Lloyd G. Carr and Carlos Westey, "Surviving Folktales and Herbal Lore among the Shinnecock Indians of Long Island," *Journal of American Folklore* 58, no. 228 (April–June 1945): 114. See also Daniel E. Moerman, *Native American Ethnobotany* (Portland: Timber Press, 1998), 29.

41. Cottrell, email conversation with the author, September 9, 2020.

42. Tantaquidgeon notes that her relatives taught her "never to gather [plants] during the hot dog days of August and never to pick more than you need. . . . Plants were gathered and carefully dried in the sun. The sun adds to their potency. Some plants are actually poison when green. They are dried, ground with a stone or wooden mortar, and gathered." Fawcett, *Medicine Trail,* 39.

43. Occom, "Samson Occom, herbal remedies," Rauner DC History, Rauner Library, Dartmouth College.

44. Tantaquidgeon and Jayne G. Fawcett, "Symbolic Motifs on Painted Baskets of the Mohegan-Pequot," in *A Key into the Language of Woodsplint Baskets,* ed. Ann McMullen and Russell G. Handsman (Washington, CT: American Indian Archaeological Institute, 1987), 98.

45. Tantaquidgeon and Fawcett, "Symbolic Motifs," 99.

46. Tantaquidgeon and Fawcett, "Symbolic Motifs," 99.

47. Tantaquidgeon and Fawcett, "Symbolic Motifs," 99.

48. Stephanie Fitzgerald, "The Cultural Work of a Mohegan Painted Basket," in *Early Native Literacies in New England: A Documentary and Critical Anthology,* ed. Kristina Bross and Hilary E. Wyss (Amherst: University of Massachusetts Press, 2008), 53.

49. Occom likely provided medical care for people in the intervening years, but I focus here on the periods he documents in his journals.

50. See Occom's comments on his care for Montaukett peoples' bodies. Occom, "Autobiographical Narrative," 55. Jason Mancini suggests that Occom sought to "document" Montaukett medicinal knowledge, naming Occom as a first Native

"ethnographer." Mancini notes that Occom never explains why he creates "Herbs & Roots," but writes: "His purpose for recording this information is not known, but one wonders if he is documenting this information because Ocus represents the last of the Indian powwows in the region or an individual familiar with the practice. It is also possible he is compiling medical information in anticipation of a Brotherton migration that is only about 10 years away." Jason Mancini, "Whose Medicine?," 7.

51. Occom, "Temperance Hannabal," in *Collected Writings*, 44.

52. Occom, "Autobiographical Narrative," 55.

53. Occom, January 12, 1786, *Collected Writings*, 323.

54. Occom, September 11, 1785, *Collected Writings*, 298.

55. Occom, October 21, 1786, *Collected Writings*, 345.

56. Occom, May 30, 1787, *Collected Writings*, 365.

57. See Occom, August 30, 1786, *Collected Writings*, 340.

58. Occom, July 25, 1785, in *Collected Writings*, 296.

59. Occom, January 13, 1786, *Collected Writings*, 323.

60. Occom, August 27, 1786, *Collected Writings*, 340.

61. On Brothertown's founding and grant of Oneida lands, see Courtney Cottrell, "NAGPRA's Politics of Recognition: Repatriation Struggles of a Terminated Tribe," *American Indian Quarterly* 44, no. 1 (2020): 62–69, and Craig N. Cipolla, *Becoming Brothertown: Native American Ethnogenesis and Endurance in the Modern World* (Tucson: University of Arizona Press, 2017), esp. chaps. 1–4.

62. New Stockbridge was, like Brothertown, an intertribal community of Christian Native people who emigrated from Massachusetts to Oneida lands to avoid colonial dispossession. On New Stockbridge, see Lisa Brooks, *Common* Pot, 113–14; Joanna Brooks, "Introduction," 24–27, and Rachel Wheeler, *To Live upon Hope: Mohicans and Missionaries in the Eighteenth-Century Northeast* (Ithaca: Cornell University Press, 2008).

63. Occom, July 16, 1787, *Collected Writings*, 373.

64. Occom, November 7, 1785, *Collected Writings*, 308–9.

65. On Brothertown's body politic, see Drew Lopenzina, "'The Whole Wilderness Shall Blossom as the Rose': Samson Occom, Joseph Johnson, and the Question of Native Settlement on Cooper's Frontier," *American Quarterly* 58, no. 4 (2006): 1122–25. See also Brooks, *Common Pot*, 103, on this description of the body politic as "recalling the relationships between all of the nations from which they came."

66. Kathleen A. Brown-Pérez, "'A Reflection of Our National Character': Structurally and Culturally Violent Federal Policies and the Elusive Quest for Federal Acknowledgment," *Landscapes of Violence* 2, no. 1, Article 5 (2012): 3.

67. Recent scholarship has pointed to the preexisting, multigenerational alliances on which Brothertown and Stockbridge founders built. See Lisa Brooks, *Common Pot*, 86–105. In turn, I build on that prior scholarship by suggesting that medicinal treat-

ment contributed to making and strengthening the relationships among Native communities on which the new communities stood.

68. I'm indebted to Wendy Wall's study of early modern recipes for this point about recipes as sites of transmission. See Wall, *Recipes for Thought*, 6. See also Sara Pennell's argument that recipes must be mobile and in use to obtain "validity." Pennell, " 'Perfecting Practice,' " 238. And see DiMeo and Pennell, who note that "both the recipes and the texts they are collected in can be seen as unfixed formats that seem to defy classification as a genre; and where transmission, as well as practice, patterns (but does not standardize) received forms." DiMeo and Pennell, "Introduction," in *Reading and Writing Recipe Books*, 10.

69. In addition to the healing and conversion narratives in Occom's journals cited above, see the more recently digitized document, "Samson Occom's Account of the Death of a Christian Indian," Yale Indian Papers Project, https://yipp.yale.edu/annotated-transcription/digcoll4471497-0. Many thanks to Jason Mancini for pointing me to this source.

70. Bruchac, *Savage Kin*, 152.

71. Senier, " 'Traditionally, Disability Was Not Seen as Such,' " 215.

72. Occom was in England between 1765 and 1768. Occom mentions Shaw's aid in several letters written in the 1760s. See December 17, 1765, to Nathaniel Shaw, *Collected Writings*, 75, and 1767, to Mary Fowler Occom, *Collected Writings*, 80–81.

73. Occom to Nathaniel Shaw, December 8, 1767, New London County Historical Society. See Hilary E. Wyss on Mary Fowler Occom's correspondence with Wheelock in *English Letters*, chap. 1.

74. For this suggestion, I thank Tricia Royston, librarian at the New London County Historical Society in 2011.

75. James Constantine Pilling, *Bibliography of the Algonquian Languages* (Washington, DC: Government Printing Office, 1891), 163. Occom's copy of the Bible is now at the Clements Library at the University of Michigan.

76. On Occom's work to obtain financial and other support for Brothertown, see Occom, January 22, January 27, February 3, February 8, February 10, February 17, 1788, *Collected Writings*, 391–92. See also Christine DeLucia, "On the Trail of Samson Occum, *Ooskcoweeg: Up-Biblum God*, Cross-Cultural Marketplaces, and the Afterlives of Translated Print Culture," book chapter in progress. Many thanks to Christine for sharing this chapter and for conversations about Occom and the Bible. Thanks also to Courtney Cottrell and Megan Fulopp for discussing the Bible in email conversations between August 31 and September 9, 2020.

77. With the sale of the Bible to Shaw, Occom created what Phillip H. Round calls "Native books": the marginalia, translations, and gift giving with which Native people "reacted to [printed Bibles and devotional books] in a number of complex ways."

Round notes that Occom's "economic marginality made books a valuable source of capital when times were tough." See Round, *Removable Type*, 36.

78. Wheelock to Samson Occom, August 25, 1764, the Occom Circle, https://collections.dartmouth.edu/occom/html/diplomatic/764475-3-diplomatic.html (accessed April 10, 2018). As Hilary E. Wyss shows in her study of Native literacies and missionary schools, Wheelock sought to create dutiful, submissive students, or "Readerly Indians," who would consume their lessons and "cheerfully embrace their newfound English identity and live out missionary expectations to the letter." Wyss, *English Letters*, 39.

79. Wyss, *English Letters*, esp. the introduction.

80. Eleazar Wheelock to George Whitefield, July 4, 1761, the Occom Circle, https://collections.dartmouth.edu/occom/html/normalized/761404-normalized.html (accessed April 3, 2018).

81. Eleazar Wheelock to George Whitefield, July 4, 1761, the Occom Circle, https://collections.dartmouth.edu/occom/html/normalized/761404-normalized.html (accessed April 3, 2018).

82. Eleazar Wheelock to Samson Occom, August 25, 1764, the Occom Circle, https://collections.dartmouth.edu/occom/html/diplomatic/764475-3-diplomatic.html, accessed April 3, 2018. This letter is enclosed with a copy of Occom's commission to the Haudenosaunee.

83. As Phillip H. Round notes, mission societies supporting Occom also required journal writing to "provide evidence of how funds were being spent and what progress was being made." See Round, *Removable Type*, 65, and Wyss, *English Letters*, 43.

84. Occom Receipts, Expenses, 1761, Rauner DC History, Rauner Library, Dartmouth College. Also available on the Occom Circle, https://collections.dartmouth.edu/occom/html/diplomatic/761290-diplomatic.html, accessed April 3, 2018.

85. See "Editorial Statement," the Occom Circle, https://www.dartmouth.edu/~occom/editorial_statement/index.html, accessed April 26, 2018. Thanks to Peter Carini and Jay Satterfield for their help researching the provenance of Occom's papers. Rauner Library holds the "largest body of Occom's papers," according to librarian Laura Braunstein. See Braunstein, "And There Was a Large Number of People," *Digital Humanities in the Library: Challenges and Opportunities for Subject Specialists*, ed. Arianne Hartsell-Gundy, Laura Braunstein, Liorah Golomb (Association of College & Research Libraries, 2015), 229.

86. "New Hampshire. Dartmouth College," *Springfield Republican*, March 16, 1898, 10.

87. *Connecticut Mirror*, September 26, 1825, 3.

88. Lindsay diCuirci, *Colonial Revivals: The Nineteenth-Century Lives of Early American Books* (Philadelphia: University of Pennsylvania Press, 2019), 2.

89. DiCuirci, *Colonial Revivals*, 4.

90. Occom, "Account of the Montauk Indians, by Rev. Sampson Occum, A.D. 1761," in *Collections of the Massachusetts Historical Society*, ser. 1, vol. 10 (Boston, 1809): 106–11.

91. Likely the Boston Board of Commissioners of the Scotch Society for Propagating the Gospel, the same body that approved Occom's post teaching school at Montauk.

92. Eleazar Wheelock to Samson Occom, January 7, 1757, the Occom Circle, https://collections.dartmouth.edu/occom/html/diplomatic/757107-diplomatic .html (accessed April 3, 2018).

93. "Circular Letter of the Historical Society" (Boston: Belknap and Young, 1791), 3.

94. See "A Letter from Rev. John Devotion of Saybrook, to Rev. Dr. Stiles, inclosing Mr. Occum's Account of the Montauk Indians," *Collections*, vol. 10, 105–6.

95. Ezra Stiles, *Extracts from the Itineraries and Other Miscellanies of Ezra Stiles* (New Haven: Yale University Press, 1916), 144 and "The Number of the Nyhantic Tribe of Indians," *Collections*, vol. 10, 103. On Stiles's collecting and its relation to and effects on Indigenous communities, see Christine DeLucia, "Fugitive Collections in New England Indian Country: Indigenous Material Culture and Early American History Making at Ezra Stiles's Yale Museum," *William and Mary Quarterly*, 3rd ser., 75, no. 1 (January 2018): 109–50.

96. The Phillips Museum currently holds Devotion's letter to Stiles that enclosed Occom's "Account" but not Occom's manuscript of the "Account" itself. Thanks to Meaghan Wright, reference assistant at the Phillips Library, for a 2018 email conversation on these questions.

97. "Memoir of the Pequots," *Collections*, vol. 10, 101. Contemporary editions of Occom's writing and scholarship on his work have reproduced this generic categorization. For example, scholars have read Occom's description of Native spiritual practitioners for insight into historical Montaukett medical and religious practices, sometimes to the exclusion of the rest of the text. For selected examples, see William S. Simmons, *Spirit of the New England Tribes: Indian History and Folklore, 1620–1984* (Hanover: University Press of New England, 1986), 92; Frank Shuffelton, "Indian Devils and Pilgrim Fathers: Squanto, Hobomok, and the English Conception of Indian Religion," *New England Quarterly* 49, no. 1 (March 1976): 113; Joanna Brooks, "Prose," in *Collected Writings*, 42; and Kelly Wisecup, *Medical Encounters: Knowledge and Identity in Early American Literatures* (Amherst: University of Massachusetts Press, 2013), 1–2. One effect of these ethnographic readings is to gloss over the status of the "Account" as a reflection of the range of duties Occom performed and of his relations to Montaukett people.

98. "Circular Letter of the Historical Society" (Boston: Belknap and Young, 1791), 2.

99. "Circular Letter," 2.

100. "Circular Letter," 3.

101. Jean M. O'Brien, *Firsting and Lasting: Writing Indians out of Existence in New England* (Cambridge: Cambridge University Press, 2010), xii and xv.

102. John W. De Forest, *History of the Indians of Connecticut, from the Earliest Known Period to 1850. Published with the Sanction of the Connecticut Historical Society* (Hartford: WM Jas Hamersley, 1851), chap. 3.

103. William DeLoss Love, *Samson Occom and the Christian Indians of New England* (Boston: Pilgrim Press, 1899), v.

104. Love, *Samson Occom,* 1.

105. Pilling, *Bibliography of the Algonquian Languages,* 379 and 125.

106. Michael Kelly's indefatigable work to trace the many reprintings of the *Sermon* has shown just how popular it was, how widely it circulated, and how savvily Occom used northeastern print networks to reprint the *Sermon.* See Michael Kelly, "Samson Occom and the Uses of Bibliography," paper presented at Rare Book School Lectures, Charlottesville, VA. June 2016.

107. See Courtney Cottrell's scholarship on the ways western museums have claimed power to determine what an "Indigenous aesthetics" is and on more "Native-centric standards" that emphasize what Scott Richard Lyons calls "rhetorical sovereignty" for evaluating and interpreting works of art. Courtney Cottrell, "Indian Made: Museum Valuation of American Indian Identity through Aesthetics," *Transmotion* 5, no. 2 (2019): 23–44. For some examples of museums and archives that reject settler categories for Mohegan and Brothertown histories and writings, see the Tantaquidgeon Museum and the Mohegan Library and Archives. https://mohegan.biblionix.com/catalog/ and https://www.mohegan.nsn.us/explore/heritage/important-sites/tantaquidgeon-museum. And see the Occom Circle project, a digital repository of writing to, from, and about Occom at Dartmouth College. As project director Ivy Schweitzer notes of the Circle, one of its aims is to demote Wheelock and center Occom in a "'circle' of diverse associations and events named for Occom." For Schweitzer, the digital format makes it possible to trace Occom's exchanges and responses to ministers, acquaintances, and friends and the "communal work and collective identity that he specifically embraced as an activist and leader." Ivy Schweitzer, "Native Sovereignty and the Archive: Samson Occom and Digital Humanities," *Resources for American Literary Study* 38 (2015), quotations on 39 and 41, respectively.

108. Love, *Samson Occom,* vi.

109. Megan Fulopp, "A Journey with Occom," *Occom's Footsteps,* https://occomsfootsteps.wordpress.com/ (accessed July 20, 2020).

110. "About this Site," *The Life of the Brothertown Indians,* https://brothertowncitizen.com/about-this-site/(accessed July 20, 2020).

111. Megan Fulopp, "July 14, 2020: The Brothertown Indian Nation Celebrates First Annual Samson Occom Day," *The Life of the Brothertown Indians,* https://

brothertowncitizen.com/2020/07/13/july-14—2020-the-brothertown-indian-nation
-celebrates-first-annual-samson-occom-day/(accessed July 20, 2020).

112. Melissa Tantaquidgeon Zobel, *Oracles* (Albuquerque: University of New Mexico Press, 2004), 51.

113. Zobel, *Oracles,* 20.

114. Zobel, *Oracles,* 97.

Interlude: William Apess's Bright Gleams

1. William Apess, *Indian Nullification of the Unconstitutional Laws of Massachusetts Relative to the Marshpee Tribe: or, The Pretended Riot Explained* (Boston: Jonathan Howe, 1835), 13, 14, and 23.

2. Apess, *Indian Nullification,* 77 and 78.

3. Apess, *Indian Nullification,* 48.

4. Lisa Brooks, *The Common Pot: The Recovery of Native Space in the Northeast* (Minneapolis, University of Minnesota Press, 2008), 163.

5. Apess, *Indian Nullification,* 89.

6. Apess, *Indian Nullification,* 61.

7. William Apess, *A Son of the Forest: The Experience of William Apes, a Native of the Forest. Comprising a Notice of the Pequod Tribe of Indians. Written by Himself* (New York, 1829), 125.

8. Apess, *Son of the Forest,* 121.

9. Apess, *Son of the Forest,* 153.

Chapter Two. Extract

1. As William G. McLoughlin points out, this treaty was signed by only eight Creek leaders; it led to leader William McIntosh's execution on the grounds that he had sold the land for his personal gain. See William G. McLoughlin, *Cherokee Renascence in the New Republic* (Princeton: Princeton University Press, 1986), 372–73. On Cherokee views of the Creek case, see Julie L. Reed, *Serving the Nation: Cherokee Sovereignty and Social Welfare, 1800–1907* (Norman: University of Oklahoma, 2016), 66–67.

2. Gallatin to McKenney, March 4, 1826, Papers of Albert Gallatin, New-York Historical Society, roll 36, frames 221–23.

3. Payne published some of his research in an article, "Ancient Cherokee Traditions and Religious Rites," that appeared in *American Quarterly Register and Magazine* (December 1849): 444–50. On Payne's collaboration with Butrick, see William L. Anderson, Jane L. Brown, and Anne F. Rogers, "Introduction," *The Payne-Butrick Papers,* vols. 1–3 (Lincoln: University of Nebraska Press, 2010), xiii–xxiii.

4. See William C. Sturtevant, "John Ridge on Cherokee Civilization in 1826," *Journal of Cherokee Studies* 6 (1981): 90, n. 8. Sturtevant placed in brackets what he

determined to be "significant variations appearing in the Newberry draft," meaning that he indicates where the draft letter departs from the sent one, but he does not indicate which sentences are unique to the sent letter. This may lead him to argue that "Ridge followed rather closely the instructions that Gallatin had transmitted to him" (80), a conclusion from which I depart. See also Theda Perdue and Michael D. Green, eds. *The Cherokee Removal: A Brief History with Documents* (New York: Bedford/ St. Martin's, 1995), 33.

5. On the Treaty of New Echota, Cherokee Removal, and the assassinations of the Ridges and Boudinot, see Daniel Heath Justice, *Our Fire Survives the Storm: A Cherokee Literary History* (Minneapolis: University of Minnesota Press, 2006), chap. 2, esp. 81–88; Joshua B. Nelson, *Progressive Traditions: Identity in Cherokee Literature and Culture* (Norman: University of Oklahoma Press, 2014), chap. 5; and Reed, *Serving the Nation,* chap. 2, esp. 72–80.

6. On the progressive vs. traditional binary, see Nelson, *Progressive Traditions.* On the limiting effects of Cherokee peoples' adoption of U.S. political structures and vocabulary of nationhood, see Mark Rifkin, *Manifesting America: The Imperial Construction of U.S. National Space* (New York: Oxford University Press, 2009), chap. 1, esp. 49–54.

7. Tiya Miles, *The House on Diamond Hill: A Cherokee Plantation Story* (Durham: University of North Carolina Press, 2010), 20. See also Rifkin, *Manifesting America,* 73.

8. Julie Reed characterizes these changes as moving from a "nation made up of autonomous towns governed by rules of kinship and connected together through seven matrilineal clans to a constitutional republic comprised of citizens operating under a constitution that administered pensions from a national treasury." She shows that these changes were part of ongoing efforts to provide "social protections" for Cherokee people, much as the clan system had for centuries, and examines the choices Cherokee people made about how to use or interact with such protections. See Reed, *Serving the Nation,* 26 and chap. 2, esp. pages 60–84. On the myriad ways that Cherokee people decided how to respond to and resist U.S. pressures to assimilate and remove, see Kirby Brown, *Stoking the Fire: Nationhood in Cherokee Writing, 1907–1970* (Norman: University of Oklahoma Press, 2018); Daniel Heath Justice, *Our Fire,* chaps. 2–3; and Nelson, *Progressive Traditions,* chaps. 4–5. See also Tiya Miles's discussion of the links between the civilization policy and U.S. protection of Cherokee borders from U.S. squatters in *House on Diamond Hill,* 53.

9. Apess, *Son of the Forest,* 121.

10. Robert Benjamin Lewis, *Light and Truth Collected from the Bible and Ancient and Modern History, Containing the Universal History of the Colored and the Indian Race, from the Creation of the World to the Present Time* (1836) and Pauline Hopkins, *Of One Blood; Or, the Hidden Self* (first pub. 1902–3), in *The Magazine Novels of Pauline Hopkins* (Oxford: Oxford University Press, 1990). On Lewis's work, see Britt Rusert, *Fugitive Science: Empiricism and Freedom and Early African American Culture* (New York: New York University Press, 2017), chap. 2.

11. See John Richard Alden, "The Eighteenth Century Cherokee Archives," *American Archivist* 5 (1942): 240–44, and Phillip H. Round, *Removable Type: Histories of the Book in Indian Country, 1663–1880* (Chapel Hill: University of North Carolina Press, 2010), 103. For the archives, see Virginia Papers, item 71, vol. 2, 156. *Papers of the Continental Congress, 1774–1789* (National Archives Microfilm Publication M247, roll 85): 141–222, National Archives and Records Administration, Washington, DC. For transcriptions of some of the archive, see James William Hagy and Stanley J. Folmsbee, eds, "The Lost Archives of the Cherokee Nation, Part I, 1763–1772," *East Tennessee Historical Society's Publications* 43 (1971): 112–22, and Hagy and Folmsbee, eds., "The Lost Archives of the Cherokee Nation, Part II, 1772–1775," *East Tennessee Historical Society's Publications* 44 (1972): 114–25.

12. Arthur Campbell to Thomas Jefferson, June 20, 1781, Virginia Papers, item 71, vol. 2, 141–42.

13. James Adair, *The History of the American Indians; Particularly Those Nations Adjoining to the Mississippi, East and West Florida, Georgia, South and North Carolina, and Virginia: containing, An Account of their Origin, Language, Manners, Religious and Civil Customs, Laws, form of Government, Punishments, conduct in War and Domestic Life, their Habits, Diet, Agriculture, Manufactures, Diseases and Method of Cure, and other Particulars, sufficient to render it A Complete Indian System* (London, 1775), 326–27. Adair does not say exactly when he saw Attakullakulla's collection, so the governor in question may have been either James Glen (1738–56) or William Henry Lyttleton (1756–60).

14. Adair, *History of the American Indians*, 326–27.

15. Justice, *Our Fire*, 26, and Jace Weaver, *That the People Might Live: Native American Literatures and Native American Community* (New York: Oxford University Press, 1997), viii.

16. Alexander Cameron, "Friends and Brothers," February 5, 1772, Virginia Papers, item 71, vol. 2, 156.

17. John Stuart to Oukonnestotah Great War Chief of the Cherokee Nation, June 1773, Virginia Papers, item 71, vol. 2, 193.

18. Ellen Cushman, "Wampum, Sequoyan, and Story: Decolonizing the Digital Archive," *College English* 76, no. 2 (2013): 117. See also Angela M. Haas, "Wampum as Hypertext: An American Indian Intellectual Tradition of Multimedia Theory and Practice," *Studies in American Indian Literatures* 19, no. 4 (2007): 77–100.

19. For just one example, see Beau Duke Carroll, Alan Cressler, Tom Belt, Julie Reed, and Jan F. Simek, "Talking Stones: Cherokee Syllabary in Manitou Cave, Alabama," *Antiquity* 93, no. 368 (2019): 519–36.

20. Reed, *Serving the Nation*, 13 and chap. 1; McLoughlin, *Cherokee Renascence*, 33–48.

21. "Treaty of Holston," *Oklahoma State Library Digital Collections*, http://digital.library.okstate.edu/kappler/vol2/treaties/che0029.htm (accessed October 15, 2015). See also Miles, *House on Diamond Hill*, 52–53, and Perdue, *Cherokee Women: Gender and*

Culture Change, 1700–1835 (Lincoln: University of Nebraska Press, 1998), chap. 3, esp. 110–11.

22. On slaveholding practices in the Cherokee Nation, see Tiya Miles, *House on Diamond Hill,* and on those practices' relation to the civilization program, see Miles, *Ties That Bind: The Story of an Afro-Cherokee Family in Slavery and Freedom* (Oakland: University of California Press, 2015), chap. 1.

23. On this marriage, and that of Elias Boudinot to the white woman Harriet Gold a few years later, see Theresa Strouth Gaul, *To Marry an Indian: The Marriage of Harriett Gold and Elias Boudinot in Letters, 1823–1839* (Chapel Hill: University of North Carolina Press, 2005).

24. Anonymous, "Speech of John Ridge, A Cherokee Chief," *The Liberator,* March 17, 1832, 44.

25. "Speech of John Ridge," 44.

26. Poems and Hymns copied by John Ridge at Cornwall Mission School, February–March 1819, John Howard Payne Papers, vol. 8, folder 2, Newberry Library, Chicago. Herman Daggett, *The American Reader: Consisting of Familiar, Instructive, and Entertaining Stories,* 2nd ed. (Poughkeepsie, NY, 1812). On the educational system at Cornwall and for a reading of one of Ridge's copied poems, see Hilary E. Wyss, *English Letters and Indian Literacies: Reading, Writing, and New England Missionary Schools, 1750–1830* (Philadelphia: University of Pennsylvania Press, 2012), chap. 2.

27. On copying as a site of discipline as well as creativity at Cornwall, see Karen Sanchez Eppler, "Copying and Conversion: An 1824 Friendship Album 'from a Chinese Youth,'" *American Quarterly* 59, no. 2 (2007): 301–39.

28. Around the same time that he was drafting the letters to Gallatin, Ridge compiled word lists in Cherokee, and other southeastern Indigenous languages, which he also sent to Gallatin. John Ridge, "Comparative Vocabulary," no date, Gallatin Papers, box 64–3, Indian Languages, Manuscripts Collection, New-York Historical Society. I've written about these word lists in "Entangled Archives: Cherokee Interventions in Language Collecting," *Afterlives of Indigenous Archives: Essays in Honor of the Occom Circle,* ed. Ivy Schweitzer and Gordon Henry (Hanover: University of New England Press, 2019), 120–38.

29. John Ridge, "Strictures on 'The Report of the Joint Committee on the State of the Republic,' in the Legislature of Georgia, on the subject of the Cherokee Lands; purporting to prove the absolute jurisdictional right of the said state to the same," *Cherokee Phoenix,* March 13, 1828, 2. I've written on Ridge's writing as Socrates in "Practicing Sovereignty: Colonial Temporalities, Cherokee Justice, and the 'Socrates' Writings of John Ridge," *NAIS: Journal of the Native American and Indigenous Studies Association* 4, no. 1 (Spring 2017): 30–60.

30. Jonathan Elliot, *Historical Sketches of the Ten Miles Square Forming the District of Columbia* (Washington, DC, 1830), 166.

31. Elliot, *Historical Sketches*, 167.

32. Elliot, *Historical Sketches*, 165.

33. Elliot, *Historical Sketches*, 166.

34. Peter du Ponceau to Albert Gallatin, April 8, 1826, Historical and Literary Committee Letter Book, vol. 3, 46, American Philosophical Society, Philadelphia. As the correspondence in its Letter Book shows, the Historical and Literary Committee made the collection of documents related to Native languages, deeds, and life central to its work.

35. James Barbour, Circular, Department of War, May 15, 1826, American Indian Vocabulary Collection, American Philosophical Society, Philadelphia, Mss.497.V85.

36. Barbour, Circular.

37. "Preface," *Archaeologia Americana, Transactions and Collections of the American Antiquarian Society*, vol. 2. (Cambridge, 1836), viii.

38. "Preface," *Archaeologia Americana*, viii. Collecting pieces of information and arranging them into a whole that could be observed all at once was a key observational strategy in the eighteenth century. See J. Andrew Mendelsohn, "The World on a Page: Making a General Observation in the Eighteenth Century," in *Histories of Scientific Observation*, ed. Lorraine Daston and Elizabeth Lunbeck (Chicago: University of Chicago Press, 2011), 404. Query lists were institutionalized as a form of data collection and knowledge production in the late seventeenth century, when the British Royal Society formed several committees to standardize queries for collecting information about various locations, in England and throughout the world. Drawing on Francis Bacon's tabulation of over one hundred topics in need of investigation and on his recommendation that "Topics or Articles of Inquiry" be proposed to "stimulate further inquiry," the Royal Society proposed to circulate queries to generate data for its members to discuss and verify. See Michael Hunter, "Robert Boyle and the Early Royal Society: A Reciprocal Exchange in the Making of Baconian Science," *British Journal for the History of Science* 40, no. 1 (2007): 6. In the United States, colonists employed query lists to collect information about the continent, especially information about Native nations. For just a few examples, François Marbois's query lists to Thomas Jefferson resulted in *Notes in the State of Virginia*, and Jefferson and physician Benjamin Rush created query lists to guide Meriwether Lewis and William Clark as they collected information about Native peoples in the western parts of the continent. Philadelphia physician Benjamin Smith Barton distributed query lists about Native American health and medical practices to his correspondents, and later in the nineteenth century, the Smithsonian Institution continued the practice of distributing query lists about Native languages, practices, and peoples to agents in the field.

39. Elizabeth Yale, "Making Lists: Social and Material Technologies in the Making of Seventeenth-Century British Natural History," in *Ways of Making and Knowing: The Material Culture of Empirical Knowledge*, ed. Pamela H. Smith, Amy R. W. Myers, and Harold J. Cook (Ann Arbor: University of Michigan Press, 2014), 280.

40. On the colonial expectation that Native people could not change and still be Indigenous, see Jean M. O'Brien, *Firsting and Lasting: Writing Indians out of Existence in New England* (Cambridge: Cambridge University Press, 2010), xxii. On the "unexpected" place of Native people in modernity, see Philip J. Deloria, *Indians in Unexpected Places* (Lawrence: University of Kansas Press, 2004).

41. Maureen Konkle, *Writing Indian Nations: Native Intellectuals and the Politics of Historiography, 1827–1863* (Chapel Hill: University of North Carolina Press, 2004), 61.

42. "Cherokee Nation v. Georgia," https://supreme.justia.com/cases/federal/us/30/1/ (accessed August 28, 2015). On the ways that Marshall's decision in *Cherokee Nation v. Georgia* reinterpreted the European doctrine of discovery, see David E. Wilkins and K. Tsianina Lomawaima, *Uneven Ground: American Indian Sovereignty and Federal Law* (Norman: University of Oklahoma Press, 2001), 25.

43. David E. Wilkins, *American Indian Sovereignty and the U.S. Supreme Court: The Masking of Justice* (Austin: University of Texas Press, 1997), 33–35. The Supreme Court had ruled in 1823 that Native people possessed only the right of occupancy to their lands. See Johnson & Graham's Lessee v. M'Intosh, U.S. Supreme Court, 21 U.S. (8 Wheat.) 543, 1823. *Justia US Supreme Court*, https://supreme.justia.com/cases/federal/us/21/543/case.html (accessed September 14, 2015).

44. Kevin Bruyneel, *The Third Space of Sovereignty: The Postcolonial Politics of U.S.-Indigenous Relations* (Minneapolis: University of Minnesota Press, 2007), xvii. See also Audra Simpson's point that "multiple sovereignties cannot proliferate robustly or equally." Audra Simpson, *Mohawk Interruptus: Political Life across the Borders of Settler States* (Durham: Duke University Press, 2014), 12.

45. Gallatin, "A Synopsis of the Indian Tribes within the United States East of the Rocky Mountains, and in the British and Russian Possessions in North America," in *Archaeologia Americana,* 155.

46. Gallatin to McKenney, March 4, 1826, Papers of Albert Gallatin, New-York Historical Society, roll 36, frames 221–23. Gallatin's initial request seems to have been in early or mid-February, since Ridge dates his draft letter February 27.

47. Gallatin to McKenney, March 4, 1826.

48. Albert Gallatin to Alexander von Humboldt, March 24, 1826, in *Alexander von Humboldt und die Vereinigten Staaten von Amerika,* ed. Ingo Schwarz (Berlin: Akademie Verlag, 2004), 178 (my translation). The original letter reads: "En attendant mieux, je vous envoye an essai de *Ridge* Cherokee pur, fils d'un des principaux chefs de la Nation, mais élevé pendant quelques années dans le Connecticut. Il est en entire de lui, écrit de sa main, sans que j'y aye change ou ajouté un seul mot. Il y a probalement un peu d'exagération; mais vous y trouverez les sentimens reels et exaltés des Indiens et leur désir de subsister comme Nation civilisée mais indépendante." Humboldt and Gallatin had corresponded for nearly a decade by 1826, and Humboldt encouraged Gallatin's linguistic collecting, asking that he send reports and classificatory essays on Native

Americans to Europe for inclusion in some of Humboldt's publications. Thanks to Sean Harvey for directing me to this source. On Gallatin's correspondence with Humboldt, see Laura Dassow Walls, *Passage to Cosmos: Alexander von Humboldt and the Shaping of America* (Chicago: Chicago University Press, 2009), 186–87.

49. John Ridge to Albert Gallatin, February 27, 1826, John Howard Payne Papers, vol. 8, folder 4, Newberry Library, Chicago.

50. Miles, *Ties That Bind*, 53. See also Reed, *Serving the Nation*, 11–14.

51. See Scott Richard Lyons, *X-Marks: Native Signatures of Assent* (Minneapolis: University of Minnesota Press, 2010), 2–3.

52. John Ridge to Albert Gallatin, February 27, 1826. The language in the sent letter is similar: "This was a principle of Government in the worst of shapes of our people. Our Chiefs were numerous and then accountability was small. Lands could then be obtained at a price most convenient to the United States, as their commissioners with the assistance of the Agent could always procure a majority for a Cession, and when this was done the patriotic Chiefs yielded to secure their share for the trifling equivalent." Ridge to Gallatin, March 10, 1826, Gallatin Papers, box 64–3, Indian Languages, Manuscripts Collection, New-York Historical Society.

53. McLoughlin, *Cherokee Renascence*, 19. The chiefs argued that they understood the transaction to be one that allowed settlers to rent the land, not to own it.

54. Reed, *Serving the Nation*, 63 (and see also chap. 1).

55. Ridge to Gallatin, February 27, 1826.

56. Gallatin to McKenney, March 4, 1826.

57. Ridge to Gallatin, March 10, 1826.

58. Ridge to Gallatin, March 10, 1826.

59. Gallatin to McKenney, March 4, 1826.

60. Ridge to Gallatin, March 10, 1826. And see "Anecdotes of Teedyuscung," *Weekly Magazine* 1 (1798): 393–94.

61. Ridge to Gallatin, February 27, 1826.

62. Ridge to Gallatin, March 10, 1826.

63. Ridge to Gallatin, March 10, 1826.

64. Ridge to Gallatin, March 10, 1826.

65. Ridge to Gallatin, March 10, 1826.

66. On U.S. American authors' consideration of "several distinct temporal dispositions," not just the homogenous time of the nation, see Lloyd Pratt, *Archives of American Time: Literature and Modernity in the Nineteenth Century* (Philadelphia: University of Pennsylvania Press, 2010), 5. On how conceptions of temporality are linked to settler colonialism, see Mark Rifkin, *Beyond Settler Time: Temporal Sovereignty and Indigenous Self-Determination* (Durham: Duke University Press, 2017), chap. 1, esp. 1–16.

67. William C. Sturtevant reproduces the dashes in his publication of Ridge's sent letter.

68. For a summary of the ways Dickinson's dashes have been read, see Edith Wylder, "Emily Dickinson's Punctuation: The Controversy Revisited," *American Literary Realism* 36, no. 3 (2004): 206–24.

69. Meredith McGill, *American Literature and the Culture of Reprinting, 1834–1853* (Philadelphia: University of Pennsylvania Press, 2003), 159. On dashes as representing silences or hesitations, see Johnnie M. Stover, "Nineteenth-Century African American Women's Autobiography as Social Discourse: The Example of Harriet Ann Jacobs," *College English* 66, no. 2 (2003): 133–54. For a different reading of blanks, not as literary devices of abstraction so much as the elements of a bureaucratic system that organizes, divides, and systematizes, see Lisa Gitelman, *Paper Knowledge: Toward a Media History of Documents* (Durham: Duke University Press, 2014), 30. Ridge's use of blanks to extract and reroute archival forms indicates how Indigenous compilations put documentary forms to very different ends than the bureaucratic, utilitarian uses Gitelman observes in nineteenth-century job printing.

70. Ridge to Gallatin, March 10, 1826. Tiya Miles, *Ties That Bind*, 23.

71. Ridge to Gallatin, March 10, 1826.

72. Ridge to Gallatin, March 10, 1826. According to Claudio Saunt, this library contained "'both ancient and modern' histories, among other books." See Saunt, "Telling Stories: The Political Uses of Myth and History in the Cherokee and Creek Nations," *Journal of American History* 93, no. 3 (2006): 681. Ridge's consultation of Vattel and regional histories in "Strictures" may give a sense of some of the books contained in the library.

73. Ridge to Gallatin, March 10, 1826.

74. Ellen Cushman has argued that Sequoyah was better acquainted with English literacy than nineteenth-century accounts posited, and this familiarity means that he made careful choices about whether and how to engage (or not engage) with alphabetic orthographies. See Ellen Cushman, *The Cherokee Syllabary: Writing the People's Persistence* (Norman: University of Oklahoma Press, 2011), 24–26. The Cherokees who removed to Arkansas Territory in the late eighteen-teens, in an early removal crisis when they faced the offer of reserves in the west or the pressure of U.S. citizenship if they remained, are sometimes called the Old Settlers. See McLoughlin, *Cherokee Renascence*, chap. 11.

75. James Mooney, "The Sacred Formulas of the Cherokees," in *Seventh Annual Report of the Bureau of Ethnology, 1885–'86 by JW Powell, Director* (Washington, DC: Government Printing Office, 1891), 316. As Christopher Teuton observes, Mooney was "placated with half-truths and adaptations of stories." Christopher B. Teuton, "Indigenous Textuality Studies and Cherokee Traditionalism: Notes toward a Gagoga Rhetoric," *Textual Cultures: Texts, Contexts, Interpretation* 6, no. 4 (2011): 133–41 (quotation on 140).

76. Justice, *Our Fire Survives*, 24. See also Ellen Cushman on embodied Cherokee archives in Cushman, "Wampum, Sequoyan, and Story."

77. My reading departs from Claudio Saunt's analysis of Hicks's letter, which he views as treating Cherokee historical narratives as "degraded stories that once contained biblical or historical truths" and thus as placing "them firmly within a European interpretive framework." See Claudio Saunt, "Telling Stories," 685. I read Hicks's letter as not merely providing historical narratives but also as commenting on Cherokee historiography and depicting Cherokee stories with metaphors specific to Cherokee contexts. On Hicks's tutoring of John Ross, see Gary E. Moulton, *John Ross, Cherokee Chief* (Athens: University of Georgia Press, 1978), 31 and 66.

78. Charles R. Hicks to John Ross, February 1, 1826, John Howard Payne Papers, vol. 7, folder 1, Newberry Library, Chicago.

79. Hicks to Ross, February 1, 1826.

80. Justice, *Our Fire*, 26.

81. Justice, *Our Fire*, 26.

82. John Ross, "To all the aged, and wise Antiquarians of the Cherokee Nation," September 15, 1835, John Howard Payne Papers, vol. 4, folder 5, Newberry Library, Chicago. Superscript and brackets in original.

83. Butrick described this process in his correspondence with Payne: "Dear Sir, as soon as convenient, after the return of MR Ross, from Washington City, I hope to lay the result of my enquiries before him. His intention I believe, is to call together some of the most noted antiquarians to assist him in examining the correctness of my writings. Should they pronounce them correct, I could then, with confidence, transmit them to you, and should rejoice to do so. In that case, sir, you might receive them as coming directly from Mr. Ross, and such antiquarians as might sanction them." Daniel S. Butrick to John Howard Payne, May 13, 1836, John Howard Payne Papers, vol. 4, Newberry Library, Chicago.

84. John Howard Payne, *Traditions of the Cherokee Indians,* unpublished manuscript, quotations on pages 116 and 120. John Howard Payne Papers, Newberry Library, Chicago.

85. On this moment, see also Konkle, *Writing Indian Nations*, 84.

86. Gallatin's claims about the Cherokee Nation were published in Adrien Balbi's *Atlas ethnographique du globe,* vol. 1 (Paris: 1826), 309–10. Gallatin's discussion of the Cherokees is reminiscent of Ridge's letter and may have drawn from it, but Ridge's name is erased from the *Atlas.* For an English translation of Gallatin's letter to Humboldt, see Sturtevant, "John Ridge," 89–90.

87. Payne wrote that his papers contained private documents, "specimen copy books" from the Missionary School at Brainerd (one of which may have been Ridge's). See "John Howard Payne to His Countrymen," *Knoxville Register,* December 23, 1835.

88. I depart here from readings that contrast Ridge's letters and Boudinot's writing with Ross's approval of Payne's and Butrick's research into Cherokee histories. See Konkle, *Writing Indian Nations*, 48.

89. Mary Kathryn Nagle, *Sovereignty* (Evanston: Northwestern University Press, 2020), 119.

90. Nagle, *Sovereignty,* 70.

91. Nagle, *Sovereignty,* 71. Italics in original.

92. John Ridge to Albert Gallatin, February 27, 1826.

93. Nagle, *Sovereignty,* 118.

94. Nagle, *Sovereignty,* 109.

95. Nagle, *Sovereignty,* 91.

96. Nagle, *Sovereignty,* 91.

97. Nagle, *Sovereignty,* 117.

98. Nagle, *Sovereignty,* 125. Nagle echoes these words in the playbill. See "From the Playwright," *Sovereignty,* Marin Theatre Company Playbill, 2.

Interlude: E. Pauline Johnson's Wild Flowers

1. E. Pauline Johnson, "A Red Girl's Reasoning," in *Tekahionwake: E. Pauline Johnson's Writings on Native North America,* ed. Margery Fee and Dory Nason (Peterborough: Broadview Press, 2016), 164.

2. Johnson, "Red Girl's," 164.

3. Johnson, "Red Girl's,"163.

4. Johnson, "Red Girl's," 165 and 166.

5. Johnson, "Red Girl's," 172.

6. Johnson, "Red Girl's," 176. On this scene, see also Beth Piatote, *Domestic Subjects: Gender, Citizenship, and Law in Native American Literature* (New Haven: Yale University Press, 2013), chap. 1.

7. Johnson, "Red Girl's," 172.

8. See James E. Johnson, "Scrapbook, 1899–1904," Northwestern Libraries Digital Collections, https://digitalcollections.library.northwestern.edu/items/0620eaca-54e6–4181-a858–39ddeaobb1c5#zoom=0.4395573195297044&x=0.5&y=0.6263810980792113. See also Charles Amera, "Autograph Album," VAULT Ayer MS 3241, Newberry Library, Chicago (the album is from the Nez Percé man Amera's time at Chemawa Indian School in Salem, Oregon, and contains autographs and notes from other Native students and teachers).

9. On these albums, see *E. Pauline Johnson, Tekahionwake: Collected Poems and Selected Prose,* ed. Carole Gerson and Veronica Strong-Boag (Toronto: University of Toronto Press, 2002), 289; Alexander Posey, Manuscript Collection, 1888–1907, Gilcrease Museum, Tulsa, OK.

10. Carlos Montezuma, "Clippings, Scrapbook of published articles by Albert Payson Terhune," n.d., Carlos Montezuma Papers, box 4, folder 219, Ayer Modern

MS Montezuma, Newberry Library, Chicago, and "Ely Samuel Parker Scrapbooks, 1828–1894," Ayer Modern MS Parker, Newberry Library, Chicago.

Chapter Three. Album

1. Charlotte Johnston, "Journal," Judge Joseph H. Steere Room, Bayliss Public Library, Sault Ste. Marie, MI, lines 1–2. The Journal's pages are not numbered. Further citations from this book will appear parenthetically. I refer to Charlotte Johnston as "Johnston" throughout this chapter since, with a few exceptions, I discuss a period before her marriage to William McMurray in 1833. I refer to Charlotte's sister Jane Johnston Schoolcraft as Johnston Schoolcraft to distinguish between the two.

2. This poem was written by Samuel Woodworth, the New York poet and publisher of literary periodicals for young ladies, such as the *Ladies Literary Cabinet,* the *Literary Casket,* and the *Parthenon;* it was published in books of Woodworth's "melodies" and in literary magazines under the title "For Viola's Album" and "Written in A Commonplace Book."

3. For Johnston stitching quires, see Jeremiah Porter, Thursday 15 [May 1832], Journal, Jeremiah Porter Papers, Chicago History Museum. Johnston's mother's name is also spelled "Oshaguscodaywayquay" in historical documents.

4. Johnston's book is referred to as a "Journal" in archival finding aids, but she wrote few, if any, of the entries in it.

5. Miscellanies like scrapbooks and friendship albums were "intended as an informal receptacle of unassociated and impromptu clumps of words and images. Each scrapbook, pocket-book, or album represents an importance that is conflated with public and private, and a scrapbook may entertain different moments or memories or may be a snapshot of a life." See Katherine D. Harris, *Forget Me Not: The Rise of the British Literary Annual, 1823–1835* (Athens: Ohio University Press, 2015), 73. On "ready-made" albums and blank books marketed with decorative covers, like those Johnston used for her albums, see Blake Bronson-Bartlett, "From Loose Leaves to Readymades: Manuscript Books in the Age of Emerson and Whitman," *J19: The Journal of Nineteenth-Century Americanists* 6, no. 2 (2018): 259–83.

There is an excellent and extensive body of scholarship on albums and their printed counterparts, gift books, and their place within literary histories, especially white women's textual production. See Sara Lodge, "Romantic Reliquaries: Memory and Irony in The Literary Annuals," *Romanticism* 10, no. 1 (2008): 23–40; *Milcah Martha Moore's Book: A Commonplace Book from Revolutionary America,* ed. Catherine La Courreye Blecki and Karin A. Wulf (University Park: Pennsylvania State University Press, 1997); Meredith McGill, *American Literature and the Culture of Reprinting, 1834–1853* (Philadelphia: University of Pennsylvania Press, 2003), 28–41; Elizabeth A. Petrino, "Presents of

Mind: Lydia Sigourney, Gift Book Culture, and the Commodification of Poetry," in *A History of Nineteenth-Century American Women's Poetry*, ed. Jennifer Putzi and Alexandra Socarides (Cambridge: Cambridge University Press, 2017), 87–105; Clare Pettit, "Topos, Taxonomy and Travel in Nineteenth-Century Women's Scrapbooks," in *Travel Writing, Visual Culture and Form, 1760–1900*, ed. Mary Henes and Brian H. Murray (Palgrave, 2016), 21–41; Dahlia Porter, "Specimen Poetics: Botany, Reanimation, and the Romantic Collection," *Representations* 139 (Summer 2017): 60–94; Britt Rusert, "Disappointment in the Archives of Black Freedom," *Social Text* 125, no. 33 (2015): 19–33; Susan M. Stabile, *Memory's Daughters: The Material Culture of Remembrance in Eighteenth-Century America* (Ithaca: Cornell University Press, 2004); Alexandra Socarides, "Rethinking the Fascicles: Dickinson's Writing, Copying, and Binding Practices," *Emily Dickinson Journal* 15, no. 2 (2006): 69–94; and Caroline Wigginton, *In the Neighborhood: Women's Publication in Early America* (Amherst: University of Massachusetts Press, 2016), chap. 4.

6. Wigginton, *In the Neighborhood*, 111. Lindsey Eckert uses the term "album verse" to describe lyric poetry transcribed in albums, arguing that this verse performed and generated intimacy and social connections. As she notes, album verse obtained its value through use and circulation. See Eckert, "Reading Lyric's Form: The Written Hand in Albums and Literary Annuals," *ELH* 85, no. 4 (2018): 973–97. Andrew Piper argues that Romantic miscellanies raised questions of and encouraged acts of textual sharing. Piper, *Dreaming in Books: The Making of the Bibliographic Imagination in the Romantic Age* (Chicago: University of Chicago Press, 2014), 133–38.

7. The French called the Anishinaabe community at Bow-e-ting the Sauteurs, a term that NAIS scholars continue to use, as I do in this chapter.

8. Robert Dale Parker, "Introduction: The World and Writings of Jane Johnston Schoolcraft," in *The Sound the Stars Make Rushing through the Sky: The Writings of Jane Johnston Schoolcraft*, ed. Parker (Philadelphia: University of Pennsylvania Press, 2007), 11.

9. Parker, "Introduction," 9–11 and 25. Johnston's brother George Johnston wrote that there was in 1815 a "very large and numerous assemblage of Indians at the foot of the falls, and on an eminence was situated the ancient village of the Chippewas, considered as a metropolis during the summer months, and where the Indians living on the southern and northern shore of Lake Superior and its interior portions of the country, congregated to meet on friendly relations." See "Reminiscences of Geo. Johnston, of Sault de Ste. Marie, 1815," in *Michigan Pioneer and Historical Collections*, 2nd ed., vol. 12 (Lansing: Wynkoop, Hallenbeck, Crawford, 1906), 606. Janet E. Chute notes that 100–300 Sauteurs lived at the Sault, depending on the time of year. See Janet E. Chute, *The Legacy of Shingwaukonse: A Century of Native Leadership* (Toronto: University of Toronto Press, 1998), 13. And as Michael Witgen points out, by 1822 only 8,675 Americans resided in Michigan Territory, far from the 60,000 white male citizens required to form a state. See Michael Witgen, *An Infinity of Nations: How the*

Native New World Shaped Early North America (Philadelphia: University of Pennsylvania Press, 2012), 339.

10. On the "high standard that emphasized reciprocity" to which Anishinaabe relatives held fur traders who married Anishinaabe women, see Brenda J. Child, *Holding Our World Together: Ojibwe Women and the Survival of Community* (New York: Penguin, 2012), 37. On Ozhaawshkodewikwe's marriage to Johnston, see Child, *Holding*, 44–45, and Jill Doerfler and Erik Redix, "Regional and Tribal Histories: The Great Lakes," in *Oxford Handbook of American Indian History,* ed. Frederick Hoxie (Oxford: Oxford University Press, 2016), 176–77.

11. See Witgen, *Infinity of Nations,* esp. 327–57 and Karl S. Hele, "The Anishinaabeg and Métis at the Sault Ste Marie Borderlands: Confronting a Line Drawn upon the Water," in *Lines Drawn upon the Water: First Nations and the Great Lakes Borders and Borderlands,* ed. Karl S. Hele (Waterloo: Wilfrid Laurier University Press, 2008), 67.

12. Parker, "Introduction," 2.

13. On Jane Johnston Schoolcraft, see the introduction, edition of her poems, and scholarly bibliography in Parker, ed., *Sound the Stars Make,* and Maureen Konkle's reading of Johnston Schoolcraft within the Anishinaabe world in Konkle, "Recovering Jane Schoolcraft's Cultural Activism in the Nineteenth Century," in *Oxford Handbook of Indigenous American Literature,* ed. James H. Cox and Daniel Heath Justice (New York: Oxford University Press, 2014), 81–101. See also Christine R. Cavalier, "Jane Johnston Schoolcraft's Sentimental Lessons: Native Literary Collaboration and Resistance," *MELUS* 38, no. 1 (2013): 98–118; Alanna Hickey, "The Forms of National Belonging: The Politics of Citizenship in Nineteenth-Century Native American Poetry" (PhD diss., Northwestern University, 2016), chap. 2; Laura Mielke, *Moving Encounters: Sympathy and the Indian Question in Antebellum Literature* (Amherst: University of Massachusetts Press, 2008), chap. 6; and Bethany Schneider, "Not for Citation: Jane Johnston Schoolcraft's Synchronic Strategies," *ESQ: A Journal of the American Renaissance* 54, no. 1–4 (2008): 111–44. On Schoolcraft and the history of anthropology, see Richard Bauman, "Representing Native American Oral Narrative: The Textual Practices of Henry Rowe Schoolcraft," *Pragmatics* 5, no. 2 (2010): 167–83; Joshua David Bellin, *The Demon of the Continent: Indians and the Shaping of American Literature* (Philadelphia: University of Pennsylvania Press, 2001), chap. 5; and Scott Michaelson, *The Limits of Multiculturalism: Interrogating the Origins of American Anthropology* (Minneapolis: University of Minnesota Press, 1999), introduction and chap. 1.

14. Attributing material in Johnston's albums to her hand is difficult, as she seems to have written few letters while she lived at Bow-e-ting. Most of her surviving letters date from the 1830s and 1840s, when she had moved away from her family to McMurray's new mission site in Dundas, Ontario. During that time away from Bow-e-ting, Johnston wrote to her sisters and George Johnston, but more frequently William McMurray conveyed messages from Johnston to her family in his letters. My attribution

of materials in the albums to Johnston rests on my analysis of the handwriting in Johnston's letters held at the Burton Historical Collection, Detroit Public Library, to which I compared handwriting in the albums.

15. Johnston has appeared primarily in studies of the Johnston family and of their relations to missionaries at Bow-e-ting. See Karl S. Hele, " 'By the Rapids': The Anishinabeg-Missionary Encounter at Bawating (Sault Ste. Marie), c. 1821–1871," PhD diss., McGill University, 2002; Hele, " 'Fully Equal to a Mission in Herself': Charlotte Johnston McMurray's Missionary Labours at Bawating, 1827–1838," *Algonquin Conference* (2008): 316–57; Hele, " 'How to Win Friends and Influence People': Missions to Bawating, 1830–1840," Historical Papers 1996: *Canadian Society of Church History* (1996): 155–76; and Colin Elder, "Changing Political and Cultural Realms in the Upper Great Lakes, 1826: A Case-Study of the Influential 'Oode' (or family) of Jane Johnston Schoolcraft" (master's thesis, Dalhousie University, 2015).

16. For reprinting as an "appropriative strategy," see Phillip H. Round, *Removable Type: Histories of the Book in Indian Country, 1663–1880* (Chapel Hill: University of North Carolina Press, 2010), chap. 7 (quotation on 184). On mid-nineteenth-century "cultures of reprinting," see Meredith McGill, *American Literature and the Culture of Reprinting, 1834–1853* (Philadelphia: University of Pennsylvania Press, 2003) and on periodical reprinting, see Ryan Cordell, "Reprinting, Circulation, and the Network Author in Antebellum Newspapers," *American Literary History* 27, no. 3 (2015): 417–45 (esp. 427). On African American citational practices, see Britt Rusert, *Fugitive Science: Empiricism and Freedom and Early African American Culture* (New York: New York University Press, 2017); Lara Langer Cohen, "Notes from the State of Saint Domingue: The Practice of Citation in *Clotel*," in *Early African American Print Culture*, ed. Cohen and Jordan Stein (Philadelphia: University of Pennsylvania Press, 2014): 161–77; and John Ernest, *Liberation Historiography: African American Writers and the Challenge of History, 1794–1861* (Durham: University of North Carolina Press, 2004).

17. See Parker, "Introduction," 14.

18. Henry R. Schoolcraft, "Memoir of John Johnston," *Historical Collections, Michigan Pioneer and Historical Society*, vol. 36 (Lansing: Wynkoop, Hallenbeck, Crawford, 1908), 60. See also Schoolcraft, *Personal Memoirs of a Residence of Thirty Years with the Indian Tribes on the American Frontiers* (Philadelphia, 1851), 240.

19. Andrew Piper, "The Art of Sharing," in *Bookish Histories: Books, Literature, and Commercial Modernity, 1700–1900*, ed. Ina Ferris and Paul Keen (Basingstroke: Palgrave Macmillan, 2009), 127.

20. John J. Bigsby, *The Shoe and Canoe: or, Pictures of Travel in the Canadas, Illustrative of Their Scenery and of Colonial Life*, vol. 2 (London: Chapman and Hall, 1850), 127. Bigsby writes that he visits the Johnstons "ten years afterwards" of the plundering of the Johnston home in 1814, in a U.S. attack on British territory during the War of 1812.

On practices of binding multiple titles together in the early modern period, see Jeffrey Todd Knight, *Bound to Read: Compilations, Collections, and the Making of Renaissance Literature* (Philadelphia: University of Pennsylvania Press, 2013).

21. See George Johnston Memorandum Book, George Johnston Papers, folders 2 and 3, box 1, Judge Joseph H. Steere Room, Bayliss Public Library, Sault Ste. Marie, MI. The four memorandum books held at the Bayliss Public Library are made of sheets of paper folded and stitched together at the centerfold; the vellum covers appear also to be cut and attached by hand.

22. See "Devotional Songs and Poems" and "Poetic Remains of John Johnston," Henry Rowe Schoolcraft Papers, box 70, Library of Congress. Parker observes that some of the dates for the hymns Jane copied, in "Devotional Songs," including 1811 and 1815, make it unlikely that she wrote the songs (as she would have been eleven and fifteen years old at those times, respectively). Instead, she was likely copying others' songs, though as of this writing, scholars have not been able to locate source texts. See Parker, "Introduction," 223–24 and 259.

23. As subagent François Audrain wrote to George Johnston in 1827, "We have had a reading society this winter, Mr S was the editor of paper [*sic*] (little Literary Voyager) which was well written and very amusing." March 27, 1827, François Audrain to George Johnston, George Johnston Papers, Burton Historical Collection, Detroit Public Library. On the *Literary Voyager,* see Hickey, "Forms of National Belonging," chap. 2; Maureen Konkle, *Writing Indian Nations: Native Intellectuals and the Politics of Historiography, 1827–1863* (Chapel Hill: University of North Carolina Press, 2004), 166–80; Mielke, *Moving Encounters,* chap. 6; Henry Rowe Schoolcraft, *The Literary Voyager, or, Muzzeniegun,* ed. Philip P. Mason (East Lansing: Michigan State University Press, 1962); and Parker, "Introduction," 33–35.

24. Rowe Schoolcraft, "Memoir of John Johnston," 63.

25. Thursday 15, [May 1832], Journal, Jeremiah Porter Papers, Chicago History Museum. "Haliday" is also spelled "Halliday" in many archival records.

26. April 5, [1832], Journal, Jeremiah Porter Papers, Chicago History Museum.

27. Jane Johnston to Henry Rowe Schoolcraft, May 19, 1823, Henry Rowe Schoolcraft Papers, box 7, Library of Congress.

28. Thomas McKenney, *Sketches on a Tour to the Lakes, of the character and customs of the Chippeway Indians, and of incidents connected with the Treaty of Fond du Lac* (Baltimore, 1827), 194.

29. Charlotte Johnston to George Johnston, May 24 1833, George Johnston Papers, Burton Historical Collection, Detroit Public Library.

30. McKenney, *Sketches,* 186.

31. Bigsby, *Shoe and Canoe,* vol. 2, 129.

32. McKenney, *Sketches,* 182.

33. For just a few such descriptions, see Ross Cox, *Adventures on the Columbia River* (New York: J&J Harper, 1832), 302; Bigsby, *Shoe and Canoe*, vol. 2, 127–30; McKenney, *Sketches*, 201; and Porter, December 27, [1831], Journal.

34. Anna Brownell Jameson, *Winter Studies and Summer Rambles in Canada*, vol. 3 (London, Saunders and Otley, 1838), 85.

35. See Schoolcraft, *Personal Memoirs*, 568, where he quotes one of Johnston Schoolcraft's letters, which in turn quotes Jameson: "I have written to Mrs. McMurray, and troubled her with several questions relative to the women. I remark generally, that the propinquity of the white man is destruction to the red man; and the farther the Indians are removed from us, the better for them. In their own woods, they are a noble race; brought near to us, a degraded and stupid race. We are destroying them off the face of the earth." George Johnston was also a frequent collaborator with colonial collectors, creating vocabularies of Anishinaabemowin and obtaining objects during his time as a trader among his relatives at La Pointe. George's fluency in Anishinaabemowin led to positions as an interpreter and subagent under Henry. Later in his life, after being dismissed from his position as subagent (due in part to Henry's deteriorating political status) and struggling to find employment, George attempted to convince Henry and other officials to hire him as a guide to mineral resources in the Great Lakes, but he appears to have been unsuccessful in this endeavor. See the letters in the George Johnston Papers, 1792–1944, Judge Joseph H. Steere Room, Bayliss Public Library, Sault Ste. Marie, esp. Johnston's Letterbook, 1832–1860.

36. See James Schoolcraft to George Johnston, January 23, 1833, Burton Historical Collection, Detroit Public Library.

37. Schoolcraft, *Personal Memoirs*, 107.

38. Schoolcraft, *Personal Memoirs*, 639.

39. On the 1826 Treaty of Fond du Lac, see Schoolcraft, *Personal Memoirs*, 243–45; McKenney, *Sketches*, 273–343. On the U.S. imperial designs that motivated the treaty and the U.S.'s failure to realize those designs in 1826, see Witgen, *Infinity of Nations*, 351–56.

40. McKenney, *Sketches*, 186.

41. McKenney, *Sketches*, 186.

42. McKenney, *Sketches*, 189. On McKenney's *Tour* and Barbour as recipient, see Herman J. Viola, *Thomas L. McKenney: Architect of America's Early Indian Policy, 1818–1830* (Chicago: Sage Books, 1974), 153. Thanks to Frank Kelderman for pointing me to this source.

43. On nineteenth-century sentimental images of flowers and their entanglement with colonialism, see Ruth B. Phillips, *Trading Identities: The Souvenir in Native North American Art from the Northeast, 1700–1900* (Seattle: University of Washington Press, 1998), chap. 5, esp. 157–62 and 185–90. As Phillips points out, flowers were not only popular among Euro-western Victorians but also among Native men and women, who

embraced floral imagery as it circulated through materials made by Quebec nuns and made the imagery their own, "inventing" a "new vocabulary of floral design" for bead- and quillwork (172).

44. McKenney, *Sketches,* 189 (flowers), 320 (relics), and 369 (allegory). McKenney writes that John and Charlotte Johnston "presented me with the skin of a Wa-ba-jick—or the White Fisher. 'This,' said Charlotte, as she handed it to me, 'is *my grand father*—at least in name.' I inquired if this animal was the *totem* of his band—and was answered, 'no,' and informed that the 'totem of his band was the rein-deer.'" See *Sketches,* 198. On McKenney's interactions with Anishinaabe diplomats, see Frank Kelderman, *Authorized Agents: Publication and Diplomacy in the Era of Indian Removal* (Albany: SUNY Press, 2019), chap. 4.

45. McKenney, *Sketches,* 185. Anna Brownell Jameson includes a very similar description of Johnston in her 1838 travel narrative: she describes Johnston's beauty even while dissecting the qualities that allegedly signify her Indianness. See Jameson, *Sketches,* vol. 2, 33–34.

46. Jane Johnston Schoolcraft also seems to have believed McKenney had improper ends in mind, for she wrote to Henry on August 3, 1827, that John Johnston "retracted his word & [will] not permit Sister Charlotte to go to Washington. So distant & alone without a single Relative near to advise & check her too innocent & unsuspecting nature, devoid as she is of any knowledge of the World—I think it is decidedly for her advantage to remain where she is." See Jane Johnston Schoolcraft to Henry Rowe Schoolcraft, August 3, 1827, Henry Rowe Schoolcraft Papers, box 7, Library of Congress.

47. McKenney, *Sketches,* 369.

48. McKenney, *Sketches,* 320.

49. Schoolcraft, *Personal Memoirs,* 264.

50. Schoolcraft, "Indian Story Tellers," in *Oneóta, or, Characteristics of the Red Race of America from Original Notes and Manuscripts* (New York: Wiley & Putnam, 1845), n.p.

51. Schoolcraft, *Oneóta,* 197.

52. Schoolcraft, *Oneóta,* 43.

53. Schoolcraft, *Oneóta,* 43.

54. Schoolcraft, *Oneóta,* 487.

55. Dian Million, *Therapeutic Nations: Healing in an Age of Indigenous Human Rights* (Tucson: University of Arizona Press, 2013), 7. See also Sarah Deer, *The Beginning and End of Rape: Confronting Sexual Violence in Native America* (Minneapolis: University of Minnesota Press, 2015), esp. the introduction.

56. Leanne Betasamosake Simpson, *As We Have Always Done: Indigenous Freedom through Radical Resistance* (Minneapolis: University of Minnesota Press, 2017), 52, and see all of chaps. 2–3.

57. McKenney, *Sketches,* 186.

58. McKenney, *Sketches*, 187. A copy of the song in Anishinaabemowin, with the literal English translation, also resides in Schoolcraft's papers at the Library of Congress. The song and translation are in Johnston Schoolcraft's hand; a note in pencil on reverse side of the paper reads: "The Literal Translation of a Young Ojibway Girl's Song [in pencil] by Mrs J. [unreadable]." See Henry Rowe Schoolcraft Papers, box 70, Library of Congress.

59. McKenney, *Sketches*, 187–88. Parker has read the poem as glossing Ojibwe women's experience of being deserted by their European husbands after their marriages were no longer expedient to the men. See Parker, "Braided Relations: Toward a History of Nineteenth-Century American Indian Women's Poetry," in *A History of Nineteenth-Century American Women's Poetry*, ed. Jennifer Putzi and Alexandra Socarides (Cambridge: Cambridge University Press, 2016), 325–26. For recently published versions of the song in Schoolcraft's papers, see *Sound the Stars Make*, 201–4; 248–49. Parker notes that Schoolcraft includes in his unpublished essay "Dawn of Literary Composition by Educated Natives of the Aboriginal Tribes" yet another version, in which an Ojibwe girl is leaving for school. See Schoolcraft, "Dawn," in *Sound the Stars Make*, 248. Colin Elder reads the multiple versions of "Ojibwe Maid" as signifying Anishinaabe practices of repetition. See Elder, "Changing Political and Cultural Realms," 117.

60. Johnston, "Journal."

61. Schoolcraft, *Literary Voyager*, ed. Mason, 103–4.

62. On the lasting power of Pocahontas stories, see Reyna Green, "The Pocahontas Perplex: The Image of Indian Women in American Culture," *Massachusetts Review* 16, no. 4 (1975): 698–714.

63. See Beth H. Piatote, *Domestic Subjects: Gender, Citizenship, and Law in Native American Literature* (New Haven: Yale University Press, 2013).

64. Johnston, "Journal."

65. McKenney, *Sketches*, 187.

66. See Renato Rosaldo, "Imperialist Nostalgia," *Representations* 26 (1989): 107–22.

67. Cohen, *Social Lives*, 86.

68. Naomi Greyser, *On Sympathetic Grounds: Race, Gender and Affective Geographies in Nineteenth-Century North America* (Oxford: Oxford University Press, 2018), introduction. See also Mielke, *Moving Encounters*, chap. 6.

69. Greyser, *On Sympathetic Grounds*, 8.

70. Porter, November 28, [1831], Journal, Autumn 1831–Spring 1932, Jeremiah Porter Papers, Chicago History Museum.

71. Peter Jones, *Life and Journals of Keh-ke-wa-guo-nā-ba: (Rev. Peter Jones)* (Toronto: A. Green, 1860), 363. See also Chute, *Legacy of Shingwaukonse*, 46–48.

72. Chute, *Legacy of Shingwaukonse*, 47; see also 42–68.

73. In the late 1820s and early 1830s, George Copway translated the book of Luke, while George Henry worked with Canadian minister James Evans (who created an

Ojibwe syllabary in the 1830s) to translate hymns. Peter Jones was the most prolific of these translators, working in collaboration with Henry and Evans. He created Anishinaabemowin versions of several books of the Bible (the gospels of Matthew and John and the book of Genesis), and several collections of hymns. Jones's hymn translations were published at the end of a Mohawk-language hymnbook in 1827; in his *Collection of Hymns for the Use of Native Christians of the Chipeway Tongue;* and in *Tracts in the Chippeway and English: Comprising Seven Hymns, the Decalogue, the Lord's Prayer, the Apostle's Creed, and the Fifth Chapter of St. Matthew* (New York: A. Hoyt, 1828). At the Sault, the white man and adopted captive John Tanner translated the New Testament, working with physician Edwin James, although Peter Jones and others (including Henry Rowe Schoolcraft) criticized the translation. See Tanner and James, *Kekitchemanitomenahn gahbemahjein-nunk Jesus Christ: otoashke wawweendummahgawin* (Albany: Packard and Van Benthuysen, 1833). See also Donald B. Smith, *Ojibwe Voices from Nineteenth-Century Canada* (Toronto: University of Toronto Press, 2013), 134–35.

74. Michael D. McNally, *Ojibwe Singers: Hymns, Grief, and a Native Culture in Motion* (Oxford: Oxford University Press, 2000), 27.

75. McNally, *Ojibwe Singers,* 27.

76. English-language hymns in translation could be put to a number of tunes, as hymnbooks did not include musical notation and provided only a note as to whether the hymn was in short, common, or long meter. It was also common practice to use hymns for devotional reading. On devotional reading, see McNally, *Ojibwe Singers,* 34.

77. McKenney, *Sketches,* 186 and Jameson, *Winter Studies,* vol. 3, 228.

78. June 18, [1832], Journal, Jeremiah Porter Papers, Chicago History Museum.

79. January 2, [1833], Journal, Jeremiah Porter Papers, Chicago History Museum.

80. June 18, [1832], Journal, Jeremiah Porter Papers, Chicago History Museum.

81. See Mark Rifkin, *The Erotics of Sovereignty: Queer Native Writing in the Era of Self-Determination* (Minneapolis: University of Minnesota Press, 2012), 3. While Rifkin is discussing twentieth-century literatures, his conceptualization of a structure that remains "unaddressed in and even constitutively excluded from the field of U.S. and tribal politics" (2) is useful for considering earlier circulations of feeling.

82. Rifkin, *Erotics of Sovereignty,* 3, and Schoolcraft, *Oneóta,* "Indian Story Tellers," n.p.

83. After establishing a mission in the Seneca Nation, Bingham received a congressional contract to build a mission and school at Bow-e-ting in 1828, according to terms McKenney and Schoolcraft helped to negotiate in the 1826 Treaty of Fond du Lac. Bingham was charged with advancing U.S. goals of Anishinaabe assimilation to western-style agriculture and gender norms. There was also a Catholic priest at the Sault during this period; the Protestant missionaries generally opposed his efforts, while struggling to find ways to share converts with each other. On Johnston's translation work, see Hele, "Fully Equal to a Mission in Herself."

84. [October] Lords Day 19th [1828]. Journal No. 1, 1828–1832, Abel Bingham Papers, Clarke Historical Library, Mt. Pleasant, MI.

85. 25 [December] 1828, Journal No. 1, Abel Bingham Papers, Clarke Historical Library.

86. 17 [January 1829], Journal No. 1, Abel Bingham Papers, Clarke Historical Library.

87. 17 [November 1830], Journal No. 1, Abel Bingham Papers, Clarke Historical Library.

88. February 18, [1832], Journal, Jeremiah Porter Papers, Chicago History Museum.

89. Craig Womack, *Red on Red: Native American Literary Separatism* (Minneapolis: University of Minnesota Press, 1999), 16.

90. Chute, *Legacy*, 61–65. Chute explains that the British side of St. Mary's River was not Shingwaukonse's preferred location; he lobbied for a site near trading posts on the Garden River but British officials denied his appeal for a move there.

91. François Audrain to George Johnston, June 18, 1833, George Johnston Papers, Burton Historical Collection, Detroit Public Library. Audrain worked under Rowe Schoolcraft.

92. Hele, "How to Win Friends," 158–59. See also Chute, *Legacy*, 53–57.

93. Chute, *Legacy*, 45.

94. Jameson, *Sketches*, vol. 3, 228.

95. Jameson, *Sketches*, vol. 3, 235.

96. Quoted in Hele, "How to Win Friends," 161, n. 43.

97. See the translation by Kayla Gonyon, with assistance from Margaret Noodin, Howard Kimewon, and Alphonse Pitawanakwat, on http://ojibwe.net/projects/prayers-teachings/namewin-prayer/. Charlotte's prayer differs as well from other translations with which she may have been familiar, such as the one Jones included in his *Tracts in the Chippeway and English,* which hews more closely to the English-language prayer.

Interlude: Jane Johnston Schoolcraft's Unfinished Scraps

1. Jane Johnston Schoolcraft, "Album," Poems of Jane Johnston Schoolcraft, 1823–28 & n.d., Henry Rowe Schoolcraft Papers, box 70, Library of Congress.

2. Heid E. Erdrich, "Introduction: June 2018," *Poetry Magazine* (June 2018). *Poetry Foundation,* https://www.poetryfoundation.org/poetrymagazine/articles/146715/introduction-5afo7ff7c1b70 (accessed December 21, 2018).

Chapter Four. List

1. On vocabulary lists as windows into encounter, see Laura J. Murray, "Vocabularies of Native American Languages: A Literary and Historical Approach to an Elusive Genre," *American Quarterly* 53, no. 4 (2001): quotation on 613. Sean Harvey argues that

colonists' linguistic collecting of Native languages provided a foundation for racial theories of difference. He notes that Native people contributed to linguistic projects as translators and informants but observes that after linguistic materials left Native hands and entered colonial institutions, Native people had little control over their meaning. Sarah Rivett, by contrast, sees colonists' interactions with Native languages as leading to the disruption of Enlightenment taxonomies and theologies. Colonists' obsession with the beauty and nature of Native languages, she argues, led to those languages being absorbed into western natural historical and literary frameworks. See Sean Harvey, *Native Tongues: Colonialism and Race from Encounter to the Reservation* (Cambridge: Harvard University Press, 2015) and Sarah Rivett, *Unscripted Americas: Indigenous Languages and the Origins of a Literary Nation* (Oxford: Oxford University Press, 2017).

2. The vocabulary book was published by Léger Brousseau, a printer and publisher who did job printing for the Catholic Church, printing catechisms, pamphlets, almanacs, and bureaucratic documents, such as registers and stationery.

3. On Laurent's education and life, see Lisa Brooks, *The Common Pot: The Recovery of Native Space in the Northeast* (Minneapolis: University of Minnesota Press, 2008), esp. 249–51, and Siobhan Senier, "'All This / Is Abenaki Country': Cheryl Savageau's Poetic Awikhiganak," *Studies in American Indian Literature* 22, no. 3 (2010): 8–9. For Abenaki histories, see Frederick Matthew Wiseman, *The Voice of the Dawn: An Autohistory of the Abenaki Nation* (Hanover: University Press of New England, 2001) and Colin G. Calloway, *The Western Abenakis of Vermont, 1600–1800: War, Migration, and the Survival of an Indian People* (Norman: University of Oklahoma Press, 1990).

4. Carl Benn, *Mohawks on the Nile: Natives among the Canadian Voyageurs in Egypt, 1884–1885* (Toronto: National Heritage Books, 2009), chap. 1, esp. page 29. Thanks to Michael Kelly, head of Archives and Special Collections at Amherst College, for the suggestion that the cover of *Dialogues* might align with interest in the Mohawk men's travels.

5. On the Bureau of American Ethnology and its focus on linguistic collecting as well as Pilling's projects, see Regna Darnell, *And Along Came Boas: Continuity and Revolution in Americanist Anthropology* (Amsterdam: John Benjamins Publishing, 2000), chaps. 1–5. On Pilling, see pages 46–49.

6. Joseph Laurent, *New Familiar Abenakis and English Dialogues* (Quebec: Léger Brousseau, 1884), Ayer PM551.L3 1884, Newberry Library, Chicago. Pilling's copy of the *Dialogues* is now held at the Newberry Library in Chicago, where it is part of the Edward E. Ayer collection, the library's enormous collection of books by and about Native American and Indigenous peoples. The book made its way to the Newberry when Pilling donated his collection on Native American linguistics to Ayer.

7. Laurent, *New Familiar Abenakis and English Dialogues*, Ayer PM551 .L3 1884. Newberry Library.

8. I've also discussed salvage bibliography in the co-authored special issue introduction (with Alyssa Mt. Pleasant and Caroline Wigginton), "Materials and Methods

in Native American and Indigenous Studies: Completing the Turn," *Early American Literature* 53, no. 2 (2018): 415.

9. Sébastian Rasles, "Letter from Father Sébastien Rasles, Missionary of the Society of Jesus in New France, to Monsieur His Brother," October 12, 1723, in *Jesuit Relations and Allied Documents,* vol. 67, ed. Reuben Gold Thwaites, 132–229 (quotation on 146).

10. John Pickering, "Introductory Memoir," in Pickering and Sébastian Rasles, "A Dictionary of the Abnaki Language in North America," *Memoirs of the American Academy of Arts and Sciences,* n.s., 1 (1833): 374.

11. The circulations of the *Dialogues* attest to the ways that, as Phillip H. Round has shown for the eighteenth-century Native Northeast, "books functioned as valuable and valued material objects, often cementing relationships as symbols of affection and esteem, as well as providing a useful form of capital." As Round points out, during the nineteenth century, books knit Native communities together through shared interests or communal acts of reading, and in the case of the *Dialogues,* language learning; books also functioned to cement relationships between Native people and Euro-American patrons, missionaries, or associates. See Phillip H. Round, *Removable Type: Histories of the Book in Indian Country, 1663–1880* (Chapel Hill: University of North Carolina Press, 2010), 62.

12. Laurent, *New Familiar Abenakis and English Dialogues,* 5. Subsequent references to this text will appear in parenthetical citations.

13. Brooks, *Common Pot,* 251.

14. Rasles, "Letter from Father Sébastien Rasles," 133.

15. Rasles, "Letter from Father Sébastien Rasles," 142.

16. Rasles, "Letter from Father Sébastien Rasles," 143–44.

17. Stephen Laurent's comments on Rasles's vocabulary appear in "Talk on Rasle's [*sic*] Dictionary-for Madison Historical," Stephen Laurent Papers, 1846–1999, series 1, box 1, folder 5, Ms.Coll.118, American Philosophical Society, Philadelphia. (August 1965 is written in pencil at the top of the typed manuscript.)

18. As Frederick Wiseman points out, Odanak's location north of the U.S. border "had the important effect of allowing people to maintain highly visible traditions of language, music, dance, art, and public ceremony" that British colonists sought to extinguish. See Wiseman, *Voice of the Dawn,* 118; and on Odanak, see Margaret M. Bruchac, "Reading Abenaki Traditions and European Records of Rogers' Raid," Department of Anthropology Papers, University of Pennsylvania Scholarly Commons, 2006, retrieved from http://repository.upenn.edu/anthro_papers/155, 1–2; Colin G. Calloway, *Dawnland Encounters: Indians and Europeans in Northern New England* (Hanover: University Press of New England, 1991), 133–77; and Senier, "'All This,'" 3. Jean L. Manore comments that "the Canadian and Quebec governments considered the Abenaki to be refugees who fled the United States, not indigenous inhabitants who had simply relocated to more northern areas within Wobanakik. These

governments chose to recognize Abenaki bands at Wolinak and Odanak but resisted extending their recognition to other Abenaki communities such as at Grand Forks (Sherbrooke), Ulverton, Megantic, and Coaticook." Jean L. Manore, "The Historical Erasure of an Indigenous Identity in the Borderlands: The Western Abenaki of Vermont, New Hampshire, and Quebec," *Journal of Borderlands Studies* 26, no. 2 (2011): 180. Day compiles a list of these claims in Gordon M. Day, "The Identity of the Saint Francis Indians," *Canadian Ethnology Service Paper*, no. 71 (Ottawa, 1981): 6–11.

19. In October 1759, British military leader Robert Rogers attacked the village in what has become known as Rogers' Raid, burning the church and all but three houses and claiming afterwards that he destroyed the town and killed all but twenty survivors. But Abenaki accounts differ greatly, suggesting that Rogers and his men killed far fewer people than they claimed and that the village was larger than they assumed. See Bruchac, "Reading Abenaki Traditions," 6; Wiseman, *Voice of the Dawn*, 105, 118; Day, "Identity of the Saint Francis Indians," 43–49.

20. Laurent family manuscripts, currently held at Cornell University, provide a glimpse into the ways that this linguistic work involved creating, using, and saving manuscript texts in Abenaki, many of them guides to religious services. The Abenaki-language manuscript books are stitched together by hand; many books have been repaired with additional stitching, indicating their extensive use. See Abenaki language collection, #9045, Division of Rare and Manuscript Collections, Cornell University Library. Notes within the collection describe it as the Joseph Laurent Abenaki Language Collection in the Huntington Free Library, collected by A. Irving Hallowell from the Laurent family, St. Francis Abenaki Reserve, Odanak, Quebec, 1923.

21. See Brooks, *Common Pot*, 249.

22. For the spelling book, see *Wobanaki kimzowi awighigan* (Boston: Crocker and Brewster, 1830); for religious texts, see Wzokhilain's translation of the book of Mark (Montreal, 1844); the instructional text *Wawasi lagidamwoganek mdala chowagidamwoganal tabtagil: onkawodokodozwal wji pobatami kidwogan* (Boston: Crocker and Brewster, 1830); and an Abenaki-language hymnbook (St. Francis du Lac, 1842). Jesse Bowman Bruchac notes that, in addition to his translation work, Wzokhilain also brought a printing press to Odanak. See Jesse Bruchac, *The Gospel of Mark: Translated into Abenaki Indian, English and French* (New York: Bowman Books, 2011), 2. On Laurent as Wzokhilain's student, see Senier, "'All This,'" 8.

23. Gordon M. Day, "Dartmouth and Saint Francis," in *In Search of New England's Native Past: Selected Essays by Gordon M. Day*, ed. Michael K. Foster and William Cowan (Amherst: University of Massachusetts Press, 1998), 51–52; see also Brooks, *Common Pot*, 249 and Jesse Bowman Bruchac, "A Brief Biography of the Minister, Schoolmaster and Interpreter of the Abenaki Pial Pol Wzokhilain," in *The Gospel of Mark Translated into Abenaki Indian, English and French* (Greenfield Center, NY: Bowman Books, 2011), 1–3.

24. Brooks, *Common Pot,* 251. Brooks analyzes the uses of *kdakinna* in Laurent's word lists; I build on her analysis here to think about the same word in Wzokhilain's book.

25. Brooks, *Common Pot,* 249. See also Senier, "'All This,'" 8.

26. John Wesley Powell, *Fourteenth Annual Report of the Bureau of Ethnology* (Washington, DC: Government Printing Office, 1896), xxix.

27. Powell argued that linguistic categories also had racial uses, suggesting that they could determine the boundaries between "red men and white." See Powell, *Fourteenth Annual Report,* xxix.

28. James Barbour, Circular, Department of War, May 15, 1826, American Indian Vocabulary Collection, Mss.497.V85, American Philosophical Society. Philadelphia.

29. Powell, *Introduction to the Study of Indian Languages with Words Phrases and Sentences to Be Collected. Second Edition—with Charts* (Washington, DC: Government Printing Office, 1880), vi.

30. Powell, *Introduction, Second Edition,* 45–46.

31. Powell, "Indian Linguistic Families," in *Seventh Annual Report of the Bureau of Ethnology* (Washington, DC: Government Printing Office, 1891), 29.

32. Powell, "Linguistic Stocks of American Indians North of Mexico," in *Bureau of American Ethnology, Seventh Annual Report, 1885–1886.*

33. See Powell, *Fourteenth Annual Report,* xxviii.

34. Albert Gallatin's map, on which Powell modeled his, is also temporally inconsistent: as Powell's caption indicates, Gallatin's map shows Indian tribes of North America at about 1600 along the Atlantic coast and about 1800 —as settlers began to push across the Ohio River valley and toward the Pacific coast—in western regions. Like Powell's map, Gallatin's relies on colonization to orient its temporality. See Albert Gallatin, *Map of the Indian Tribes of North* America (1836).

35. Powell, "Indian Linguistic Families," 29.

36. On British and French Canadian denials of Abenaki land rights, see Alain Beaulieu, "'An Equitable Right to Be Compensated': The Dispossession of the Aboriginal Peoples of Quebec and the Emergence of a New Legal Rationale, 1760–1860," *Canadian Historical Review* 94, no. 1 (2013): 1–27 (esp. 8, 10, and 16, on Odanak and other Abenaki towns in the St. Lawrence River valley); Julia Lewandowski, "'The Same Force, Authority, and Effect': Formalizing Native Property and British Plurality in Lower Canada," *Quebec Studies,* Supplemental Issue (2016): 149–70; Bruchac, "Reading Abenaki Traditions"; Calloway, *Dawnland Encounters,* 133–77; and Manore, "Historical Erasure," 180.

37. Joseph Nicolar, *The Life and Traditions of the Red Man* (Bangor, ME: C.H. Glass, 1893), iii.

38. James E. Francis, Sr., Penobscot Nation tribal historian, conversation with the author, June 2016. Thanks to Francis for discussing Nicolar's reliance on Penobscot

traditions, and thanks as well to Charles Norman Shay for his generosity in talking with me about his grandfather, Joseph Nicolar in June 2016.

39. Nicolar, *Life and Traditions*, iii.

40. Nicolar, *Life and Traditions*, iv.

41. Nicolar, *Life and Traditions*, v.

42. Nicolar, *Life and Traditions*, 27–28.

43. Nicolar, *Life and Traditions*, 13.

44. Nicolar, *Life and Traditions*, 98.

45. Nicolar, *Life and Traditions*, 101.

46. Nicolar, *Life and Traditions*, 105.

47. Nicolar, *Life and Traditions*, 105.

48. Nicolar, *Life and Traditions*, 95.

49. Nicolar, *Life and Traditions*, 99.

50. Nicolar, *Life and Traditions*, 105.

51. Gordon M. Day, vol. 1 of *Western Abenaki Dictionary* (Hull, Quebec: Canadian Museum of Civilization, 1993), 64. On Thunder Beings or Birds, see Kathleen J. Bragdon, *Native People of Southern New England, 1500–1650* (Norman: University of Oklahoma Press, 1996), 188–89.

52. Nicolar, *Life and Traditions*, 99.

53. Nicolar, *Life and Traditions*, 86.

54. Nicolar, *Life and Traditions*, 86.

55. Nicolar, *Life and Traditions*, 99.

56. Many thanks to Lisa Brooks for her suggestion to think about the fog as both atmospheric phenomena and a state of being.

57. Colonial writers position the comets preceding colonists as evidence for their claims that Native peoples struggled to interpret Europeans' technology, from ships to guns, and colonists' very presence. Thomas Harriot suggests that Roanoke Algonquian people interpreted a comet as presaging a deadly illness, while Edward Johnson and Thomas Morton insist that astronomical phenomena portended diseases that followed and that the comets were signs of divine approval for English colonization. See Thomas Harriot, *A Briefe and True Report of the New Found Land of Virginia* (London, 1590), 29, and Edward Johnson, *A History of New-England. From the English planting in the yeere 1628. Untill the yeere 1652 . . . With the names of all their governours, magistrates, and eminent ministers* (London, 1653), 15.

58. Nicolar, *Life and Traditions*, 105.

59. This interaction, or "contention," in Nicolar's words, disrupts or disorders Abenaki kinship relations, the "reciprocal networks" that facilitated the "formal and practical exchange of resources and the renewal of longstanding agreements." As Abenaki scholars Lisa Brooks and Cassandra M. Brooks point out in their reading of

relations between Abenaki people and the Presumpscot River, renewing kinship relations involved a "clear responsibility to ensure the continuance of the Presumpscot's people and the non-human relations with whom their survival was entwined." See Lisa Brooks and Cassandra M. Brooks, "The Reciprocity Principle and Traditional Ecological Knowledge: Understanding the Significance of Indigenous Protest on the Presumpscot River," *International Journal of Critical Indigenous Studies* 3, no. 2 (2010): 15 and 17. See also Lisa Brooks's discussion of the common pot, within "which shared space means shared consequences and shared pain." Brooks, *Common Pot*, 6. On the multiple effects of colonization on Abenaki people, see Wiseman, *Voice of the Dawn*, chap. 6.

60. Nicolar, *Life and Traditions*, 105. In this sense, the *Dialogues* act as *awikhigan*, a "tool for image making, for writing, for transmitting an image or idea from one mind to another, over waterways, over time." Brooks, *Common Pot*, xxii.

61. Lisa Brooks, *Our Beloved Kin: A New History of King Philip's War* (New Haven: Yale University Press, 2018), 4.

62. Adrian Johns, *The Nature of the Book: Print and Knowledge in the Making* (Chicago: University of Chicago Press, 1998), 59. On the capacity for circulation to alter an object's meaning, see also Arjun Appadurai, "Introduction: Commodities and the Politics of Value," in *The Social Life of Things*, ed. Arjun Appadurai (Cambridge: Cambridge University Press, 1986), 3–63.

63. Mishuana Goeman, "(Re)Mapping Indigenous Presence on the Land in Native Women's Literature," *American Quarterly* 60, no. 2 (2008): 295. See also Goeman, *Mark My Words: Native Women Mapping Our Nations* (Minneapolis: University of Minnesota Press, 2013).

64. Goeman, "(Re)Mapping," 297.

65. Joseph Laurent, *New Familiar Abenakis and English Dialogues* (Quebec, 1884), Younghee Kim-Wait (Class of 1982)/Pablo Eisenberg Native American Literature Collection, Amherst College Library, Archives and Special Collections. The postcard is dated 1893. One of Amherst's copies of the *Dialogues* may be viewed here: https://acdc.amherst.edu/view/asc:705029.

66. Gary Hume notes that Laurent maintained the camp until his death in 1917; about twelve to eighteen men from Odanak traveled to and worked at the camp. See Gary W. Hume, "Joseph Laurent's Intervale Camp: Post-Colonial Abenaki Adaptation and Revitalization in New Hampshire," *Algonkians of New England, Past and Present: Proceedings of the Dublin Seminar for New England Folklife, 1989*, ed. Peter Benes (Boston: Boston University Press, 1991), 105 and 107. On the camp, see also Wiseman, *Voice of the Dawn*, 132. On Odanak Abenaki basketmakers, including members of Laurent's extended family, and their summer travels, see Alyssa Mt. Pleasant, "Salt, Sand, and Sweetgrass: Methodologies for Exploring the Seasonal Basket Trade in Southern Maine," *American Indian Quarterly* 38, no. 4 (2014): 411–26. As Mt. Pleasant shows,

Laurent's travels to Pequaket participated in the broader practices of Abenaki people selling baskets to tourists throughout their homelands, including on the Maine coast.

67. Hume, "Joseph Laurent's Intervale Camp," 106.

68. I'm grateful to Rhonda Besaw and Margaret M. Bruchac for conversations about Octavie Laurent.

69. Nicolar, *Life and* Traditions, 27–28.

70. Hume, "Joseph Laurent's Intervale Camp," 105 and 113.

71. Wiseman, *Voice of the Dawn*, 118. See also Hume, who notes that the camp allowed the community to continue seasonal labor practices, with men hunting and trapping and women making baskets in the winter and with the community traveling south to sell these materials in the summer. Hume, "Joseph Laurent's Intervale Camp," 106.

72. Brooks, *Common Pot*, 250.

73. "Stephen Laurent (Atian Lolo): Lexicographer of the Abenaki," Stephen Laurent Papers, 1846–1999, series 3, box 7, folder 1, Ms.Coll.118, American Philosophical Society, Philadelphia.

74. "Centennial of the Abenakis in Intervale," Stephen Laurent Papers, 1846–1999, series 1, box 1, folder 5, Ms.Coll.118, American Philosophical Society, Philadelphia.

75. Frank G. Speck, "Abnaki Text," *International Journal of American Linguistics* 11, no. 1 (1945): 45.

76. Stephen Laurent, "The Abenakis: Aborigines of Vermont-Part I," Stephen Laurent Papers, 1846–1999, series 1, box 1, folder 5, Ms.Coll.118, American Philosophical Society, Philadelphia.

77. Stephen Laurent, "Abenakis: Aborigines of Vermont-Part I."

78. Stephen Laurent, "Abenakis: Aborigines of Vermont-Part I."

79. See Brooks, *Common Pot*, 250. See also the map of Penobscot Abenaki words and stories, which shows how stories locate people in place, created by Margaret Pearce and the Penobscot Cultural & Historical Preservation Department. Margaret Pearce and Penobscot Cultural & Historic Preservation Department, Penobscot Nation, *Iyoka Eli-Wihtamakw Kətahkinawal / This Is How We Name Our Lands* (4-color, 2-sided, 44 x 60 inches, folded), Indian Island, ME: Penobscot Cultural & Historic Preservation Department, 2015. On this map and the relations among place names, stories, and places, see Margaret Wickens Pearce, "The Last Piece Is You," *Cartographic Journal* 51, no. 2 (2014): 107–22.

80. Gordon Day, who compiled a two-volume Abenaki-English Dictionary, noted in correspondence to Stephen Laurent that the *Dialogues* had been pivotal to his research. Day marveled at Joseph Laurent's ability to perform translations apparently "out of his head," and commented, "I use your father's book a lot. It is still the easiest place to find an Abenaki form I can't think of, since my own data is arranged only in Abenaki order, and I am relying on the computer to provide an English index one day. And I sometimes wonder at your father producing this marvel out of his head and apparently

unassisted. You don't by chance have any family tradition about his working on it or his methods, do you?" See Gordon Day to Stephen Laurent, June 18, 1987, Stephen Laurent Papers, 1846–1999, series 1, box 1, Ms.Coll.118, American Philosophical Society, Philadelphia.

81. "Stephen Laurent (Atian Lolo): Lexicographer of the Abenaki." Stephen's annotations of the *Dialogues* are in the Stephen Laurent Papers, series 3, box 7, folder 2. For Masta, see Henry Lorne Masta, *Abenaki Indian Legends, Grammar and Place Names* (Victoriaville: La Voix des boisfrancs, 1932).

82. For Stephen's map annotations, see Laurent, series 3, box 7, folder 2. We can see such remapping work continuing in Penobscot Abenaki mapping projects. On such projects, see Pearce, "Last Piece."

83. "Stephen Laurent (Atian Lolo): Lexicographer of the Abenaki." In 1985, the Pequawket Foundation deeded the camp area to the town of Conway, New Hampshire, with the provisions that only Stephen and Emmanuel Laurent had a life estate to use the area and that the town must preserve the camp for "public use and benefit as a public forest reserve forever." This deed recognized the Laurent family's longstanding relationship to Pequaket, even as it claimed the camp for "public" use as well. See Hastings Law Office to Town of Conway Selectmen, July 25, 1994, Stephen Laurent Papers, 1846–1999, series 1, box 1, folder 4, Ms.Coll.118, American Philosophical Society, Philadelphia.

84. Program for Dedication Ceremonies in Honor of Abenaki Chief Joseph Laurent, 1839–1917, Grounds of the Abenaki Indian Shop Intervale N.H. August 30 1959 4:30 PM. Stephen Laurent Papers, series 2, box 4, Ms.Coll.118, American Philosophical Society, Philadelphia.

85. Besaw speculates that the book may have been stolen from the camp when someone broke into its buildings in the late 1990s. Rhonda Besaw, email message to author, June 18, 2015.

86. Besaw, email message to author, June 18, 2015.

87. Besaw, email message to author, June 18, 2015.

88. On uses for books that extend beyond acts of literacy, see Leah Price, *How to Do Things with Books in Victorian England* (Princeton: Princeton University Press, 2012). While Price focuses on the ways that handling and reading were activities with social ramifications in Victorian Britain, her work is a helpful foundation for considering how Laurent's attention to books' "material affordances" played a key role in his educational activities and political advocacy for Abenaki people (16).

Interlude: Carlos Montezuma's Famous Indians

1. Carlos Montezuma, "Clippings, Scrapbook of published articles by Albert Payson Terhune," n.d., Carlos Montezuma Papers, box 4, folder 219, Ayer Modern MS

Montezuma, Newberry Library, Chicago. The Newberry has digitized the scrapbook, and it can be viewed here: http://collections.carli.illinois.edu/cdm/compoundobject/collection/nby_eeayer/id/5454/rec/.

2. Montezuma, "Clippings."

3. Montezuma, Speech, "Flash Lights on the Indian Question," n.d., series 2, box 4, folder 207, Ayer Modern MS Montezuma, Newberry Library, Chicago. "Flash Lights" may be viewed here: https://collections.carli.illinois.edu/digital/collection/nby_eeayer/id/5554.

4. Montezuma, Speech, "Flash Lights."

5. Montezuma, Speech, "Let My People Go," 1915, box 4, folder 210, Ayer Modern MS Montezuma, Newberry Library, Chicago. "Let My People Go" may be viewed here: https://collections.carli.illinois.edu/digital/collection/nby_eeayer/id/5413.

6. Tommy Orange, *There There* (New York: Penguin, 2018).

Chapter Five. Account

1. See Frederick Jackson Turner's speech "The Significance of the Frontier in American History," published in Turner, *The Frontier in American History* (New York: Henry Holt, 1921) and Ida B. Wells, ed. *The Reason Why the Colored American Is Not in the World's Columbian Exposition* (Chicago, 1893). On Du Bois's data portraits, see Whitney Battle-Baptiste and Britt Rusert, eds., *W. E. B. Du Bois's Data Portraits: Visualizing Black America* (Princeton: Princeton Architectural Press, 2018).

2. On this debate, see Curtis M. Hinsley, "Afterward: The Ironies of the Fair, the Uncertainties of Anthropology," in *Coming of Age in Chicago: The 1893 World's Fair and the Coalescence of American Anthropology,* ed. Hinsley and David R. Wilcox (Lincoln: University of Nebraska Press, 2016), 492. Franz Boas and Otis T. Mason debated whether arranging objects in evolutionary types (Mason) or culture areas (Boas) most accurately represented the human past in a June 1887 issue of *Science.* Otis T. Mason, "The Occurrence of Similar Inventions in Areas Widely Apart," *Science* 9 (1887) 534-35, and Franz Boas, "Museums of Ethnology and Their Classification," *Science* 9 (1887): 587-89. See also Curtis M. Hinsley, "The World as Marketplace: Commodification of the Exotic at the World's Columbian Exposition, Chicago," in *Exhibiting Cultures: The Poetics and Politics of Museum Display,* ed. Ivan Karp and Steven D. Lavine (Washington, DC: Smithsonian Books, 1991): 344-66; and George Stocking, ed., *The Shaping of American Anthropology, 1883-1911: A Franz Boas Reader* (New York: Basic Books, 1974).

3. A short pamphlet of twenty-eight pages tied with a yellow ribbon, the *Greeting* circulated as a popular souvenir item at the fair and afterwards, going through at least two printings in 1893. Chicago newspaper articles published in early May 1893 reference the pamphlet as a "poem" in preparation, so it may have circulated in Chicago between May and October 1893. It was certainly doing so by October. See "Poem

by an Indian Chief," *Chicago Daily Tribune,* May 4, 1893, 1, and "Pokagon the Poet," *Chicago Daily Tribune,* October 4, 1893, 1. Scholars have argued that the book was reissued as *Red Man's Greeting* (perhaps for diplomatic purposes), while Pokagon's publisher Cenius H. Engle writes that the book was first issued as *Greeting* and later retitled *Red Man's Rebuke.* See Cenius H. Engle, "Publisher's Notes," *O-gî-mäw-kwĕ Mit-i-gwä-kî/Queen of the Woods,* (1899), 10; Jonathan Berliner, "Written in the Birch Bark: The Linguistic-Material Worldmaking of Simon Pokagon," *PMLA* 125, no. 1 (2010): 73; and John N. Low, *Imprints: The Pokagon Band of Potawatomi Indians & the City of Chicago* (East Lansing: Michigan State University Press, 2016), 44. For Engle's claim, see his contribution to Oran W. Rowland, *History of Van Buren County, Michigan* (Chicago, 1912), 4. Native scholars have provided useful analyses of Pokagon by considering him within Anishinaabe and specifically Neshnabek (or Potawatomi) resistance to colonialism and advocacy. John N. Low (Pokagon Band of Potawatomi Indians) positions Pokagon in a long history of Potawatomi people who successfully argued for the right to remain on their homelands and for annuities owed for land ceded to the United States. Similarly, Kiara M. Vigil considers Pokagon as part of a history of twentieth-century Indigenous intellectuals. See Low, *Imprints,* and Kiara M. Vigil, *Indigenous Intellectuals: Sovereignty, Citizenship, and the American Imagination, 1880–1930* (New York: Oxford University Press, 2015), 5. For the broader context of Anishinaabe people strategically arguing for their rights to remain on their lands, see Michael Witgen, *An Infinity of Nations: How the Native New World Shaped Early North America* (Philadelphia: University of Pennsylvania Press, 2012), and Brenda J. Child, *Holding Our World Together: Ojibwe Women and the Survival of Community* (New York: Penguin, 2012).

4. See Teresa Dean, "Pokagon, the Indian Poet, Apt in Latin and Greek," *Daily Inter Ocean,* October 11, 1893, 7, which states: "On sale at the American Indian village on the Midway is a little booklet with its leaves and cover made of birch bark."

5. Boyd Cothran, *Remembering the Modoc War: Redemptive Violence and the Making of American Innocence* (Chapel Hill: University of North Carolina Press, 2014), 14–15.

6. See, for example, John Cumming, "Pokagon's Birch Bark Books," *American Book Collector* 18, no. 8 (1968): 14–17.

7. Some scholars have characterized Pokagon as representing the last gasp of Native diplomacy as it gave way to "mediated representation"; others have suggested that he did not write his own books and articles; and still others have misread *Rebuke/Greeting* as containing the text of Pokagon's speech at the fair. On "mediated representation" and the *Rebuke/Greeting* as reprinting Pokagon's speech, see Nancy Bentley, *Frantic Panoramas: American Literature and Mass Culture, 1870–1920* (Philadelphia: University of Pennsylvania Press, 2009), 151 and 156. Jonathan Berliner argues that the birchbark pages of the pamphlet offer a "material resolution to a rhetorical problem" (73) and that they allow Pokagon to capitalize on Native peoples' "cultural connection to na-

ture" (74). For Berliner, it is the material form of the book that carries the text's political meaning. See Berliner, "Written in the Birch Bark."

8. Jodi A. Byrd, *The Transit of Empire: Indigenous Critiques of Colonialism* (Minneapolis: University of Minnesota Press, 2011), xiii.

9. I use "Anishinaabe" to refer to the Confederacy of Three Fires, which includes the Ojibwe, Odawa, and Potawatomi peoples, and I use "Neshnabek" to refer specifically to Potawatomi people. Thanks to John Low for advice on language.

10. Nicholas Hopwood, Simon Schaffer, and Jim Secord, "Seriality and Scientific Objects in the Nineteenth Century," *History of Science* 18 (2010): 252.

11. Bentley, *Frantic Panoramas*, 5–6, and Hopwood et al., "Seriality," 263.

12. Hopwood et al., "Seriality," 263.

13. On "evolutionary typology," see Hinsley, "Afterward," 269, and on "tribal arrangements," see Franz Boas, "Museums of Ethnology and Their Classification," *Science* 9, no. 228 (June 17, 1887): 588. See also Tony Bennett, Fiona Cameron, Nélia Dias, Ben Dibly, Rodney Harrison, Ira Jacknis, and Conal McCarthy, *Collecting, Ordering, Governing: Anthropology, Museums, and Liberal Government* (Durham: Duke University Press, 2017), chap. 1, esp. pages 10–15. Exhibits were curated by staff from competing institutions: the Government Building cases were arranged by the National Museum (Smithsonian) and the Bureau of American Ethnology (Goode and Mason) and Department M by Frederic Ward Putnam (and his protégé Franz Boas) from the Peabody Museum at Harvard University. In July 1893 (three months after the fair opened), a separate "Anthropology Building" was opened to accommodate the overwhelming number of objects contributed by Putnam.

14. Hubert Howe Bancroft, *The Book of the Fair: An Historical and Descriptive Presentation of the World's Science, Art, and Industry, as Viewed through the Columbian Exposition at Chicago in 1893* (Chicago, 1893), 631.

15. Frederic Ward Putnam, "Draft of Speech to Committee on the Liberal Arts, Sept. 21," F. W. Putnam Papers, Harvard University Archives, cited in Hinsley and Wilcox, *Coming of Age in Chicago*, 16. As George R. Davis and Putnam explained in their published guide to Department M, "The object of this ethnographical exhibit, as before stated, is to present the means of studying the native peoples in a scientific manner; and, by representing the people who were in America 400 years ago, to form a background to the other departments of the Exposition in which will be illustrated the developments made during the past four centuries." George R. Davis and F. W. Putnam, *World's Columbian Exposition, Chicago, U.S.A., 1893. Plan and Classification Department M* (Chicago: World's Columbian Exposition, 1892), 8. Steven Conn has identified an "object-based epistemology," in which objects "tell stories" to viewers, that orients museum exhibits starting in the mid-nineteenth century. Objects were "illustrations of facts" that represented both the categories and the bodies of knowledge in which

they were arranged. For Conn, the "sentence" and grammar are the organizing principles of object-based epistemologies. I build on Conn's work as I study the fair's "object lessons," but I find that these displays require us to account as well for the series and its categories of time and type. See Steven Conn, *Museums and American Intellectual Life, 1876–1926* (Chicago: University of Chicago Press, 1998): quotations on 4 and 5, respectively.

16. Franz Boas, "Ethnology at the Exposition," *A World's Fair, 1893: A Special Issue of Cosmopolitan Magazine* (December 1893), 81. Meanwhile, Davis and Putnam noted in their description of Department M that, "this gathering of the different natives of the continent at such a time and place can but be beneficial to them, as it will afford them a grand opportunity to see and understand the relations of different nations and the material advantages which civilization brings to mankind." Davis and Putnam, *World's Columbian Exposition*, 9. Commentators also caught on to this "comparative object lesson," noting how the fair juxtaposed "evidence of the latest steps taken in the world's advancement, [with] the objects that show how the rude forefathers of a thousand tribes delved, dug, and builded." See Benjamin Cummings Truman, *History of the World's Fair, Being a Complete and Authentic Description of the Columbian Exposition* (Chicago, 1893), 262.

17. Otis T. Mason, "Ethnological Exhibit of the Smithsonian Institution at the World's Columbian Exposition," in *Memoirs of the International Congress of Anthropology*, ed. C. Staniland Wake (Chicago, 1894), 211.

18. Mason, "Ethnological Exhibit," 211.

19. Mason, "Ethnological Exhibit," 211.

20. Putnam, "Draft of Speech to Committee on the Liberal Arts, Sept. 21."

21. Truman, *History of the World's Fair*, 256. Curtis M. Hinsley reads the displays in the Government Building as evidence that a paradigm shift was underway in aesthetics and perception: "The typological evolutionism of the previous decade ('Kulturgeschichte' or culture history) was ceding organizational authority and interest to new emphases on actual fieldwork experiences (e.g., Cushing, Mooney, Boas), attention to environmental factors, and emerging recognition of culture areas." See Hinsley, "Afterward," 492. See also David Jenkins, "Object Lessons and Ethnographic Displays: Museum Exhibitions and the Making of American Anthropology," *Comparative Studies in Society and History* 36, no. 2 (1994): 260–66, and Regna Darnell, *And Along Came Boas: Continuity and Revolution in Americanist Anthropology* (Amsterdam: John Benjamins Publishing, 2000), esp. the preface. On expositions as places for reading the world, and the use of displays as spaces for such reading, see Alexander C. T. Geppert, *Fleeting Cities: Imperial Expositions in Fin-de-Siécle Europe* (New York: Palgrave, 2010).

22. On some of these doubles, see Ira Jacknis, "Refracting Images: Anthropological Display at the Chicago World's Fair, 1893," in *Coming of Age*, 261–336. Jacknis notes that representations of Native people circulated throughout so many sections of the

fair in part because of the representational technologies appropriating Native people and materials for "art and decoration, advertising, entertainment, and as commodities." See Jacknis, "Refracting," 272. For a comprehensive study of the spaces in which Native people appeared at the fair and their work to control their representation, see David Beck, *Unfair Labor? American Indians and the 1893 World's Columbian Exposition in Chicago* (Lincoln: University of Nebraska Press, 2019); see also Melissa Rhinehart, "To Hell with the Wigs!: Native American Representation and Resistance at the World's Columbian Exposition," *American Indian Quarterly* 36, no. 4 (2012): 403–42.

23. Bancroft, *Book of the Fair*, 107.

24. Truman, *History of the World's Fair*, 259. On the fair's disorder, see also Bancroft, *Book of the Fair*, 646: "As already stated, the bureaus of charities and corrections and of hygiene and sanitation, including in the department of Liberal Arts, were installed in the Anthropological building, this being due to the urgent demand for space by the educational institutions of the United States and foreign countries."

25. Jean M. O'Brien describes this framing of the only authentic history as that of settlers in *Firsting and Lasting: Writing Indians Out of Existence in New England* (Minneapolis: University of Minneapolis Press, 2010), 2.

26. These descriptions appeared in newspapers throughout Illinois, Wisconsin, and Missouri. For just a few examples, see *Nashville (Illinois) Journal*, October 13, 1893, 1, and *Mt. Carmel Register*, October 12, 1893, 3. In 1899, Pokagon's publisher Cenius H. Engle described him in the publisher's notes to *O-gî-mäw-kwĕ Mit-i-gwä-kî* in similar terms, as the "great master link between She-gog-ong as an Indian village and Chicago as one of the greatest commercial cities of the world," and wrote that Pokagon "'link[ed] the present with the past.'" Engle, "Publisher's Notes," 13 and 19.

27. On Chicago Day events, see *Chicago Daily Tribune*, October 9, 1893, and "Triumph of Peace," *Chicago Daily Tribune*, October 10, 1893, 9. For the treaty, see "Chicago, 1833," https://www.cmich.edu/library/clarke/ResearchResources/Native _American_Material/Treaty_Rights/Text_of_Michigan_Related_Treaties/Pages/ Chicago,-1833.aspx.

28. *Chicago Daily Tribune*, October 10, 1893, 9.

29. Michael Zimmerman, Jr., telephone conversation with the author, February 5, 2019. Zimmerman is a former Pokagon Band of Potawatomi Indians tribal historic preservation officer and tribal historian.

30. All descriptions of the float from "Official Chicago Day Program," *Chicago Daily Tribune*, October 10, 1893, 1. On the battle at Fort Dearborn and its interpretations, see Anne Durkin Keating, *Rising Up from Indian Country: The Battle of Fort Dearborn and the Birth of Chicago* (Chicago: University of Chicago Press, 2012).

31. O'Brien, *Firsting and Lasting*, 2.

32. Reports of Chicago Day and of the float consistently identify Pokagon as a representative of the treaty of 1833. To take just one example, the *Illinois State Register*'s

October 10 report on incorrectly identified Pokagon as the "Pottawattomie chief who sold the site on which Chicago is situated." "An Awful Crush," *Illinois State Register,* October 10, 1893, 1. By associating Simon and Leopold Pokagon exclusively with Fort Dearborn and Potawatomi removal, the press and fair organizers obfuscated the other Native nations on whose homelands Chicago rests and their presence at the signing of the treaty of 1833. Michael Zimmerman notes that evidence does not place the Pokagon Band at Fort Dearborn during the battle. Zimmerman, Jr., telephone conversation with the author, February 5, 2019. See also Low, *Imprints,* chap. 1.

33. These temporal relations between "Indians" and U.S. or European "civilizations" oriented a sense of the emergent discipline of anthropology as the study of "culture" defined temporally, that is, a study of peoples over time. On the relations between anthropology and Indigenous dispossession, see Audra Simpson, *Mohawk Interruptus: Political Life across the Borders of Settler States* (Durham: Duke University Press, 2014), 67, and Simpson, "Why White People Love Franz Boas; or, the Grammar of Indigenous Dispossession," in *Indigenous Visions: Rediscovering the World of Franz Boas,* ed. Ned Blackhawk and Isaiah Lorado Wilner (New Haven: Yale University Press, 2018): 166–81.

34. Pokagon says there was a partial payment in 1866, but the balance of $150,000 was not paid until 1896 after appeal to the United States Supreme Court. See Low, *Imprints,* 32, 43, and 227, n. 12.

35. These newspapers reported—inaccurately—that the Potawatomis would receive $200,000 from the government "in full settlement of all claims of the once powerful tribe." "State Items," *Evansville Courier,* October 19, 1889, 2.

36. "Settling Their Claims," *Daily Nebraska State Journal,* December 2, 1889, 5. The right of the Pokagon Potawatomis to remain on part of their homelands was secured by a series of strategic decisions in the early nineteenth century on the part of leader Leopold Pokagon and other Band members. Leopold won these concessions from U.S. treaty officials by insisting that they negotiate with the Pokagon Band individually, rather than applying the treaty's stipulations broadly to all Potawatomi people, and he insisted on exceptions to treaties requiring removal for his Band, actions supported by his strategic political and religious alliances with local Michigan businessmen and the Catholic Church. This insistence forced the U.S. commissioners to negotiate terms specifically for Pokagon's Band, which allowed them to remain in Michigan, on 874 acres that Leopold had purchased. See Low, *Imprints,* 29. On Leopold's Catholicism and strategic alliances, see Gregory Evans Dowd, "Indigenous Catholicism and St. Joseph Potawatomi Resistance in 'Pontiac's War,' 1763–1766," *Ethnohistory* 63, no. 1 (January 2016): 143–66, and Christopher Wetzel, *Gathering the Potawatomi Nation: Revitalization and Identity* (Norman: University of Oklahoma Press, 2015), chap. 1.

37. "Indian Claims Allowed," *Morning Star,* April 15, 1892, 7.

38. Simon Pokagon, *The Red Man's Greeting* (Hartford, MI, 1893), 1. Subsequent references to this text will appear in parenthetical citations. Zimmerman, telephone conversation with the author, February 5, 2019.

39. Pokagon was familiar with these printed histories and their authors, as shown by the fact that he frequently excerpts or references material from Blackbird's *History* in his novel and writings for periodicals. He and Blackbird also attended a boarding school for Native students near Twinsburg, Ohio; for at least part of this period, they attended the school at the same time. For records of their presence at the school, see Samuel Bissell Papers, Western Reserve Historical Society, Cleveland, Mss 116, box 4, folder 1.

40. William Whipple Warren, "History of the Ojibway People," in *Collections of the Minnesota Historical Society* 5 (St. Paul: Minneapolis Historical Society, 1885), 298.

41. Margaret Noodin, "Megwa Baabaamiiaayaayaang Dibaajomoyaang: Anishi-naabe Literature as Memory in Motion," in *Oxford Handbook of Indigenous American Literature*, ed. James H. Cox and Daniel Heath Justice (Oxford: Oxford University Press, 2014), 177. Additionally, the Neshnabek word "gazhëwe'bêk," translated as what happened in the past, is relevant to describing the task of collecting stories about the past. Thanks to Pokagon Band of Potawatomi Indians language specialist Kyle Malott for discussing these words and translations. Malott, conversation with the author, April 9, 2018.

42. These histories also emerged out of ongoing Anishinaabe sovereignty. American, British, and French colonists only slowly made political claims to the western Great Lakes that had force beyond paper claims (see chapter 3). Indigenous languages and political sovereignty remained dominant during much of the nineteenth century, making the book format and the English or French language of uncertain value as materials of diplomacy, history, or literature. By the time Warren and other Anishi-naabe men created their histories, Anishinaabe lands had only recently been forcibly and violently claimed by the U.S. Warren writes about twelve years before the 1862 U.S.-Dakota War and the largest mass execution in U.S. history, of thirty-eight Dakota men accused of killing colonists in the war. Moreover, as we have already seen, Potawatomi people like Leopold Pokagon resisted removal by negotiating to remain on their lands; other Native communities joined relations in Canada or refused to move west. See Witgen, *Infinity of Nations*, esp. 10–12; Susan Sleeper Smith, *Indian Women and French Men: Rethinking Cultural Encounter in the Western Great Lakes* (Amherst: University of Massachusetts Press, 2001), 100–147; Wetzel, *Gathering the Potawatomi Nation*, 31–32; and Mark R. Schurr, Terrance J. Martin, and W. Ben Secunda, "How the Pokagon Band Avoided Removal: Archaeological Evidence from the Faunal Assemblage of the Pokagon Village Site (20BE13)," *Midcontinental Journal of Archaeology* 31, no. 1 (2006): 143–63.

43. Noodin, "Megwa Baabaamiiaayaayaang Dibaajomoyaang," 180. On nonlinear approaches to Indigenous history that emphasize the stories embedded in place, see also Lisa Brooks, "The Primacy of the Present, the Primacy of Place: Navigating the Spiral of History in the Digital World," *PMLA* 127, no. 2 (2012): 308–16.

44. Warren, *History*, 104; annals on 108, 255, 305, and 314.

45. Andrew J. Blackbird, *History of the Ottawa and Chippewa Indians of Michigan: A Grammar of Their Language, and Personal and Family History of the Author* (Ypsilanti, MI, 1887), chap. 2.

46. Blackbird, *History*, 16.

47. Blackbird, *History*, 74.

48. Noodin, "Megwa Baabaamiiaayaayaang Dibaajomoyaang," 180.

49. Noodin, "Reading *Queen of the Woods* Today," in Simon Pokagon, *Ogimawkwe Mitigwaki-Queen of the Woods* (East Lansing: Michigan State University Press, 2011), 68.

50. Noodin, "Megwa Baabaamiiaayaayaang Dibaajomoyaang," 183.

51. Noodin, "Megwa Baabaamiiaayaayaang Dibaajomoyaang,"183–84.

52. Noodin, "Megwa Baabaamiiaayaayaang Dibaajomoyaang," 177.

53. As Claudia Stokes has shown, influential American literature anthologies, such as Brander Matthews's *Introduction to the Study of American Literature* (1896), appeared first in serial form. See Stokes, *Writers in Retrospect: The Rise of American Literary History, 1875–1910* (Chapel Hill: University of North Carolina Press, 2006), 41. First published in 1828, Irving's book was republished many times before 1893; it was printed in New York, Philadelphia, and London in the late nineteenth century, including an 1892 New York edition and 1893 Philadelphia edition from which Pokagon could have drawn his excerpts. Irving's *History* was also excerpted and serialized in periodicals, including the children's magazine *Robert Merry's Museum,* published in Boston. Irving's *History* described for nineteenth-century readers Columbus's so-called discovery of the Americas and the various measures he took to conquer Indigenous peoples.

54. Lindsay diCuirci, *Colonial Revivals: The Nineteenth-Century Lives of Early American Books* (Philadelphia: University of Pennsylvania Press, 2019), chap. 5. DiCuirci argues that Irving's historical romance must be understood in relation to his antiquarianism, especially his attempt to work in a Spanish archive that was not only voluminous and disorganized but that also cast the United States as an heir to the violence of conquest.

55. Washington Irving, *History of the Life and Voyages of Christopher Columbus,* vol. 1 (London: John Murray, 1828), 313. Columbus's journals were first transcribed and edited by Bartolomé de las Casas; Martyr composed his own history of Spanish colonization in 1511 based on Columbus's letters and other Spanish reports, including an account of Columbus's fourth voyage (Martyr's work on Columbus was part of his ten-volume reports on Spanish travels and colonial ventures, *Decades of the New World*). Richard Eden translated Martyr's first three decades (or books) into English in 1555,

and in the nineteenth century, Edward Arber edited Eden's versions and published them in 1895 as *The First Three English Books on America.*

56. See diCuirci, *Colonial Revivals*, 153–54, and Elise Bartosik-Velez, *The Legacy of Christopher Columbus in the Americas: New Nations and a Transatlantic Discourse of Empire* (Nashville, Vanderbilt University Press, 2014).

57. Irving, *History*, vol. 2, 278.

58. Irving, *History*, vol. 2, 283.

59. Simon Pokagon, "The Future of the Red Man," *Forum* (August 1897), 701.

60. Noodin, "Reading *Queen of the Woods* Today," 68.

61. Pokagon is perhaps referring here to the Hotchkiss guns (a Gatling-style rapid-fire gun) used at the Wounded Knee Massacre in 1890 as well as at other U.S. massacres of Native people in the nineteenth century.

62. Pokagon, "Old Simon Pokagon," *Sunday Inter Ocean*, October 20, 1893, 6.

63. Pokagon, *O-gî-mäw-kwĕ Mit-i-gwä-kî*, 107, n. 1.

64. Pokagon, *O-gî-mäw-kwĕ Mit-i-gwä-kî*, 135, n. 1.

65. Pokagon, *O-gî-mäw-kwĕ Mit-i-gwä-kî*, 107.

66. Pokagon, *O-gî-mäw-kwĕ Mit-i-gwä-kî*, 135. I depart here from Berliner's reading of this moment as one in which Ashtaw and Pokagon convey a "reformist message." See Berliner, "Written in the Birch Bark," 77.

67. Pokagon, *O-gî-mäw-kwĕ Mit-i-gwä-kî*, 135–36.

68. Pokagon, "Indian Native Skill," *The Chautauquan* 26, no. 5 (February 1898): 541.

69. Pokagon, "Indian Native Skill," 540.

70. Pokagon, "Indian Native Skill," 540.

71. Cothran, *Remembering the Modoc War*, 14.

72. Ann Durkin Keating, *Rising Up from Indian Country: The Battle of Fort Dearborn and the Birth of Chicago* (Chicago: University of Chicago Press, 2012), 2.

73. John Tanner, *A Narrative of the Captivity and Adventures of John Tanner (U.S. Interpreter at the Saut [sic] de Ste. Marie) during Thirty Years Residence among the Indians in the Interior of North America* (London, 1830), 60.

74. Tanner, *Narrative*, 175.

75. Heidi Bohaker, "Indigenous Histories and Archival Media in the Early Modern Great Lakes," in *Colonial Mediascapes: Sensory Worlds of the Early Americas*, ed. Matt Cohen and Jeffrey Glover (Lincoln: University of Nebraska Press, 2014), 109. See also Louise Erdrich, *Books and Islands in Ojibwe Country: Traveling through the Land of My Ancestors* (New York: Harper Collins, 2003), 3 and 8, and Francis Densmore, *Chippewa Customs: Smithsonian Institution Bureau of Ethnology Bulletin 86* (Washington, DC, 1929), 176–80.

76. Bohaker, "Indigenous Histories," 115. I depart here once again from Jonathan Berliner's reading of the *Greeting*, in my argument that Pokagon models his book on account books and Anishinaabe historiographies. Berliner argues that the texts

NOTES TO PAGES 200–207

of Anishinaabe "medewewin" (also spelled midewiwin) and North American tourist art offer generic contexts for the *Greeting*. But, despite the fact that both the *Greeting* and medewewin texts were inscribed on birchbark, Pokagon's text has more in common generically with the birchbark maps put to everyday use, especially because medewewin texts were interpreted by people who had undergone ceremonial training. See Berliner, "Written in the Birch Bark," esp. 74.

77. Zitkála-Šá, *American Indian Stories* (Lincoln: University of Nebraska Press, 2003), 159.

78. Zitkála-Šá, *American Indian Stories*, 168.

79. Zitkála-Šá, *American Indian Stories*, 63.

80. Zitkála-Šá, *American Indian Stories*, 64.

81. Zitkála-Šá, *American Indian Stories*, 155–56.

82. Zitkála-Šá, *American Indian Stories*, 157.

83. Zitkála-Šá, *American Indian Stories*, 157–58.

Epilogue

1. Susan Power, *Roofwalker* (Minneapolis: Milkweed Editions, 2002), 161.

2. Power, *Roofwalker*, 163.

3. See, for more information, https://www.chicagoparkdistrict.com/parks-facilities/signal-peace; http://chicagopublicart.blogspot.com/2013/08/worlds-fair-bison.html; and https://www.artic.edu/artworks/111661/the-end-of-the-trail.

4. Power, *Roofwalker*, 164.

5. Power, *Roofwalker*, 161.

6. Power, *Roofwalker*, 165.

7. Pokagon, "Indian Native Skill," *The Chautauquan* 26, no. 5 (February 1898): 540.

8. On the history of Chicago's Native community in the twentieth century, see Rosalyn R. LaPier and David R. M. Beck, *City Indian: Native American Activism in Chicago, 1893–1934* (Lincoln: University of Nebraska Press, 2015); John N. Low, *Imprints: The Pokagon Band of Potawatomi Indians & the City of Chicago* (East Lansing: Michigan State University Press, 2016); and William "Buddy" Scarborough, Faith R. Kares, Iván Arenas, and Amanda E. Lewis, "Adversity and Resiliency for Chicago's First: The State of Racial Justice for American Indian Chicagoans Report," Institute for Research on Race & Public Policy, University of Illinois at Chicago (2019), https://stateofracialjusticechicago.com/.

9. The exhibit was held in November–December 2018 at the American Indian Center of Chicago. The digital archive created by the interns may be viewed here: http://hub.madstudio.northwestern.edu/aica/. The project was funded by a 2018 NEH Common Heritage grant titled "The American Indian Center of Chicago and Urban Native American Histories." The grant team consisted of Heather Miller (then

executive director, AIC), Dave Spencer (development and arts coordinator, AIC), Monica Boutwell (AIC intern), Naomi Harvey-Turner (AIC intern), Eli Suzukovich (AIC and NU), John Bresland (NU Media and Design Studio), Matthew Taylor (NU Media and Design Studio), Josh Honn (NU Libraries), and Kelly Wisecup.

10. Power, *Roofwalker,* 163.

11. Thanks to Chris Pappan for discussing the exhibit with me and sharing details about the works displayed in an email conversation on September 13, 2019.

BIBLIOGRAPHY

Primary Texts

Adair, James. *The History of the American Indians; Particularly Those Nations Adjoining to the Mississippi, East and West Florida, Georgia, South and North Carolina, and Virginia: containing, An Account of their Origin, Language, Manners, Religious and Civil Customs, Laws, form of Government, Punishments, conduct in War and Domestic Life, their Habits, Diet, Agriculture, Manufactures, Diseases and Method of Cure, and other Particulars, sufficient to render it A Complete Indian System.* London, 1775.

Amera, Charles. "Autograph Album." Ayer MS 3241. Newberry Library, Chicago.

"An Awful Crush." *Illinois State Register.* October 10, 1893, 1. *Readex: America's Historical Newspapers.* Accessed December 2016.

"Anecdotes of Teedyuscung." *Weekly Magazine* 1 (1798): 393–94. *Readex: America's Historical Newspapers.* Accessed November 2015.

Apess, William. *Indian Nullification of the Unconstitutional Laws of Massachusetts Relative to the Marshpee Tribe: or, The Pretended Riot Explained.* Boston: Jonathan Howe, 1835.

———. *On Our Own Ground: The Complete Writings of William Apess, a Pequot,* edited by Barry O'Connell. Amherst: University of Massachusetts Press, 1992.

————. *Son of the Forest: The Experience of William Apes, A Native of the Forest. Comprising a Notice of the Pequod Tribe of Indians. Written by Himself.* New York, 1829.

Audrain, François. François Audrain to George Johnston. March 27, 1827, and June 18, 1833. George Johnston Papers. Burton Historical Collection, Detroit Public Library.

Balbi, Adrien. *Atlas ethnographique du globe.* Vol. 1. Paris, 1826.

Bancroft, Hubert Howe. *The Book of The Fair: An Historical and Descriptive Presentation of the World's Science, Art, and Industry, as Viewed through the Columbian Exposition at Chicago in 1893.* Chicago, 1893.

Barbour, James. "Circular, Department of War." May 15, 1826. American Indian Vocabulary Collection. Mss.497.V85. American Philosophical Society, Philadelphia.

Bigsby, John J. *The Shoe and Canoe: or, Pictures of Travel in the Canadas, Illustrative of Their Scenery and of Colonial Life.* Vol. 2. London: Chapman and Hall, 1850.

Bingham, Abel. Journals. Abel Bingham Papers. Clarke Historical Library, Mt. Pleasant, MI.

Blackbird, Andrew J. *History of the Ottawa and Chippewa Indians of Michigan: A Grammar of Their Language, and Personal and Family History of the Author.* Ypsilanti, MI, 1887.

Blecki, Catherine La Courreye, and Karin A. Wulf, eds. *Milcah Martha Moore's Book: A Commonplace Book from Revolutionary America.* University Park: Pennsylvania State University Press, 1997.

Boas, Franz. "Ethnology at the Exposition." *A World's Fair, 1893: A Special Issue of Cosmopolitan Magazine.* December 1893. In *Coming of Age in Chicago: The 1893 World's Fair and the Coalescence of American Anthropology,* edited by Curtis M. Hinsley and David R. Wilcox, 78–83. Lincoln: University of Nebraska Press, 2016.

————. "Museums of Ethnology and Their Classification." *Science* 9 (1887): 587–89.

Bross, Kristina, and Hilary E. Wyss, eds. *Early Native Literacies in New England: A Documentary and Critical Anthology.* Amherst: University of Massachusetts Press, 2008.

Brown, Catharine. *Cherokee Sister: The Collected Writings of Catharine Brown, 1818–1823,* edited by Theresa Strouth Gaul. Lincoln: University of Nebraska Press, 2014.

Butrick, Daniel S., to John Howard Payne. May 13, 1836. John Howard Payne Papers. Vol. 4. Newberry Library, Chicago.

"Cherokee Nation v. Georgia." https://supreme.justia.com/cases/federal/us/30/1/. Accessed August 28, 2015.

"Circular Letter of the Historical Society." Boston: Belknap and Young, 1791.

Copway, George. *Life, Letters and Speeches,* edited by LaVonne Brown Ruoff and Donald B. Smith. Lincoln: University of Nebraska Press, 2006.

Cox, Ross. *Adventures on the Columbia River.* New York: J&J Harper, 1832.

Daggett, Herman. *The American Reader: Consisting of Familiar, Instructive, and Entertaining Stories.* 2nd ed. Poughkeepsie, NY, 1812.

Davis, George R., and F. W. Putnam. *World's Columbian Exposition, Chicago, USA, 1893. Plan and Classification Department M.* Chicago: World's Columbian Exposition, 1892.

Day, Gordon, to Stephen Laurent. June 18, 1987. Stephen Laurent Papers, 1846–1999. Ms.Coll.118. Series 1, box 1. American Philosophical Society, Philadelphia.

De Forest, John W. *History of the Indians of Connecticut, from the Earliest Known Period to 1850. Published with the Sanction of the Connecticut Historical Society.* Hartford: WM Jas Hamersley, 1851.

Densmore, Francis. *Chippewa Customs. Smithsonian Institution Bureau of Ethnology Bulletin 86.* Washington, DC, 1929.

Eastman, Charles. *From the Deep Woods to Civilization.* Lincoln: University of Nebraska Press, 1977.

Elliot, Jonathan. *Historical Sketches of the Ten Miles Square Forming the District of Columbia.* Washington, DC, 1830.

Engle, Cenius H. "Publisher's Notes." *O-gî-mäw-kwĕ Mit-i-gwä-kî (Queen of the Woods),* 5–33. Hartford, MI, 1899.

Erdrich, Heid E. "Introduction: June 2018." *Poetry Magazine* (June 2018). https://www.poetryfoundation.org/poetrymagazine/articles/146715/introduction-5afo7ff7c1b70. Accessed December 21, 2018.

Erdrich, Louise. *Books and Islands in Ojibwe Country: Traveling through the Land of My Ancestors.* New York: Harper Collins, 2003.

Fulopp, Megan. "A Journey with Occom," *Occom's Footsteps.* https://occomsfootsteps.wordpress.com/. Accessed August 31, 2020.

———. "July 14, 2020: The Brothertown Indian Nation Celebrates First Annual Samson Occom Day." *The Life of the Brothertown Indians.* https://brothertowncitizen.com/2020/07/13/july-14–2020-the-brothertown-indian-nation-celebrates-first-annual-samson-occom-day/. Accessed August 31, 2020.

Gallatin, Albert. *Map of the Indian Tribes of North America, about 1600 A.D. along the Atlantic and about 1800 A.D. Westwardly.* 1836. GA405 .W5 1957 v. 2. Newberry Library, Chicago.

———. Papers of Albert Gallatin. New-York Historical Society. Microfilm, roll 36, frames 221–23. New York. Accessed April 2016.

Gaul, Theresa Strouth, ed. *To Marry an Indian: The Marriage of Harriett Gold and Elias Boudinot in Letters, 1823–1839.* Chapel Hill: University of North Carolina Press, 2005.

Gonyon, Kayla, Margaret Noodin, Howard Kimewon, and Alphonse Pitawanakwat. "Namewin." http://ojibwe.net/projects/prayers-teachings/namewin-prayer/. Accessed March 15, 2018.

Harriot, Thomas. *A Briefe and True Report of the New Found Land of Virginia.* London, 1590.

Hastings Law Office to Town of Conway Selectmen. July 25, 1994. Stephen Laurent Papers, 1846–1999. Series 1, box 1, folder 4. Ms.Coll.118. American Philosophical Society, Philadelphia.

Hicks, Charles R., to John Ross. February 1, 1826. John Howard Payne Papers. Vol. 7, folder 1. Newberry Library, Chicago.

Hopkins, Pauline. "Of One Blood; Or, the Hidden Self." (1902–3). In *The Magazine Novels of Pauline Hopkins.* Oxford: Oxford University Press, 1990.

Horton, Azariah. "Second Journal of Mr. Azariah Horton, Missionary in the Province of New York, from 22nd November 1741, to 16th May 1742." In *History and Archaeology of the Montauk,* edited by Gaynell Stone, 198–205. Vol. 3. 2nd ed. Suffolk County Archaeological Association, 1993.

"Indian Claims Allowed." *Morning Star.* April, 15, 1892, 7. *Readex: America's Historical Newspapers.* Accessed December 2016.

Irving, Washington. *History of the Life and Voyages of Christopher Columbus.* Vol. 1. London: John Murray, 1828.

Jameson, Anna Brownell. *Winter Studies and Summer Rambles in Canada.* Vol. 3. London: Saunders and Otley, 1838.

Jefferson, Thomas. *Notes on the State of Virginia,* edited by Frank Shuffelton. New York: Penguin, 1999.

Johnson & Graham's Lessee v. M'Intosh. U.S. Supreme Court. 21 U.S. (8 Wheat.) 543, 1823. *Justia US Supreme Court.* https://supreme.justia.com/cases/federal/us/21/543/case.html. Accessed September 14, 2015.

Johnson, Edward. *A History of New-England. From the English planting in the yeere 1628. Untill the yeere 1652 . . . With the names of all their governours, magistrates, and eminent ministers.* London, 1653.

Johnson, E. Pauline. *E. Pauline Johnson, Tekahionwake: Collected Poems and Selected Prose,* edited by Carole Gerson and Veronica Strong-Boag. Toronto: University of Toronto Press, 2002.

———. *Tekahionwake: E. Pauline Johnson's Writings on Native North America,* edited by Margery Fee and Dory Nason. Peterborough, ON: Broadview Press, 2016.

Johnson, James E. "Scrapbook, 1899–1904." Northwestern University Libraries Digital Collections. Accessed October 15, 2019.

Johnson, Joseph. *To Do Good to My Indian Brethren: The Writings of Joseph Johnson, 1751–76,* edited by Laura J. Murray. Amherst: University of Massachusetts Press, 1998.

Johnston, Charlotte. Charlotte Johnston to George Johnston. May 24, 1833. George Johnston Papers. Burton Historical Collection. Detroit Public Library.

———. "Journal." George Johnston Papers, 1792–1944. Judge Joseph H. Steere Room. Bayliss Public Library, Sault Ste. Marie, MI.

———. "Ojibwa Book." George Johnston Papers, 1792–1944. Judge Joseph H. Steere Room. Bayliss Public Library, Sault Ste. Marie, MI.

Johnston, George. George Johnston Memorandum Book. George Johnston Papers, 1792–1944. Folders 2 and 3, box 1. Judge Joseph H. Steere Room. Bayliss Public Library, Sault Ste. Marie, MI.

———. "Reminiscences of Geo. Johnston, of Sault de Ste. Marie, 1815." In *Michigan Pioneer and Historical Collections,* edited by Henry S. Bartholomew, 605–11. Vol. 12. 2nd ed. Lansing, MI: Wynkoop, Hallenbeck, Crawford, 1906.

Jones, Peter. *Collection of Hymns for the Use of Native Christians of the Iroquois. To which are Added a Few Hymns in the Chipeway Tongue,* translated by Peter Jones. New York: A. Hoyt, 1827.

———. *Life and Journals of Keh-ke-wa-guo-nā-ba: (Rev. Peter Jones).* Toronto: A. Green, 1860.

———. *Tracts in the Chippeway and English: Comprising Seven Hymns, the Decalogue, the Lord's Prayer, the Apostle's Creed, and the Fifth Chapter of St. Matthew.* New York, 1828.

Laurent, Joseph. *New Familiar Abenakis and English Dialogues.* Quebec: Léger Brousseau, 1884.

Laurent, Stephen. "The Abenakis: Aborigines of Vermont-Part I." Stephen Laurent Papers, 1846–1999. Ms.Coll.118. Series 1, box 1, folder 5. American Philosophical Society, Philadelphia.

———. "Centennial of the Abenakis in Intervale." Stephen Laurent Papers, 1846–1999. Ms.Coll.118. Series 1, box 1, folder 5. American Philosophical Society, Philadelphia.

————. "Stephen Laurent (Atian Lolo): Lexicographer of the Abenaki." Stephen Laurent Papers, 1846–1999. Ms.Coll.118. Series 3, box 7, folder 1. American Philosophical Society, Philadelphia.

————. "Talk on Rasle's [*sic*] Dictionary-for Madison Historical." Ms.Coll.118. Series 1, box 1, folder 5. Stephen Laurent Papers, 1846–1999. American Philosophical Society, Philadelphia.

Lewis, Robert Benjamin. *Light and Truth Collected from the Bible and Ancient and Modern History, Containing the Universal History of the Colored and the Indian Race, from the Creation of the World to the Present Time.* Boston, 1844.

Long, Stephen. *Account of An Expedition from Pittsburgh to the Rocky Mountains, Performed in the Years 1819 and '20, by order of the Hon. J. C. Calhoun, Sec'y of War, under the command of Major Stephen H. Long, from the Notes of Major Long, Mr. T. Say, and other Gentlemen of the Exploration Party. Compiled by Edwin James, Botanist and Geologist for the Expedition.* Vol. 1. Philadelphia, 1823.

Love, William DeLoss. *Samson Occom and the Christian Indians of New England.* Boston: Pilgrim Press, 1899.

Mason, Otis T. "Ethnological Exhibit of the Smithsonian Institution at the World's Columbian Exposition." In *Memoirs of the International Congress of Anthropology,* edited by C. Staniland Wake, 208–16. Chicago, 1894.

————. "The Occurrence of Similar Inventions in Areas Widely Apart." *Science* 9 (1887): 534–35.

Masta, Henry Lorne. *Abenaki Indian Legends, Grammar and Place Names.* Victoriaville: La Voix des boisfrancs, 1932.

Mayhew, Experience. *Indian Converts: Or, Some Account of the Lives and Dying Speeches of a considerable Number of the Christianized Indians of Martha's Vineyard, in New-England.* London: Samuel Gerrish, 1727.

McKenney, Thomas. *Sketches on a Tour to the Lakes, of the Character and Customs of the Chippeway Indians, and of Incidents Connected with the Treaty of Fond du Lac.* Baltimore, 1827.

Montezuma, Carlos. "Clippings, Scrapbook of published articles by Albert Payson Terhune, n.d." Carlos Montezuma Papers. Box 4, folder 219. Ayer Modern MS Montezuma. Newberry Library, Chicago.

————. "Flash Lights on the Indian Question," n.d. Series 2, box 4, folder 207. Ayer Modern MS Montezuma. Newberry Library, Chicago.

————. "Let My People Go." 1915. Box 4, folder 210. Ayer Modern MS Montezuma. Newberry Library, Chicago.

Nagle, Mary Kathryn. *Sovereignty.* Evanston: Northwestern University Press, 2020.

Nicolar, Joseph. *The Life and Traditions of the Red Man.* Bangor, ME: CH Glass, 1893.

Occom, Samson. *The Collected Writings of Samson Occom, Mohegan: Leadership and Literature in Eighteenth-Century America*, edited by Joanna Brooks. Oxford: Oxford University Press, 2006.

"Official Chicago Day Program." *Chicago Daily Tribune.* October 9, 1893, 1. *Readex: America's Historical Newspapers.* Accessed December 2016.

Orange, Tommy. *There There.* New York: Penguin, 2018.

Parker, Ely S. "Ely Samuel Parker Scrapbooks, 1828–1894." Ayer Modern MS Parker. Newberry Library, Chicago.

Payne, John Howard. "Ancient Cherokee Traditions and Religious Rites." *American Quarterly Register and Magazine* (December 1849): 444–50. *Readex: America's Historical Newspapers.* Accessed December 2016.

———. "John Howard Payne to His Countrymen." *Knoxville Register.* December 2, 1835. *Readex: America's Historical Newspapers.* Accessed December 2016.

Pearce, Margaret, and Penobscot Cultural & Historic Preservation Department, Penobscot Nation. *Iyoka Eli-Wihtamakw Kətahkinawal / This Is How We Name Our Lands.* Indian Island, ME: Penobscot Cultural & Historic Preservation Department, 2015.

Perdue, Theda. *Cherokee Women: Gender and Culture Change, 1700–1835.* Lincoln: University of Nebraska Press, 1998.

Perdue, Theda, and Michael D. Green, eds. *The Cherokee Removal: A Brief History with Documents.* New York: Bedford/St. Martin's, 1995.

Pickering, John. "Introductory Memoir." In *Memoirs of the American Academy of Arts and Sciences,* n.s., 1 (1833): 370–74.

Pilling, James Constantine. *Bibliography of the Algonquian Languages.* Washington, DC: Government Printing Office, 1891.

"Poem by an Indian Chief." *Chicago Daily Tribune.* May 4, 1893, 9. *Readex: America's Historical Newspapers.* Accessed December 2016.

Pokagon, Simon. "The Future of the Red Man." *Forum* (August 1897): 698–708.

———. "Indian Native Skill." *The Chautauquan* 26, no. 5 (February 1898): 540–43.

———. *O-gî-mäw-kwĕ Mit-i-gwä-kî (Queen of the Woods).* Hartford, MI: C. H. Engle, 1899.

———. "Old Simon Pokagon." *Sunday Inter Ocean.* October 20, 1893, 6. *Readex: America's Historical Newspapers.* Accessed December 2016.

———. *The Red Man's Greeting* (alt. title *The Red Man's Rebuke*). Hartford, MI: C. H. Engle, 1893.

"Pokagon the Poet." *Chicago Daily Tribune.* October 4, 1893, 1. *Readex: America's Historical Newspapers.* Accessed December 2016.

Ponceau, Peter du, to Albert Gallatin. April 8, 1826. Historical and Literary Committee Letter Book. Vol. 3. American Philosophical Society, Philadelphia.

Porter, Jeremiah. Journal. Jeremiah Porter Papers. Chicago History Museum. Chicago.

Posey, Alexander. Manuscript Collection, 1888–1907. Gilcrease Museum, Tulsa.

"Preface." In *Archaeologia Americana, Transactions and Collections of the American Antiquarian Society,* viii–x. Vol. 2. Cambridge, 1836.

Powell, John Wesley. *Fourteenth Annual Report of the Bureau of Ethnology.* Washington, DC: Government Printing Office, 1896.

———. "Indian Linguistic Families." In *Seventh Annual Report of the Bureau of Ethnology.* Washington, DC: Government Printing Office, 1891.

———. *Introduction to the Study of Indian Languages with Words Phrases and Sentences to Be Collected. Second Edition—with Charts.* Washington, DC: Government Printing Office, 1880.

———. "Linguistic Stocks of American Indians North of Mexico." In *Bureau of American Ethnology, Seventh Annual Report, 1885–1886.* Washington, DC: Government Printing Office, 1891.

Program for Dedication Ceremonies in Honor of Abenaki Chief Joseph Laurent, 1839–1917. Grounds of the Abenaki Indian Shop Intervale, NH, August 30, 1959. 4:30 PM. Stephen Laurent Papers. Series 2, box 4. Ms.Coll.118. American Philosophical Society, Philadelphia.

Power, Susan. *Roofwalker.* Minneapolis: Milkweed Editions, 2002.

Rasles, Sébastian. "A Dictionary of the Abnaki Language in North America." In *Memoirs of the American Academy of Arts and Sciences,* n.s., 1 (1833): 375–574.

———. "Letter from Father Sébastien Rasles, Missionary of the Society of Jesus in New France, to Monsieur his Brother," October 12, 1723. In *The Jesuit Relations and Allied Documents: Travels And Explorations of the Jesuit Missionaries in New France 1610–1791,* edited by Reuben Gold Thwaites, 84–119. Vol. 67. Cleveland: Burrow Brothers, 1900.

Ridge, John. "Comparative Vocabulary." Gallatin Papers. Box 64–3, Indian Languages. Manuscripts Collection. New-York Historical Society.

———. John Ridge to Albert Gallatin. February 27, 1826. John Howard Payne Papers. Vol. 8, folder 4. Newberry Library. Chicago.

———. John Ridge to Albert Gallatin. March 10, 1826. Gallatin Papers. Box 64–3, Indian Languages. Manuscripts Collection. New-York Historical Society.

———. "Poems and Hymns copied by John Ridge at Cornwall Mission School, February–March, 1819." John Howard Payne Papers. Vol. 8, folder 2. Newberry Library, Chicago.

————. [Socrates, pseud.] "Strictures on 'The Report of the Joint Committee on the State of the Republic,' in the Legislature of Georgia, on the subject of the Cherokee Lands; purporting to prove the absolute jurisdictional right of the said state to the same." *Cherokee Phoenix* (Cherokee Nation), March 13, 1828.

Rosier, James. *A True Relation of the most prosperous voyage made this present yeere 1605, by Captaine George Waymouth, in the discovery of the land of Virginia* (London, 1605). In *The English New England Voyages, 1602–1608*, edited by David B. Quinn and Alison M. Quinn, 250–311. London: Hakluyt Society, 1983.

Ross, John. "To all the aged, and wise Antiquarians of the Cherokee Nation." September 15, 1835. John Howard Payne Papers. Vol. 4, folder 5. Newberry Library, Chicago.

Rowland, Oran W. *History of Van Buren County, Michigan.* Chicago, 1912.

Schoolcraft, James. James Schoolcraft to George Johnston. January 23, 1833. George Johnston Papers. Burton Historical Collection. Detroit Public Library.

Schoolcraft, Jane Johnston. "Album." Poems of Jane Johnston Schoolcraft, 1823–28 & n.d. Henry Rowe Schoolcraft Papers. Box 70. Library of Congress, Washington, DC.

————. "Devotional Songs and Poems." Henry Rowe Schoolcraft Papers. Box 70. Library of Congress, Washington, DC.

————. Jane Johnston to Henry Rowe Schoolcraft. May 19, 1823. Henry Rowe Schoolcraft Papers. Box 7. Library of Congress, Washington, DC.

————. "Poetic Remains of John Johnston." Henry Rowe Schoolcraft Papers. Box 70. Library of Congress, Washington, DC.

Schoolcraft, Henry Rowe. "Dawn of Literary Composition by Educated Natives of the Aboriginal Tribes." In *The Sound the Stars Make Rushing through the Sky: The Writings of Jane Johnston Schoolcraft*, edited by Robert Dale Parker, 241–56. Philadelphia: University of Pennsylvania Press, 2007.

————. *Historical and Statistical Information Respecting the History, Condition, and Prospects of the Indian Tribes of the United States.* 6 vols. Philadelphia: Lippincott, Grambo, 1851.

————. *The Literary Voyager, or, Muzzeniegun*, edited by Philip P. Mason. East Lansing: Michigan State University Press, 1962.

————. "Memoir of John Johnston." *Historical Collections, Michigan Pioneer and Historical Society* 36 (Lansing, MI: Wynkoop, Hallenbeck, Crawford, 1908): 53–101.

————. *Oneóta or, Characteristics of the Red Race of America from Original Notes and Manuscripts.* New York, 1845.

————. *Personal Memoirs of a Residence of Thirty Years with the Indian Tribes on the American Frontiers.* Philadelphia, 1851.

Senier, Siobhan, ed. *Dawnland Voices: An Anthology of Indigenous Writing from New England.* Lincoln: University of Nebraska Press, 2014.

"Settling Their Claims." *Daily Nebraska State Journal.* December 2, 1889, 5. *Readex: America's Historical Newspapers.* Accessed December 2016.

"Speech of John Ridge, A Cherokee Chief." *The Liberator.* March 17, 1832, 44. *Readex: America's Historical Newspapers.* Accessed December 2015.

"State Items." *Evansville Courier.* October 19, 1889, 2. *Readex: America's Historical Newspapers.* Accessed December 2016.

Tanner, John, and Edwin James. *Kekitchemanitomenahn gahbemahjeinnunk Jesus Christ: otoashke wawweendummahgawin.* Albany: Packard and Van Benthutsen, 1833.

Tanner, John. *A Narrative of the Captivity and Adventures of John Tanner (U.S. Interpreter at the Saut [sic] de Ste. Marie) during Thirty Years Residence among the Indians in the Interior of North America.* London, 1830.

"Treaty of Holston." *Oklahoma State Library Digital Collections.* http://digital.library .okstate.edu/kappler/vol2/treaties/che0029.htm. Accessed October 15, 2015.

"Triumph of Peace." *Chicago Daily Tribune.* October 10, 1893, 9. *Readex: America's Historical Newspapers.* Accessed December 2016.

Truman, Benjamin Cummings. *History of the World's Fair, Being a Complete and Authentic Description of the Columbian Exposition.* Chicago, 1893.

Turner, Frederick Jackson. *The Frontier in American History.* New York: Henry Holt, 1921.

Virginia Papers. Item 71, vol. 2, 156. Papers of the Continental Congress, 1774– 1789 (National Archives Microfilm Publication M247, roll 85): 141–222. National Archives and Records Administration, Washington, DC. Accessed June 2015.

Warren, William Whipple. *History of the Ojibways, Based upon Traditions and Oral Statements.* St. Paul: Minnesota Historical Society, 1885.

Wells, Ida B., ed. *The Reason Why the Colored American Is Not in the World's Columbian Exposition.* Chicago, 1893.

"White City Chips. Pokagon, the Indian Poet, Apt in Latin and Greek." *Daily Inter Ocean.* October 11, 1893, 7. *Readex: America's Historical Newspapers.* Accessed December 2016.

Wzokhilain, Pierre Paul. *Wawasi lagidamwoganek mdala chowagidamwoganal tabtagil: onkawodokodozwal wji pobatami kidwogan.* Boston: Crocker and Brewster, 1830.

————. *Wobanaki kimzowi awighigan.* Boston: Crocker and Brewster, 1830.

Zitkála-Šá. *American Indian Stories*. Lincoln: University of Nebraska Press, 2003.

Zobel, Melissa Tantaquidgeon. *Oracles*. Albuquerque: University of New Mexico Press, 2004.

Scholarly Texts

Adams-Campbell, Melissa, Ashley Glassburn Falzetti, and Courtney Rivard. "Introduction: Indigeneity and the Work of Settler Archives." *Settler Colonial Studies* 5, no. 2 (2015): 109–16.

Alden, John Richard. "The Eighteenth Century Cherokee Archives." *American Archivist* 5 (1942): 240–44.

Anderson, Jane, and James Eric Francis, Sr. "Decolonial Futures of Sharing: 'Protecting Our Voice,' Intellectual Property and Penobscot Language Materials." In *Indigenous Languages and the Promise of Archives*, edited by Adrianna Link, Abigail Shelton, and Patrick Spero. Nebraska: University of Nebraska Press, 2021.

Anderson, William L., Jane L. Brown, and Anne F. Rogers. "Introduction." In *The Payne-Butrick Papers*, edited by William L. Anderson, Jane L. Brown, and Anne F. Rogers, xiii–xxiii. Vols. 1–3. Lincoln: University of Nebraska Press, 2010.

Appadurai, Arjun. "Introduction: Commodities and the Politics of Value." In *The Social Life of Things*, edited by Arjun Appadurai, 3–63. Cambridge: Cambridge University Press, 1986.

Battle-Baptiste, Whitney, and Britt Rusert, eds. *W. E. B. Du Bois's Data Portraits: Visualizing Black America*. Princeton: Princeton Architectural Press, 2018.

Bartosik-Velez, Elise. *The Legacy of Christopher Columbus in the Americas: New Nations and a Transatlantic Discourse of Empire*. Nashville: Vanderbilt University Press, 2014.

Bauman, Richard. "Representing Native American Oral Narrative: The Textual Practices of Henry Rowe Schoolcraft." *Pragmatics* 5, no. 2 (2010): 167–83.

Beaulieu, Alain. "'An Equitable Right to be Compensated': The Dispossession of the Aboriginal Peoples of Quebec and the Emergence of a New Legal Rationale, 1760–1860." *Canadian Historical Review* 94, no. 1 (2013): 1–27.

Beck, David R. M. *Unfair Labor? American Indians and the 1893 World's Columbian Exposition in Chicago*. Lincoln: University of Nebraska Press, 2019.

Bellin, Joshua David. *The Demon of the Continent: Indians and the Shaping of American Literature*. Philadelphia: University of Pennsylvania Press, 2001.

Ben-Zvi, Yael. "Ethnography and the Production of Foreignness in Indian Captivity Narratives." *American Indian Quarterly* 32, no. 1 (2008): 5–32.

Benn, Carl. *Mohawks on the Nile: Natives among the Canadian Voyageurs in Egypt, 1884 – 1885*. Toronto: National Heritage Books, 2009.

Bennett, Tony, Fiona Cameron, Nélia Dias, Ben Dibly, Rodney Harrison, Ira Jacknis, and Conal McCarthy. *Collecting, Ordering, Governing: Anthropology, Museums, and Liberal Government*. Durham: Duke University Press, 2017.

Bentley, Nancy. *Frantic Panoramas: American Literature and Mass Culture, 1870 –1920*. Philadelphia: University of Pennsylvania Press, 2009.

Berliner, Jonathan. "Written in the Birch Bark: The Linguistic-Material World-making of Simon Pokagon." *PMLA* 125, no. 1 (2010): 73 –91.

Best, Stephen, and Sharon Marcus. "Surface Reading: An Introduction." *Representations* 108, no. 1 (2009): 1 –21.

Bohaker, Heidi. "Indigenous Histories and Archival Media in the Early Modern Great Lakes." In *Colonial Mediascapes: Sensory Worlds of the Early Americas*, edited by Matt Cohen and Jeffrey Glover, 99 –140. Lincoln: University of Nebraska Press, 2014.

Bragdon, Kathleen J. *Native People of Southern New England, 1500 –1650*. Norman: University of Oklahoma Press, 1996.

Bronson-Bartlett, Blake. "From Loose Leaves to Readymades: Manuscript Books in the Age of Emerson and Whitman." *J19: The Journal of Nineteenth-Century Americanists* 6, no. 2 (2018): 259 –83.

Brooks, Lisa. *The Common Pot: The Recovery of Native Space in the Northeast*. Minneapolis: University of Minnesota Press, 2008.

———. *Our Beloved Kin: A New History of King Philip's War*. New Haven: Yale University Press, 2018.

———. "The Primacy of the Present, the Primacy of Place: Navigating the Spiral of History in the Digital World." *PMLA* 127, no. 2 (2012): 308 –16.

———. "Turning the Looking Glass on King Philip's War: Locating American Literature in Native Space." *American Literary History* 25, no. 4 (2013): 718 –50.

Brooks, Lisa, and Cassandra M. Brooks. "The Reciprocity Principle and Traditional Ecological Knowledge: Understanding the Significance of Indigenous Protest on the Presumpscot River." *International Journal of Critical Indigenous Studies* 3, no. 2 (2010): 11 –28.

Brown, Kirby. *Stoking the Fire: Nationhood in Cherokee Writing, 1907 –1970*. Norman: University of Oklahoma Press, 2018.

Brown-Pérez, Kathleen A. " 'A Reflection of Our National Character': Structurally and Culturally Violent Federal Policies and the Elusive Quest for Federal Acknowledgment." *Landscapes of Violence* 2, no. 1, Article 5 (2012): 1 –12.

Brown, Matthew P. "Blanks: Data, Method, and the British American Print Shop." *American Literary History* 29, no. 2 (2017): 228–47.

Bruchac, Jesse. "A Brief Biography of the Minister, Schoolmaster and Interpreter of the Abenaki Pial Pol Wzokhilain." In *The Gospel of Mark Translated into Abenaki Indian, English and French*, 1–3. Greenfield Center, NY: Bowman Books, 2011.

———. *The Gospel of Mark: Translated into Abenaki Indian, English and French.* Greenfield Center, NY: Bowman Books, 2011.

Bruchac, Margaret M. "Reading Abenaki Traditions and European Records of Rogers' Raid." Department of Anthropology Papers, University of Pennsylvania Scholarly Commons. 2006. Retrieved from http://repository.upenn.edu/anthro_papers/155, 1–12.

———. *Savage Kin: Indigenous Informants and American Anthropologists.* Tucson: University of Arizona Press, 2018.

Bruyneel, Kevin. *The Third Space of Sovereignty: The Postcolonial Politics of U.S.-Indigenous Relations.* Minneapolis: University of Minnesota Press, 2007.

Byrd, Jodi A. *The Transit of Empire: Indigenous Critiques of Colonialism.* Minneapolis: University of Minnesota Press, 2011.

Calcaterra, Angela. *Literary Indians: Aesthetics and Encounter in American Literature to 1920.* Chapel Hill: University of North Carolina Press, 2018.

Calloway, Colin G. *Dawnland Encounters: Indians and Europeans in Northern New England.* Hanover: University Press of New England, 1991.

———. *The Western Abenakis of Vermont, 1600–1800: War, Migration, and the Survival of an Indian People.* Norman: University of Oklahoma Press, 1990.

Carr, Lloyd G., and Carlos Westey. "Surviving Folktales and Herbal Lore among the Shinnecock Indians of Long Island." *Journal of American Folklore* 58, no. 228 (April–June 1945): 113–23.

Carroll, Beau Duke, Alan Cressler, Tom Belt, Julie Reed, and Jan F. Simek. "Talking Stones: Cherokee Syllabary in Manitou Cave, Alabama." *Antiquity* 93, no. 368 (2019): 519–36.

Cavalier, Christine R. "Jane Johnston Schoolcraft's Sentimental Lessons: Native Literary Collaboration and Resistance." *MELUS* 38, no. 1 (2013): 98–118.

Certeau, Michel de. *The Practice of Everyday Life.* Berkeley: University of California Press, 2011.

Chartier, Roger. *The Order of Books: Readers, Authors, and Libraries in Europe between the 14th and 18th Centuries.* Stanford: Stanford University Press, 1994.

Child, Brenda J. *Holding Our World Together: Ojibwe Women and the Survival of Community.* New York: Penguin, 2012.

Christen, Kimberly. "Opening Archives: Respectful Repatriation." *American Archivist* 74 (2011): 185–210.

Christen, Kimberly, and Jane Anderson, "Toward Slow Archives." *Archival Science* 19 (2019): 87–116.

Chute, Janet E. *The Legacy of Shingwaukonse: A Century of Native Leadership*. Toronto: University of Toronto Press, 1998.

Cipolla, Craig N. *Becoming Brothertown: Native American Ethnogenesis and Endurance in the Modern World*. Tucson: University of Arizona Press, 2017.

Cohen, Lara Langer. "Notes from the State of Saint Domingue: The Practice of Citation in *Clotel*." In *Early African American Print Culture*, edited by Lara Langer Cohen and Jordan Stein, 161–77. Philadelphia: University of Pennsylvania Press, 2014.

Cohen, Matt. *The Networked Wilderness: Communicating in Early New England*. Minneapolis: University of Minnesota Press, 2010.

Cohen, Matt, and Jeffrey Glover, eds. *Colonial Mediascapes: Sensory Worlds of the Early Americas*. Lincoln: University of Nebraska Press, 2014.

Cohen, Michael C. *The Social Lives of Poems in Nineteenth-Century America*. Philadelphia: University of Pennsylvania Press, 2015.

Conn, Steven. *Museums and American Intellectual Life, 1876–1926*. Chicago: University of Chicago Press, 1998.

Cormack, Bradin, and Carla Mazzio. *Book Use, Book Theory: 1500–1700*. Chicago: University of Chicago Press, 2005.

Cothran, Boyd. *Remembering the Modoc War: Redemptive Violence and the Making of American Innocence*. Chapel Hill: University of North Carolina Press, 2014.

Cottrell, Courtney. "Indian Made: Museum Valuation of American Indian Identity through Aesthetics." *Transmotion* 5, no. 2 (2019): 23–44.

———. "NAGPRA's Politics of Recognition: Repatriation Struggles of a Terminated Tribe." *American Indian Quarterly* 44, no. 1 (2020): 59–85.

Crain, Patricia. *The Story of A: The Alphabetization of America from* The New England Primer *to* The Scarlet Letter. Stanford: Stanford University Press, 2000.

Cruikshank, Julie. "Oral History, Narrative Strategies, and Native American Historiography: Perspectives from the Yukon Territory, Canada." In *Clearing a Path: Theorizing the Past in Native American Studies*, edited by Nancy Shoemaker, 3–28. New York: Routledge, 2002.

Cumming, John. "Pokagon's Birch Bark Books." *American Book Collector* 18, no. 8 (1968): 14–17.

Cushman, Ellen. *The Cherokee Syllabary: Writing the People's Persistence*. Norman: University of Oklahoma Press, 2011.

————. "Wampum, Sequoyan, and Story: Decolonizing the Digital Archive." *College English* 76, no. 2 (2013): 115–35.

Darnell, Regna. *And Along Came Boas: Continuity and Revolution in Americanist Anthropology*. Amsterdam: John Benjamins Publishing, 2000.

Day, Gordon M. "Dartmouth and Saint Francis." In *In Search of New England's Native Past: Selected Essays by Gordon M. Day,* edited by Michael K. Foster and William Cowan, 51–52. Amherst: University of Massachusetts Press, 1998.

————. "The Identity of the Saint Francis Indians." *Canadian Ethnology Service Paper,* no. 71 (Ottawa, 1981): 1–117.

————. *Western Abenaki Dictionary*. Vol 1. Hull, Quebec: Canadian Museum of Civilization, 1993.

Deer, Sarah. *The Beginning and End of Rape: Confronting Sexual Violence in Native America*. Minneapolis: University of Minnesota Press, 2015.

Delbourgo, James, and Staffan Müller-Wille. "Introduction: Listmania." *Isis* 103, no. 4 (2012): 710–15.

Deloria, Philip J. *Indians in Unexpected Places*. Lawrence: University of Kansas Press, 2004.

Den Ouden, Amy E. *Beyond Conquest: Native Peoples and the Struggle for History in New England*. Lincoln: University of Nebraska Press, 2005.

Derrida, Jacques. "Archive Fever: A Freudian Impression." *Diacritics* 25, no. 2 (1995): 9–63.

diCuirci, Lindsay. *Colonial Revivals: The Nineteenth-Century Lives of Early American Books*. Philadelphia: University of Pennsylvania Press, 2019.

DiMeo, Michelle, and Sara Pennell. "Introduction." In *Reading and Writing Recipe Books, 1550–1800,* edited by Michelle DiMeo and Sara Pennell, 1–22. Manchester: Manchester University Press, 2013.

Doerfler, Jill, and Erik Redix. "Regional and Tribal Histories: The Great Lakes." In *Oxford Handbook of American Indian History,* edited by Frederick Hoxie, 173–98. Oxford: Oxford University Press, 2016.

Dowd, Gregory Evans. "Indigenous Catholicism and St. Joseph Potawatomi Resistance in 'Pontiac's War,' 1763–1766." *Ethnohistory* 63, no. 1 (January 2016): 143–66.

Ernest, John. *Liberation Historiography: African American Writers and the Challenge of History, 1794–1861*. Durham: University of North Carolina Press, 2004.

Eckert, Lindsey. "Reading Lyric's Form: The Written Hand in Albums and Literary Annuals." *ELH* 85, no. 4 (2018): 973–97.

Elder, Colin. "Changing Political and Cultural Realms in the Upper Great Lakes, 1826: A Case-study of the Influential 'Oode' (or Family) of Jane Johnston Schoolcraft." Master's thesis, Dalhousie University, 2015.

Eppler, Karen Sanchez. "Copying and Conversion: An 1824 Friendship Album 'from a Chinese Youth.'" *American Quarterly* 59, no. 2 (2007): 301–39.

Fawcett, Melissa Jayne. *The Lasting of the Mohegans: Part I, The Story of the Wolf People*. Uncasville, CT: Mohegan Tribe and Pequot Printing, 1995.

———. *Medicine Trail: The Life and Lessons of Gladys Tantaquidgeon*. Tucson: University of Arizona Press, 2000.

Fitzgerald, Stephanie. "The Cultural Work of a Mohegan Painted Basket." In *Early Native Literacies in New England: A Documentary and Critical Anthology*, edited by Kristina Bross and Hilary E. Wyss, 52–56. Amherst: University of Massachusetts Press, 2008.

Fuentes, Marisa. *Dispossessed Lives: Enslaved Women, Violence, and the Archive*. Philadelphia: University of Pennsylvania Press, 2016.

Geppert, Alexander C. T. *Fleeting Cities: Imperial Expositions in* Fin-de-Siécle *Europe*. New York: Palgrave, 2010.

Green, Reyna. "The Pocahontas Perplex: The Image of Indian Women in American Culture." *Massachusetts Review* 16, no. 4 (1975): 698–714.

Gitelman, Lisa. *Paper Knowledge: Toward a Media History of Documents*. Durham: Duke University Press, 2014.

Goeman, Mishuana. *Mark My Words: Native Women Mapping Our Nations*. Minneapolis: University of Minnesota Press, 2013.

———. "(Re)Mapping Indigenous Presence on the Land in Native Women's Literature." *American Quarterly* 60, no. 2 (2008): 295–302.

Gore, Amy. "Material Matters: Paratextual Bodies in Nineteenth-Century Indigenous Book History." PhD diss., University of New Mexico, 2019.

Greyser, Naomi. *On Sympathetic Grounds: Race, Gender and Affective Geographies in Nineteenth-Century North America*. Oxford: Oxford University Press, 2018.

Haas, Angela M. "Wampum as Hypertext: An American Indian Intellectual Tradition of Multimedia Theory and Practice." *Studies in American Indian Literatures* 19, no. 4 (2007): 77–100.

Hagy, James William, and Stanley J. Folmsbee, eds. "The Lost Archives of the Cherokee Nation, Part I, 1763–1772." *East Tennessee Historical Society's Publications* 43 (1971): 112–22.

———. "The Lost Archives of the Cherokee Nation, Part II, 1772–1775." *East Tennessee Historical Society's Publications* 44 (1972): 114–25.

Harris, Katherine D. *Forget Me Not: The Rise of the British Literary Annual, 1823 – 1835*. Athens: Ohio University Press, 2015.

Hartman, Saidiya V. *Scenes of Subjection: Terror, Slavery, and Self-Making in Nineteenth-Century America*. New York: Oxford University Press, 1997.

———. "Venus in Two Acts." *Small Axe* 12, no. 2 (2008): 1–14.

Harvey, Sean. *Native Tongues: Colonialism and Race from Encounter to the Reservation*. Cambridge: Harvard University Press, 2015.

Hele, Karl S. "The Anishinaabeg and Métis at the Sault Ste Marie Borderlands: Confronting a Line Drawn upon the Water." In *Lines Drawn upon the Water: First Nations and the Great Lakes Borders and Borderlands*, edited by Karl S. Hele, 65–84. Waterloo: Wilfrid Laurier University Press, 2008.

———. " 'By the Rapids': The Anishinabeg-Missionary Encounter at Bawating (Sault Ste. Marie), c. 1821–1871." PhD diss., McGill University, 2002.

———. " 'Fully Equal to a Mission in Herself': Charlotte Johnston McMurray's Missionary Labours at Bawating, 1827–1838." *Algonquian Conference* (2008): 316–57.

———. " 'How to Win Friends and Influence People': Missions to Bawating, 1830–1840." *Historical Papers 1996: Canadian Society of Church History* (1996): 155–76.

Hickey, Alanna. "The Forms of National Belonging: The Politics of Nineteenth-Century Native American Poetry." PhD diss., Northwestern University, 2016.

Hinsley, Curtis M. "Afterward: The Ironies of the Fair, the Uncertainties of Anthropology." In *Coming of Age in Chicago: The 1893 World's Fair and the Coalescence of American Anthropology*, edited by Curtis M. Hinsley and David R. Wilcox, 489–96. Lincoln: University of Nebraska Press, 2016.

———. "The World as Marketplace: Commodification of the Exotic at the World's Columbian Exposition, Chicago." In *Exhibiting Cultures: The Poetics and Politics of Museum Display*, edited by Ivan Karp and Steven D. Lavine, 344–66. Washington, DC: Smithsonian Books, 1991.

Hinsley, Curtis M., and David R. Wilcox, eds. *Coming of Age in Chicago: The 1893 World's Fair and the Coalescence of American Anthropology*. Lincoln: University of Nebraska Press, 2016.

Hopwood, Nicholas, Simon Schaffer, and Jim Secord. "Seriality and Scientific Objects in the Nineteenth Century." *History of Science* 18 (2010): 251–85.

Hume, Gary W. "Joseph Laurent's Intervale Camp: Post-Colonial Abenaki Adaptation and Revitalization in New Hampshire." In *Algonkians of New*

England, Past and Present: Proceedings of the Dublin Seminar for New England Folklife, 1989, edited by Peter Benes, 101–113. Boston: Boston University Press, 1991.

Hunter, Michael. "Robert Boyle and the Early Royal Society: A Reciprocal Exchange in the Making of Baconian Science." *British Journal for the History of Science* 40, no. 1 (2007): 1–23.

Jacknis, Ira. "Refracting Images: Anthropological Display at the Chicago World's Fair, 1893." In *Coming of Age in Chicago: The 1893 World's Fair and the Coalescence of American Anthropology,* edited by Curtis M. Hinsley and David R. Wilcox, 261–336. Lincoln: University of Nebraska Press, 2016.

Jenkins, David. "Object Lessons and Ethnographic Displays: Museum Exhibitions and the Making of American Anthropology." *Comparative Studies in Society and History* 36, no. 2 (1994): 260–66.

Johns, Adrian. *The Nature of the Book: Print and Knowledge in the Making.* Chicago: University of Chicago Press, 1998.

Justice, Daniel Heath. *Our Fire Survives the Storm: A Cherokee Literary History.* Minneapolis: University of Minnesota Press, 2006.

Keating, Anne Durkin. *Rising Up from Indian Country: The Battle of Fort Dearborn and the Birth of Chicago.* Chicago: University of Chicago Press, 2012.

Kelderman, Frank. *Authorized Agents: Publication and Diplomacy in the Era of Indian Removal.* Albany: SUNY Press, 2019.

Kelly, Michael. "Samson Occom and the Uses of Bibliography." Paper presented at Rare Book School Lectures, Charlottesville, VA. June 2016.

Knight, Jeffrey Todd. *Bound to Read: Compilations, Collections, and the Making of Renaissance Literature.* Philadelphia: University of Pennsylvania Press, 2013.

Konkle, Maureen. "Recovering Jane Schoolcraft's Cultural Activism in the Nineteenth Century." In *Oxford Handbook of Indigenous American Literature,* edited by James H. Cox and Daniel Heath Justice, 81–101. New York: Oxford University Press, 2014.

———. *Writing Indian Nations: Native Intellectuals and the Politics of Historiography, 1827–1863.* Chapel Hill: University of North Carolina Press, 2004.

Krupat, Arnold, ed. *Native American Autobiography: An Anthology.* Madison: University of Wisconsin Press, 1994.

LaPier, Rosalyn R., and David R. M. Beck, *City Indian: Native American Activism in Chicago, 1893–1934.* Lincoln: University of Nebraska Press, 2015.

Lewandowski, Julia. "'The Same Force, Authority, and Effect': Formalizing Native Property and British Plurality in Lower Canada." *Quebec Studies,* Supplemental Issue (2016): 149–70.

Lodge, Sara. "Romantic Reliquaries: Memory and Irony in *The Literary Annuals*." *Romanticism* 10, no. 1 (2008): 23–40.

Lonetree, Amy. *Decolonizing Museums: Representing Native America in National and Tribal Museums*. Chapel Hill: University of North Carolina Press, 2012.

Lopenzina, Drew. *Red Ink: Native Americans Picking Up the Pen in the Colonial Period*. Albany: SUNY University Press, 2012.

———. "'The Whole Wilderness Shall Blossom as the Rose': Samson Occom, Joseph Johnson, and the Question of Native Settlement on Cooper's Frontier." *American Quarterly* 58, no. 4 (2006): 1122–45.

Low, John N. *Imprints: The Pokagon Band of Potawatomi Indians & the City of Chicago*. East Lansing: Michigan State University Press, 2016.

Lyons, Scott Richard. *X-Marks: Native Signatures of Assent*. Minneapolis: University of Minnesota Press, 2010.

Mancini, Jason. "Whose Medicine?: Observations on the Transformation of Native American Medicinal Practices in the Context of European-American Medical Theory, Religion, and Law." Paper presented at the 3rd Mashantucket Pequot History Conference, September 20, 2002.

Manore, Jean L. "The Historical Erasure of an Indigenous Identity in the Borderlands: The Western Abenaki of Vermont, New Hampshire, and Quebec." *Journal of Borderlands Studies* 26, no. 2 (2011): 179–96.

McGill, Meredith. *American Literature and the Culture of Reprinting, 1834–1853*. Philadelphia: University of Pennsylvania Press, 2003.

McLoughlin, William G. *Cherokee Renascence in the New Republic*. Princeton: Princeton University Press, 1986.

McNally, Michael D. *Ojibwe Singers: Hymns, Grief, and a Native Culture in Motion*. Oxford: Oxford University Press, 2000.

Mendelsohn, J. Andrew. "The World on a Page: Making a General Observation in the Eighteenth Century." In *Histories of Scientific Observation*, edited by Lorraine Daston and Elizabeth Lunbeck, 396–425. Chicago: University of Chicago Press, 2011.

Michaelson, Scott. *The Limits of Multiculturalism: Interrogating the Origins of American Anthropology*. Minneapolis: University of Minnesota Press, 1999.

Mielke, Laura. *Moving Encounters: Sympathy and the Indian Question in Antebellum Literature*. Amherst: University of Massachusetts Press, 2008.

Miles, Tiya. *The House on Diamond Hill: A Cherokee Plantation Story*. Durham: University of North Carolina Press, 2010.

———. *Ties That Bind: The Story of an Afro-Cherokee Family in Slavery and Freedom*. Oakland: University of California Press, 2015.

Million, Dian. *Therapeutic Nations: Healing in an Age of Indigenous Human Rights.* Tucson: University of Arizona Press, 2013.

Moerman, Daniel E. *Native American Ethnobotany.* Portland, OR: Timber Press, 1998.

Monaghan, E. Jennifer. *Learning to Read and Write in Colonial America.* Amherst: University of Massachusetts Press, 2007.

Mooney, James. "The Sacred Formulas of the Cherokees." In *Seventh Annual Report of the Bureau of Ethnology, 1885–'86 by JW Powell, Director,* 307–97. Washington, DC: Government Printing Office, 1891.

Morgan, Jennifer L. "Archives and Histories of Racial Capitalism: An Afterword." *Social Text* 33, no. 4 (2018): 153–61.

Moretti, Franco. *Distant Reading.* London: Verso, 2013.

Moulton, Gary E. *John Ross, Cherokee Chief.* Athens: University of Georgia Press, 1978.

Mt. Pleasant, Alyssa. "Salt, Sand, and Sweetgrass: Methodologies for Exploring the Seasonal Basket Trade in Southern Maine." *American Indian Quarterly* 38, no. 4 (2014): 411–26.

Mt. Pleasant, Alyssa, Caroline Wigginton, and Kelly Wisecup. "Materials and Methods in Native American and Indigenous Studies: Completing the Turn." *Early American Literature* 53, no. 2 (2018): 407–44.

Murray, Laura J. "Vocabularies of Native American Languages: A Literary and Historical Approach to an Elusive Genre." *American Quarterly* 53, no. 4 (2001): 590–623.

Nelson, Joshua B. *Progressive Traditions: Identity in Cherokee Literature and Culture.* Norman: University of Oklahoma Press, 2014.

Newman, Andrew. *Allegories of Encounter: Colonial Literacy and Indian Captives.* Chapel Hill: University of North Carolina Press, 2019.

Noodin, Margaret. "Megwa Baabaamiiaayaayaang Dibaajomoyaang: Anishinaabe Literature as Memory in Motion." In *Oxford Handbook of Indigenous American Literature,* edited by James H. Cox and Daniel Heath Justice, 175–84. Oxford: Oxford University Press, 2014.

———. "Reading *Queen of the Woods* Today." In Simon Pokagon, *Ogimawkwe Mitigwaki-Queen of the Woods,* 57–76. East Lansing: Michigan State University Press, 2011.

O'Brien, Jean M. *Firsting and Lasting: Writing Indians out of Existence in New England.* Cambridge: Cambridge University Press, 2010.

Parker, Robert Dale. "Braided Relations: Toward a History of Nineteenth-Century American Indian Women's Poetry." In *A History of Nineteenth-Century*

American Women's Poetry, edited by Jennifer Putzi and Alexandra Socarides, 313–28. Cambridge: Cambridge University Press, 2016.

———. "Introduction: The World and Writings of Jane Johnston Schoolcraft." In *The Sound the Stars Make Rushing through the Sky: The Writings of Jane Johnston Schoolcraft,* edited by Robert Dale Parker, 1–84. Philadelphia: University of Pennsylvania Press, 2007.

Pearce, Margaret Wickens. "The Last Piece Is You." *Cartographic Journal* 51, no. 2 (2014): 107–22.

Pennell, Sara. "Perfecting Practice?: Women, Manuscript Recipes and Knowledge in Early Modern England." In *Early Modern Women's Manuscript Writing: Selected Papers from the Trinity/Trent Colloquium,* edited by Victoria E. Burke and Jonathan Gibson, 237–55. Burlington, VT: Ashgate, 2004.

Piatote, Beth. *Domestic Subjects: Gender, Citizenship, and Law in Native American Literature.* New Haven: Yale University Press, 2013.

Piper, Andrew. "The Art of Sharing." In *Bookish Histories: Books, Literature, and Commercial Modernity, 1700–1900,* edited by Ina Ferris and Paul Keen, 126–47. Basingstroke: Palgrave Macmillan, 2009.

———. *Dreaming in Books: The Making of the Bibliographic Imagination in the Romantic Age.* Chicago: University of Chicago Press, 2014.

Petrino, Elizabeth A. "Presents of Mind: Lydia Sigourney, Gift Book Culture, and the Commodification of Poetry." In *A History of Nineteenth-Century American Women's Poetry,* edited by Jennifer Putzi and Alexandra Socarides, 87–105. Cambridge: Cambridge University Press, 2017.

Pettit, Clare. "Topos, Taxonomy and Travel in Nineteenth-Century Women's Scrapbooks." In *Travel Writing, Visual Culture and Form, 1760–1900,* edited by Mary Henes and Brian H. Murray, 21–41. London: Palgrave, 2016.

Phillips, Ruth B. *Trading Identities: The Souvenir in Native North American Art from the Northeast, 1700–1900.* Seattle: University of Washington Press, 1998.

Porter, Dahlia. "Specimen Poetics: Botany, Reanimation, and the Romantic Collection." *Representations* 139 (Summer 2017): 60–94.

Powell, Malea. "Dreaming Charles Eastman: Cultural Memory, Autobiography, and Geography in Indigenous Rhetorical Histories." In *Beyond the Archives: Research as a Lived Process,* edited by Gesa E. Kirsch and Liz Rohan, 115–27. Carbondale: Southern Illinois University, 2008.

Powell, Timothy B., William Weems, and Freeman Owle. "Native/American Digital Storytelling: Situating the Cherokee Oral Tradition within American Literary History." *Literature Compass* 4, no. 1 (2007): 1–23.

Pratt, Lloyd. *Archives of American Time: Literature and Modernity in the Nineteenth Century*. Philadelphia: University of Pennsylvania Press, 2010.

Price, Leah. *How to Do Things with Books in Victorian England*. Princeton: Princeton University Press, 2012.

Radus, Daniel M. "Writing Native Pasts in the Nineteenth Century." PhD diss., Cornell University, 2017.

Rasmussen, Birgit Brander. *Queequeg's Coffin: Indigenous Literacies and Early American Literature*. Durham: Duke University Press, 2012.

Reed, Julie L. *Serving the Nation: Cherokee Sovereignty and Social Welfare, 1800 –1907*. Norman: University of Oklahoma, 2016.

Rhinehart, Melissa. "To Hell with the Wigs!: Native American Representation and Resistance at the World's Columbian Exposition." *American Indian Quarterly* 36, no. 4 (2012): 403 –42.

Richmond, Trudi Lamb. "'Put Your Ear to the Ground and Listen': The Wigwam Festival is the Green Corn Ceremony." *Artifacts* 17, no. 4 (1989): 24 –34.

Rifkin, Mark. *Beyond Settler Time: Temporal Sovereignty and Indigenous Self-Determination*. Durham: Duke University Press, 2017.

———. *The Erotics of Sovereignty: Queer Native Writing in the Era of Self-Determination*. Minneapolis: University of Minnesota Press, 2012.

———. *Manifesting America: The Imperial Construction of U.S. National Space*. New York: Oxford University Press, 2009.

Rivett, Sarah. *Unscripted Americas: Indigenous Languages and the Origins of a Literary Nation*. Oxford: Oxford University Press, 2017.

Rosaldo, Renato. "Imperialist Nostalgia." *Representations* 26 (1989): 107 –22.

Round, Phillip H. "Early Native Literature as Social Practice." In *The Oxford Handbook of Native American Literature,* edited by James H. Cox and Daniel Heath Justice, 65 –80. Oxford: Oxford University Press, 2014.

———. *Removable Type: Histories of the Book in Indian Country, 1663 –1880*. Chapel Hill: University of North Carolina Press, 2010.

Rusert, Britt. "Disappointment in the Archives of Black Freedom." *Social Text* 33, no. 4 (2018): 19 –33.

———. *Fugitive Science: Empiricism and Freedom and Early African American Culture*. New York: New York University Press, 2017.

Saunt, Claudio. "Telling Stories: The Political Uses of Myth and History in the Cherokee and Creek Nations." *Journal of American History* 93, no. 3 (2006): 673 –97.

Scarborough, William "Buddy," Faith R. Kares, Iván Arenas, and Amanda E. Lewis. "Adversity and Resiliency for Chicago's First: The State of Racial Justice for American Indian Chicagoans Report." Institute for Research on Race & Public Policy, University of Illinois at Chicago (2019). https://stateofracialjusticechicago.com/.

Schwarz, Ingo, ed. *Alexander von Humboldt und die Vereinigten Staaten von Amerika.* Berlin: Akademie Verlag, 2004.

Schneider, Bethany. "Not for Citation: Jane Johnston Schoolcraft's Synchronic Strategies." *ESQ: A Journal of the American Renaissance* 54, no. 1–4 (2008): 111–44.

Schurr, Mark R., Terrance J. Martin, and W. Ben Secunda. "How the Pokagon Band Avoided Removal: Archaeological Evidence from the Faunal Assemblage of the Pokagon Village Site (20BE13)." *Midcontinental Journal of Archaeology* 31, no.1 (2006): 143–63.

Schweitzer, Ivy. "Native Sovereignty and the Archive: Samson Occom and Digital Humanities." *Resources for American Literary Studies* 38 (2015): 21–52.

Schweitzer, Ivy, and Gordon Henry, eds. *Afterlives of Indigenous Archives: Essays in Honor of the* Occom Circle. Hanover: Dartmouth College Press, 2019.

Senier, Siobhan. "'All This / Is Abenaki Country': Cheryl Savageau's Poetic Awikhiganak." *Studies in American Indian Literature* 22, no. 3 (2010): 1–25.

———. "Commentary: Sovereignty and Sustainability in Mohegan Ethnobotanical Literature." *Journal of Ecocriticism* 6, no. 1 (Spring 2014): 1–15.

———. "'Traditionally, Disability Was Not Seen as Such': Writing and Healing in the Work of Mohegan Medicine People." *Journal of Literary & Cultural Disability Studies* 7, no. 2 (2013): 213–29.

Sherman, William H. *Used Books: Marking Readers in Renaissance England.* Philadelphia: University of Pennsylvania Press, 2008.

Shuffelton, Frank. "Indian Devils and Pilgrim Fathers: Squanto, Hobomok, and the English Conception of Indian Religion." *New England Quarterly* 49 no. 1 (March 1976): 108–116.

Simmons, William S. *Spirit of the New England Tribes: Indian History and Folklore, 1620–1984.* Hanover: University Press of New England, 1986.

Simpson, Audra. *Mohawk Interruptus: Political Life across the Borders of Settler States.* Durham: Duke University Press, 2014.

———. "Why White People Love Franz Boas; or, the Grammar of Indigenous Dispossession." In *Indigenous Visions: Rediscovering the World of Franz Boas,* edited by Ned Blackhawk and Isaiah Lorado Wilner, 166–81. New Haven: Yale University Press, 2018.

Simpson, Leanne Betasamosake. *As We Have Always Done: Indigenous Freedom through Radical Resistance.* Minneapolis: University of Minnesota Press, 2017.

Smallwood, Stephanie E. *Saltwater Slavery: A Middle Passage from Africa to American Diaspora.* Cambridge: Harvard University Press, 2008.

Smith, Donald B. *Ojibwe Voices from Nineteenth-Century Canada.* Toronto: University of Toronto Press, 2013.

Smith, Susan Sleeper. *Indian Women and French Men: Rethinking Cultural Encounter in the Western Great Lakes.* Amherst: University of Massachusetts Press, 2001.

Socarides, Alexandra. "Rethinking the Fascicles: Dickinson's Writing, Copying, and Binding Practices." *Emily Dickinson Journal* 15, no. 2 (2006): 69–94.

Speck, Frank G. "Abnaki Text." *International Journal of American Linguistics* 11, no. 1 (1945): 45–46.

———. "Medicine Practices of the Northeastern Algonquians." *Proceedings of the 19th International Congress of Americanists,* 303–21. Washington, DC, 1917.

Spry, Adam. *Our War Paint Is Writers' Ink: Anishinaabe Literary Transnationalism.* Albany: SUNY Press, 2018.

Stabile, Susan M. *Memory's Daughters: The Material Culture of Remembrance in Eighteenth-Century America.* Ithaca: Cornell University Press, 2004.

Stallybrass, Peter. "Little Jobs: Broadsides and the Printing Revolution." In *Agent of Change: Print Culture Studies after Elizabeth L. Eisenstein,* edited by Sabrina Alcorn Baron, Eric N. Lindquist, and Eleanor F. Shevlin, 315–41. Amherst: University of Massachusetts Press, 2008.

Stocking, George, ed. *The Shaping of American Anthropology, 1883–1911: A Franz Boas Reader.* New York: Basic Books, 1974.

Stokes, Claudia. *Writers in Retrospect: The Rise of American Literary History, 1875–1910.* Chapel Hill: University of North Carolina Press, 2006.

Stoler, Ann Laura. *Along the Archival Grain: Epistemic Anxieties and Colonial Common Sense.* Princeton: Princeton University Press, 2010.

Stover, Johnnie M. "Nineteenth-Century African American Women's Autobiography as Social Discourse: The Example of Harriet Ann Jacobs." *College English* 66, no. 2 (2003): 133–54.

Strong, John. "How the Montauk Lost Their Land." In *History and Archaeology of the Montauk,* edited by Gaynell Stone, 77–120. Vol. 3. 2nd ed. Suffolk County Archaeological Association, 1993.

Sturtevant, William C. "John Ridge on Cherokee Civilization in 1826." *Journal of Cherokee Studies* 6 (1981): 79–91.

Tantaquidgeon, Gladys. *Folk Medicine of the Delaware and Related Algonkian Indians.* Harrisburg, Pennsylvania Historical and Museum Commission, 1972.

———. "Mohegan Medicinal Practices, Weather-Lore and Superstition." In *Annual Report of the Bureau of American Ethnology to the Secretary of the Smithsonian Institution, 1925–1926.* Washington, DC: 1926.

Tantaquidgeon, Gladys, and Jayne G. Fawcett, "Symbolic Motifs on Painted Baskets of the Mohegan-Pequot." In *A Key into the Language of Woodsplint Baskets,* edited by Ann McMullen and Russell G. Handsman, 95–123. Washington, CT: American Indian Archaeological Institute, 1987.

Taylor, Marie Balsley. "Diplomatic Conversions: Recovering Sachem Influence in Seventeenth-Century New England Missionary Writings." PhD diss., Purdue University, 2017.

Teuton, Christopher B. "Indigenous Textuality Studies and Cherokee Traditionalism: Notes Toward a Gagoga Rhetoric." *Textual Cultures: Texts, Contexts, Interpretation* 6, no. 4 (2011): 133–41.

Thomas, Deborah A. "Caribbean Studies, Archive Building, and the Problem of Violence." *Small Axe* 17, no. 2 (2013): 27–42.

Tonkovich, Nicole. *The Allotment Plot: Alice C. Fletcher, E. Jane Gay, and Nez Perce Survivance.* Lincoln: University of Nebraska Press, 2012.

Vigil, Kiara M. *Indigenous Intellectuals: Sovereignty, Citizenship, and the American Imagination, 1880–1930.* New York: Oxford University Press, 2015.

Viola, Herman J. *Thomas L. McKenney: Architect of America's Early Indian Policy: 1818–1830.* Chicago: Sage Books, 1974.

Wall, Wendy. *Recipes for Thought: Knowledge and Taste in the Early Modern English Kitchen.* Philadelphia: University of Pennsylvania Press, 2016.

Walls, Laura Dassow. *Passage to Cosmos: Alexander von Humboldt and the Shaping of America.* Chicago: Chicago University Press, 2009.

Warrior, Robert. *The People and the Word: Reading Native Nonfiction.* Minneapolis: University of Minnesota Press, 2005.

———. *Tribal Secrets: Recovering American Indian Intellectual Traditions.* Minneapolis: University of Minnesota Press, 1995.

Weaver, Jace. *That the People Might Live: Native American Literatures and Native American Community.* New York: Oxford University Press, 1997.

Wetzel, Christopher. *Gathering the Potawatomi Nation: Revitalization and Identity.* Norman: University of Oklahoma Press, 2015.

Weyler, Karen A. *Empowering Words: Outsiders and Authorship in Early America.* Athens: University of Georgia Press, 2013.

Wheeler, Rachel. *To Live upon Hope: Mohicans and Missionaries in the Eighteenth-Century Northeast.* Ithaca: Cornell University Press, 2008.

Wigginton, Caroline. *In the Neighborhood: Women's Publication in Early America.* Amherst: University of Massachusetts Press, 2016.

Wilkins, David E. *American Indian Sovereignty and the U.S. Supreme Court: The Masking of Justice.* Austin: University of Texas Press, 1997.

Wilkins, David E., and K. Tsianina Lomawaima. *Uneven Ground: American Indian Sovereignty and Federal Law.* Norman: University of Oklahoma Press, 2001.

Williams, Dana A., and Marissa K. López. "More Than a Fever: Toward a Theory of the Ethnic Archive." *PMLA* 127, no. 2 (2012): 357–59.

Wisecup, Kelly. "Encounters, Objects, and Commodity Lists in Early English Travel Narratives." *Studies in Travel Writing* 17, no. 3 (2013): 264–80.

———. "Entangled Archives: Cherokee Interventions in Language Collecting." In *Afterlives of Indigenous Archives: Essays in Honor of the* Occom Circle, edited by Ivy Schweitzer and Gordon Henry, 120–38. Hanover: University Press of New England, 2019.

———. *Medical Encounters: Knowledge and Identity in Early American Literatures.* Amherst: University of Massachusetts Press, 2013.

———. "Practicing Sovereignty: Colonial Temporalities, Cherokee Justice, and the 'Socrates' Writings of John Ridge." *NAIS: Journal of the Native American and Indigenous Studies Association* 4, no. 1 (Spring 2017): 30–60.

Wiseman, Frederick Matthew. *The Voice of the Dawn: An Autohistory of the Abenaki Nation.* Hanover: University Press of New England, 2001.

Witgen, Michael. *An Infinity of Nations: How the Native New World Shaped Early North America.* Philadelphia: University of Pennsylvania Press, 2012.

Womack, Craig. *Red on Red: Native American Literary Separatism.* Minneapolis: University of Minnesota Press, 1999.

Wylder, Edith. "Emily Dickinson's Punctuation: The Controversy Revisited." *American Literary Realism* 36, no. 3 (2004): 206–24.

Wyss, Hilary E. *English Letters and Indian Literacies: Reading, Writing, and New England Missionary Schools, 1750–1830.* Philadelphia: University of Pennsylvania Press, 2012.

———. *Writing Indians: Literacy, Christianity, and Native Community in Early America.* Amherst: University of Massachusetts Press, 2000.

Yale, Elizabeth. "Making Lists: Social and Material Technologies in the Making of Seventeenth-Century British Natural History." In *Ways of Making and Knowing: The Material Culture of Empirical Knowledge,* edited by Pamela H. Smith, Amy R. W. Myers, and Harold J. Cook, 280–301. Ann Arbor: University of Michigan Press, 2014.

Zobel, Melissa Tantaquidgeon. *The Lasting of the Mohegans.* Mohegan: Little People Publications, 1995.

INDEX

An italicized f *after a page number indicates a figure.*